18th Joint ACL-ISO Workshop on Interoperable Semantic Annotation (ISA-18)

Held at LREC 2022

Marseille, France
20 - 25 June 2022

Editor:

Harry Bunt

ISBN: 978-1-7138-6123-2

Printed from e-media with permission by:

Curran Associates, Inc.
57 Morehouse Lane
Red Hook, NY 12571

Some format issues inherent in the e-media version may also appear in this print version.

Association for Computational Linguistics
209 N. Eighth Street
Stroudsburg, Pennsylvania 18360

Phone: 1-570-476-8006
Fax: 1-570-476-0860

acl@aclweb.org

Additional copies of this publication are available from:

Curran Associates, Inc.
57 Morehouse Lane
Red Hook, NY 12571 USA
Phone: 845-758-0400
Fax: 845-758-2633
Email: curran@proceedings.com
Web: www.proceedings.com

LREC 2022 Workshop
Language Resources and Evaluation Conference
20-25 June 2022

18th Joint ACL - ISO Workshop on Interoperable Semantic Annotation (ISA-18)

Monday, June 20, 2022

PROCEEDINGS

Editor: Harry Bunt

Proceedings of the 18th Joint ACL - ISO workshop on Interoperable Semantic Annotation (ISA-18)

Edited by Harry Bunt

EAN: 9791095546818

For more information:
European Language Resources Association (ELRA)
9 rue des Cordelières
75013, Paris
France
http://www.elra.info
Email: lrec@elda.org

Preface

Welcome to the proceedings of the 18th Joint ACL - ISO Workshop on Interoperable Semantic Annotation (ISA-18), held on site in Marseille at LREC 2022. At last, the ISA workshop series is back to its preferred physical form, after two years of struggle with the COVID-19 virus. In 2020, when LREC was originally scheduled to take place in Marseille, the ISA-16 workshop (like the LREC conference) was canceled altogether, and only the proceedings with the accepted submissions were a reality. In 2021, ISA-17 was held in online form as part of the IWCS 2021 conference, which at the time felt as a step forward. Now at last the workshop could take place in Marseille in physical form, even though Covid-related travel restrictions still prevent participants from some countries to attend. Maybe partly because of this return to almost normal, the number of submissions to this ISA workshop was higher than it was for several years, and with very few exceptions they were of excellent quality. As a result, the workshop has a packed full-day program, of which the order of the presentations matches the order of the papers in these proceedings.

We thank the members of the ISA-18 program committee for reviewing the submitted papers timely and thoroughly, and we thank the authors of accepted papers for revising their contributions according to the very tight time schedule, taking the review comments into account. Thank you!

The ISA-18 organizers,

Harry Bunt
Nancy Ide
Kiyong Lee
Volha Petukhova
James Pustejovsky
Laurent Romary

Organizers

Harry Bunt - Tilburg University (Netherlands)
Nancy Ide - Vassar College, Poughkeepsie, NY (USA)
Kiyong Lee - Korea University, Seoul (South Korea)
Volha Petukhova - Saarland University, Saarbrücken (Germany)
James Pustejovsky - Brandeis University, Waltham, MA (USA)
Laurent Romary - INRIA/Humboldt University, Berlin (Germany)

Program Committee:

Jan Alexandersson, DFKI, Saarbrücken (Germany)
Johan Bos, University of Groningen (Netherlands)
Harry Bunt, Tilburg University (Netherlands)
Jae-Woong Choe, Korea University, Seoul (South Korea)
Robin Cooper, University of Gothenburg (Sweden)
Ludivine Crible, University of Edinburgh (Scotland)
Rodolfo Delmonte, Università Ca Foscari, Venezia (Italy)
David DeVault, USC Institute for Creative Technologies, Playa Vista, CA (USA)
Simon Dobnik, University of Gothenburg (Sweden)
Jens Edlund, KTH, Stockholm University (Sweden)
Alex Fang, City University of Hong Kong
Robert Gaizauskas, University of Sheffield (UK)
Koiti Hasida, Tokyo University (Japan)
Nancy Ide, Vassar College, Poughkeepsie, NY (USA)
Elisabetta Jezek, Università degli Studi di Pavia (Italy)
Nikhil Krishnaswamy, Brandeis University, Waltham, MA (USA)
Kiyong Lee, Korea University, Seoul (South Korea)
Paul Mc Kevitt, University of Ulster, Londonderry (Northern Ireland)
Philippe Muller, IRIT, Université Paul Sabatier, Toulouse (France)
Rainer Osswald, Heinrich-Heine University, Düsseldorf (Germany)
Patrizia Paggio, L-University of Malta, Msida (Malta)
Catherine Pelachaud, Sorbonne University, Paris (France)
Guy Perrier, Universityé de Lorraine, INRIA/LORIA, Nancy (France)
Volha Petukhova, Saarland University, Saarbrücken (Germany)
Massimo Poesio, Queen Mary University, London (UK)
Andrei Popescu-Belis, University of Applied Sciences of Western Switzerland
Laurent Prévot, Aix-Marseille University (France)
Stephen Pulman, Apple, Oxford (UK)
Maria da Purificação Silvano, University of Porto, INESC TEC (Portugal)
James Pustejovsky, Brandeis University, Waltham, MA (USA)
Laurent Romary, INRIA/Humboldt University, Berlin (Germany)
Ielka van der Sluis, University of Groningen (Netherlands)
Matthew Stone, Rutgers, the State University of New Jersey, Piscataway NJ (USA)
Thorsten Trippel, University of Tübingen (Germany)
Carl Vogel, Trinity College, Dublin (Ireland)
Menno van Zaanen, North West University South Africa,Mahikeng (RSA)
Annie Zaanen, Stanford University, Palo Alto, CA (USA)
Heike Zinsmeister, Universität Hamburg (Germany)

Table of Contents

Program

09:00 ***Opening***

09:10 **Session 1**

What Is Going through Your Mind? Metacognitive Events Classification in Human-Agent Interactions
Hafiza Erum Manzoor and Volha Petukhova

Assessment of Sales Negotiation Strategies with ISO 24617-2 Dialogue Act Annotations
Jutta Stock, Volha Petukhova and Dietrich Klakow

Guidelines and a Corpus for Extracting Biographical Events
Marco Antonio Stranisci, Enrico Mensa, Rossana Damiano, Daniele Radicioni and Ousmane Diakite

10:30 ***Coffee break***

11:00 **Session 2**

Levels of Non-Fictionality in Fictional Texts
Florian Barth, Hanna Varachkina, Tillmann Dönicke and Luisa Gödeke

10:55 **Session 3: Flash presentations**

Event Sequencing Annotation with TIE-ML
Damir Cavar, Ali Aljubailan, Ludovic Mompelat, Yuna Won, Billy Dickson, Matthew Fort, Andrew Davis and Soyoung Kim

Measuring Similarity by Linguistic Features rather than Frequency
Rodolfo Delmonte and Nicolò Busetto

Testing the Annotation Consistency of Hallidayan Transitivity Processes: A Multi-variable Structural Approach
Min Dong, Xiaoyan Liu and Alex Chengyu Fang

The place of ISO-Space in Text2Story multilayer annotation scheme
António Leal, Purificação Silvano, Evelin Amorim, Inês Cantante, Fátima Silva, Alípio Mario Jorge and Ricardo Campos

Do machines dream of artificial agreement?
Anna Lindahl

CroaTPAS: A Survey-based Evaluation
Costanza Marini

Simplifying Semantic Annotations of SMCalFlow
Joram Meron

Multilingual Reference Annotation: A Case between English and Mandarin Chinese
Ut Seong Sio and Luís Morgado da Costa

12:15 **Session 4: Poster visits**

13:00 ***Lunch break***

14:00 **Session 5**

Graph Querying for Semantic Annotations
Maxime Amblard, Bruno Guillaume, Siyana Pavlova and Guy Perrier

Intuitive and Formal Transparency in Annotation Schemes
Harry Bunt

How much of UCCA can be predicted from AMR?
Siyana Pavlova, Maxime Amblard and Bruno Guillaume

Towards Practical Semantic Interoperability in NLP Platforms
Julian Moreno-Schneider, Rémi Calizzano, Florian Kintzel, Georg Rehm, Dimitris Galanis and Ian Roberts

Annotating Japanese Numeral Expressions for a Logical and Pragmatic Inference Dataset
Kana Koyano, Hitomi Yanaka, Koji Mineshima and Daisuke Bekki

16:00 ***Coffee/tea break***

16:30 **Session 6**

Annotating Propositional Attitude Verbs and their Arguments
Marta Ricchiardi and Elisabetta Jezek

Annotating complex words to investigate the semantics of derivational processes
Rossella Varvara, Justine Salvadori and Richard Huyghe

17:20 ***Closing***

Proceedings of ISA-18 Workshop at LREC2022, pages 1–9
Marseille, 20 June 2022

What Is Going through Your Mind?
Metacognitive Events Classification in Human-Agent Interactions

Hafiza Erum Manzoor, Volha Petukhova
Spoken Language Systems Group, Saarland Informatics Campus
Saarland University, Saarbrücken, Germany
{hemanzoor,v.petukhova}@lsv.uni-saarland.de

Abstract

For an agent, either human or artificial, to show intelligent interactive behaviour implies assessments of the reliability of own and others' thoughts, feelings and beliefs. Agents capable of these robust evaluations are able to adequately interpret their own and others' cognitive and emotional processes, anticipate future actions, and improve their decision-making and interactive performances across domains and contexts. Reliable instruments to assess interlocutors' mindful capacities for monitoring and regulation - metacognition - in human-agent interaction in real-time and continuously are of crucial importance however challenging to design. The presented study reports Concurrent Think Aloud (CTA) experiments in order to access and evaluate metacognitive dispositions and attitudes of participants in human-agent interactions. A typology of metacognitive events related to the 'verbalized' monitoring, interpretation, reflection and regulation activities observed in a multimodal dialogue has been designed, and serves as a valid tool to identify relation between participants' behaviour analysed in terms of ISO 24617-2 compliant dialogue acts and the corresponding metacognitive indicators.

Keywords: metacognitive events, dialogue acts, metacognition assessment in human-agent interaction

1. Introduction

Human interactions are regulated by the participants' abilities to attribute mental and emotional states to self and others. These metacognitive abilities allude to higher order thinking that involves active control over the cognitive processes (Livingston, 2003). Metacognition helps people identify gaps in their knowledge and create strategies to fill those gaps (Dunning, 2011). Metacognition governs decision-making processes (Yeung and Summerfield, 2012) and plays an important role in guiding and regulating human intelligent behaviour and social functioning (Frith, 2012).

With tremendous increase in computational power and significant advances in sensing technologies, many multimodal dialogue systems claim to offer the mode of interaction that is more intuitive and natural for their users. Behaviour of such systems, however, most of the time presents only a rough approximation of what would be considered as intelligent. The incorporation of metacognitive processes into the dialogue model has a potential to make dialogue systems genuinely more intelligent: enable proactive cognitive control, anticipate future task demands and actions, improve knowledge transfer and task switching, enhance interactivity, and enable social and cognitive adaptation in behaviour and decision making (Malchanau et al., 2018).

In order to bring metacognition into the dialogue system design and to exploit the full potential of efficient regulation and control strategies, it is crucial to have appropriate real-time continuous measurement of metacognition. An access to own and others' cognitive processes through offline prospective or retrospective *self-reports* is not always accurate (Schraw, 2009). Introspective online methods include *verbalization* and *reflection when prompting*, and provide rich information about the metacognitive processes when performing a task. They are powerful predictors of task performance (Bannert and Mengelkamp, 2008), but also disclose current sensations, emotions, focus of attention, plans, intentions (Ericsson and Simon, 1980). However, elicitation of explicit monitoring, reflection and regulation moments may disrupt or even break down the interaction process and cannot be used as real-time continuous assessment tool. *Observational* approaches, where authentic multimodal interaction and social processes are recorded, have advantages over self-report and think-aloud methods (Whitebread et al., 2009). Observations may be more ecologically valid than the other methods, because they are independent of interlocutor's verbal ability and working memory capacity. Nevertheless, metacognition is not directly accessible through observations. Multimodal data has to be transformed in a meaningful way to understand the relationships between components of metacognition. Thus, a multi-method approach is required. This study investigates what verbalised data adds to the understanding of metacognitive processes and corresponding behaviours enabling a real-time continuous assessment of metacognition by the system. For this, a series of human-agent interactions experiments have been performed that involved concurrent probing and thinking aloud. The collected multimodal data was annotated with dialogue act information as having a certain communicative function and semantic content with explicitly defined metacognitive components. The semantic framework of Dynamic Interpretation Theory (DIT, (Bunt, 1999)) and the ISO 24617-2 dialogue act annotation standard (2. Edition, (ISO, 2020)) was applied

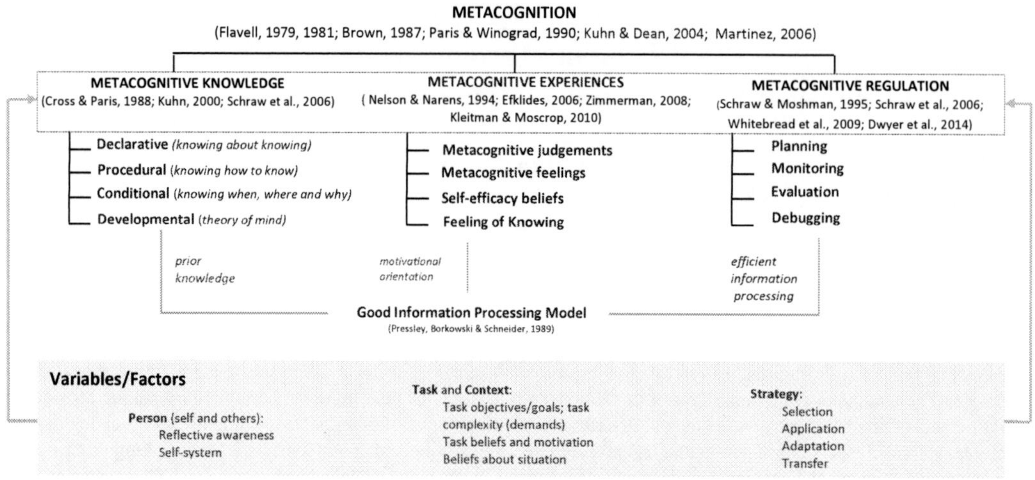

Figure 1: Conceptual overview of metacognition.

and extended to model the metacognitive events. We identified a number of associated metacognitive indicators that we will use in the future task of metacognitive states classification.

The paper is organized as follows. Section 2 discusses the key concepts of metacognition and presents the DIT/ISO 24617-2 based taxonomy of metacognitive acts by specifying their functions and contents. Section 3 outlines the experimental design. We discuss the think-aloud protocols for human-agent negotiation scenarios. The multimodal data collection, processing, dialogue act annotations and the obtained results are presented. Section 5 summarises important findings and limitations, draws conclusions and outlines future research.

2. Metacognition: Conceptual Overview and Events

There are various definitions and models proposed featuring fuzziness, expansiveness and complexity of the construct of metacognition (Tarricone, 2011). The general concept of metacognition as cognition about cognition (the 2nd order cognition: thoughts about thoughts, knowledge about knowledge) has been gradually broadened to include anything psychological, rather than just anything cognitive: knowledge of one's knowledge, processes, cognitive and affective states, the ability to consciously and deliberately monitor and regulate one's knowledge, processes, cognitive and affective states (Flavell, 1979; Flavell, 1981; Efklides, 2006; Zimmerman, 2008). Metacognition is at best described as a multidimensional construct comprising metacognitive knowledge, metacognitive experiences and the respective regulation. *Metacognitive knowledge* consists of beliefs of one's cognitive abilities, of particular tasks and of different strategies that are available and appropriate to the task. *Metacognitive experiences* are concerned with self-efficacy beliefs, confidence, feelings and accuracy as the degree of correspondence between the subjective judgement and the actual performance. *Metacognitive regulation* involves conscious control and strategies such as planning, progress monitoring, effort allocation, strategy use and regulation of cognition, i.e. the ability to recognize and reflect on one's own and others mental states, as well as the ability to use metacognitive knowledge to tackle the difficulties in social interactions (Petty et al., 2007; Brune et al., 2011). Three major factors or variables interact to affect the course and outcome of cognitive enterprises: *person*, *task* and *strategy*. Discrete acts of metacognition, i.e. cognitive acts of monitoring and the respective behavioural regulation are complemented by synthetic forms of metacognition in which an array of intentions, thoughts, feelings, and connections between events are integrated into larger complex representations of self and others developed over time (Brune et al., 2011). Figure 1 depicts the conceptual overview of metacognition with references to the most cited research work in the area.

2.1. Metacognitive Events: Functions and Contents

In (Petukhova and Manzoor, 2021), *metacognitive events* are defined as reflexive activities that express any level of the sender's mindful awareness of own and others cognitive processes: pay attention, monitor, interpret and verify understanding, evaluate contents and feelings, and regulate and plan actions. These functional aspects of information processing concern *metacognitive functions* - abilities to recognize the various elements of one's mental state, and the ability to comprehend other's behaviour in terms of intentionality, variations and changes in intentional states.

Metacognitive events can be annotated using the Metacognition Assessment Scale (MAS) protocols designed to analyse interview transcripts with psy-

Metacognition Assessment Scale (MAS)		DIT/ISO24617-2 Dialogue Act	
Domain	**Function**	**Dimension**	**Communicative function**
Understanding One's Own Mind	Basic requirements	Auto-Feedback	pos./neg. attention
	Identification		pos./neg. recognition
	Relating variables		pos./neg. interpretation
	Differentiation		
	Integration		
	Decentration		
Understanding Other's Mind	Basic requirements	Allo-Feedback	pos./neg. attention
	Identification		pos./neg. recognition
	Relating variables		pos./neg. interpretation
	Differentiation		
	Integration		
	Decentration		
Master	Basic requirements	Auto-Feedback	pos./neg. evaluation
	1st level strategy	Auto-Feedback	pos./neg. execution
		Own Communication	error signal, retraction, self-correction
		Time Management	stalling
	2nd level strategy	Task& Task Management	various + (implied) Auto-Execution
		Interaction Management	various+ (implied) Auto-Execution
	3rd level strategies	Allo-Feedback	pos./neg. execution
			feedback elicitation (higher levels)
		Task& Task Management	various + (implied) Auto-& Allo-Execution
		Interaction Management	various+ (implied) Auto-& Allo-Execution

Table 1: Mapping between MAS domains and functions and DIT/ISO24617-2 dialogue acts.

chotherapy patients (Semerari et al., 2003). To the best of our knowlegde, this is the only taxonomy that can serve as a basis for our annotation efforts as it is suitable for our interactive setting. We compared concepts defined in the DIT^{++} (Bunt, 2006) and its subset, the ISO 24617-2 dialogue act annotation standard (ISO, 2020)[1], and the MAS metacognitive domains and functions. Table 1 provides an overview of our mapping efforts.

In both taxonomies, a special attention is paid to *feedback* acts which are crucial for the successful metacognitive functioning. DIT/ISO 24617-2 defines positive and negative feedback about sender's own (*auto*-feedback) and the partner's processing (*allo*-feedback). They correspond to the two MAS domains: (1) mental operations which involve knowing one's own mental states (*understanding one's own mind*), and (2) knowing mental states of the others (*understanding other's mind*), with six functions:

1. *basic requirements* refer to the ability to acknowledge own mental functions and existence of those in others, and to represent self and others as persons with autonomous thoughts and feelings;
2. *identification* – the ability to recognize one's own and other's cognitive and emotional states;
3. *relating variables* – the ability to establish relations among the separate components of one's own and other's mental state and between the components of mental states and behaviour;
4. *differentiation* – the ability to distinguish one's own and other individuals' mental states;
5. *integration* – the ability to work out coherent descriptions of one's own and other's mental states;
6. *decentration* – the ability to produce interpretations independent of other people's knowledge.

The first two MAS functions concern *monitoring* activities and involve gaining *attention* and setting *recognition* of each other's behaviour. The last three MAS functions concern *interpretation* processes. Higher processing levels involve *mastery* of regulation and control activities based on the ability to assess one's representations and mental states (*evaluation* as a *mastery basic requirement*, MBR), and the ability to implement effective action strategies to accomplish cognitive tasks or to cope with problematic mental states (*task execution*). Levels of mastery regulation and control strategies reflect the complexity of the metacognitive operations needed to be executed. For example, if an interlocutor acts directly on her/his own understanding and evaluation of the current dialogue state slightly modifying her/his mental states, this concerns the *1st level strategies*. Interlocutor may **report** (in-)consistencies in her/his mental state, successes or failures in execution of certain action. *Own communication* and *time management* acts are typically concerned with this level strategies. When an interlocutor performs a certain type of behaviour actively **modify**ing one's own level of attention, concentration, interpretation and evaluation, voluntarily thinking or not thinking about a problem, and adjusting her/his previous mental state, these acts require the *2nd level strategies*. The *3rd level strategies* involve **adopt**ing a rational and critical attitude to the beliefs that are behind a problematic state using one's knowledge about others' mental states, e.g. regulate interpersonal problems accepting one's personal limits and errors, or influencing events. These three levels strategies imply various reflection and regulation efforts.

[1]DIT, Release 5.2 and ISO 24617-2, 2nd Edition are available on `https://dit.uvt.nl/`

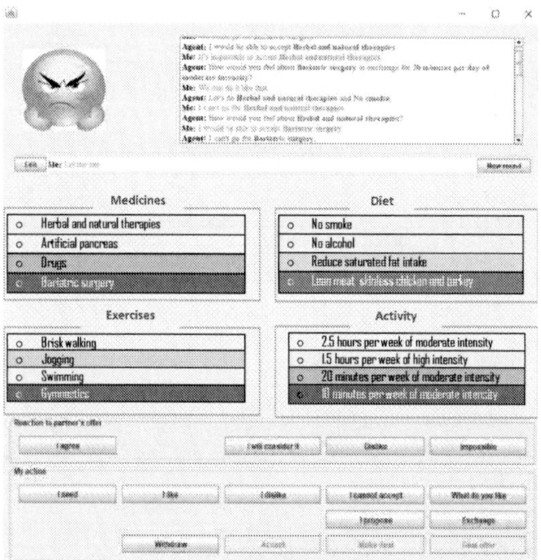

Figure 2: Agent Graphical User Interface. From up to down: dialogue window with an emoji depicting the agent's satisfaction with the partner's strategies; generated preference profile for a human participant, with brighter orange colours for increasingly negative options and brighter blue - for positive ones; set of actions in response to agent's offers, to request agent's preferences, to propose (counter-)offers, concessions, final deals or terminate negotiation.

Metacognitive contents are the ideas and beliefs linked to beliefs about beliefs and are task dependent. They are concerned with beliefs about the current state of the world including partners' states (what do I know, what do I know about others, what am I asked, what can I do, what has happened before), and an action to be taken in that situation (e.g. give information, run tests, examine something, reason about others, change attitude). In our think aloud experiments, it is assumed that participants will verbalize metacognitive contents making them accessible for further modelling and assessments.

3. Experimental Design

In dialogue, to directly access participants' metacognitive knowledge, experiences and regulation strategies, and to understand partner's cognitive processes, Concurrent Think-Aloud (CTA) protocols were designed (Ericsson and Simon, 1980). Participants were encouraged to verbalize their experiences, thoughts, actions, and feelings whilst interacting with an artificial agent through its graphical interface. This method provides direct "real-time" insight into the cognitive processes employed by the participants. Participants were asked/prompted to not only verbalize their decisions and what they think about the decisions of their partners but also explain why they think these decision lead to certain outcomes or try to look ahead and predict how certain decisions will influence the outcomes.

3.1. Use Case and Scenario

Negotiations are chosen as the use case, a domain where the importance of metacognition has been empirically proven to significantly influence decision-making processes (Galluccio and Safran, 2015). In the designed scenario, the human participant - Doctor - negotiates with an Interactive Cognitive Agent - Simulated Patient (SP)- various plans for treatment of diabetes of Type 2. SPs hold different preferences and are trained to take actions and make decisions that people would take and make in real-life scenarios (Petukhova et al., 2019). The patient-doctor negotiation scenario is based on the recommendations of the International Diabetes Federation (IDF, 2017) addressing four issues: (1) medication, (2) diet, (3) activity and (4) exercise recommendations. Interaction concerns multi-issue bargaining where each issue involves multiple negotiation *options* with preferences representing parties negotiation positions. Preferences are weighted in order of importance and defined as the participant's beliefs about *attitudes* towards certain behaviour and *abilities* to perform this behaviour. The goal of each partner is to find out preferences of each other and to search for the best possible mutual agreement.

3.2. Set Up and Experimental Protocols

A negotiation *session* consists of six think-aloud *rounds* featuring scenarios of various complexity. Human participant is assigned the role of a doctor and receives the background story and an automatically generated preference profile as depicted in Fig. 2. The task is to negotiate an agreement with an SP (agent) - select exactly one value for each issue, exchange and elicit offers concerning the agent's options. No further rules on the negotiation process, order of discussion of issues, or time constraints are imposed. Negotiators are allowed to withdraw or re-negotiate previously made agreements within a round, or terminate a negotiation. Participants were asked to verbalize everything what is on their mind: explain what action they are going to perform and why, and what they think about the agent's actions and the rationales/strategies behind.
Prior to experiments, participants are educated about the purpose and the course of the study. Subsequently, a declaration of informed consent is signed. The anonymity of the participants is guaranteed followed by European laws on personal data protection (GDPR, 2018`https://gdpr-info.eu/`). During the experiment, the participant sits in a comfortable chair in front of a laptop monitor. Participants are briefed on how to interact with the agent using the GUI.
10 subjects (aged between 19 and 25 years, 4 male and 6 female, proficient but non-native speakers of English) participated in the experiments, each involved in one negotiation session. Interactions were recorded with LENOVO THINKPAD E570 (Core i7) equipped with the webcam (720p) and dual microphones. The lighting and sound conditions were close to the conditions

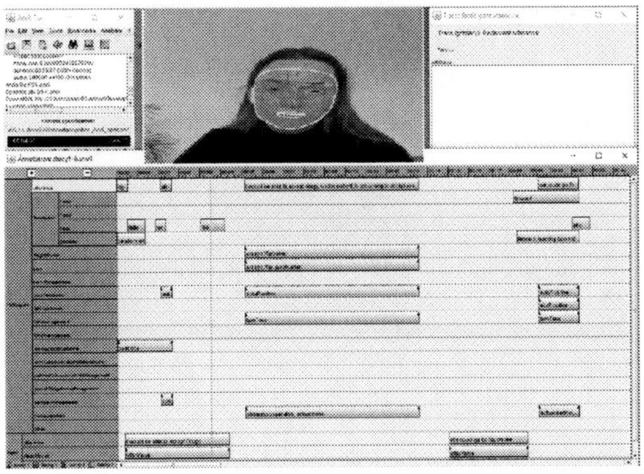

Figure 3: Example of Anvil annotations with video featuring OpenFace facial landmark detection.

of the intended interactive application entailing a fairly good but not perfect acoustic and video quality. Video background was white. The goal of the **technical set-up** was to let participants interact as free as possible keeping them away from any distraction and enabling stable continuous recording and logging of multimodal data.

3.3. Data Collection and Processing

Participants behaviour was video and audio recorded. The mouse and keyboard GUI actions were captured automatically and time aligned using the python library `atbswp`[2]. Video recordings (640x480, 30fps) were done with `ffmpeg`[3] tool applying the MPEG codec; audio signals were stored in `wav` format having frame per buffer (fpb) 1024 at rate of 44100. The video quality was sufficient to be further processed using `OpenFace`[4] and `MediaPipe`[5] libraries to extract features and facial landmarks reliably, see Fig. 3.

Participants nonverbal behaviour, mainly gaze re-direction, facial expressions, head gestures, posture shifts were coded using the scheme proposed in (Petukhova and Bunt, 2012) which supports a rather detailed characterization of movements in terms of low-level behavioural features, such as changes in muscular activity and types of these changes, direction, trajectory, speed, intensity and periodicity of movements. A moderate inter-coder agreement coding type of visible movement was observed (standard Cohen's kappa of 0.62). We measured the coding RealTime Factor (RTF), the amount of time spent on transcriptions and coding, as being RTF 19 on average and meaning that a coder spent 19 minutes annotating 1 minute of video. The detected mouse and 'on-screen' (touch screen) actions were categorized as 'mouse up', 'scroll', 'move to', 'mouse down' and 'sleep'. Timing, duration, speed and direction of movements were computed automatically. The coding scheme is recently finalised, quality assessment as well as neural network based classification experiments are in progress.

Video, GUI logs and audio signals were synchronised and mixed using `FFmpeg`[6]. Participants' speech was transcribed in `PRAAT`[7]. Annotations were performed in `Anvil`[8].

3.4. Annotations

The collected multimodal data was annotated with multidimensional DIT/ISO 24617-2 tagset taking into account MAS categories specified in Section 2.1. Ten DIT/ISO 24617-2 dimensions address the information about a negotiation (*Task*); the sender's processing of dialogue contributions, awareness of her/his mental states and knowledge of the basic regulation strategies (*Auto Feedback*) or similar cognitive processing by the partner (*Allo Feedback*); the management of difficulties in the sender's contributions (*Own Communication Management*), or similar difficulties of the partner (*Partner Communication Management*); maintaining contact (*Contact Management*); need for time (*Time Management*); the allocation of the sender role (*Turn Management*); the *Structuring* of the *Dialogue*; and the *Management* of *Social Obligations*. A recently added ISO 24617-2 dimension (2. Edition) deals with the management of the negotiation, but also with the management of decision-making processes and metacognitive tasks (*Task Management*). In Task Management utterances, the sender verbalizes beliefs concerning her/his understanding and evaluation of the current negotiation state, procedures and strategies, anticipated (un-)favourable actions, explains why certain own and partner's decisions are or should be made. Dialogue act annotations were linked to different type of primary data: to verbal and (non)verbal behaviour and logged GUI actions. The inter-annotator agreement was measured and ranges from moderate to almost perfect for specific dimensions, see Table 2.

To annotate metacognitive contents, we enriched functional aspects of dialogue act with specifications of semantic content related to *reflection* and *decision*. These two categories were empirically observed when analysing think aloud dialogue transcripts. In their (meta)cognitive thinking verbalizations, participants mostly refer to their understanding of own and partner's mental states as the basis for their past and future decisions which concern (i) the sender's beliefs about her/his own and partner's past and future *actions*, (ii) the interpretation of the participants' *preferences*, (iii) own and partners' applied or to apply negotiation *strategies*, and (iv) *consequences* or *conditions* under which certain intermediate and final outcomes can be reached.

[2] https://awesomeopensource.com/project/RMPR/atbswp

[3] https://ffmpeg.org/

[4] https://cmusatyalab.github.io/openface/

[5] https://google.github.io/mediapipe/

[6] https://ffmpeg.org

[7] https://www.fon.hum.uva.nl/praat/

[8] http://www.anvil-software.org/

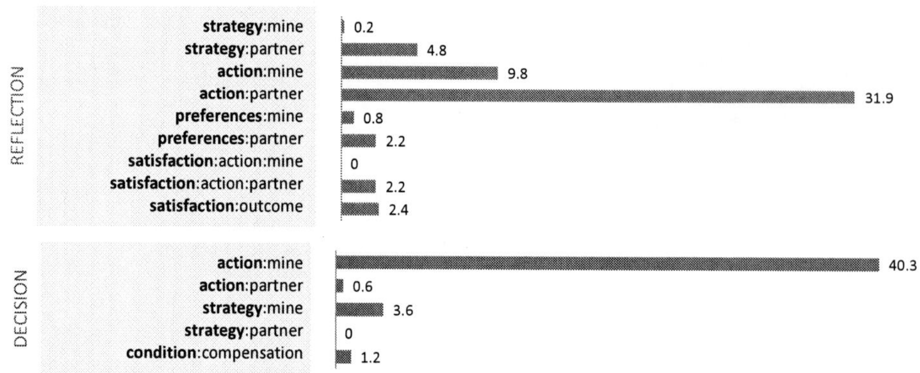

Figure 4: Dialogue acts with metacognitive content annotated in think-aloud interactions.

To sum up, dialogue acts were annotated across eleven DIT/ISO 24617-2^{++} dimensions as having a *communicative function* which specifies the sender's intention expressed in a dialogue utterance, and *semantic content* which indicates what the utterance is about. DIT^{++} tagset of possibly *qualified* communicative functions was applied. We distinguished two types of semantic content: (1) negotiation specific content which concerns negotiation moves such as offer, counter-offer, compromise as defined in (Petukhova et al., 2017); and (2) metacognitive content which concerns the sender's reflection efforts and decision related beliefs. The `Anvil` multi-tier annotations functionality was exploited to establish temporal, structural and semantic dependence relations of various types: (i) between (parts of) two or more segments in primary data; (ii) between functional components of two or more dialogue acts; (iii) between functional and semantic components of two or more dialogue acts; and (iv) between domain related and metacognitive components of two or more dialogue acts.

4. Experimental Results

The analysis of the annotated data shows that think-aloud interactions are mostly concerned with task-related exchanges, i.e. task and task management acts prevail constituting from 16.6% to 27% of all dialogue acts performed (see Table2). The more task management acts were performed the higher success rate in negotiations was achieved, only 4% of all interactions resulted in negotiation termination. This confirms previous findings that explicit metacognitive thinking positively effects negotiation task performance and outcomes. The other important aspect of interactions concerns the understanding and communication of interlocutor's intentions related to one's own and partner's preferences, strategies and actions, as well as the assessment of the ongoing (meta)cognitive processes. Auto- and Allo-Feedback acts were therefore frequently observed in think aloud experiments, 19.2% and 9.6% respectively. Task management and feedback acts are directly concerned with metacognitive processes, with reflection efforts and regulation strategies, as illustrated in examples in (1):

(1) (i) Human: I will try to meet in the middle [preferences]
(ii) Human: I would be stubborn too
(iii) Human: I think now the patient wants to ...

We represent metacognitive contents as a set of attribute-value pairs corresponding to one's beliefs encoding reflections and decisions about preferences, strategies, actions and conditions, and one's beliefs about other's beliefs of the same kind. Following the ISO 24617-2 guidelines, a simple plug-in for representing semantic content as a list of attribute-value pairs is used. In the example in (2), the `<avContent>` element specifies this semantic information in terms of attribute-value pairs of an utterance in (1i).
The example in 2 illustrates this.

(2)

```
<dialogueAct xml:id="dap2TSKM74"
   sender="#p2" addressee="#p1"
   dimension="taskManagement"
   communicativeFunction="inform"
   target="#fsp2TSKMCV74">
     <avContent xml:id="av74"
     target="#fsp2TSKMCV74"
     attribute="decision:strategy:mine"
     value="middle"/>
     <contentLink dialAct="#dap2TSKM74"
     content="#c74"/>
</dialogueAct>
```

We were able to identify a range of feedback-related metacognitive indicators which often concerned various head movements, e.g. head nodding, shaking and waggles accompanied by a noticeable smile, lip pout or compression, raising or lowering eyebrows, conjugated lateral eye movements (CLEMs), and posture shifts, e.g. leaning forward, backward or aside, shifting one's weight in the chair.
Turn and time management acts were frequently observed (9.5% to 17.9%) to co-occur with and often precede metacognitive events concerned with sender's reflection about the partner's action as in (3):

DIT/ISO 24617-2 dimension	Relative frequency (in %)	Inter-annotator agreement (Cohne's kappa)
Task	16.6	0.71
Task Management	19.2	0.59
Auto-Feedback − >	9.6	0.72
... *attention*	12.3	
... *recognition*	7.1	
... *interpretation*	16.8	
... *evaluation*	18.7	
... *execution*	45.1	
Allo-Feedback − >	13.7	0.86
... *attention*	0.3	
... *recognition*	2.1	
... *interpretation*	44.1	
... *evaluation*	52.9	
... *execution*	0.6	
Turn Management	17.9	0.71
Time Management	12.6	0.96
Contact Management	1.7	0.96
Discourse Structuring	5.9	0.77
Own Communication Man.	2.5	0.97
Partner Communication Man.	0.0	0.91
Social Obligation Management	0.3	1.0

Table 2: Distribution and inter-annotator agreement of the annotated dialogue acts across ISO 24617-2^{++} dimensions in think-aloud interactions.

(3) (i) Human: He wants ... *uhm* something bad for him
(ii) Human: ... *uhm* $_{smile}$ ... I don't agree with this

Our experiments showed that the content of participants' metacognitive events was largely concerned with the **reflection** beliefs (54.3%) compared to the verbalised **decisions** (45.7%). The interpretation and evaluation of *partner's actions* (31.9%) predominantly occupied the sender's mind. Participants often reflected on their *own actions* (9.8%), partner's *strategies* (4.8%), interlocutors' *preferences* (3.0%), and on how *valuable* the performed actions were for the sender and for the overall negotiation outcome (4.6%). The metacognitive events concerning reflection beliefs were annotated as feedback acts and were used by the sender as a basis to decide what *action* to perform next (40.3%), and what strategy to follow (3.6%) based on the accumulated utility and values of alternative options to compensate for possible own or partner's loses (1.2%). Figure4 depicts distribution of metacognitive content expressed in dialogue acts.

The analysis of mouse movements and clicking behaviour largely shows the following pattern: slowing down and pausing in mouse movements indicated reflection moments, revealed sender's lower confidence and often happened around decision points; changes in the direction of mouse movements after pausing indicated retractions, while continuation in the same direction were often interpreted as gain in confidence; and sudden termination of any movement or GUI activity meant either technical problems or unexpected situations experienced by the sender. The more in-depth analysis of GUI and verbalised actions is required and will be performed in the nearest future for which the initial technical set up will be extended, more data collection and machine learning experiments carried out.

5. Conclusion

The paper provides methodological insights and experimental design to assess metacognitive processes and contents relevant for human-agent interaction. We reviewed existing models of metacognition and available metacognition assessment instruments. Metacognitive events were defined by mapping and using the systematic analysis of concepts related to metacognitive activities, metacognitive domains and functions, and open assessment protocols. The identified metacognitive concepts were mapped to DIT/ISO 24617-2 dialogue acts - the concepts that the dialogue research community is used to operate on in dialogue modelling and system design. Subsequently, metacognitive functions and contents of dialogue acts were explicitly defined, plugged into the DIT/ISO 24617-2^{++} representations and annotated in multimodal interactive data collection experiments.

Experiments comprised behavioural observations, pragmatic and semantic analysis in think-aloud human-agent interactions. Doing this, we aimed at establishing relations between overall and task-specific metacognitive thinking, the complexity of metacognitive processes activated in social interactive setting and their multimodal behavioural indicators. We aimed at understanding to what extend and how dialogue participants use their metacognitive knowledge and regulation strategies in dialogue. Participants were asked to verbalise their metacognitive thinking to make metacognitive processes directly accessible and assessible through the use of any metacognitive indicators associated with certain type of dialogue acts in human-agent interactions. The identified indicators can serve in the future as a basis for data-driven metacognitive states classification needed for real-time monitoring and continuous metacognitive assessment pursuing two purposes: (1) to enable the system's behaviour which is intelligent, human-like and adaptive to their users, and (2) to encourage and support users to behave in the same way.

There are certain limitations of this study and much room for improvement and further research. Participants demography needs to be more diverse in age group. In the follow up experiments, we aim to replicate gender and age differences in a human-agent setting, e.g. to manipulate the agent's respective characteristics. A severe limitation of think-aloud experiments was that participants were non-native English speakers and sometimes not that verbally fluent, however metacognition may be confounded with verbal ability.

Our future research efforts will focus on the automatic detection and classification of nonverbal and GUI metacognitive indicators using modern machine learning algorithms and deep neural networks. We will refine our OpenFace based models and perform an in-depth quantitative and qualitative analysis of the logged GUI data.

Acknowledgments

The authors are very thankful to anonymous reviewers for their valuable comments.

6. References

Bannert, M. and Mengelkamp, C. (2008). Assessment of metacognitive skills by means of instruction to think aloud and reflect when prompted. does the verbalisation method affect learning? *Metacognition and Learning*, 3(1):39–58.

Brown, A. (1987). Metacognition, executive control, self-regulation, and other more mysterious mechanisms. *Metacognition, motivation, and understanding*.

Brune, M., Dimaggio, G., and H Lysaker, P. (2011). Metacognition and social functioning in schizophrenia: Evidence, mechanisms of influence and treatment implications. *Current Psychiatry Reviews*, 7(3):239–247.

Bunt, H. (1999). Dynamic interpretation and dialogue theory. *The structure of multimodal dialogue*, 2:139–166.

Bunt, H. (2006). Dimensions in dialogue act annotation. In *LREC*, pages 919–924.

Cross, D. R. and Paris, S. G. (1988). Developmental and instructional analyses of children's metacognition and reading comprehension. *Journal of educational psychology*, 80(2):131.

Dunning, D. (2011). The dunning–kruger effect: On being ignorant of one's own ignorance. In *Advances in experimental social psychology*, volume 44, pages 247–296. Elsevier.

Dwyer, C. P., Hogan, M. J., and Stewart, I. (2014). An integrated critical thinking framework for the 21st century. *Thinking skills and Creativity*, 12:43–52.

Efklides, A. (2006). Metacognition and affect: What can metacognitive experiences tell us about the learning process? *Educational research review*, 1(1):3–14.

Ericsson, K. A. and Simon, H. A. (1980). Verbal reports as data. *Psychological review*, 87(3):215.

Flavell, J. H. (1979). Metacognition and cognitive monitoring: A new area of cognitive–developmental inquiry. *American psychologist*, 34(10):906.

Flavell, J. H. (1981). Cognitive monitoring. *Children's oral communication skills*.

Frith, C. D. (2012). The role of metacognition in human social interactions. *Philosophical Transactions of the Royal Society B: Biological Sciences*, 367(1599):2213–2223.

Galluccio, M. and Safran, J. D. (2015). Mindfulness-based training for negotiators: Fostering resilience in the face of stress. In *Handbook of International Negotiation*, pages 209–226. Springer.

ISO. (2020). *Language resource management – Semantic annotation framework – Part 2: Dialogue acts. ISO 24617-2, Second Edition*. ISO Central Secretariat, Geneva.

Kleitman, S. and Moscrop, T. (2010). Self-confidence and academic achievements in primary-school children: Their relationships and links to parental bonds, intelligence, age, and gender. In *Trends and prospects in metacognition research*, pages 293–326. Springer.

Kuhn, D. and Dean, Jr, D. (2004). Metacognition: A bridge between cognitive psychology and educational practice. *Theory into practice*, 43(4):268–273.

Kuhn, D. (2000). Metacognitive development. *Current directions in psychological science*, 9(5):178–181.

Livingston, J. A. (2003). Metacognition: An overview.

Malchanau, A., Petukhova, V., and Bunt, H. (2018). Towards integration of cognitive models in dialogue management: designing the virtual negotiation coach application. *Dialogue & Discourse*, 9(2):35–79.

Martinez, M. E. (2006). What is metacognition? *Phi delta kappan*, 87(9):696–699.

Nelson, T. O. and Narens, L. (1994). Why investigate metacognition. *Metacognition: Knowing about knowing*, 13:1–25.

Paris, S. G., Winograd, P., et al. (1990). How metacognition can promote academic learning and instruction. *Dimensions of thinking and cognitive instruction*, 1:15–51.

Petty, R. E., Briñol, P., Tormala, Z. L., and Wegener, D. T. (2007). *The role of metacognition in social judgment.* The Guilford Press.

Petukhova, V. and Bunt, H. (2012). The coding and annotation of multimodal dialogue acts. In *Proceedings of the Eighth International Conference on Language Resources and Evaluation (LREC'12)*, pages 1293–1300.

Petukhova, V. and Manzoor, H. E. (2021). Towards the iso 24617-2-compliant typology of metacognitive events. In *Proceedings of the 17th Joint ACL-ISO ISA Workshop*, pages 14–19.

Petukhova, V., Bunt, H., and Malchanau, A. (2017). Computing negotiation update semantics in multi-issue bargaining dialogues. In *Proceedings of the SemDial*, Saarbrücken, Germany.

Petukhova, V., Sharifullaeva, F., and Klakow, D. (2019). Modelling shared decision making in medical negotiations: Interactive training with cognitive agents. In *Proceeding PRIMA Conference*, pages 251–270. Springer.

Pressley, M., Borkwski, J. G., and Schneider, W. (1989). Good information processing: What it is and how education can promote it. *International Journal of Educational Research*, 13(8):857–867.

Schraw, G. and Moshman, D. (1995). Metacognitive theories. *Educational psychology review*, 7(4):351–371.

Schraw, G., Crippen, K. J., and Hartley, K. (2006). Promoting self-regulation in science education: Metacognition as part of a broader perspective on learning. *Research in science education*, 36(1):111–139.

Schraw, G. (2009). A conceptual analysis of five measures of metacognitive monitoring. *Metacognition and learning*, 4(1):33–45.

Semerari, A., Carcione, A., Dimaggio, G., Falcone, M., Nicolo, G., Procacci, M., and Alleva, G. (2003). How to evaluate metacognitive functioning in psychotherapy? the metacognition assessment scale and its applications. *Clinical Psychology & Psychotherapy*, 10(4):238–261.

Tarricone, P. (2011). *The taxonomy of metacognition*. Psychology Press.

Whitebread, D., Coltman, P., Jameson, H., and Lander, R. (2009). Play, cognition and self-regulation: What exactly are children learning when they learn through play? *Educational and Child Psychology*, 26(2):40.

Yeung, N. and Summerfield, C. (2012). Metacognition in human decision-making: confidence and error monitoring. *Philosophical Transactions of the Royal Society*, 367(1594):1310–1321.

Zimmerman, B. J. (2008). Investigating self-regulation and motivation: Historical background, methodological developments, and future prospects. *American educational research journal*, 45(1):166–183.

Proceedings of ISA-18 Workshop at LREC2022, pages 10–19
Marseille, 20 June 2022

Assessment of Sales Negotiation Strategies with ISO 24617-2 Dialogue Act Annotations

Jutta Stock[1,2], Volha Petukhova[2], Dietrich Klakow[2]
[1]DPV Deutscher Pressevertrieb GmbH, Hamburg, Germany
[2]Saarland University, Spoken Language Systems, Saarbrücken, Germany
stock.jutta@dpv.de; {v.petukhova,dietrich.klakow}@lsv.uni-saaarland.de

Abstract

Call centres endeavour to achieve the highest possible level of transparency with regard to the factors influencing sales success. Existing approaches to the quality assessment of customer-agent sales negotiations do not enable in-depths analysis of sales behaviour. This study addresses this gap and presents a conceptual and operational framework applying the ISO 24617-2 dialogue act annotation scheme, a multidimensional taxonomy of interoperable semantic concepts. We hypothesise that the ISO 24617-2 dialogue act annotation framework adequately supports sales negotiation assessment in the domain of call centre conversations. Authentic call centre conversations are annotated and a range of extensions/modifications are proposed making the annotation scheme better fit this new domain. We concluded that ISO 24617-2 serves as a powerful instrument for the analysis and assessment of sales negotiation and strategies applied by a call centre agent.

Keywords: call centre, semantic annotations, interaction analysis

1. Introduction

For companies and their associated call centres, information about service quality, sales success factors and customer satisfaction is a valuable asset. Call centres routinely record interactions with their customers, such as phone calls and emails. To record, track and analyse conversational data, Speech Analytics Tools (SAT) are used, such as AVOKE[1], Talkdesk[2], NICE [3], and VERINT [4]. The current SAT applications for call centre interactions incorporate speech-to-text and text mining functionalities. However, most of them do not enable in-depths analysis of persuasive communicative and sale strategies that account for social and interpersonal aspects, affected cognitive states of interlocutors, and the corporate organisational rules and business logic. Being able to plan, monitor and evaluate appropriate interactive and sales negotiation strategies while optimising customer satisfaction for inbound service calls are the core skills and tasks of call centre agent in order to gain high economic and reputation advantages for their company.

In the challenging call centre environment, agents are advised to regard any service call as an opportunity for sales and an option to connect the customer to the corporate brands and products. At the same time, agents need to preserve customer satisfaction and choose the most efficient strategy to keep the Average Handling Time (AHT) as short as possible. To support this, agents have a set of special offers, including discounts and vouchers. Agents may experience a variety of situations with angry, difficult, extreme wordy or helpless customers or those whose context or needs are not clear. Call centre agents have to be aware that their interactions and attitudes will influence the outcome of a call, both negatively and positively. This leads to the following question: why are some agents successful while others cannot finalise a single deal, despite the fact that they share the same set of special offers and vouchers or even have high activity indexes.

To obtain a better understanding of the exact nature of strong and weak communicative and sales negotiation strategies, a comprehensive analysis of authentic conversations is required. While there are different opinions and guidelines concerning what constitutes human-like intelligent communicative behaviour, supported by formal (qualitative and quantitative) studies, data driven studies of authentic human-human interactions in many domains, especially those sensitive to personal data, are very scarce. Call centre conversations usually contain private data, such as full name and address, often also much more sensitive and legally protected data, such as bank and credit card details. Call centres are very careful about their data and are even obliged to purge it regularly, e.g. every 3-6 months; they are reluctant to share it for research purposes. On the other hand, the lack of comprehensive, theoretically well motivated, and potentially automatable analysis methods play a major role in hindering large scale data driven research in this area. The study reported in this paper is the first step in addressing this gap and developing a conceptual and operational framework for a comprehensive multidimensional, multi-level and multi-factor interaction analysis of call centre interactions. The analysis involves annotations with dialogue act information. Annotation schemes have been constructed to be useful for both empirically-based studies of interactive and task-related phenomena, and for the data-driven design of interactive systems. We hypothesise that the ISO

[1]https://www.intrado.com/
[2]https://www.talkdesk.com/
[3]https://www.nice.com/
[4]https://www.verint.com/

24617-2 dialogue act annotation framework will adequately support sales negotiation assessment in the domain of call centre conversations. The presented study tests this assumption and performs a comprehensive analysis of the annotated communicative behaviour applying the ISO-24617-2 taxonomy (Second Edition, (ISO, 2020)). We extend the ISO 24617-2 repository of communicative functions specific to a given application domain and enrich functional aspects of dialogue act specifications with domain-specific semantic content in various forms and degrees of detail. This allows customising the ISO 24617-2 dialogue act taxonomy as a tool to support effective understanding and assessment of call centre inbound interactions accounting for the relationship between language-specific schemes and emotional, social and cognitive determinants of sales negotiation strategies.

The remainder of this paper is structured as follows. Section 2 discusses the domain of sales negotiations and the related work performed in the analysis and modelling of call centre conversations. Section 3 addresses the complexity of call centre sales negotiations and specifies a number of use cases. In Section 4, the ISO 24617-2 annotation framework and previous relevant annotation efforts are presented. Section 5 presents annotation experiments performed to assess the applicability and coverage of concepts defined in the ISO 24617-2 taxonomy to the target domain, whereby we specify the corpus data and discuss the results obtained. Section 6 proposes extensions to ISO 24617-2 to make it powerful and accurate, as required for the use cases to analyse and model call centre interactions. Finally, Section 7 summarises our findings and outlines directions for future research and development.

2. Domain of Sales Negotiations

People negotiate daily, often without considering it to be a negotiation (Fisher et al., 2011). The study of negotiation has been an active research field for a long time, pursued from the perspectives of several disciplines including psychology, organisational behavior, decision sciences, game theory, communication, and others. The overall questions concern what drives several parties to negotiate, how they behave when doing so, how they should handle negotiations to obtain specific results, and how disputants can be helped reaching joint, mutually satisfactory decisions (Borbély et al., 2017). It can be further observed that negotiation wisdom remains rather distributed in its disciplines and practices of origin.

To understand communicative negotiation behaviour in call centre interactions, we consider it important that negotiation is always a process (Lax and Sebenius, 1986). For instance, (Weingart and Olekalns, 2004) mentions that the negotiation process is related to tactics that are not used in isolation but rather in combination to form a strategy. The way in which tactics are combined to form a strategy or strategies are employed to reach a goal is reflected in the form of the communication.

The actual negotiation phase in such interactions is called the *sales approach* which reflects the step-by-step proposition developed by a sales person or company to improve the selling process. The sales process can be defined as a linear process with chronological steps of interest generation, presentation and closing (Freese, 2000). A properly developed sales approach is what sometimes differentiates an amateur salesperson from an experienced one. Top-performing salespeople treat customer interactions like a hierarchical set of if-then choices, while other salespeople treat customer interactions as a linear dialogue (Leigh et al., 2014).

The particular challenge with incoming service calls is that the customer has a service request and does not expect a sales offer. It is therefore all the more important that the agent consciously chooses his strategy. Like many others in marketing literature, (McFarland et al., 2006) refers to the importance of rapport building, consultative communication, presenting tangible benefits, using financial incentives and creating an emotional response in customers as strategic tools to support successful sales negotiations.

Communication strategies are not well explored within the call centre scenarios. Call centre conversational data has been analysed from many perspectives, including: to classify call types (Tang et al., 2003), assist and monitor agents′ performances (Mishne et al., 2005), filter problematic conversations (Hastie et al., 2002), develop domain models (Roy and Subramaniam, 2006), and enable automatic user-specified analysis (Takeuchi et al., 2009). There is also a steady growing research interest in automatic assessment of call centre service quality relating agents characteristics (including their personalities and communication skills) to the negotiation outcome. In (Clark, 2011), it has been observed that communication strategies for call centre agents are a missing area of research. With this study, we aim to outline an approach to close this gap accordingly.

3. Use Cases

Limitations of pure text-based speech analytics software solutions have been described by (Pallotta and Delmonte, 2013). It was emphasised that conversational speech is fundamentally different from written text and that the analysis of conversations can not be only focused on semantics. In our view, there are at least three important techniques used by a sales agent that may significantly influence sales success, namely the agent's: (1) pervasive questioning methods, (2) specific customer-oriented behaviour and (3) power of persuasion.

3.1. Pervasive Questioning

According to (Kellermann, 2007), questioners put words in the answerer's mouth, shaping their responses. Even small changes in word choice and order, presuppositions and framing effects upon which questions are based, the implications that they carry and their surface form may trigger major changes in answers.

In the marketing literature, there are numerous references to the importance of questioning techniques. A salesperson's questioning skill is the act of asking customers probing and insightful questions that uncover their buying situation and needs (Shoemaker and Johlke, 2002). In the need identification stage of a sales encounter, customer oriented sales people engage in behaviors to identify the customer´s interests, goals, and other product-related needs (Homburg et al., 2011). The most straightforward way to identify customer needs is to ask questions.

Furthermore, it is underlined that effective questioning skills should yield immediate performance benefits, compared to customer orientation (CO) and adaptive selling (AD)(Arndt et al., 2018). Methodologies such as the SPIN model (Rackham, 2020) or (Freese, 2000) are commonly used to support salesperson training to effectively ask questions. It is emphasised that questions persuade more powerfully than any other form of verbal behaviour. Open and closed questions are distinguished, whereby the latter are acknowledged as stronger instrument to persuade the customer to disclose more and initially not-intended information about his/her preferences and constraints.

3.2. Customer Oriented Behaviour

From experience, we know that some agents are capable of seizing any opportunity and successfully closing a deal, even if they face negatively loaded, complaining customers. Customer-oriented behaviours (COB) that an agent can show will significantly increase customer satisfaction and therefore influence sales success. While intuitively there should be significant effects of being 'customer oriented' on service performance perceptions and sales outcomes, there is a lack of a clear understanding of what it means for a service organisation to be 'customer oriented' and how it fits into established service marketing paradigms(Brady and Cronin Jr, 2001). COB can be defined as the ability to identify, evaluate, understand, and meet customer needs (Reychav and Weisberg, 2009). (Mechinda and Patterson, 2011) define it as specific behaviors shown by front-line employees to increase customer satisfaction. Rafaeli (2008) defines five types of COB for call centre settings and relates them to the service quality as evaluated by customers: (1) anticipating customer requests; (2) providing explanations and justifications; (3) educating customers; (4) creating an emotional bound with a customer; and (5) offering personalised information.

Within the framework of adaptive selling, (Weitz et al., 1986) explain sales negotiation effectiveness by the knowledge of customer types and sales strategies, as well as the motivation of salespeople to flexibly adapt their behavior and to alter their sales goals.

3.3. Persuasive Negotiation

In our view, one of the most powerful impact factors on the sales success is the persuasive power of an agent's arguments. Salespeople can adapt their persuasion strategies to reach the deal acceptance by the customer. Successful salespeople know which persuasion strategies are most appealing to their customers. Knowing certain customers' characteristics and preferences associated with those characteristics could inform agents what message strategies are optimal for which specific customers. The persuasiveness of messages can be affected by many factors and needs to be experimentally investigated.

People accept certain suggestions if they receive additional relevant information. Due to powerful rhetorical devices, messages may be perceived as strongly persuasive. People generally associate certain speech, personality and interaction features with what they think is a persuasive argument, e.g. related to audibility, engagement, conviction, authority and likability (AECAL) criteria, (see the overview provided by (Petukhova et al., 2017)).

People respond to persuasion strategies based on their distinct personality (Adler et al., 2016). There are also interpersonal social factors that influence persuasion preferences.

Messages conveying competence arguments have been shown to be more persuasive for higher power audiences while messages conveying warmth arguments are more persuasive for low power audiences. The big two of social cognition are *communion/warmth* and *agency/competence* (Fiske et al., 2002). Warmth subsumes characteristics like cooperativeness, trustworthiness, and likeability, whereas competence includes dominance, capability and status (Fiske, 2018).

Further, the role of psychological power in the persuasion process and the relationship between power and persuasion have been investigated by (Dubois et al., 2016). The authors outline a theoretical model to demonstrate that the persuasiveness of messages can be affected by the alignment between the psychological sense of power of the communicator and the audience. To model the specified use cases, we apply the ISO 24617-2 dialogue act taxonomy and propose the necessary domain-specific extensions. We expect to gain a better understanding of the interaction structure and establish reliable indicators for specific negotiation behavior.

4. Semantic Framework of the ISO 24617-2 Dialogue Act Taxonomy

Dialogue is a complex activity in the sense that it requires participants not only to understand and perform actions towards joint goals or underlying tasks, but also to continuously share background information about the processing of each other's messages, elicit feedback, manage the use of time, take turns, and monitor contact and attention, often simultaneously (Allwood, 2000; Bunt et al., 2012). Similarly, in call centre sales negotiations, dialogues serve at least three core functions: (1) to determine, monitor and resolve a customer-related sales problems (*Task* and *Task Management*), (2) to carry out and manage the successful interaction (*Dialogue Control*); and (3) to develop and maintain relationship between an agent, also in fact between an organization and a customer (*Interpersonal Relations Management*). These aspects can be addressed simultaneously in one utterance contributing to its multifunctionality and requiring multidimensional analysis. Multidimensional approaches to dialogue act annotation, that incorporate a multifunctional view of dialogue behavior, have been recognised by many researchers as empirically better motivated, and allowing a more accurate modelling of theoretical distinctions (Allwood, 2000; Core and Allen, 1997; Bunt, 1999; Klein, 1999; Larsson, 1998; Popescu-Belis, 2005).

ISO 24617-2 (Second Edition, (ISO, 2020)) presents the semantic framework for the systematic analysis of behaviour of dialogue participants, taking a multidimensional view on dialogue in the sense that participation in a dialogue is viewed as performing several activities in parallel, such as pursuing the dialogue task or activity, providing and eliciting feedback, and taking turns. These activities in various 'dimensions' are called *dialogue acts* and are semantic units in the description of dialogue behaviour, characterising how the information state(s) of the participant(-s) at whom the behaviour is directed are changed when he/they understands the behaviour. Dialogue acts have two main components: a *semantic content*, which corresponds to what the utterance is about, e.g. objects, events, etc.; and a *communicative function*, which specifies how an addressee updates his information state with the semantic content when he understands the corresponding aspect of the meaning of a dialogue utterance. ISO 24617-2 includes the specification of the XML-based Dialogue Act Markup Language (DiAML) for the representation of dialogue act annotations (Bunt et al., 2012).

Assigning communicative functions to utterances in multiple dimensions can help represent the meaning of dialogue contributions at an adequate level of complexity for interaction analysis, resulting in multi-layered annotations. Nine dimensions are distinguished, addressing information about *tasks*, the processing of utterances by the speaker (*auto-feedback*) or the addressee (*allo-feedback*), managing difficulties in the contributions of the speaker (*own communication management*) or that of the addressee (*partner communication management*), the speaker's need for time to continue the dialogue (*time management*), the allocation of the speaker role (*turn management*), topic management (*dialogue structuring*), and managing social obligations (*social obligations management*).

The ISO 24517-2 dialogue act annotation scheme is an open domain-independent taxonomy. The multidimensional nature of the ISO taxonomy enables various extensions and offers the opportunity to tailor it to specific applications and domains. It has been successfully used to analyse and model interactive games (Petukhova et al., 2014), multi- and two-party political debates (Petukhova et al., 2015; Petukhova et al., 2018), multi-issue bargaining dialogues (Petukhova et al., 2016), and robot-assisted disaster responses (Anikina and Kruijff-Korbayová, 2019). Plug-ins have been defined in (Bunt, 2019) that allow DiAML expressions to be enriched with (a) articulate semantic content representations, tailored to the semantic complexity of a specific application domain, e.g. specifying negotiation and debate semantics (Malchanau, 2019), modality-specific semantics (Lapina and Petukhova, 2017); and (b) descriptions of emotions, for example following EmotionML (Burkhardt et al., 2017). Finally, additional specific types of communicative action for a given application domain can be defined. For example, as shown when modelling medical consultations (Petukhova and Bunt, 2020).

5. Annotation Experiments

The goal of our annotation experiments is to identify key dialogue phenomena specific to the call centre interactions and mainly related to participants' strategies.

5.1. Corpus Data

The analysed corpus presents a selection of inbound service calls from a publishing house where call centre agents communicate with various customers. These interactions are initiated by the customer, calling the contact centre for a wide range of services like ordering, cancelling their magazine subscription, expressing a complaint or changing their address. Using the in-house speech analytics application of VONAGE [5], the data collection process is organised to extract specific rather than random dialogue recordings. For instance, to find typical call centre situations featuring rich sales negotiation behavior, we selected dialogues where the customer intends to cancel the subscribed service and the call centre agent applies at least one sales approach to prevent the customer from cancelling. To achieve this, keyword lexicon functionality is used to extract dialogues containing the customer's utterances "I'd like to cancel the subscription of magazine XX" and those of an agent's "We have very attractive proposals with a discount...".

The final analysed corpus includes 60 call centre interactions with a total duration of 4 hours. The dialogue data is provided with the metadata concerning: call duration, agent ID and time stamp per turn. The speech signals (audio recordings, one channel per

[5] `https://www.vonage.com`

Dimension	Functional segments (in%)		
	ALL	from those	
		Company	Customer
Task	41.0	53.6	464
rhetoricalRelation	8.9	63.9	36.1
qualifier	3.2	34.7	36.1
autoFeedback	8.8	59,5	40.5
turnManagement	20.0	52.2	47.8
timeManagement	3.2	68.0	32.0
ownCommunicationManagement	1.1	46.8	53.2
discourseStructuring	2.9	80.1	19.9
socialObligationsManagement	10.8	57.1	42.9

Dimension	Communicative Function	Relative frequency in %
Task	request	11.6
	answer	5.8
	confirm	19.9
	inform	28.5
	setQuestion	6.4
	checkQuestion	5.1
	choiceQuestion	1.1
Turn Management	turn-unit-initial functions	46.0
	turn-unit-final functions	50.1
discourseStructuring	opening	34.2
	closing	35.4
	topicShift	13.7
	interactionStructuring	16.8

Table 1: Distribution of functional segments across dimensions produced by the Customer and Company, in terms of relative frequency (in %), Distribution of the most frequent dialogue acts, in terms of relative frequency (in %)

speaker) were automatically transcribed and manually corrected.

5.2. Annotations

The ISO 24617-2 annotations were performed segmenting participant's turns into functional segments as having one or more (potentially qualified) communicative functions, dependence and rhetorical relations between segments and/or dialogue acts. The corpus contains 29,954 tokens, segmented into 3,572 functional segments from which the customer produced 1,590 segments (45%) and the company about 1,982 (55 %). An average call duration comprises 3.7 minutes.
From all dialogues that feature subscription cancellations by the customer, about 40% of the interactions were successfully completed by a call centre agent, i.e a cancellation was avoided or an alternative product was successfully offered. Dialogues have a similar structure and compromise (i) the opening, (ii) customer identification, (iii) the discussion of an issue related to the subscription, e.g. mostly subscription cancellations, (iv) the sales approach by the agent, and (v) closing.
Semantic content specifications can be plugged in into the ISO 24617-2 standard as proposed by (Bunt, 2019). Table 1 provides an overview of dialogue act distribution addressing ISO 24617-2 dimensions as well as three dimensions in detail. It can be observed that agent-customer interactions are dominated by task-related exchanges. The Task dimension was addressed in 41.0% of all functional segments.
Within the Task dimension, the largest share of the categories compromise Request, Answer, Confirm and Inform with a total share of 65,8%, expressing a focused exchange of information. They are predominantly related to concerns about customer identification, information regarding the cancellation procedure or eliciting customer's interests. The next big part compromises tags in the question categories of Set Question, Check Question and Choice Question with a share of 12,6 %, with the majority being part of the sales negotiation, or detailed questions about offers or re-negotiations. The remaining 21,6 % are distributed among categories that focus on the sales negotiation, mostly presentation of Offers and Suggestions, and corresponding responses to them such as Decline- or Accept Offer or Suggest respectively.
The Turn Management dimension is dominated by *turn-unit-initial* functions when the customer agrees to take the turn, which the agent has given to him/her and *turn-unit-final* functions when the agent wants the customer to take the turn. This is due to a high share of request and information exchange dialogue acts.
Discourse Structuring categories like opening and closing the conversation, topic shift and active interaction structuring are clearly dominated by the agent (80,1 %) as the leading participant of the communication.
In summary, the standard functions of the ISO 24617-2 taxonomy provide a comprehensive view of the structure, the process steps and the actions of the participants in the conversation.
Examples:

(1) Company: Is there a particular reason why you no longer wish to read the magazine? *<Task;setQuestion(cancellation:reason)>*
Customer: I don't have the time *<Task; answer(cancellation:reason:lack_of_time)>*

(2) Company: I will use your email address to send you the cancellation confirmation. I think it will take 48 hours at the latest. With a bit of luck, it will be in your e-mail box this evening. Then you'll have it in black and white. *<Task; inform (cancellation:procedure); rhetoricalRelation (explanation)>*

(3) Company: Of course, we don't want to lose you as a customer. So that you don't cancel, I could offer that you read another 8 months, but only pay for 6. Then you will have two full months of the magazine free of charge. *<Task; suggest (sales:offer:advantage:price); rhetoricalRelation(elaboration))>*

6. ISO 24617-2 Extensions and Modifications

Applying the ISO 24617-2 scheme with its rich inventory of dialogue act tags to call centre interactions has shown that there remain a number of uncovered sections for assessing sales negotiation behavior. To identify and understand the communicative behavior described in the use cases, we propose the following extensions and modifications.

Semantic Content		
1st Level	2nd Level	3rd level
customerIdentification	name	
	contactDetails	address
		phoneNumber
		email
		other
	callReason	delivery
		cancellation
		other
subscriptionDetails	conditions	
	invoice	
	service	satisfaction
	product	satisfaction
cancellationDetails	subscription	
	procedure	
	payment	
	reason	lackOfTime
		content
		age
		advertising
		volume
		financial
		changeInterest
		pausing
		other
salesOffer	alternative	product
		condition
	advantage	specialPrice
		flexibility
		digitalProduct
		service

Table 2: Semantic content categories at multiple levels of specificity.

6.1. Semantic Content

ISO 24617-2 focuses on the functional aspects of dialogue acts and supports the annotation of semantic content by means of plug-ins. To model participants intentions and sales negotiation strategies in the call centre domain, the semantic content is essential. Discussed topics were observed to reflect the aforementioned dialogue structure. The distribution of all functional segments addresses the main topics of the cancellation procedure and the sales approach undertaken by the call centre agent. Other information is concerned with customer identification, contact details and addressing social and structural aspects, e.g. greetings, thanking, topic shifts, see Table 2. Functional segments addressing subscription cancellation and sales approach are of particular interest.

It merged that this structure, containing up to three level of semantic content, supports the understanding of the communicative intentions, as well as the strategic components of sales negotiation behavior. By annotating, for example, a cancellation reason such as cancellationDetails:reason:lackOfTime, see example in (1) rather than only a cancellation, the agent's decision on which products and offers to present to the customer becomes transparent. Furthermore, we have differentiated various sales offers. It is interesting to observe which product advantages such as price, flexibility or alternatives are incorporated into the sales approach argumentation, and how clients respond to them. Strategic approach, questions and corresponding answers, as well as argumentation and objection handling become evident. In these parts of the conversation, strategic aspects of sales negotiations, flexible and adaptive behaviour (Weitz et al., 1986) become transparent as well as the agent's ability to think in if-then dependencies in their sales approach (Leigh et al., 2014) . Overall, analysis of various approaches leading to particular outcomes can be compared and the most successful sales strategies can be identified.

Table 2 provides the list of defined semantic content categories at multiple levels of specificity.

6.2. Interpersonal Relations Management

Successful relationship building is one of the prerequisites for sales negotiation. Therefore, it is important to capture all clues that express developing and maintaining a relationship between an agent and a customer. In the conversations analysed, the main challenge is that two strangers are trying to address their concerns and build a relationship in a very limited period of time. Still challenging is that customers are often suspicious about subscriptions, because they fear long, inflexible contract terms. Therefore, building trust is significant. Clients expect proper management and precise information especially regarding their termination modalities and possible new contracts.

6.3. Rhetorical Relations

Concerning rhetorical relations, ISO 24617-2 (ISO, 2020) does not propose a specific set of relations to be used, but defines a plug-in for ISO 24617-8 discourse relations annotation standard (Bunt and Prasad, 2016) to be incorporated into dialogue act annotations. In (Bunt et al., 2017), it is explained that rhetorical relations can optionally be annotated to express how one dialogue act motivates the performance of another dialogue act.

In linguistic literature there is a wide field of research on discourse relations, also described as *coherence relations* or *rhetorical relations* (Prasad and Bunt, 2015). Relations bind contiguous segments of text into a global structure for the text as a whole with elaborations, explanations, contrasts, parallelisms, etc. (Hobbs, 1985) We applied rhetorical relations categories offered by the ISO 24617-8 taxonomy and focused on those that have relevance for the domain specific use cases.

The following categories were the most frequently observed: explanation, restatement, elaboration, cause and recommendation, see Table 3. Explanations, elaborations and recommendations are mostly used by the agent. (S)he often explains offers proposed and why communication needs to be terminated or resumed/repeated , see examples in (2) and (3). At the same time, the customer mostly provides reasons and restatements. This behaviour is closely related to the client's desire to be understood by the agent, e.g. by

Rhetorical Relations		Company	Customer
explanation	51.2	73.2	26.8
restatement	14.5	39.4	60.6
elaboration	13.1	85.9	14.1
cause	9.2	17.8	82.2
recommendation	3.7	100	0

Qualifier		Company	Customer
happy	27.4	35.4	64.6
uncertain	25.7	8.9	91.1
dissatisfied	11.4	0	100
pleased	10.9	63.2	36.8
satisfied	8.6	93.3	6.7

Table 3: Top five rhetorical relations and qualifiers, distributions in relative frequency in (%).

specifying the purpose of his call or explaining the reason for subscription cancellation. It has been observed that rhetorical relations mostly connect consecutive segments.

6.4. Qualifiers

Agents should be aware of the customer's feelings and insecurities, and this ideally at the very beginning of the phone call. In cases of complaint, feelings are obviously mostly negative. However, many customers do not openly express their sentiment and it is not always easy to determine it. Recognizing and understanding such behaviour is important to gain and maintain customer acceotance and satisfaction, and initiate successful sales negotiations.

To model these aspects of communicative behavior, we incorporated qualifiers into our annotations and further analysis. In the ISO 24617-2, sentiment qualifiers, that we mostly are interested in, are underspecified and negative-neutral-positive values are defined. Finer distinctions would be required to model our use case, in particular when addressing COB strategies. For instance, positive sentiments qualifiers such as amused, happy or pleased may be important to compute the degree of customer satisfaction.

Similarly, sentiment (emotions, affect) analysis may be highly relevant for sales negotiations addressing customer complaints. In the analysed subscription cancellations, about 175 segments are annotated with qualifiers. With a total of 3,572 segments, however, this is a very small proportion. Table 3 provides an overview of the top five qualifier categories. The main share of the qualifiers *happy*, *dissatisfied* and *uncertain* lies on the customer side. Situations in which these sentiments could be observed are, for example, uncertainties about the cancellation process. Expressing happiness is often related with the outcome of the conversation, when the customer is delighted to have either successfully cancelled subscription or is excited about having ordered a new product in combination with an attractive offer. On the agent side, the categories *pleased* and *satisfied* are most frequent, these occur especially at the end of the conversation.

An emotion has an experiencer and an object that the emotion is directed to. While in ISO 24617-2 qualifiers are attached to communicative functions modifying/strengthening its force, sender's attitudes can be expressed towards other participants and towards the utterance content. The former should be modelled as part of the Interpersonal Relations Management, and the latter as part of the semantic content.

Applying qualifier as an open category brings the advantage to be flexible in description of various domain-specific phenomena. For these fine-grained descriptions, many different approaches to emotions and affective states classification can be used. One of the best known taxonomies of emotions, which is still relevant nowadays, is defined in Ekman´s work (Ekman, 1999), (Ekman, 1992), where six basic emotions such as anger disgust, fear, happiness, sadness and surprise are distinguished. There is no agreed benchmark in the form of emotion terms, therefore he proposes an everyday emotion vocabulary (Cowie et al., 1999). It is recommended in ISO 24617-2 to define a plug-in using EmotionML (Schröder et al., 2011), which is a flexible scheme offering a wide range of possibilities to annotate affective aspects of dialogue behaviors. Emotions are represented in terms of 'emotion categories', 'dimensions', 'action-tendencies'. Other values that can be considered is the confidence of human annotator as well as related to valence and arousal dimensions defined in circumplex model of (Russell, 1980) .

7. Conclusion

In this study, call centre conversations were under investigation, sales negotiation behaviour in particular. Taking the complexities of sales negotiation into account, we considered several use cases which support assessment of the sales success: questioning techniques, customer oriented behaviour and the power of persuasion.

Based on the obvious limitations of the existing speech analytics solutions, we applied the ISO 24617-2 dialogue act taxonomy in order to reply our research questions. The ISO 24617-2 has been already proven to be useful in qualitative and quantitative detailed studies of communication behavior. Due to the multidimensional nature and flexibility in terms of possible extensions, we aimed to obtain a deeper understanding of the participants negotiation behaviour. Customer-agent human-human dialogues were annotated and the occurrences of dialogue acts, their semantic content and relations between them were analysed. Such detailed multidimensional ISO 24617-2 based annotations provided insights into the structure, processing steps and communicative behaviour of the negotiation participants. Already at this initial research stage, the advantages of the standard procedures became apparent. However, as enabled by the framework and specified by the standard procedures, certain domain-specific extensions or modifications are necessary including modelling important social and interpersonal aspects of sales negotiation and customer-oriented behaviour. The application of qualifier and rhetorical relations are essential for the processing of the use cases, but require further specification to close gaps in . Hereby we established a framework that enables in-depth analysis of sales negotiation behaviour.

For future research, we suggest the following perspectives and application development on the basis of our outcomes. All three use cases will be explored in individual studies; specific research questions and hypotheses will be formulated and empirical experiments designed.

The annotation methodology will consistently rely on the ISO 24617-2 guidelines for semantic and discourse information annotations (Second Edition, (ISO, 2020)). Annotation costs, quality as well as the individual processing steps will be documented in detail. In the follow-up annotation experiments, trained and (domain) expert annotators will be involved. Due to practically unlimited access to the call centre data, a wide range of various interactive scenarios will be investigated. Existing marketing theories and models will be empirically validated and novel models or their components may emerge.

Acknowledgments

The authors are very thankful to anonymous reviewers for their valuable comments.

8. References

Adler, R. F., Iacobelli, F., and Gutstein, Y. (2016). Are you convinced? a wizard of oz study to test emotional vs. rational persuasion strategies in dialogues. *Computers in Human Behavior*, 57:75–81.

Allwood, J. (2000). An activity-based approach to pragmatics. *Abduction, Belief and Context in Dialogue*, pages 47–81.

Anikina, T. and Kruijff-Korbayová, I. (2019). Dialogue act classification in team communication for robot assisted disaster response. In *Proceedings of the 20th Annual SIGdial Meeting on Discourse and Dialogue*, pages 399–410.

Arndt, A. D., Rippé, C. B., and Castleberry, S. B. (2018). Any questions? questioning skill as a selling tactic for sales students. *Journal for Advancement of Marketing Education*, 26(2).

Borbély, A., Ebner, N., Honeyman, C., Kaufman, S., and Schneider, A. K. (2017). A grand unified negotiation theory: In context. *J. Disp. Resol.*, page 145.

Brady, M. K. and Cronin Jr, J. J. (2001). Customer orientation: Effects on customer service perceptions and outcome behaviors. *Journal of service Research*, 3(3):241–251.

Bunt, H. and Prasad, R. (2016). Iso dr-core (iso 24617-8): Core concepts for the annotation of discourse relations. In *Proceedings 12th Joint ACL-ISO Workshop on Interoperable Semantic Annotation (ISA-12)*, pages 45–54.

Bunt, H., Alexandersson, J., Choe, J.-W., Fang, A. C., Hasida, K., Petukhova, V., Popescu-Belis, A., and Traum, D. (2012). Iso 24617-2: A semantically-based standard for dialogue annotation. In *Proceedings of the Eighth International Conference on Language Resources and Evaluation (LREC'12)*, pages 430–437.

Bunt, H., Petukhova, V., Traum, D., and Alexandersson, J. (2017). Dialogue act annotation with the iso 24617-2 standard. In *Multimodal interaction with W3C standards*, pages 109–135. Springer.

Bunt, H. (1999). Dynamic interpretation and dialogue theory. *The structure of multimodal dialogue*, 2:139–166.

Bunt, H. (2019). Plug-ins for content annotation of dialogue acts. In *Workshop on Interoperable Semantic Annotation (ISA-15)*, page 33.

Burkhardt, F., Pelachaud, C., Schuller, B. W., and Zovato, E. (2017). Emotionml. In *Multimodal interaction with W3C standards*, pages 65–80. Springer.

Clark, C. M. (2011). *Communication strategies of call center agents: a multi-method study of solidarity building and conversation control on agent performance*. Ph.D. thesis, Nanyang Technological University.

Core, M. G. and Allen, J. (1997). Coding dialogs with the damsl annotation scheme. In *AAAI fall symposium on communicative action in humans and machines*, volume 56, pages 28–35. Boston, MA.

Cowie, R., Douglas-Cowie, E., Apolloni, B., Taylor, J., Romano, A., Fellenz, W., et al. (1999). What a neural net needs to know about emotion words. *Computational intelligence and applications*, 404:5311–5316.

Dubois, D., Rucker, D. D., and Galinsky, A. D. (2016). Dynamics of communicator and audience power: The persuasiveness of competence versus warmth. *Journal of Consumer Research*, 43(1):68–85.

Ekman, P. (1992). Are there basic emotions? *Psychological Review*, 99(3):550–553.

Ekman, P. (1999). Basic emotions. *Handbook of cognition and emotion*, 98(45-60):16.

Fisher, R., Ury, W. L., and Patton, B. (2011). *Getting to yes: Negotiating agreement without giving in.* Penguin.

Fiske, S. T., Cuddy, A. J., Glick, P., and Xu, J. (2002). A model of (often mixed) stereotype content: competence and warmth respectively follow from perceived status and competition. *Journal of personality and social psychology*, 82(6):878.

Fiske, S. T. (2018). Stereotype content: Warmth and competence endure. *Current directions in psychological science*, 27(2):67–73.

Freese, T. (2000). *Secrets of question-based selling: How the most powerful tool in business can double your sales results.* Sourcebooks, Inc.

Hastie, H., Prasad, R., and Walker, M. (2002). What's the trouble: automatically identifying problematic dialogues in darpa communicator dialogue systems. In *Proceedings of the 40th Annual Meeting of the Association for Computational Linguistics*, pages 384–391.

Hobbs, J. R. (1985). On the coherence and structure of discourse.

Homburg, C., Müller, M., and Klarmann, M. (2011). When should the customer really be king? on the optimum level of salesperson customer orientation in sales encounters. *Journal of marketing*, 75(2):55–74.

ISO. (2020). *Language resource management – Semantic annotation framework – Part 2: Dialogue acts. ISO 24617-2, Second Edition.* ISO Central Secretariat, Geneva.

Kellermann, K. (2007). Persuasive question asking: how question wording influences answers. In *Annual Meeting of the State Bar Association of California, Anaheim, CA.*

Klein, M. (1999). Standardisation efforts on the level of dialogue act in the mate project. In *Towards Standards and Tools for Discourse Tagging.*

Lapina, V. and Petukhova, V. (2017). Classification of modal meaning in negotiation dialogues. In *Proceedings of the 13th Joint ISO-ACL Workshop on Interoperable Semantic Annotation (ISA-13).*

Larsson, S. (1998). Using a type hierarchy to characterize reliability of coding schemas for dialogue moves.

Lax, D. A. and Sebenius, J. K. (1986). Interests: The measure of negotiation. *Negotiation Journal*, 2(1):73–92.

Leigh, T. W., DeCarlo, T. E., Allbright, D., and Lollar, J. (2014). Salesperson knowledge distinctions and sales performance. *Journal of Personal Selling & Sales Management*, 34(2):123–140.

Malchanau, A. (2019). *Cognitive architecture of multimodal multidimensional dialogue management.* Saarländische Universitäts-und Landesbibliothek.

McFarland, R. G., Challagalla, G. N., and Shervani, T. A. (2006). Influence tactics for effective adaptive selling. *Journal of Marketing*, 70(4):103–117.

Mechinda, P. and Patterson, P. G. (2011). The impact of service climate and service provider personality on employees' customer-oriented behavior in a high-contact setting. *Journal of Services Marketing.*

Mishne, G., Carmel, D., Hoory, R., Roytman, A., and Soffer, A. (2005). Automatic analysis of call-center conversations. In *Proceedings of the 14th ACM international conference on Information and knowledge management*, pages 453–459.

Pallotta, V. and Delmonte, R. (2013). Interaction mining: the new frontier of customer interaction analytics. In *New challenges in distributed information filtering and retrieval*, pages 91–111. Springer.

Petukhova, V. and Bunt, H. (2020). Adapting the iso 24617-2 dialogue act annotation scheme for modelling medical consultations. In *16th Joint ACL-ISO Workshop on Interoperable Semantic Annotation PROCEEDINGS*, pages 75–87.

Petukhova, V., Gropp, M., Klakow, D., Schmidt, A., Eigner, G., Topf, M., Srb, S., Motlicek, P., Potard, B., Dines, J., et al. (2014). The dbox corpus collection of spoken human-human and human-machine dialogues. In *Proceedings of the Ninth International Conference on Language Resources and Evaluation (LREC'14)*. European Language Resources Association (ELRA).

Petukhova, V., Malchanau, A., and Bunt, H. (2015). Modelling argumentative behaviour in parliamentary debates: data collection, analysis and test case. In *Principles and Practice of Multi-Agent Systems*, pages 26–46. Springer.

Petukhova, V., Stevens, C., de Weerd, H., Taatgen, N., Cnossen, F., and Malchanau, A. (2016). Modelling multi-issue bargaining dialogues: Data collection, annotation design and corpus. In *Proceedings of the Tenth International Conference on Language Resources and Evaluation (LREC'16)*, pages 3133–3140.

Petukhova, V., Mayer, T., Malchanau, A., and Bunt, H. (2017). Virtual debate coach design: assessing multimodal argumentation performance. In *Proceedings of the 19th ACM International Conference on Multimodal Interaction*, pages 41–50.

Petukhova, V., Malchanau, A., Oualil, Y., Klakow, D., Luz, S., Haider, F., Campbell, N., Koryzis, D., Spiliotopoulos, D., Albert, P., et al. (2018). The metalogue debate trainee corpus: Data collection and annotations. In *Proceedings of the Eleventh International Conference on Language Resources and Evaluation (LREC 2018).*

Popescu-Belis, A. (2005). Dialogue acts: One or more dimensions. *ISSCO WorkingPaper*, 62.

Prasad, R. and Bunt, H. (2015). Semantic relations in discourse: The current state of iso 24617-8. In *Proceedings of the 11th Joint ACL-ISO Workshop on Interoperable Semantic Annotation (ISA-11).*

Rackham, N. (2020). *SPIN®-selling.* Routledge.

Rafaeli, A., Ziklik, L., and Doucet, L. (2008). The impact of call center employees' customer orientation behaviors on service quality. *Journal of service research*, 10(3):239–255.

Reychav, I. and Weisberg, J. (2009). Going beyond technology: Knowledge sharing as a tool for enhancing customer-oriented attitudes. *International Journal of Information Management*, 29(5):353–361.

Roy, S. and Subramaniam, L. V. (2006). Automatic generation of domain models for call-centers from noisy transcriptions. In *Proceedings of the 21st International Conference on Computational Linguistics and 44th Annual Meeting of the Association for Computational Linguistics*, pages 737–744.

Russell, J. A. (1980). A circumplex model of affect. *Journal of personality and social psychology*, 39(6):1161.

Schröder, M., Baggia, P., Burkhardt, F., Pelachaud, C., Peter, C., and Zovato, E. (2011). Emotionml–an upcoming standard for representing emotions and related states. In *International Conference on Affective Computing and Intelligent Interaction*, pages 316–325. Springer.

Shoemaker, M. E. and Johlke, M. C. (2002). An examination of the antecedents of a crucial selling skill: Asking questions. *Journal of Managerial Issues*, pages 118–131.

Takeuchi, H., Subramaniam, L. V., Nasukawa, T., and Roy, S. (2009). Getting insights from the voices of customers: Conversation mining at a contact center. *Information Sciences*, 179(11):1584–1591.

Tang, M., Pellom, B., and Hacioglu, K. (2003). Call-type classification and unsupervised training for the call center domain. In *2003 IEEE Workshop on Automatic Speech Recognition and Understanding (IEEE Cat. No. 03EX721)*, pages 204–208. IEEE.

Weingart, L. R. and Olekalns, M. (2004). Communication processes in negotiation: Frequencies, sequences, and phases. *The handbook of negotiation and culture*, pages 143–157.

Weitz, B. A., Sujan, H., and Sujan, M. (1986). Knowledge, motivation, and adaptive behavior: A framework for improving selling effectiveness. *Journal of marketing*, 50(4):174–191.

Proceedings of ISA-18 Workshop at LREC2022, pages 20–26
Marseille, 20 June 2022

Guidelines and a Corpus for Extracting Biographical Events

Marco A. Stranisci*, **Enrico Mensa***, **Ousmane Diakite***,
Daniele P. Radicioni*, **Rossana Damiano***
*Department of Computer Science - University of Turin, Turin, Italy
{marcoantonio.stranisci, enrico.mensa, daniele.radicioni, rossana.damiano}@unito.it
ousmane.diakite@edu.unito.it

Abstract

Despite biographies are widely spread within the Semantic Web, resources and approaches to automatically extract biographical events are limited. Such limitation reduces the amount of structured, machine-readable biographical information, especially about people belonging to underrepresented groups. Our work challenges this limitation by providing a set of guidelines for the semantic annotation of life events. The guidelines are designed to be interoperable with existing ISO-standards for semantic annotation: ISO-TimeML (SO-24617-1), and SemAF (ISO-24617-4). Guidelines were tested through an annotation task of Wikipedia biographies of underrepresented writers, namely authors born in non-Western countries, migrants, or belonging to ethnic minorities. $1,000$ sentences were annotated by 4 annotators with an average Inter-Annotator Agreement of 0.825. The resulting corpus was mapped on OntoNotes. Such mapping allowed to to expand our corpus, showing that already existing resources may be exploited for the biographical event extraction task.

Keywords: Event Extraction, Semantic Annotation, Interoperability

1. Introduction

The Semantic Web shift led in few years to a growth of biographical information online. Knowledge Graphs (KG), such as Dbpedia (Auer et al., 2007) and Wikidata (Vrandečić and Krötzsch, 2014), allow the gathering of structured socio-demographic attributes and facts about people. Notwithstanding, many unstructured data conveying biographical information are still not mapped in KGs. Wikipedia pages express more content than their corresponding Wikidata profile: for instance, all the places where a person lived within their life and all their migrations. The enrichment of existing KGs with such information would be crucial in improving several tasks such as community detection (Wang et al., 2018), prosopography (Booth, 2008), and social bias detection (Sun and Peng, 2021).

Although several semantic models have been proposed to formally represent a biographical event (Krieger and Declerck, 2015; Tuominen et al., 2018), computational resources for the automatic extraction of biographical events from text are still missing, and there are no annotated corpora, nor annotation schemes specifically designed for this task.

In this paper, we describe a novel set of annotation guidelines specifically developed for this task, built on two Semantic Annotation Frameworks, ISO 24617-1 (Pustejovsky et al., 2010), and ISO 24617-4 (Bunt and Palmer, 2013). The guidelines have been adopted to annotate a corpus of $1,000$ sentences extracted from Wikipedia pages of under-represented writers, namely writers born in non-Western countries, migrants or belonging to ethnic minorities (Stranisci et al., 2021b). The resource is designed to be interoperable with existing language resources (Pustejovsky et al., 2003; Hovy et al., 2006), in order to augment the corpus with additional data through a systematic mapping. Such data augmentation is crucial for the future implementation of a pipeline for the automatic extraction of biographical events.

The paper is structured as follow. In Section 2, a review of works on biographical encoding and event extraction is provided. Section 3 describes data collection and annotation guidelines design. In Section 4, results of the annotation are presented. Section 5 presents the mapping of the resource with existing corpora. Finally, Section 6 concludes the paper with some insights on future work.

2. Related Work

The extraction of biographical events from text brings into play two main research lines, namely...

Semantic Roles and Events Annotation Frameworks. The annotation of semantic roles has been addressed by a number of approaches with specific focuses (see Petukhova and Bunt (2008)). FrameNet (FN) (Baker et al., 1998) and PropBank (PB) (Kingsbury and Palmer, 2002) are two databases of semantic roles: the former is not syntactically bounded and relies on a detailed taxonomy of semantic roles; the latter is centered on verbs and the classification of arguments is coarse-grained. Other approaches are focused on a general notion of semantic role. VerbNet's (VN) (Schuler, 2005) aim is the classification of English verbs on the basis of semantic-syntactic properties; LIRICS identifies 'relational notions which link a participant to some real or imagined situation ('event')' (Bunt and Romary, 2002). In last years, attempts to unify such resources have been made. The Semantic Annotation Framework (SemAF) (Bunt and Palmer, 2013) provides an unifying framework according to which a semantic annotation relies on a finite set of eventualities (EV) and participants (PT) that form entity structure pairs with *markables*, namely tokens to which an EV or PT can be attached. Pairs are then combined in links through link structure. For instance, in the sentence 'she published poetry' three entity structure pairs may be annotated: $\epsilon_1 = <$ She, POET $>$; $\epsilon_2 = <$ published, PUBLISH $>$, and $\epsilon_3 = <$ poetry, POEM $>$. A link structure triple connect ϵ_1 and ϵ_2, assigning to the former the role of agent: $L_1 = < \epsilon_1, \epsilon_1,$ Agent$>$.

Frameworks for the annotation of events are heterogeneous, reflecting the high variety of existing event extraction tasks (see Xiang and Wang (2019)). The ACE/ERE initiative (Song et al., 2015) resulted in a series of news corpora in which textual triggers were annotated and labelled by referring to a close set of event types. For instance, the word 'migration' triggers an event of the type 'Movement'. The Topic Detection and Tracking initiative (TDT) (Allan, 2012) led to a corpus in which the story rather is annotated and labelled with reference to actual historical events (eg: Death of Kim Jong II, Cuban Riot in Panama, etc.) rather than general categories. The ISO-TimeML framework (Pustejovsky et al., 2010) is a standard for the annotation of temporal expressions, events, and temporal relations between events. According to such approach, an instance of the type 'EVENT' must be used to annotate a situation that happens or occurs. Furthermore, events are categorized by some linguistic properties. For instance, the word 'start' triggers an event of the type 'ASPECTUAL', whereas 'say' is a 'REPORTING' event. The Richer Event Description (RED) guidelines (O'Gorman et al., 2016) is a reformulation of ISO-TimeML in which the taxonomy of event properties is simplified, but further annotation layers are defined: entities, causal relations between events, and link between entities.

Our annotation guidelines for biographies take inspiration from two existing frameworks. On one side, they adopt the semantic formalism of SemAF (Bunt and Palmer, 2013), while on the other side they partly inherit the taxonomy of events proposed in ISO-TimeML (Pustejovsky et al., 2010).

Biographical Events Extraction. Despite the existence of several semantic models for biographical events encoding, few works focused on the extraction of biographical information. Russo et al. (Russo et al., 2015) collected 782 biographies of people deported to Nazi concentration camps with the aim of extracting a predefined set of information from both raw text and DBpedia. Then, all information was arranged into a structured representation by using the TimeML framework (Pustejovsky et al., 2010). Menini et al. (2017) defined a set of verbal motion frames and used it to extract migration events from Wikipedia biographies.

Both works adopt a top-down approach. First, a number of information to be retrieved is defined, then an event extraction pipeline is built.

Our guidelines rely on a bottom-up approach: instead of a predetermined classification of event types to be extracted, the focus is on all events in which the entity of the type *writer* is involved as a participant.

3. Data Collection and Annotation Scheme Design

In this section, the data gathering and preprocessing from Wikipedia is described; then, the annotation guidelines are presented.

3.1. Data Gathering

The corpus is a collection of sentences extracted from $8,047$ Wikipedia English pages of under-represented writer, namely authors born in non-Western countries, migrants or ethnic minorities. Specifically, Wikidata properties 'place of birth', 'occupation', and 'ethnic group' were exploited in order to identify all writers born in a former colony or writers belonging to a minority group that were born in a Western country. The data gathering process was performed in four steps: (i) each biography was split in sentences using Stanford Core NLP (Manning et al., 2014); (ii) for each sentence, all the named entities of the type Location or Organization were identified using the same tool; (iii) an automatic semantic role labelling was performed on each sentence, using SRL Bert (Shi and Lin, 2019). The resulting dataset of $218,198$ tuples of predicates and semantic arguments contains at least one Location or one Organization. Below some examples are reported:

- **predicate**:move,**ARG2**:to New York City;
- **predicate**:study,**ARGM-LOC**:in the Convent of Jesus and Mary School in New Delhi;
- **predicate**:confer,**ARG0**:by the municipality of Kautokeino and the Kautokeino Sámi Association.

In the final step (iv), we identified the most frequently occurring combinations of 'predicate,ARG0', 'predicate,ARG1', and 'predicate,ARG2' in order to select a sample representative of the sentences in the data set for annotation.

3.2. Annotation Guidelines

Annotation guidelines were developed in order to annotate all events in which the subject of the biography is a participant in the event. It is important to notice that there is no one-to-one correspondence between a tuple of the type <predicate,argument> and a sentence, since most sentences contain more than one predicate, as it can be observed in the following example:
"In 1974 he left South Africa, living in North America, Europe and the Middle East, before returning in 1986". Hence, a separate annotation for each relevant subject-predicate pair was made.

The selection of the most significant semantic arguments in biographical events is guided by previous work (Stranisci et al., 2021a) in which a set of combinations of life events and named entities types were recognized as salient for biographies: locations for migrations; organizations for education and career events. Therefore, our guidelines mainly focus on events in which the subject of the biography is involved with such named entities. Moreover, since time is a crucial feature for biographical narratives, guidelines includes the identification of temporal expressions.

Identification of the entity and their semantic role. The prerequisite for an event to be annotated was that it had to involve the biography subject. This involvement was not always direct, though: an author could be mentioned through their works, as in "Her third novel, Missing in Machu Picchu (2013), was awarded" or through a group they were part of, as in "At the age of nine, her family moved to Ghana". According to the RED guidelines[1], the former case was a BRIDGING relation, while the latter was a SET-MEMBER link. In our guidelines all these types of entity had to be annotated as if they were an instance of the writer, in order to consider important biographical events of the type 'his book win a prize', in which the writer is only indirectly mentioned.

Together with the identification of the writer, annotators had to specify her/his semantic role, in order to classify their participation in the event. Two labels were created for this purpose, both inspired by the Propbank framework: 'writer-ARG0', when the entity plays roles covered by this argument, such as 'Agent' or 'Perceiver', 'writer-ARGx', if they play roles covered by other argument types, like 'Patient'. Even though grouping such arguments slightly reduces the expressiveness of the PropBank framework, it has the advantage of helping the annotators to focus on a more general distinction between events in which writers have an active role and events in which they have not.

Identification of events, and their taxonomy. Events had to be annotated according to the TimeML scheme and were categorized according to a subset of TimeML event types tag: 'ASP-EVENT' to mark all verbs conveying aspectual information, and 'REP-EVENT', for verbs reporting other states and events, 'STATE', 'EVENT' respectively. The last two are mutually exclusive in each annotation. For instance, in the sentence "Then, she traveled to Venezuela, where she worked in linguistics at the Department of Justice of Venezuela" two separate annotations had be provided: one for the pair 'she-traveled', and another one for the pair 'she-worked'. 'ASP-EVENT' and 'REP-EVENT' may occur jointly with another 'STATE' or 'EVENT', in expressions such as 'he started working', which results in the link structure $< started, working, ASP >$ and 'he said he moved', which is encoded as $< said, moved, REP >$

Since some sentences contained nominal utterances and there were semantically empty verbs like the copular *be*, guidelines allowed for the annotation of names as events or states in subordinate clauses like "After a brief time in Toronto", or in nominal predicates such "He was a professor". The annotation of nominal events was supported by NomBank frames (Meyers et al., 2004).

Identification of arguments containing a location or an organization. The third component of the guidelines was aimed at identifying the relation between the writer and some named entities that may signal their migration or their condition of being a migrant in a given place. Annotators were asked to select the entire argument containing a location or an organization, and to mark the latter as 'ARGx-ORG', and the former 'ARGx-LOC'. The focus of this annotation stage was not to identify the specific semantic argument, but to label the cases in which a named entity is part of a semantic role. This allowed to refine clusters of arguments and map them onto existing taxonomies. For instance, in 'He works for $organization', the ARGx-ORG may be mapped onto the VerbNet 'Beneficiary' thematic role.

Identification of temporal arguments. Finally, the guidelines establish the annotation of temporal arguments. Rather than identifying only the token triggering a time expression, the entire argument had to be selected and labelled as 'ARGM-TIME'. For instance, in the example "In 1974 he left South Africa" the entire semantic argument "in 1974" had to be annotated.

A fully annotated example of the sentence below is the following:

"In 1974 he left South Africa, living in North America, Europe and the Middle East, before returning in 1986".

ϵ_1 = <he, WRITER>
ϵ_2 = <left, LEAVE>
ϵ_3 = <South Africa, LOCATION>
ϵ_4 = <living, LIVE>
ϵ_5 = <in South Africa, LOCATION>
ϵ_6 = <in 1974, TIME>
L_1 = <ϵ_1, ϵ_2, writer-ARG0>
L_2 = <ϵ_3, ϵ_2, ARGx-LOC>
L_3 = <ϵ_1, ϵ_4, writer-ARG0>
L_4 = <ϵ_5, ϵ_4, ARGx-LOC>
L_5 = <ϵ_6, ϵ_2, ARGM-TIME>

4. Annotation Task and Results

The annotation task involved 4 annotators who evaluated $1,000$ sentences sampled from $8,047$ Wikipedia English pages of under-represented writers. One of them (ann_01 in Table 1) evaluated all sentences 1000, while the others annotated respectively 200 (ann_02), 100 (ann_03), and 200 (ann_04) sentences. The annotation has been performed on Label Studio[2], an Open Source platform that easily allows to organize chunk annotation tasks. Annotators were asked to provide one

[1] https://github.com/timjogorman/RicherEventDescription

[2] https://labelstud.io/

Table 1: Inter-Annotator Agreement (F-measure).

annotator	Event	State	Writer-ARG0	Writer-ARGx	ARGx-LOC	ARGx-ORG	ARGM-TIME
ann_01 (baseline ann_02)	0.83	0.72	0.90	0.87	0.78	0.75	0.91
ann_01 (baseline ann_03)	0.83	0.76	0.91	0.92	0.38	0.75	0.94
ann_01 (baseline ann_04)	0.84	0.66	0.91	0.90	0.65	0.83	0.85
ann_02 (baseline ann_01)	0.83	0.66	0.91	0.89	0.85	0.94	0.94
ann_03 (baseline ann_01)	0.82	0.64	0.93	0.95	0.91	0.92	0.94
ann_04 (baseline ann_01)	0.84	0.61	0.91	0.89	0.75	0.70	0.87
Average	**0.83**	**0.67**	**0.91**	**0.90**	**0.75**	**0.81**	**0.91**

separate annotation for every EVENT or STATE identified in each sentence. As it is shown in Figure 1, the same sentence has received two separated annotations. The first is the chunk 'jailed' labelled as an EVENT, the second is the chunk 'detained', labelled as a STATE.
The IAA was computed through averaged pairwise F-measure: in this setting, the annotations of one annotator are used as the reference against which the annotations of the other annotator are compared. In order to maximize the agreement between annotators, we did not only consider the exact match between chunk, but also the cases in which one chunk contained the other. Adopting such an approach has allowed to resolve some recurrent inconsistencies. Let us consider the two pairs of annotations:

1. awarded / was awarded
2. the United Nations / to the United Nations

In the first one (1) all the smaller chunk was kept. Conversely, in (2) the larger chunk was kept, in order to preserve the semantic role of the argument containing an entity of the type location.
Table 1 shows the F-measure of the agreement between annotators for each class. Agreement is larger than 0.8 in almost all classes, with the exception of STATE and ARGx-LOC. From a qualitative analysis we observed a mismatch in the recognition of nominal events in proposition such as in (3). Lower agreement in ARGx-ORG identification seems to be caused by the broadness of such a type of entity that results in a variety of irrelevant usages for the annotation task, as in (4).

3. after one year of studies
4. when Sri Lanka banned the burka on 2019, Nasrin took to Twitter to show her support for the decision

The resulting corpus contains $1,489$[3] semantic annotations. Table 2 summarizes the number of ST in the corpus, in which there are 894 events and 695 states. Furthermore, 215 aspectual or reported events were annotated; they occurred in 72 semantic annotations. In 143 cases, they jointly appear with an event or a state (eg: 'he $[started]^{ASP-EVENT}$ $[working]^{STATE}$'). Writers hold the semantic role of agent in $1,205$ annotations, other roles in 445. Arguments containing an organization or a location are $1,203$. More specifically, there are 281 sentences in the corpus in which the presence of a named entity of the type LOCATION or ORGANIZATION was not relevant, despite the corpus to annotate was created by relying on a combination of Named Entity Recognition and Semantic Role Labelling (see Section 3).

Table 2: All the occurrences of Semantic Types in the corpus.

Semantic Type	Occurrences
EVENT	894
STATE	695
ASP-EVENT	114
REP-EVENT	101
writer-ARG0	$1,205$
writer-ARGx	445
ARGx-LOC	532
ARGx-ORG	671
TIME	525

In Table 3 the 10 most frequently occurring events and states are shown. Some of them are related to the writers' educational journey (eg: graduate, hold, attend, study), others to their career (eg: publish, serve, teach, win, work, write). Finally, there is a set of events framing personal events (eg: bear, die, live, move). From such clusters of predicates, a set of biographical frames may be derived. This is the inverse process of existing works on biographical knowledge extraction from text (Menini et al., 2017; Russo et al., 2015). Rather than selecting a prior number of frames to be used for data gathering, this approach extracts knowledge that must subsequently be aligned to existing resources.

5. Mapping

The annotation guidelines and the corpus presented in this paper constitute a first, yet essential step towards the development of a system for the automatic extraction of biographical events. While such system will be addressed in future work, in this Section we illustrate

[3]The corpus is available at: `https://github.com/marcostranisci/biographicalEvents`

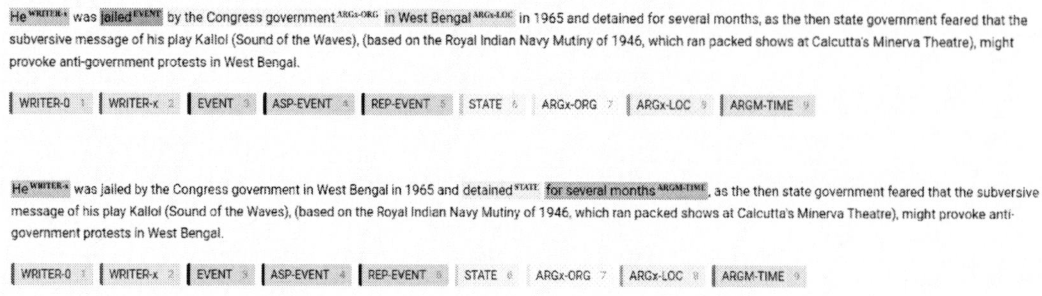

Figure 1: Two examples of annotation in Label Studio.

Table 3: The ten most frequent events and states within the corpus.

Event	occ.	State	occ.
receive	56	work	60
publish	39	write	46
win	36	study	41
award	34	teach	28
write	25	attend	28
move	25	live	21
bear	22	serve	20
graduate	21	hold	15
take	20	spend	14
die	20	writer	13

Table 4: The distribution of arguments containing a Organization (ORG), a Person, or a Geo Political Entity (GPE) for the work.01 PropBank sense in OntoNotes.

argument	n.	ORG	PERSON	GPE
ARG0	996	6.0%	8.1%	3.5%
ARG1	347	7.8%	2.0%	7.2%
ARGM-LOC	248	7.7%	0.4%	18.5%
ARGM-MNR	239	0.4%	0.8%	0.0%
ARGM-TMP	148	1.4%	1.4%	0%
ARGM-DIS	122	0.8%	3.3%	0.0%
ARG2	107	29.0%	8.4%	11.2%
ARG3	99	17.2%	13.1%	8.1%

how the current corpus could be extended to obtain an appropriate training dataset. We show how the data from OntoNotes (Hovy et al., 2006) can be mapped onto our annotation schema, and report some figures regarding this process. Although OntoNotes was selected as the first target for this mapping, the same process could also be applied to other PropBank-like datasets, such as (Kim and Klinger, 2018), for the enrichment of our original corpus.

OntoNotes (Hovy et al., 2006) contains a multi-layer annotation of texts from several domains (e.g., newswires, magazine articles, broadcast news). For each such domain, a PropBank-based semantic annotation and the annotation of named entities is provided. The data set is composed of 99,974 sentences, 249,157 rolesets, and 554,307 semantic arguments. Given a verb, rolesets represent all roles possibly associated to each of its senses according to the PropBank model (Bonial et al., 2014).

In order to align the two corpora, we extracted all verb occurrences and their arguments. Then, we computed the percentage of arguments containing a named entity of the type ORG, GPE, or PERSON. Table 4 shows the 8 most frequently recurring instances for the roleset associated to work.01, which expresses the sense "work, being employed, acts, deeds". As it can be observed, in some of them there is a predominance of GPE and ORG compared to entities of the type PERSON. This enables the identification of some arguments that are more likely to be aligned with our corpus: it is the case of ARG1 and ARG2, which respectively correspond to 'job, project' and 'employer, benefactive'. Let us consider the following examples.

5. <*work*, to improve China's nickel industry's level of technology, technique and equipment, ARG1>

6. <*work*, for the Justice Department, ARG2>

In the former case, the GPE simply adds information about the argument, as in (5). In the latter case, it is directly linked to the verb with the role of 'benefactive', as in (6).

We analyzed the distribution for the 10 most frequently occurring events and states in our corpus (Table 5): they amount to 430 events, covering the 27% of the overall number of instances. Besides the widespread presence of the ARGM-LOC modifier, some patterns emerge. There is a set of events in which an ORG or a GPE has agency on the event: publish.01, award.01. The 60% of the ARG0 linked to publish.01 and the 80% linked to award.01 contain a GPE or a ORG. In fact, many books are published and many prizes are awarded by an organization or a geopolitical entity.

Other patterns may imply the 'benefactive' role: as mentioned before, work.01 is often linked to a benefactive as in (6). Conversely, the presence of GPE or ORG in arguments of the type 'benefactive' linked to award.01 seems to be not informative. In some cases, they have an appositive function, as in 'to Waring & LaRosa, New York'. At times, the mapping is less interesting for the specific task, since in some cases organizations are the recipient of a prize, which is not consistent with the biographical domain.

Some arguments are specific to single verbs. For instance, receive.01 always presents an ARG2 associated with the role 'received from', while attend.01 ARG1 always presents instances of type 'thing attended'. Both combinations are common in sentences like 'he attends an institution' and 'he received a degree from an institution'. The distribution confirms such pattern, since the 45.1% of ARG1 linked to attend.01 and the 31.7% paired with receive.02 contain a ORG or a GPE.

Finally, move.02, win.01, and work.01 show a similar behavior when an ARG1 is present. GPE and ORG Entities in this argument are not directly linked to the verb, but rather to further entities within the argument, such as in the example (7):

7. <'win', 'the New York Drama Critics' Circle Award', ARG1>

By definition, the ARG1 of the verb 'win' represents a prize; however, since the organization 'New York Drama Critics' is part of the argument, the entity type ORG is mistakenly considered as a value for the argument in our statistics. Although this behaviour represents an issue when recording descriptive statistics and for the mapping process, such dependency structures should be considered to collect precious and more subtle biographical information that needs further investigation.

Despite the actual limitations, the results of the mapping process is encouraging. In fact, even considering only non-ambiguous argument types, 851 instances may be mapped from OntoNotes to the top ten instances of our corpus, tripling the initial size of the corpus. At the same time, we observed the emergence of patterns helpful to automatically extract and understand events and states from raw text biographies. Further studies may focus on the automatic implementation of such patterns.

6. Conclusions and Future Work

In this paper we presented a novel schema for the annotation of biographical events in free text. We have also built a new corpus for this task, containing 1,000 annotated sentences sampled from 8,047 Wikipedia English pages pertaining underrepresented writers. Finally, we have shown how existing resources, such as OntoNotes, can be mapped onto our annotation schema in order to increase significantly the size of the corpus.

The developed corpus and the proposed schema are preparatory for the development of an automatic system for the extraction of biographical events from free text, which constitutes the main focus of our future work. Ideally, we could start from existing systems performing semantic role labeling (such as (Shi and Lin, 2019)), and then adapt the results in a manner similar to the one adopted in the mapping process. The mapping process itself also needs to be strengthened with a more thorough evaluation and with the development of specific rules to better detect the entities filling the arguments. Our final focus consists in a study aimed at better understanding and quantifying how the biographical information extracted by the system can be beneficial to tackle other downstream tasks.

Table 5: The most recurring link structures of the type <verb,argument containing ORG or GPE> for the 10 events and states with more occurrences in our corpus.

verb	argument(s)	description
work.01	ARG2 ARG1	benefactive project
write.01	ARG2	benefactive
receive.01	ARG2	received from
publish.01	ARG0	publisher
win.01	ARG1	prize
award.01	ARG0, ARG2	giver, beneficiary
attend.01	ARG1	thing attended
move.01	ARG2	destination
move.02	ARG1	measures
study.01	ARGM-LOC	location
teach.01	ARGM-LOC	location

7. Bibliographical References

Allan, J. (2012). *Topic detection and tracking: event-based information organization*, volume 12. Springer Science & Business Media.

Auer, S., Bizer, C., Kobilarov, G., Lehmann, J., Cyganiak, R., and Ives, Z. (2007). Dbpedia: A nucleus for a web of open data. In *The semantic web*, pages 722–735. Springer.

Baker, C. F., Fillmore, C. J., and Lowe, J. B. (1998). The berkeley framenet project. In *COLING 1998 Volume 1: The 17th International Conference on Computational Linguistics*.

Bonial, C., Bonn, J., Conger, K., Hwang, J. D., and Palmer, M. (2014). Propbank: Semantics of new predicate types. In *Proceedings of the Ninth International Conference on Language Resources and Evaluation (LREC'14)*, pages 3013–3019.

Booth, A. (2008). Orlando: Women's writing in the british isles from the beginnings to the present.

Bunt, H. and Palmer, M. (2013). Conceptual and representational choices in defining an iso standard for semantic role annotation. In *Proceedings Ninth Joint ISO-ACL SIGSEM Workshop on Interoperable Semantic Annotation (ISA-9), Potsdam*, pages 41–50.

Bunt, H. and Romary, L. (2002). Requirements on multimodal semantic representations. In *Proceed-*

ings of ISO TC37/SC4 Preliminary Meeting, pages 59–68. KAIST.

Hovy, E., Marcus, M., Palmer, M., Ramshaw, L., and Weischedel, R. (2006). Ontonotes: the 90% solution. In *Proceedings of the human language technology conference of the NAACL, Companion Volume: Short Papers*, pages 57–60.

Kim, E. and Klinger, R. (2018). Who feels what and why? annotation of a literature corpus with semantic roles of emotions. In *Proceedings of the 27th International Conference on Computational Linguistics*, pages 1345–1359.

Kingsbury, P. R. and Palmer, M. (2002). From treebank to propbank. In *LREC*, pages 1989–1993. Citeseer.

Krieger, H.-U. and Declerck, T. (2015). An owl ontology for biographical knowledge. representing time-dependent factual knowledge. In *BD*, pages 101–110.

Manning, C. D., Surdeanu, M., Bauer, J., Finkel, J. R., Bethard, S., and McClosky, D. (2014). The stanford corenlp natural language processing toolkit. In *Proceedings of 52nd annual meeting of the association for computational linguistics: system demonstrations*, pages 55–60.

Menini, S., Sprugnoli, R., Moretti, G., Bignotti, E., Tonelli, S., and Lepri, B. (2017). Ramble on: Tracing movements of popular historical figures. In *Proceedings of the Software Demonstrations of the 15th Conference of the European Chapter of the Association for Computational Linguistics*, pages 77–80.

Meyers, A., Reeves, R., Macleod, C., Szekely, R., Zielinska, V., Young, B., and Grishman, R. (2004). The nombank project: An interim report. In *Proceedings of the workshop frontiers in corpus annotation at hlt-naacl 2004*, pages 24–31.

O'Gorman, T., Wright-Bettner, K., and Palmer, M. (2016). Richer event description: Integrating event coreference with temporal, causal and bridging annotation. In *Proceedings of the 2nd Workshop on Computing News Storylines (CNS 2016)*, pages 47–56.

Petukhova, V. and Bunt, H. (2008). LIRICS semantic role annotation: Design and evaluation of a set of data categories. In *Proceedings of the Sixth International Conference on Language Resources and Evaluation (LREC'08)*, Marrakech, Morocco, May. European Language Resources Association (ELRA).

Pustejovsky, J., Lee, K., Bunt, H., and Romary, L. (2010). Iso-timeml: An international standard for semantic annotation. In *LREC*, volume 10, pages 394–397.

Russo, I., Caselli, T., and Monachini, M. (2015). Extracting and visualising biographical events from wikipedia. In *BD*, pages 111–115.

Schuler, K. K. (2005). *VerbNet: A broad-coverage, comprehensive verb lexicon*. University of Pennsylvania.

Shi, P. and Lin, J. (2019). Simple bert models for relation extraction and semantic role labeling. *arXiv preprint arXiv:1904.05255*.

Song, Z., Bies, A., Strassel, S. M., Riese, T., Mott, J., Ellis, J., Wright, J., Kulick, S., Ryant, N., Ma, X., et al. (2015). From light to rich ere: Annotation of entities, relations, and events. In *EVENTS@ HLP-NAACL*, pages 89–98.

Stranisci, M. A., Basile, V., Damiano, R., and Patti, V. (2021a). Mapping biographical events to odps through lexico-semantic patterns? In *12th Workshop on Ontology Design and Patterns, WOP 2021*, volume 3011, pages 1–12. CEUR-WS.

Stranisci, M. A., Patti, V., and Damiano, R. (2021b). Representing the under-represented: A dataset of post-colonial, and migrant writers. In *3rd Conference on Language, Data and Knowledge, LDK 2021*, volume 93, pages 1–14. Schloss Dagstuhl-Leibniz-Zentrum fur Informatik GmbH, Dagstuhl Publishing.

Sun, J. and Peng, N. (2021). Men are elected, women are married: Events gender bias on wikipedia. In *Proceedings of the 59th Annual Meeting of the Association for Computational Linguistics and the 11th International Joint Conference on Natural Language Processing (Volume 2: Short Papers)*, pages 350–360.

Tuominen, J. A., Hyvönen, E. A., Leskinen, P., et al. (2018). Bio crm: A data model for representing biographical data for prosopographical research. In *Proceedings of the Second Conference on Biographical Data in a Digital World 2017 (BD2017)*. CEUR Workshop Proceedings.

Vrandečić, D. and Krötzsch, M. (2014). Wikidata: a free collaborative knowledgebase. *Communications of the ACM*, 57(10):78–85.

Wang, R., Yan, Y., Wang, J., Jia, Y., Zhang, Y., Zhang, W., and Wang, X. (2018). Acekg: A large-scale knowledge graph for academic data mining. In *Proceedings of the 27th ACM international conference on information and knowledge management*, pages 1487–1490.

Xiang, W. and Wang, B. (2019). A survey of event extraction from text. *IEEE Access*, 7:173111–173137.

8. Language Resource References

Pustejovsky, J., Hanks, P., Sauri, R., See, A., Gaizauskas, R., Setzer, A., Radev, D., Sundheim, B., Day, D., Ferro, L., et al. (2003). The timebank corpus. In *Corpus linguistics*, volume 2003, page 40. Lancaster, UK.

Proceedings of ISA-18 Workshop at LREC2022, pages 27–32
Marseille, 20 June 2022

Levels of Non-Fictionality in Fictional Texts

Florian Barth[1], Hanna Varachkina[2], Tillmann Dönicke[1], Luisa Gödeke[2]
[1]Göttingen Centre for Digital Humanities, [2]Department of German Philology
University of Göttingen
florian.barth@uni-goettingen.de, hanna.varachkina@stud.uni-goettingen.de,
tillmann.doenicke@uni-goettingen.de, luisa.goedeke@uni-goettingen.de

Abstract

The annotation and automatic recognition of non-fictional discourse within a text is an important, yet unresolved task in literary research. While non-fictional passages can consist of several clauses or sentences, we argue that 1) an entity-level classification of fictionality and 2) the linking of Wikidata identifiers can be used to automatically identify (non-)fictional discourse. We query Wikidata and DBpedia for relevant information about a requested entity as well as the corresponding literary text to determine the entity's fictionality status and assign a Wikidata identifier, if unequivocally possible. We evaluate our methods on an exemplary text from our diachronic literary corpus, where our methods classify 97% of persons and 62% of locations correctly as fictional or real. Furthermore, 75% of the resolved persons and 43% of the resolved locations are resolved correctly. In a quantitative experiment, we apply the entity-level fictionality tagger to our corpus and conclude that more non-fictional passages can be identified when information about real entities is available.

Keywords: Named Entities, Fictionality, Semantic Web, Automatic Annotation, German

1. Introduction

One can easily distinguish three levels of (non-) fictionality in a text: First, a text might be classified as a work of fiction or a work of non-fiction according to whether it describes imaginary or actual events, people or places. Second, it is a common observation that a fictional text does not only consist of fictional discourse but also contains passages that suggest assertions or hypotheses about the real world.[1] And third, the people or places mentioned in a text may exist in the real world even if the text or the story is overall fictional.

Non-fictional passages within a fictional text are of special interest in literary studies because they often contain central messages of a work or correspond with specific statements or intentions of the author. However, although the automatic classification of texts into fiction and non-fiction can be considered a solved problem (e.g. Piper (2016)), the identification of non-fictionality within a fictional text remains an open task. While our ultimate goal is to identify non-fictional passages, we assume that the fictionality status of named entities can serve us as feature and we further consider the automatic annotation of (non-)fictional entities in a text to be a useful application on its own (cf. van Dalen-Oskam et al. (2014), Chu et al. (2020)).

In this paper, we briefly describe the theoretical background and working hypotheses on non-fictional passages (Sec. 2), our still-growing corpus with manual annotations (Sec. 3), the automatic annotation of fictionality for named entities (Sec. 4–6), and an analysis of the interplay between entity-level and passage-level fictionality (Sec. 7).

[1]Likewise, a non-fictional text might contain passages that make assertions about fictional people or events.

2. Theoretical Background

In fictional literature, fictional discourse builds the fictional world, e.g. introduces characters and describes actions and scenes. From a linguistic perspective, it has been repeatedly observed that fictional discourse challenges the semantic notion of truth and reference. This is because fictional discourse is obviously not true and does not refer to real entities in the real world. In (1), for example, for us readers it is clear that the character Gustav (the protagonist of the work) does not correspond to any real-world entity and all the other information concerning this character are not true, either.

(1) He [Gustav] loved the ocean for deep-seated reasons: because of that yearning for rest, when the hard-pressed artist hungers to shut out the exacting multiplicities of experience and hide himself on the breast of the simple, the vast; and because of a forbidden hankering—seductive, by virtue of its being directly opposed to his obligations—after the incommunicable, the incommensurate, the eternal, the non-existent. (Mann, 2021)

Therefore, the most influential view on fictional discourse is that fictional utterances are invitations to imagine things (cf. Currie (1990), Konrad (2017), Stock (2017), Maier (2017)).

This approach, however, neglects a certain macrostructural property of some passages in fictional texts that do not prima facie contribute to building the fictional world: so-called non-fictional-passages (NfPs). Let us consider the continuation of example (1):

(2) [...], the non-existent. To be at rest in the face of perfection is the hunger of everyone who is aiming at excellence; (Mann, 2021)

The last sentence poses problems for the imagination hypothesis on the one hand and for the truth notion on the other: The utterance, after all, may indeed be true beyond the fictional world. Thus, unlike a purely fictional utterance, it obviously does not serve exclusively to create the fictional world. Therefore, it is misleading to assume this utterance to exclusively serve the imagination. From this, we conclude that fictional works can consist of both fictional and non-fictional discourse.

Non-fictional discourse in itself can come in different varieties. In our example, it is a kind of generic, aphoristic wisdom (cf. Konrad (2017)). Another form of NfPs can refer to real places or people, sometimes with detailed descriptions apparently researched by the author, e.g. this description of a slaughterhouse in Berlin:

(3) In the northeast part of the city, from Eldenaer Strasse across Thaerstrasse across Landsberger Allee as far as Cotheniusstrasse along the Belt Line Railway, run the houses, halls, and stables of the slaughter- and stock-yards. They cover an expanse of 44.78 hectares, equal to 118.31 acres. Not counting the structures behind Landsberger Allee, 27,083,492 marks were sunk into its construction, [...]. (Döblin, 2003)

Konrad (2017) argues that these two forms of NfPs are characterised by certain linguistic features, including generalisation/abstraction, researched details and technical language. In addition to various forms of generalisation, we consider immigrant objects (Parsons, 1981) to be crucial, i.e. objects that migrated from the real world to the fictional world.[2] We therefore assume that non-fictional discourse mainly consists of generalisations and named entities referring to the real world.

3. Data and Annotation

We currently construct a diachronic corpus of German fictional literature from 1600 to 1950. Most of the texts originate from the KOLIMO corpus (Herrmann and Lauer, 2017), which is a subsample of prose texts extracted from TextGrid-Repository[3] and Project Gutenberg (Reu, 2013) encoded in TEI-XML and enriched with metadata such as identifiers from the Integrated Authority File (GND, German for "Gemeinsame Normdatei") for the author of each corpus record.[4]

As of now, we annotated 22 texts (6,555 sentences). Our annotation procedure is as follows: Each text is first annotated by four out of six student assistants (in varying constellations), all having a background in German philology. Two annotators each annotate either non-fictional passages (NfPs) or generalising passages (GenPs), where we define a passage to span at least one and potentially an open number of subsequent clauses. In a second step, the initial annotations are discussed and then confirmed, corrected or deleted by two researchers, yielding our gold standard.

Tagset	Tags	γ (multi)	γ (binary)
NfP	2	.73	.79
GenP	6	.65	.68

Table 1: Inter-annotator agreement considering subclasses (multi) or merging all classes into one (binary).

The annotation of NfPs includes all passages that suggest assertions or hypotheses about the real world (considering the time when the text was written). An example is shown in (4), which is a free translation from May (1888). The boldfaced passage makes the assertion that confederate prisoners were interned in Fort Jefferson at the time of the story. Since this makes a reference to events during the American Civil War, which the author presumably had knowledge of, the assertion can be understood to be about real world's Fort Jefferson. Note that Fort Jefferson is not called by name in the boldfaced passage but referenced by the anaphoric pronoun *this*. In such cases, where some context is required to properly interpret an NfP, we additionally annotate a larger span (with a separate tag) that includes the NfP and the minimal reference context (underlined in the example). Although the first sentence mentions two real-world entities, *Tortuga* and *Fort Jefferson*, we do not consider it to be non-fictional discourse because it describes fictional events and does not suggest assertions about the real world.

(4) The storm had driven our ship against the Tortugas, against the island on which Fort Jefferson is located. **Confederate prisoners of war were interned in this at the time**. The fishermen took care of me in the friendliest way and provided me with fresh linen and the most necessary clothes, for I was only dressed in the way *in which one goes to bed during a sea voyage*.

The annotation of GenPs is independent of fictionality and driven by mainly linguistic criteria. For example, the italicised passage in (4) makes a generalising claim about how one used to be dressed for sleep during a sea voyage. We use the tagset of Dönicke et al. (2021) to annotate subcategories of GenPs but these are not relevant for this paper.

The average inter-annotator agreement measured with γ (Mathet et al., 2015) is shown in Table 1. NfPs and GenPs are annotated with substantial agreement.[5]

4. External Resources

To use external knowledge about fictional and real entities, we integrate knowledge graph databases, Wikidata

[2]We use the terms "immigrant object" and "real(-world) entity" synonymously in this paper.

[3]https://textgridrep.de/

[4]https://www.dnb.de/EN/Professionell/Standardisierung/GND/gnd_node.html.

[5]Our corpus and annotation guidelines are published in Barth et al. (2021).

and DBpedia, that can be queried via SPARQL.

4.1. Wikidata

Wikidata is a free, multilingual, collaborative and open knowledge base developed by the Wikimedia Foundation that can be read and edited by both humans and machines.[6] Wikidata was launched in 2012 (Vrandečić and Krötzsch, 2014) and currently holds more than 97 million items. It consists mainly of items with a label (name), their description and aliases (alternative names). The structure of the data is the following: item – property – value, e.g. *Harry Potter* (Q3244512) – *instance of* (P31) – *literary character* (Q3658341) or *Globe Theatre* (Q272434) – *located in the administrative territorial entity* (P131) – *London Borough of Southwark* (Q730706). This structure corresponds to the graph format (semantic triples: Subject – Predicate – Object) and can be queried using a SPARQL query service that Wikidata provides.

4.2. DBpedia

DBpedia is a community-based platform that aims to extract structured information from Wikipedia articles so that Semantic Web techniques can be employed such as SPARQL queries or an interlinking of datasets (Auer et al., 2007). The DBpedia dataset currently consists of 850 million facts (RDF triples)[7] and it is interlinked with several open datasets from a wide range of domains such as lexical resources (WordNet), spatial knowledge bases (Geonames, LinkedGeoData), social networks (FOAF), literary resources (Project Gutenberg), and other encyclopedias (Wikidata).

5. Metadata Extraction and Enrichment

Based on the GND-identifier for a work's author within the KOLIMO corpus, we identify the author's Wikidata entry and, if existent, the Wikidata entry of the current text that we process. We employ this metadata later for the classification of fictionality and the linking of Wikidata entries to named entities, which is why we developed an own metadata structure to store and process metadata from the original corpus and own enrichments – enriched metadata can be, furthermore, serialised back to TEI-XML format.

6. Entity Classification and Linking

We parse our texts with spaCy, which also contains a named entity (NE) recogniser.[8] The NE recogniser assigns the labels PER, LOC, ORG and MISC to denote persons, locations, organisations and miscellaneous, respectively. We also use an advanced version of Krug et al. (2015)'s algorithm for coreference resolution on all noun phrases, including NEs.

Building on the preprocessing, we aim to solve two tasks: 1) determine if an NE is fictional or real and 2) assign a specific Q-identifier from Wikidata to the NE. For now, we only consider NEs tagged as PER or LOC, because persons and locations are the most relevant categories in novels, while organisations and miscellaneous are less common. In a first step, we create a set of variant forms for each NE and request information about them via the SPARQL interface of Wikidata and DBpedia. Beside the form of the NE that appears in the text, we add a variant based on the longest mention in the NE's coreference chain.[9] Furthermore, we add variants to queries by constructing the nominative form for NEs in genitive case, deleting function words using part-of-speech tags, considering only tokens with the suffix *-isch* (that might indicate locations) and normalising old spelling by substituting the *ß*-ligature.

To identify and differentiate PER entities (PERs), we check if one of the queried variants equals or is part of a description or an alias of an item (subject) that has an *instance of* property (P31) corresponding with an item (object) that we regard as either fictional or real. Relevant fictional items are among others *literary character* (Q3658341) and *fictional human* (Q15632617). Real items correspond especially with an instance of *human* (Q5). Since querying a large amount of *human* items exceeds the Wikidata API, we query DBpedia for *foaf:Person* entries that are supplied by a Wikidata identifier that has an *instance of* relation to the Wikidata item *human*. We further regard certain real-world concepts as immigrant objects, e.g. mythological PERs such as god in monotheistic religions (inter alia: Q190, Q2095353, Q2155501, Q825, Q5576009) or Greek deities (Q22989102, Q878099). Besides the direct identification of Wikidata items corresponding to the set of queries, we utilise Wikidata entries for author and work from our enriched metadata record to identify and scrape the Wikipedia article of the current text. If literary characters do not have an own Wikidata entry to link them, we can instead identify them within the Wikipedia article. In this case, no linking is applied, but corresponding PERs will be classified as fictional.

The Wikidata property that helps identify real locations the best is *coordinate location* (P625). If a query that contains this property does not yield any results, other properties are used: *located in the administrative territorial entity* (P131), *located in or next to body of water* (P206), *located in time zone* (P421), *country* (P17), *area* (P2046), *significant place* (P7153) and *located in the statistical territorial entity* (P8138). The search is conducted among labels of Wikidata items first, and — if it yields no results— continues among aliases of item labels.

The collected Wikidata entries serve as candidates for which we extract features for the classification of fictionality and the entity linking. These features are based on the requests for the query variants and the enriched metadata. Thereupon, we apply a scoring sys-

[6]https://www.wikidata.org/wiki/Wikidata:Main_Page

[7]https://www.dbpedia.org/blog/snapshot-2021-12-release

[8]https://spacy.io/api/entityrecognizer

[9]This variant consists of nominal phrases including adjectives and strips other tokens (like verbs, pronouns etc.).

Type	Tot.	Fict.	Real	None	A.	Link.	A.
PER	149	125 (.84)	6 (.04)	18 (.12)	.97	8 (.06)	.75
LOC	90	19 (.21)	36 (.40)	35 (.39)	.62	46 (.84)	.43
both	239	144 (.60)	42 (.18)	53 (.22)	.87	54 (.29)	.48

Table 2: Evaluation of classified and linked NEs: total number of NEs; number (percentage) of fictional / real / incorrectly recognised NEs; accuracy for classifying fictional and real NEs; number (percentage) of linked fictional and real NEs; accuracy for linking NEs.

Type	Gold	P.	R.	F1	Link.	A.
PER	Fict.	1.00	.97	.98	.02	.00
	Real	.60	1.00	.75	1.00	1.00
LOC	Fict.	.45	.47	.46	–	–
	Real	.71	.69	.70	.69	.80
both	Fict.	.92	.90	.91	–	–
	Real	.69	.74	.71	.74	.84

Table 3: Evaluation separated by fictionality status (as labelled in the gold standard): precision / recall / F1 for classifying NEs; percentage of linked NEs; accuracy for linking NEs.

tem for both tasks that weights indicators for either fictional or real items and assigns a Wikidata entry if possible. For PERs, the scoring considers the amount fictional and real items that have an *instance of* relation to the entry candidate. If an entry candidate is *instance of human* or is associated with other figurative concepts of the real world, the Wikidata sitelinks are applied in an item-class-adjusted manner to estimate the importance of this Wikidata entry. The higher scoring value for fictional or real determines the fictionality classification and if the corresponding Wikidata entry candidate holds a defined minimal value of sitelinks it will be linked to the NE. For LOCs, the scoring relies on sitelinks as well as the NE's context (its clause), which we compare with the Wikidata description of an entry candidate. The minimal amount of sitelinks to accept a linking can be lower for locations since locations seem less interlinked than persons or fictional characters.

7. Evaluation and Analysis

We test our classifier on one text from our corpus—Fontane (2012)—where we manually classified each LOC and PER (as found by the NE recogniser) as fictional or real and compared the manual annotation with the automatic one. As Table 2 shows, 239 entities are recognised in the text, from which we labelled 60% as fictional and 18% as real. The remaining 22% constitute errors by the NE recogniser, which we exclude from the evaluation. From the correctly recognised NEs, 87% are correctly classified as fictional or real, including all 6 real persons; 29% are linked to a Wikidata entry, where 48% of the links are correct. We achieve

	RE	GenP	RE ∪ GenP	RE ∩ GenP
$P(x\|\text{NfP})$	.14	.72	.78	.08
$P(\text{NfP}\|x)$	.15	.29	.23	.68

Table 4: Observed probabilities for cooccurrences of NfPs with immigrant objects (REs) and/or GenPs, based on 10 texts of our corpus.

higher accuracies for PERs than for LOCs in both tasks. Table 3 shows separate results for fictional and real entities. Overall, fictional and real entities are identified with 91% and 71% F1, respectively. 74% of the real entities are linked to a Wikidata entry, where 62% of the links are correct. On the other hand, we do not link fictional LOCs to a Wikidata entry so far. For fictional PERs there are no NEs in the text that have a Wikidata entry and therefore no fictional PERs that should be linked. The accuracy for only correct links would therefore be 0/0=NaN (not 100%). Still, 2 fictional PERs are incorrectly linked to a Wikidata entry, which produces an accuracy of 0/2=0%.
Table 5 presents the results for the fictionality classification and the NE linking. For PERs, we correctly identify historic entities such as "Fiedrich Wilhelms IV" (Frederick William IV; Q57180) for which the alternative spellings help to formulate a query including the nominative ("Wilhelm"). Furthermore, simple forenames like Dubslav (the main character) can be identified as characters of the novel through Wikipedia scraping based on enriched metadata. "Berlin" (Q64) is correctly recognised as an instance of real location in text. Although multiple entities with this label are found on Wikidata, the number of sitelinks helps to assign it to the correct one as capital of Germany. "Schloß Stechlin" is a fictional castle. Even though the spelling was adapted to the modern grammar for a query, it could not be found among real locations on Wikidata, correctly so. Interestingly, the NE "Stechlin" appears multiple times in the novel: as a real lake, a fictional village, the main character by his surname and as a family name that is not linked to any entity, which poses a lot of problems to the NE recogniser and for disambiguation of the entities existing in the real world.
The evaluation results suggest that the entity-level fictionality classification works adequately enough to perform a quantitative analysis of non-fictionality on the passage level in our corpus. Our hypothesis from Section 2 is that NfPs are usually generalising or contain a real entity (RE). The first row in Table 4 shows that indeed 72% NfPs (including the minimal reference context) overlap with a GenP, 14% contain an RE, and 8% do both. Returning all passages overlapping with an RE or GenP, would correctly find 78% of the NfPs. However, as the second row in Table 4 shows, both REs and GenPs occur far more often in purely fictional than in non-fictional passages,[10] which means that the returned

[10]Since we do not annotate "purely fictional passages", we

Named Entity	Entity Type	Queries	Count	Real	Wikidata item	Wikidata Description	Sitelinks
'Friedrich Wilhelms IV.'	PER	{'Friedrich Wilhelms IV.', 'Friedrich Wilhelm IV.', 'Regierungsantritt Friedrich Wilhelms IV.', [...] }	1	True	Q57180	King of Prussia (1795-1861)	65
'Dubslav'	PER	{'Dubslav', 'Regiment Garde du Corps'}	10	False	None	None	None
'Berlin'	LOC	{'Berlin'}	2	True	Q64	federal state, capital and largest city of Germany	410
'Schloß Stechlin'	LOC	{'Schloß Stechlin', 'Schloss Stechlin'}	1	False	None	None	None

Table 5: Examples of PER and LOC NEs in Theodor Fontane's *Der Stechlin* with query variants for Wikidata and query results (item, description, sitelinks)

passages still have to be filtered to get a good precision.

8. Conclusion and Future Work

We observe that the spaCy model recognises a solid number of named entities, but also makes a considerable number of mistakes. We plan to evaluate the NE recogniser used in spaCy on the domain of fictional literature. So far, we excluded wrongly recognised NEs from the analysis, in the future, we will also consider those NEs that were missed by the model. The mistakes are likely caused by the fact that the spaCy model was trained on data from a different domain, namely Wikipedia articles. For comparison, Jannidis et al. (2015) report a performance decrease of 65% F-score and as much as 74% recall for a system trained on newspaper texts and applied to a corpus of German novels, while precision remains similar. Therefore, we plan to adapt the existing NE recogniser for characters in fiction[11] by extending it to locations.

We have seen that 78% of non-fictional passages contain either a real-world entity or a generalisation. While this paper presents methods for the identification of real entities,[12] the identification of generalising statements (e.g. Friedrich et al. (2016), Gödeke et al. (to appear)) and the combination of both into a passage-level fictionality recogniser constitute another task which we have to solve in the future.

9. Acknowledgements

Our special thanks go to our fellow members of the MONA project group, who were actively involved in developing the foundations of this work: Benjamin Gittel, Anke Holler, Caroline Sporleder, and Anna Weimer. We further thank our student assistants for their engagement, and the anonymous reviewers for their valuable comments. This work is funded by the Deutsche Forschungsgemeinschaft (DFG, German Research Foundation) – 424264086 (Barth, Varachkina) and Volkswagen Foundation (Dönicke, Gödeke).

treat REs and GenPs that do not overlap with an NfP as purely fictional passages for the calculation.

[11] https://github.com/MarkusKrug/NERDetection

[12] Our implementation is available at https://gitlab.gwdg.de/mona/pipy-public/-/releases/v2.0.

10. Bibliographical References

Auer, S., Bizer, C., Kobilarov, G., Lehmann, J., Cyganiak, R., and Ives, Z. (2007). Dbpedia: A nucleus for a web of open data. In *The semantic web*, pages 722–735. Springer.

Barth, F., Dönicke, T., Gittel, B., Gödeke, L., Hofmann, A. M., Holler, A., Sporleder, C., and Varachkina, H. (2021). MONACO: Modes of narration and attribution corpus. https://gitlab.gwdg.de/mona/korpus-public.

Chu, C. X., Razniewski, S., and Weikum, G. (2020). ENTYFI: A system for fine-grained entity typing in fictional texts. In *Proceedings of the 2020 Conference on Empirical Methods in Natural Language Processing: System Demonstrations*, pages 100–106, Online, October. Association for Computational Linguistics.

Currie, G. (1990). *The nature of fiction*. Cambridge University Press.

Dönicke, T., Gödeke, L., and Varachkina, H. (2021). Annotating quantified phenomena in complex sentence structures using the example of generalising statements in literary texts. In *Proceedings of the 17th Joint ACL - ISO Workshop on Interoperable Semantic Annotation*, pages 20–32, Groningen, The Netherlands (online), June. Association for Computational Linguistics.

Döblin, A. (2003). *Berlin Alexanderplatz. The story of Franz Biberkopf [1929]. Translated by Eugene Jolas*. Continuum.

Fontane, T. (2012). Der Stechlin. In *TextGrid Repository*. Digitale Bibliothek.

Friedrich, A., Palmer, A., and Pinkal, M. (2016). Situation entity types: automatic classification of clause-level aspect. In *Proceedings of the 54th Annual Meeting of the Association for Computational Linguistics (Volume 1: Long Papers)*, pages 1757–1768,

Berlin, Germany, August. Association for Computational Linguistics.

Gödeke, L., Barth, F., Dönicke, T., Weimer, A. M., Varachkina, H., Gittel, B., Holler, A., and Sporleder, C. (to appear). Generalisierungen als literarisches Phänomen. Charakterisierung, Annotation und automatische Erkennung. *Zeitschrift für digitale Geisteswissenschaften.*

Herrmann, B. and Lauer, G. (2017). Kolimo. a corpus of literary modernism for comparative analysis.

Jannidis, F., Reger, I., Weimer, L., Krug, M., and Puppe, F. (2015). Automatische Erkennung von Figuren in deutschsprachigen Romanen.

Konrad, E.-M. (2017). Signposts of factuality: On genuine assertions in fictional literature. *Art and Belief, London*, pages 42–62.

Krug, M., Puppe, F., Jannidis, F., Macharowsky, L., Reger, I., and Weimar, L. (2015). Rule-based coreference resolution in German historic novels. In *Proceedings of the Fourth Workshop on Computational Linguistics for Literature*, pages 98–104, Denver, Colorado, USA, June. Association for Computational Linguistics.

Maier, E. (2017). Fictional names in psychologistic semantics. *Theoretical Linguistics*, 43(1-2):1–45.

Mann, T. (2021). *Death in Venice [1911]. Translated by Kenneth Burke.* Project Gutenberg.

Mathet, Y., Widlöcher, A., and Métivier, J.-P. (2015). The unified and holistic method gamma (γ) for inter-annotator agreement measure and alignment. *Computational Linguistics*, 41(3):437–479.

May, K. (1888). Winnetou II. In *Projekt Gutenberg*. Haffmans.

Parsons, T. (1981). Nonexistent objects. *Yale University Press.*

Piper, A. (2016). Fictionality. *Journal of Cultural Analytics*, 12.

(2013). Gutenberg-de edition 13 dvd-rom. klassische literatur in deutscher sprache. DVD-ROM.

Stock, K. (2017). *Only imagine: Fiction, interpretation, and imagination.* Oxford University Press.

van Dalen-Oskam, K., de Does, J., Marx, M., Sijaranamual, I., Depuydt, K., Verheij, B., and Geirnaert, V. (2014). Named entity recognition and resolution for literary studies. *Computational Linguistics in the Netherlands Journal*, 4:121–136.

Vrandečić, D. and Krötzsch, M. (2014). Wikidata: A free collaborative knowledgebase. *Commun. ACM*, 57(10):78–85, sep.

Proceedings of ISA-18 Workshop at LREC2022, pages 33–41
Marseille, 20 June 2022

Event Sequencing Annotation with TIE-ML

Damir Cavar, Ali Aljubailan, Ludovic Mompelat, Yuna Won, Billy Dickson, Matthew Fort, Andrew Davis, Soyoung Kim
Indiana University
Bloomington, USA
{dcavar, aaaljuba, lmompela, yunawon, dicksonb, mattfort, ad7, sk135}@iu.edu

Abstract

TIE-ML (Temporal Information Event Markup Language) first proposed by Cavar et al. (2021) provides a radically simplified temporal annotation schema for event sequencing and clause level temporal properties even in complex sentences. TIE-ML facilitates rapid annotation of essential tense features at the clause level by labeling simple or periphrastic tense properties, as well as scope relations between clauses, and temporal interpretation at the sentence level. This paper presents the first annotation samples and empirical results. The application of the TIE-ML strategy on the sentences in the Penn Treebank (Marcus et al., 1993) and other non-English language data is discussed in detail. The motivation, insights, and future directions for TIE-ML are discussed, too. The aim is to develop a more efficient annotation strategy and a formalism for clause-level tense and aspect labeling, event sequencing, and tense scope relations that boosts the productivity of tense and event-level corpus annotation. The central goal is to facilitate the production of large data sets for machine learning and quantitative linguistic studies of intra- and cross-linguistic semantic properties of temporal and event logic.

Keywords: TIE-ML, event sequencing, semantic annotation, temporal logic

1. Introduction

Natural languages provide different means to encode properties of events and their relative order along the time axis in discourse. Tense, aspect, mood, and modality make up the foundations of this encoding, and various combinations of these tools are employed cross-linguistically. Whether these features are expressed lexically, morphologically, as prosodic properties, or whether they need to be induced from semantic or pragmatic cues during a conversational process, we assume that tense places events on a timeline and establishes relations between them, while aspect describes the flow of time respective to the event.

1.1. Cross-linguistic Variation

When comparing different languages, we can identify significant differences between expressions of events and time which we aim to capture for both quantitative studies, and for the development of machine learning tools that automatically annotate and process text.

English and other Germanic languages for example inflect the main verb for past and present tenses and use a modal auxiliary to form the future tense. Perfect aspect is expressed using periphrastic forms though the auxiliary construction *have + past participle* and progressive aspect is expressed through the combination of *to be + -ing*. To contrast, Japanese and Korean mark for past and non-past, and rely on adverbials or context to place events in the future. They can also employ an intention construction in the present tense to indicate future events, and Korean additionally allows the reduplication of the past tense suffix to place events in the remote past. In Semitic languages, for example Arabic and Hebrew, there is an ambiguous association between tense and aspect in verb conjugation.

This diversity of grammatical properties related to tense and event interpretation was one of the motivations for the corpus project discussed in this article. The other motivation was to compare the observed effects of scope relations between predicates in complex sentences (multi-clause structures) on the interpretation of tense for each individual clause. In this context we observe that there are differences between types of subordinate clauses such that some are subject to *Tense Agreement*, while others are not restricted with respect to their tense by any dominating clause. In other words, while some clauses have to agree in tense with their dominating clause, for others, the semantic tense is determined by the dominating clause, and the morphological or periphrastic tense interpretation is altered. In the following section we explain these aspects of the impact of structural scope relations on the interpretation of tense, and the need for corpora to study the qualitative and quantitative properties of those cross-linguistically.

1.2. Interactions between Syntax and Semantics

Interesting research questions related to events and tense emerge from the study of the interaction of temporal and event properties in complex sentences. Scope relations between clauses determine the interpretation of tense associated with a clause level predicate, see for example the discussion of the sequence of tense puzzle in Kiparsky (2002).

The interpretation of the past tense predicate in (1) includes the assumption that an event occurred that resulted in the fact that *Apple* and *Alphabet* are now a single organization. The past tense implies factivity or a positive truth value.

(1) *Apple merged with Alphabet.*

Placing this clause in the scope of a simple matrix clause with a past tense predicate does not change this interpretation, as example (2) shows.

(2) *Reuters reported*
[*that Apple merged with Alphabet*]

The interpretation of the embedded clause in example (2) does not change significantly in comparison to example (1). However, if we alter the tense of the matrix clause, the interpretation of the temporal properties of the embedded predicate is altered significantly, as example (3) shows.

(3) *Reuters will report*
[*that Apple merged with Alphabet*]

Example (3) no longer allows for the assumption that *Apple* indeed *merged with Alphabet* at speaker time, nor is it possible to exclude this possibility. The future tense of the matrix clause provides a new time frame that affects the past tense interpretation of the embedded clause.

We also observe that some clauses that are syntactically assumed to modify a predicate, tend to agree with respect to tense with the modified predicate. Clauses that are selected by the predicate, as with *report* and the subordinate clause in (3), do not have to agree for tense in the same way. We assume that example (5) in contrast to (4) should be considered deviant and semantically problematic, if not completely ungrammatical.

(4) *While I will be in Paris, Reuters will report*
[*that Apple merged with Alphabet*]

(5) ? [*While I was in Paris*] *Reuters will report*
[*that Apple merged with Alphabet*]

Similarly, deeper clause embedding of modifying predicates as in (6) is subject to the same kind of constraint. The ungrammaticality of (7) is due to the mismatch between the tense in the modifier headed by *visit* and the matrix clause head predicate *reported.*

(6) *During the time that I visited Paris, Reuters reported that Apple merged with Alphabet.*

(7) **During the time that I will visit Paris, Reuters reported that Apple merged with Alphabet.*

In some cases this compatibility of tense properties between modifier clause and modified predicate is even more complex, as the *if*-clauses in (8) and (9) show.

(8) *If I visit Paris, Reuters will report that...*

(9) **If I will visit Paris, Reuters will report that...*

Without going into details why present tense of the modifier predicate is compatible with the future tense of the modified predicate, we observe that morpho-syntactic present tense is compatible and often used as semantic future tense.

We observe that modifying temporal adverbial clauses (adjuncts) need to agree in tense with the head predicate that they modify. Selected predicates either have to have tense or be infinitival, but the tense of a selected finite clause is not part of the selection.

To be able to capture the clause-level tense properties and the complex interactions of tense scope induced via syntactic properties, we have to take into account multiple annotation levels or tiers, to describe for example:

- syntactic scope relations (dominance and precedence at least),
- the tense of the particular clauses, and
- the semantic relations between clauses in terms of selection vs. modification.

Thus in the annotation approach discussed here, the information about clause hierarchy, selection or modification, as well as linear sequencing have to be captured.

1.3. Sequencing and Duration of Events

As emphasized in Cavar et al. (2021), sequencing of predicates and events along the time axis is a phenomenon related to tense and the temporal interpretation of predicates. In example (10) we observe that the linear order of sub-events as presented in syntax correlates with the semantic alignment of the sub-events along the time axis.

(10) *Wash the veggies, chop them, and fry them.*
1 2 3

Example (11) on the other hand exhibits a mismatch between the linear presentation sequence of sub-events and the underlying temporal alignment on the time axis.

(11) *Before you fry the veggies, make sure to wash*
3 1
and chop them.
2

Capturing the empirical sequencing of events along the time axis, their potential coincidence, or their overlap is relevant at various levels in semantically aware Natural Language Processing (NLP) or Artificial Intelligence (AI) applications. In computational reasoning, the temporal sequence of events is often relevant for the analysis of causality or intention.

The central focus in the first phase of this effort was to provide temporal sequencing annotations for events in complex sentences. There are many other highly relevant issues related to this, as for example duration of events. By breaking the temporal annotation effort and ML model training into atomic tasks, we expect to achieve faster much better results. In the next project phase we are extending the effort to annotation of duration and overlaps of events.

We have not identified any other resource that could provide enough cross-linguistic data sufficiently large to train ML models and that would be able to provide temporal sequencing and duration annotations of events at the clause level. This is another motivation for the corpus project discussed here.

1.4. Previous Work

There are two dimensions to the annotation task discussed here. One is concerned with theoretical approaches to tense and event description that are useful in theoretical linguistic studies, and that facilitate the understanding and theorizing about intra- and cross-linguistic semantics of tense and event logic. The other dimension is related to annotation standards and proposals suggested for time and event description augmentation of text corpora that can facilitate the generation of corpora for data-driven machine learning for NLP. In the following, each of these dimensions is discussed separately.

For annotation purposes, there are various theoretical candidates that appear appropriate from a perspective that aims at the maximization of annotated data and minimization of annotation mistakes when focusing on events and time properties. Annotation of common tense properties and related features using grammatical concepts like present, past, and future is useful, but insufficient for the tasks at stake here, viz., event sequencing and interpretation of tense in complex sentences.

In the current approach and as part of the TIE-ML annotation schema, a variant of the Reichenbach Model (Reichenbach, 1947) has been adopted. The reason for selecting the Reichenbach model is explained in the following section. A discussion of the numerous other alternatives would be beyond the scope of this article.

1.4.1. The Reichenbach Model

Reichenbach (1947) introduces a theory of tense that provides the building blocks for developing a method to capture or describe time and event information in language. The theory presents three time variables: E for *event time*, R for *reference time*, and S for *speaker time*.

Event time refers to the time of the event in question. *Reference time* refers to a reference point or point of focus for that event, which can be expressed overtly via an adverbial such as *now* or *yesterday*, but can also be covert or implicit. *Speaker time* refers to the time of the utterance itself. These variables are ordered via two ordering relations with ',' denoting simultaneous, and '_' denoting separated sequencing.

(12)
- a. Simple Present (E,R,S where R = now)
  I see Ross now.
- b. Simple Past (E,R_S where R = yesterday)
  I saw Ross yesterday.
- c. Simple Future (S_E,R where R = tomorrow)
  I will see Ross tomorrow.
- d. Present Perfect (E_S,R where R = now)
  I have seen Ross now.
- e. Past Perfect (E_R_S where R = yesterday)
  I had seen Ross yesterday.
- f. Future Perfect (S_E_R where R = tomorrow)
  I will have seen Ross tomorrow.

All three variables are explicit in each example above, regardless of whether perfect aspect is present. Note, however, that if we consider examples without perfect aspect—i.e., consider examples with simple past, simple present, or simple future tenses—only two of the three variables, speaker time S and event time E, are needed to distinguish the tenses. It is only when we introduce a second aspect category (here, the perfect) that we need a third time variable, reference time R, to distinguish between the resulting tense-aspect combinations. The TIE-ML annotation schema incorporates this variant of the Reichenbach model. See Comrie (1985) for a related variant of the Reichenbach model where reference time only appears in relative tenses.

The hypothesis in this project is that scope relations and other temporal properties such as tense, aspect, and temporal adverbials affect ordering relations between the variables expressed in the Reichenbach model. For example, where using a concrete temporal expression that anchors the predicate's reference time does not affect the relation between speaker time and event time, other properties such as scope relations, tense, and aspect from a dominating matrix clause may alter the Reichenbach variable ordering of subordinate clauses. To be able to study such effects cross-linguistically and over large corpora, as well as develop efficient models for the analysis or generation of tense and event-related expressions, the granularity in this project's approach to capturing temporal information has been extended from simple labels like *past*, *present*, and *future* to these Reichenbach variables.

The enterprise of offering a fine-grained annotation schema that entails scope relations and other temporal properties has been undertaken by Pustejovsky et al. (2003b) and their Time Markup Language project. In the next section, we introduce the project, discuss its characteristics and potential limitations, especially regarding the complexity of its annotation schema, and how TIE-ML offers a good compromise between details of annotations and limited effort.

1.5. TimeML and Annotation Standards

TimeML (Pustejovsky et al., 2003a; Pustejovsky et al., 2005) is an XML-based markup language and metadata standard developed for annotating events and temporal expressions in natural language or time information in general. It is the most detailed and theoretically grounded framework.

Historically, TimeML seems to have its roots in the workshop Time and Event Recognition for Question Answering Systems (TERQUAS) in 2002. At the TERQUAS workshop, recommendations for the enhancement of question answering systems were developed. Pustejovsky et al. (2003b) proposed TimeML for the annotation of events and temporal relations integrating for example the TIMEX2 tag (see for example Wilson et al. (2001)), a proposed inline XML tag with six attributes, and various other suggestions, along with other emerging schemata (Katz and Arosio, 2001). See Cavar et al. (2021) for a more detailed overview of the different standards and how they relate to TimeML.

TimeML is concerned with two major objectives. The first is to map predicates to events. The second is to establish a relative ordering between events.

In TimeML there are separate annotations for events and temporal expressions, and the specific anchoring or ordering dependencies are expressed in language. It provides four core annotation tags, i.e., EVENT, TIMEX3, SIGNAL, and LINK. EVENT encodes events that are punctual or that have a duration associated with them. The SIGNAL tag can be used to mark up function words with a temporal reference. Relationships between events are encoded via LINK tags. Each of these tags provides sophisticated annotation properties that can cover complex events and temporal relations. The complexity of TimeML can be seen when considering for example the EVENT tag. It is broken down into types of events like *Reporting*, *Perception*, *Aspectual*, *I Action*, *I State*, *State*, and *Occurrence* events.

TimeML introduces not just new extensions to the TIMEX2 tag via new attributes. It also introduces temporal functions to allow intentionally specified expressions like *five months ago* or *in five days*. It allows for the annotations of SIGNALS that are relevant for the interpretation of temporal expressions, like temporal prepositions (e.g., *at*, *on*, *during*, *for*) or connectives (e.g., *while*, *after*, *before*). Event expressions that can be specified include a rich set of types like tensed verbs (e.g., *has left*, *was captured*, *will resign*), stative adjectives (e.g., *landed*, *sunken*, *stalled*), or event nominals (e.g., *destruction*, *merger*, *Military Operation*, *Gulf War*). It provides instruments to express dependencies between events and times, for example *anchoring*, *embeddings*, or *orderings*.

Although these sophisticated instruments facilitate the annotation of extremely detailed temporal information in language, their complexity requires extensive training of annotators to provide sufficient and useful data sets with acceptable annotation quality. We found the overall annotation process to demand significantly more effort than necessary when focusing on a subset of details related to event and time annotation required for our downstream machine learning applications.

The simplified TIE-ML schema presented in the next section aims to solve these issues while providing comprehensive annotations for time and event information that can easily be mapped and translated into the theoretically far superior annotation standard of TimeML

2. TIE-ML Standard and Approach

TIE-ML (Temporal Information Event Markup Language) (Cavar et al., 2021) is a simplified temporal annotation schema that focuses on event sequencing annotation and clause level temporal properties of main predicates. The goal of TIE-ML is to improve upon previous markup strategies' accuracy and productivity via simplification. Increasing the production of *good data* with the event and temporal properties annotated will facilitate the development of machine learning models for applications that can benefit from specific semantic analytics. This increase of productivity can also be achieved through simplifying the task for annotators.

Breaking tasks down to simple annotations of predicate tense, enumeration of events expressed by predicates, and labeling temporal expressions that encode duration or temporal anchoring simplifies the process, requires less training of annotators and reduces annotation errors.

TIE-ML was designed as an XML markup language that provides sentence and clause level annotations of text using the `S` and `C` tag respectively. While XML is a possible way to augment text with event and temporal information, the same approach can be achieved with a JSON-variant of TIE-ML. Alternative formats like CoNLL(-U)[1] (Buchholz and Marsi, 2006) can be generated as well.

TIE-ML focuses on the annotation of events expressed by individual predicates at the clause level. By enumerating each clause or independent predicate, an event is identified with an (`eventid`) as shown in the XML sample in Figure (1).

```
<tieml>
<s> <c eventid="1">
    Danny watched the movie
    </c>
    <c eventid="2">
    and ate popcorn
    </c>. </s>
<s> <c eventid="3">
    Josh brought the pizza
    </c>. </s>
</tieml>
```

Figure 1: TIE-ML example

While `eventid` reflects the presentation order of events in a text, temporal ordering is annotated by providing a `timeslot` identifier that reflects the relative

[1]See `https://universaldependencies.org/format.html` for a detailed explanation of the CoNLL-U format.

position of events on the time axis. For point-wise events, this is a concrete location of the event on the time axis. For events with an associated duration, this reflects the start point of the event on the time axis. These two properties are defined as attributes of the C (or S) tag in XML, as shown in Figure (2).

```
<s> <c eventid="1" timeslot="2">
    Before you fry the vegetables </c>
    <c eventid="2" timeslot="1">
    chop them into cubes
    </c>. </s>
```

Figure 2: TIE-ML timeslot example

In Figure ((2) the enumerated eventid does not correspond with the temporal order timeslot as reflected in their differing values amongst each respective clause.

The tense properties of the predicates are labeled using the Reichenbach variables *event time* E, *speaker time* S, and *reference time* R, which are introduced as XML attributes to the C tag at the clause level as shown in Figure (3). The values of these attributes are integers that reflect the relative order of coincidence or precedence, e.g., an S-value of 0 and an E-value of 0 represent present tense, an S-value of 0 and an E-value of -1 represent past tense, and an S-value of 0 and an E-value of 1 represent future tense.

```
<s> <c e="-1" s="0">
    Danny watched the movie.
</c> </s>
```

Figure 3: TIE-ML Reichenbach variables simple example

Note that because Figure ((3) is a simple past tense sentence, the *reference time* R does not appear. Values of -1 and 0 for *event time* and *reference time* respectively correspond to the Reichenbach notation of E_S. Figure (4) presents an annotation example of a future perfect sentence in which *reference time* R does appear.

```
<s> <c e="1" r ="2" s="0">
    Danny will have watched the movie.
</c> </s>
```

Figure 4: TIE-ML Reichenbach variables perfect example

Values of 1, 2, and 0 for *event time*, *reference time*, and *speaker time* respectively correspond to the Reichenbach notation of S_E_R.

Concrete expressions of reference time in the clause are encoded as attributes using the reference attribute in the C-tag. as shown in Figure (5).

```
<s> <c reference = "Monday">
    Jacob visited his mother on Monday.
</c> </s>
```

Figure 5: TIE-ML reference example

This XML annotation schema is kept intentionally simple to allow for efficient annotation of sequencing of events, as well as temporal features of predicates and temporal expressions in each respective clause. To be precise, our prediction is that TIE-ML is more efficient and leads to cleaner results much faster than alternative annotation approaches both when it comes to creating a resource that provides annotations of predicate properties and clausal relationships in particular geared toward the development of machine learning models, as well as when it comes to the quantitative and qualitative study of intra- and cross-linguistic temporal properties. To validate our prediction, we decided to use the Penn Treebank (Marcus et al., 1999) as a base-corpus and augment the syntactic and functional annotations with the proposed event and temporal properties.

XML as such, however, was not a convincing data format for annotators to work with or produce, even though powerful XML editors and tools can simplify the editing task tremendously. Instead of using XML as the annotation format, we decided to use TIE-ML XML as an exchange and conversion format, one that can be generated from formats provided by sophisticated annotation tools like INCEpTION, or one that can be converted into the extremely powerful TimeML annotation format.

In the following, we describe the adaptation and use of a specific configuration of INCEpTION for the TIE-ML style of annotation.

2.1. Annotation Implementation using INCEpTION

The INCEpTION platform (Klie et al., 2018) served for the annotation of the Penn Treebank corpus using the TIE-ML standard. The main reason for using it was the expectation that the annotation effort could be simplified and facilitated even more. In addition to providing excellent annotation instruments, INCEpTION also offers advanced management of annotators, corpora, and statistical tools for inter-annotator agreement analysis.

The specification of the three specific layers of annotations, namely: predicate, clausal, and temporal named entity annotations, is straightforward in INCEpTION. The predicate annotation layer is used to annotate predicates (whether finite or non-finite) and has an *Aspect* feature and a *Tense* feature.

The *Aspect* feature includes the following tags: *Simple*,

Progressive, *Perfect*, *Perfect Progressive*. In addition, annotation of *Voice* features is provided in form of an optional *Passive* tag.
The *Tense* feature includes the following tags: *Present*, *Past*, and *Future*. These tags are converted in the back-end when transferring the annotations to the TIE-ML XML format to the corresponding Reichenbach variables.
The Temporal named entity annotation layer is used to mark temporal referents which anchor a given clause in a specific point in time. It includes the following tags: `TEMP` (for a temporal element in its pure form), `TEMPderiv` (for a temporal element as a derivational element), and `TEMPpart` (for a temporal element as part of a bigger token). These tags corresponds to the TIE-ML `reference` tag.
In periphrastic tense forms, the temporal cues are expressed as a sequence of verbal elements, i.e., auxiliaries and verbs. In copula constructions, the copula element and an additional adjectival or nominal head form the predicate of a clause. As an additional problem, Multi-word expressions in periphrastic tense forms can be realized discontinuously in a clause, as shown in example (13). To annotate the properties of the predicate in clauses with such discontinuities, each element of the predicate is labeled with the full predicate feature set independently, while adjacent sequences of lexical items are marked as one multi-word predicate unit.

(13) *John* ***was*** *mostly* ***reading*** *newspapers.*

Finally, for non-finite verb forms or for cases in which the copula or auxiliary is missing as shown in example (14), the verbal element that is overt is only labeled for Aspect (Simple, Perfect, Progressive, or Passive) and not for Tense since the tense marking is present on the auxiliary/copula.

(14) [*John is reading a book*] *and*
[---- -- *drinking tea.*]

The core annotation assumption is that each clause has only one core predicate. In some cases, this predicate can be opaque, for example, due to *ellipsis* or *gapping* applied to the clause or sentence (see for example Johnson (2008)). Opaque predicates are not yet annotated in this version of the corpus.
The individual lexical items are independently labeled with a part-of-speech tag in the Penn Treebank, which allows for automatic detection of inversion and deviation from canonical word order. This is relevant for the annotation of languages that allow for auxiliary verb inversions, for example, German (see also *VP topicalization* in Haider (1990)) or Croatian (Cavar and Wilder, 1994).
The clausal annotation layer is used to annotate clause boundaries. Each clause can be identified as main- or subordinate clause, including differentiation between complement, adjunct, or relative clauses. Clausal features that can be used in the annotation include the following:

- Clause ID (unique integer per clause within one sentence)
- Time Slot of an event (sequence of events using integer enumeration)
- Speaker Time
- Event Time (determines the tense of each clause predicate)
- Reference Time expressed by a tagged Temporal Named Entity in the clause (optional)
- Level of Embedding (integer indicating the depth of embedding of a clause in a sentence)
- Selected by ID (the ID of the clause containing the predicate that selects the clause, if the clause is a selected complement)

Each clause is given a clause ID corresponding to the TIE-ML `eventid` tag, and a Time Slot corresponding to the TIE-ML `timeslot` tag). The Speaker Time and Event Time correspond to the TIE-ML `s` and `e` tags and are determined for the main clause based on the characterization of the main clause's predicate and its *Tense* and *Aspect* tags.The Speaker Time and Event Time of a relative, complement or adjunct clause depend on those of the main clause. The Level of Embedding and Selected by ID features relate to the clausal hierarchy. The Level of Embedding of each main clause is 0 while that of each complement, adjunct, and relative clause is always 1 more than the clause they depend on. Relative, adjunct, and main clauses are by definition not selected elements, thus the *Selected by ID* label should always be 0, while in the case of a complement clause, the label should reflect the ID of the selecting clause.
Each clause contains a list of lexical items. Clauses can be rendered discontinuous within a complex sentence as in a (15). Segments of tokens with the same clause ID are assumed to be parts of the same clause.

(15) **Which car** did John say **that Mary will like** ?
clause$_1$ clause$_2$ clause$_1$

To exemplify the annotations we will use an export format for our data set. We utilize an interim format data exchange format from INCEpTION to Machine Learning algorithms to encode sentences and clauses similar to the CoNLL[2] Tab Separated Values (TSV) format. We separate sentences with an empty line and encode clauses by line, followed by tab-separated clause ID and time slot assignment. The enumeration of clauses starts with 1 for each sentence and it is expressed in the

[2]See `https://www.clips.uantwerpen.be/conll2006/`.

second column. The temporal order of the predicates (per clause just one) is encoded as the time-slot (TS) in the third column. The clauses are tokenized. The filenames correspond to the Penn Treebank filenames.

```
CLAUSE                          ID   TS
Which car                        1    2
did John say                     2    1
that Mary will like?             1    2

She will like the blue car.      1    1
```

This format is only one of many possible export formats that we generate from the INCEpTION output or storage format.

Using annotation IDs as in this case, it is possible to capture different types of very common discontinuities or dislocations in syntax and their relevance for semantic interpretation. This way it is also possible to cope with covert or incomplete predicates that are semantically implied in clauses that are subject to ellipsis or to similar phenomena.

Since the underlying sentence collection for the first level annotation for English is based on the Penn Treebank, all the annotations from the treebank (e.g., part of speech tags and syntactic structures) are available in addition to the clause level segmentation, temporal features, and sequencing provided in this project. This syntactic information provides hierarchical and scope information that can be utilized in various automatic conversions or machine learning tasks.

Additionally, we developed our own tense annotator for various Indo-European languages for clause level tense annotation to validate the user accuracy.

Note, however, that our focus is on the annotation of predicate sequencing along the time axis using a simple enumeration strategy, and additionally, on the tense information of each individual clause given its context, scope of dominance relation to other tenses and potential temporal expressions.

3. Data and Corpora

The corpora, samples, and scripts are made available at the public TIE-ML GitHub repository:

`https://github.com/dcavar/tieml`

More documentation and information about the project can be found at the website of the NLP-Lab:

`https://nlp-lab.org/timeevents/`

The annotations for English based in the first version on the Penn Treebank are made available in the GitHub repository. The dataset covers the freely available 10% of the Penn Treebank that are distributed in the Natural Language Toolkit (NLTK)[3] (Bird et al., 2009) data set. The full Penn Treebank annotation is available as a script that reads an existing treebank data set and generates the TIE-ML annotations.

A full linked data set for the treebank will be generated and made available in the TIE-ML GitHub repository. Samples from different languages and other tools are accessible there as well, including the INCEpTION to TIE-ML XML conversion script.

Contributions from volunteers and other teams or individuals are welcome. Please use GitHub pull requests as an instrument, and feel free to contact the NLP-Lab team.

Similar datasets are being developed for Arabic, Korean, Croatian, and other languages.

3.1. Copyrights

The code produced by this project is shared in the public GitHub repository under the Apache License Version 2.0.

All texts and corpora in the public GitHub repository are licensed under the Attribution-ShareAlike 4.0 International (CC BY-SA 4.0) license, or – in case of third party data – under the specific license of the copyright holder, as noted in the README or LICENSE file in the corresponding sub-folder.

4. Results

For the evaluation of the claim that the TIE-ML annotation approach and utilization of INCEpTION the output and annotation quality per annotator can be maximized, we took the 10% portion of the Penn Treebank in the NLTK data set. This part consists of 199 files from the treebank, with a total of 3914 sentences and 93838 tokens. The number of clauses and overt main predicates will be updated here for the final paper when the validation of the annotations is complete and approved.

num. files	199
num. tokens	93838
num. sentences	3914

Table 1: Properties of the Pen Treebank Portion Annotated

For annotation, we used the adapted INCEpTION interface. The current number of annotators is 9. The scores in Table (2) reflect the current average while the 9 annotators have processed different sections of the corpus. The majority of the annotators are students in computational linguistics and linguistics at Indiana University - Bloomington, with varying experience and basic training in the syntax and semantics of events and temporal relations.

The time for annotation at each different level is given in table 2. This table reflects the average time scores after a first annotation round over a corpus sample.

The scores in Table (2) reflect the complexity of annotations of clause features such as selection relations, hierarchical depth, and time-slot assignment. Clause

[3] See `https://www.nltk.org/` for more details.

Annotation type	Avg. time
Predicate labeling	13 sec./predicate
Clause boundaries	8.8 sec./clause
Clause features	50 sec./clause
Sentence	122 sec./clause

Table 2: Average Annotation Times by Annotation Type

boundary markup and predicate tense labeling are the fastest processes in the described setting. Note that clause boundary and predicate labeling also involves enumeration of events and sequencing, that is, assigning Reichenbach features to clause-level predicates and sequencing of events can be achieved with the described approach efficiently.

5. Conclusion

Overall, TIE-ML, a simple annotation schema focused on event sequencing annotation through the incorporation of Reichenbach variables, has been presented, and initial experiments with TIE-ML annotation using INCEpTION as a graphical front-end have proven to be highly informative.

Although, in the current stage, the main focus was on enriching existing English corpora, our ultimate goal is to report on intra- and cross-linguistic insights in hierarchical interpretation of tense and event sequencing in different language types (e.g., SVO, SOV, VSO), with variation in placement of embedded clauses and predicates (e.g., placement position and interpretation of adjunct vs. complement clauses).

In addition, generating large data sets using TIE-ML will provide the necessary data for training machine learning models in downstream event labeling applications that are able to guess the temporal sequencing and relation of events.

Finally, this project will apply the simple annotation scheme for temporal sequencing with some simple tweaks also to temporal duration annotation of events. By breaking the annotations down into simple tasks, we expect to improve the quantitative and qualitative properties of our resulting data sets. Temporal sequencing and duration are essential for commonsense reasoning models, which fall in the core focus of our research interest.

6. Acknowledgements

We are grateful to all the team members of the Indiana University NLP-Lab (`https://nlp-lab.org/`). Special thanks go to Steven Franks, Thomas Grano, Larry Moss, and Zoran Tiganj for helpful discussions, suggestions, and comments related to theoretical issues, approaches, and the project goals.

Some excellent suggestions and comments from reviewers will be worked into subsequent publications and material, and summarized on the project website. Due to time limitations it was not possible to take some of the suggestions into account and integrate them in this version of the article.

7. Bibliographical References

Bird, S., Klein, E., and Loper, E. (2009). *Natural Language Processing with Python: Analyzing Text with the Natural Language Toolkit.* O'Reilly Media.

Buchholz, S. and Marsi, E. (2006). CoNLL-X shared task on multilingual dependency parsing. In *Proceedings of the Tenth Conference on Computational Natural Language Learning (CoNLL-X)*, pages 149–164, New York City, June. Association for Computational Linguistics.

Cavar, D. and Wilder, C. (1994). Clitic third in croatian. In H. van Riemsdijk et al., editors, *Clitics: Their Origin, Status and Position*, volume 6 of *Eurotype Woking Papers, Theme Group 8*. Mouton de Gruyter, Berlin.

Cavar, D., Dickson, B., Aljubailan, A., and Kim, S. (2021). Temporal information and event markup language: TIE-ML markup process and schema version 1.0.

Comrie, B. (1985). *Tense*, volume 17. Cambridge university press.

Haider, H. (1990). Topicalization and other puzzles of german syntax. In G. Grewendorf et al., editors, *Scrambling and Barriers*, pages 93–112. Benjamins, Amsterdam.

Johnson, K. (2008). *Topics in ellipsis*. Cambridge University Press, Cambridge; New York.

Katz, G. and Arosio, F. (2001). The annotation of temporal information in natural language sentences. In *Proceedings of the ACL 2001 Workshop on Temporal and Spatial Information Processing*.

Kiparsky, P. (2002). Event structure and the perfect. *The Construction of Meaning*, pages 113–136.

Klie, J.-C., Bugert, M., Boullosa, B., Eckart de Castilho, R., and Gurevych, I. (2018). The INCEpTION platform: Machine-assisted and knowledge-oriented interactive annotation. In *Proceedings of the 27th International Conference on Computational Linguistics: System Demonstrations*, pages 5–9, Santa Fe, New Mexico.

Marcus, M. P., Santorini, B., and Marcinkiewicz, M. A. (1993). Building a large annotated corpus of English: The Penn Treebank. *Computational Linguistics*, 19(2):313–330.

Pustejovsky, J., Hanks, P., Saurí, R., See, A., Gaizauskas, R., Setzer, A., Radev, D., Sundheim, B., Day, D., ferro, L., and Lazo, M. (2003a). The timebank corpus. *Proceedings of Corpus Linguistics*, pages 28–34, 01.

Pustejovsky, J., no, J. C., Robert Ingria, R. S., Gaizauskas, R., Setzer, A., Katz, G., and Radev, D. (2003b). Timeml: Robust specification of event and temporal expressions in text. Technical Report SS-03-07, AAAI.

Pustejovsky, J., Ingria, R., Sauri, R., Castaño, J. M., Littman, J., Gaizauskas, R. J., Setzer, A., Katz, G., and Mani, I. (2005). The specification language TimeML.

Reichenbach, H. (1947). *Elements of Symbolic Logic*. The Free Press, New York.

Wilson, G., Mani, I., Sundheim, B., and Ferro, L. (2001). A multilingual approach to annotating and extracting temporal information. In *Proceedings of the ACL 2001 Workshop on Temporal and Spatial Information Processing*.

8. Language Resource References

Marcus, M. P., Santorini, B., Marcinkiewicz, M. A., and Taylor, A. (1999). Treebank-3 ldc99t42. Web Download.

Proceedings of ISA-18 Workshop at LREC2022, pages 42–52
Marseille, 20 June 2022

Measuring Similarity by Linguistic Features rather than Frequency

Rodolfo Delmonte
Ca Foscari University
Venice (Italy)
delmont@unive.it

Nicolò Busetto
Accenture
Text To Speech Computational Linguist
nicolo.busetto@accenture.com

Abstract

In the use and creation of current Deep Learning Models the only number that is used for the overall computation is the frequency value associated with the current word form in the corpus, which is used to substitute it. Frequency values come in two forms: absolute and relative. Absolute frequency is used indirectly when selecting the vocabulary against which the word embeddings are created: the cutoff threshold is usually fixed at 30/50K entries of the most frequent words. Relative frequency comes in directly when computing word embeddings based on co-occurrence values of the tokens included in a window size 2/5 adjacent tokens. The latter values are then used to compute similarity, mostly based on cosine distance. In this paper we will evaluate the impact of these two frequency parameters on a small corpus of Italian sentences whose main features are two: presence of very rare words and of non-canonical structures. The results computed on the basis of a perusal of BERT's raw embeddings shows that the two parameters conspire to decide the level of predictability.

1 Introduction

This paper presents work carried out to verify whether current Transformer based models like BERT(Ashish Vaswani and Polosukhin, 2017) are able to cope with linguistically highly complex datasets and to what degree. In particular, BERT tries to predict the next word or sentence on the basis of word embeddings as they have been represented in the pre-trained model: in the experiment we used only the output of the first projection layer of a Deep Learning model, the raw word embeddings. We organized an experiment on a small number of Italian sentences taken from two domains: newspapers and poetry domain. They represent two levels of increasing difficulty in the possibility to predict the masked word that we intended to test. The experiment is organized on the hypothesis of increasing difficulty in predictability at the three levels of linguistic complexity that we intend to monitor: lexical, syntactic and semantic level. Whereas lexical predictability may be based on word frequency and not just context, syntax and semantics strictly constrain meaning understanding. To test this hypothesis we alternate canonical and non-canonical version of the same sentence before processing them with the same DL model. In particular, we expect the poetry domain to introduce additional restrictions on the local word context due to the need to create metaphors which require non-literal meaning compositional processes.

The notion of "similarity" which cosine measure is supposed to represent is very poorly defined. It can represent "semantic" similarity of a candidate word proposed by the model to the target one, in the sense of being semantically "related" or just semantically "associated" to the target word. However, whenever the two items are not identical nor semantically close in any sense they might still exhibit "linguistic" similarity which is shown by lexical, morphological, and syntactic features. These features are very important in their ability to reveal how close the prediction has been on the basis of frequency of (co)-occurence - the Context, as it is being measured by word embeddings and their vector space models. In fact, the only number that is being used by Neural Networks and Deep Learning Models is frequency of occurrence, that substitutes words in the overall computation. Now, frequency of (co)-occurence which characterizes the Context, is strictly dependent on absolute frequency and even though the corpora being used nowadays to build and train the models are huge and number by the terabytes, they will always be subjected to the Zipfian laws that establish that the frequency of any word is inversely proportional to its rank in the frequency table. As a consequence, the reference dictionary on which basis the embeddings are built - usually comprising only the first 30/50K most frequent word forms - will always be a very partial picture of the corpus it should represent, and the use of subword units does not solve the problem (see (Delmonte, 2021)).

In order to evaluate fine-grained levels of similarity between the predicted outcome and the expected result we devised a graded scale of linguistically based scoring table which is then used to produce a "predictability parameter". This parameter is highly correlated with the cosine measure used to gauge the similarity between predicted and expected, but produces a better distinction between linguistically evaluated classes.

A further important element contributing to define the kind of response Italian language exhibits to Deep Learning is its inherent language structure which is very different from English as discussed in what follows.

1.1 English and Italian are totally different languages

It is a fact that the great majority of experimental works on Deep Learning Models is made on English, which is in no way a good representative of the variety of languages spoken in Europe, where Slavic and Romance languages prevail. In particular Italian, a Romance language, is a morphologically rich language thus possessing a very large vocabulary of unique wordforms which, if compared to the total number of wordforms obtainable from the WordNet list of citation forms for English is an order of magnitude higher – from 500K to 5 million wordforms in Italian, only considering the corresponding number of grammatical categories(Delmonte, 2014). It has already been shown elsewhere(Tripodi and Pira., 2017) that languages like Italian, which have a rich morphology, need embeddings with higher dimensions and a vocabulary size more than doubled in order to account for the variety of semantically relevant wordforms. In order to evaluate frequency values associated to each masked word, we cleaned the frequency list of Italian wordforms compiled on the basis of ItWaC [1], deleting all numbers and websites, which now counts 1,700,000 entries. Then we extracted the first 50000 most frequent wordforms to be used to check what words would be included by a model created on the basis of BERT tokenization module. In this way, wordforms included are up to a frequency value of 1377. The remaining portion of the frequency list is then cut at frequency value 4, thus leaving out Rare words, made up of Trislegomena, Dislegomena and Hapaxlegomena, which is by far the longest list: it counts 1,642,949 entries. The Upper List – the list that includes the 50000 plus the rest of wordforms down to and including words with frequency 4, is made up of 513,427 entries.

Thus, we consider as the most frequent part of our 50,000 dictionary wordforms with frequency equal to 10000, and we mark them with a degree sign (°)-, second less frequent part of the list goes from 10000 to 1377 we call "low" frequency words that we mark with one asterisk (*). We then consider as "very-low" frequency words those ranging from 1377 down to 4 occurrences that we mark with two asterisks (**)-, and the wordforms in the remaining long tail are classified as "Rare Words" that we mark with three asterisks (***). The final classification is then organized into four classes: High, Low, Very Low and Rare. In this way, words with more than one asterisk will not be present in the dictionary and would have to be dissected into subunits thus losing its semantics. This is discussed in detail below in those sentences where it happens (see sentences 2A, 4A, 5A, 8B, 9B, 13A, 14A, 15B, 18B).

To compare English with Italian word lists, we now consider the lemmata list and not the wordform one we just commented. The first 100 entries in the lemmata frequency list summed together could be used to produce 926 wordforms. The list contains 50 invariable wordforms, mainly grammatical or function words - with one proper noun, "Italia"/Italy. If we look into the frequency list made available by the same project web page for UK English, we only find 20 words belonging to the class of variable words, the remaining 80 words are invariable. Summing up all possible wordforms we come up with a total of 92, again one level of magnitude less. An important feature which has been used frequently in the cognitive literature is the relevance of the effort/time required to pronounce/read a word: a short word, both phonetically and as grapheme, is preferred and confirmed in an experiment based on semantic grounds by Ma-

[1] The corpus contains approximately 388,000 documents from 1,067 different websites, for a total of about 250M tokens. All documents contained in the PAISA‘ corpus date back to Sept./Oct. 2010. The itWaC corpus is available at https://wacky.sslmit.unibo.it/ accessed on October, 2021

howald et al. (Mahowald et al., 2012), where pairs of near synonym words inserted in frame sentences and user have consistently chosen the shortest ones as the most predictable. This seems to be confirmed by the well-known fact that the top range of frequency lists of wordforms are occupied by short words thus confirming the inverse correlation existing between word length and frequency. Most frequent words are not only the shortest but the ones with more senses as confirmed in a paper by Piantadosi et al. (Piantadosi et al., 2012), hence the more frequent. To verify this we inspected the top 200 words in the frequency lists of ItWac for Italian and English and counted their number of syllables with the following results: Italian has 75 monosyllabic words and 125 words with more than one syllable; English has 149 monosyllabic words and 51 words with more syllables. The two languages have an opposite distribution as has also been documented in a previous paper (Delmonte, 2014). In addition, English top 200 words contain only 30 content words, while Italian contains 61 content words, ten of which are morphological variants, English has only one morphological variant.

1.2 The Dataset and Non-Canonical Structures

The most important feature of the experiment is that all sentences are characterized by non-canonical structures. Italian is a language in which non-canonical structures are fairly common due to the weakly configurational nature of the language and to the existence of the pro-drop parameter that allows sentences to freely omit lexically expressed subjects(Delmonte et al., 2007). We then operated on the dataset in two ways: at first we reformulated the text obtained modifying each sentence structure in order to make it canonical. The inclusion of sentences from poetry has been done in order to focus on the effects of context in conjunction with word level frequency effects [2]. The reason for this choice is that poetry is the only domain where rare words are used consistently thus making available a full real context of use for (very) low frequency words. The combined effect of using rare words in a non-canonical syntactic configuration and then restructuring the same sentence with a canonical structure allowed us to make important comparisons. Non-canonical sentences in Italian can be found in great number due to the pro-drop nature of the language which thus resembles Chinese and Japanese (Delmonte, 2009).

As said above, Italian is very rich in number and types of non-canonical structures. This is mainly due to its being a direct derivation from Latin, a free word-order language (see (Delmonte, 2018)). Our approach has been previously adopted by other researchers but with slightly different aims that we describe in what follows. The first work is by (Paccosi et al., 2022) where the authors present a new dataset of Italian based on "marked" sentences, which is then used to verify the performance of a neural parser of Italian (TINT) on the dataset. The result for LAS dependency structures is 77%, 3 points below the best results previously obtained on the UD corpus of Italian, which was 80% accuracy. This result confirm previous work documented also in (Delmonte, 2016) with a small dataset containing strongly marked sentences, which have been included in the text used in this paper, where the results were well below 50% accuracy. The authors make a detailed description of the type of marked structures they annotated in their treebank corpus. It is a list of seven structures - cleft, left dislocated, right dislocated, presentative "ci", inverted subject, pseudo-clefts, hanging topic - with a majority of Cleft sentences and Left dislocated sentences.

Similar result is obtained by the experiment presented in the paper by (Pedinotti et al., 2021) where in Section IV they test the ability of Transformers - they use RoBERTa - on a small dataset with surface syntactic structures different from the recurrent word order. They modify the sentences to produce cleft and interrogative versions of the same sentences. The result for core semantic roles - this is what they are testing - is a dramatic drop of performance from 0.65 of correlation in canonical transitive versions down below 0.35. Compared to the corpuses above, our dataset is smaller but it contains many more types of marked constructions, which makes it more difficult to come to terms with, and this is due mainly to presence of sentences from the poetry domain. [3]

[2]For a thorough syntactic and semantic description of these sentences, (Delmonte, 2018)

[3]We present here the structures contained in our dataset: ***complete argument inversion*** (the complement is fronted and the subject is in post verbal position) in sentence 7B - with copula deletion, and in sentence 17B with infinitival structure as subject;

2 The Experimental Setup: (Co)-Frequency and Cosine Measures do not coincide

We assume that word predictability can be characterized by two parameters: word (co-occurrence) frequency/ies and linguistic complexity measured by the Context, or a syntactic/semantic related scoring function. We evaluate word co-occurrence frequencies by means of embeddings as the cosine value made available by BERT[4] in its first projection layer, using pretrained models and no fine-tuning.

As said above, we used BERT – with the Italian model taken from UWAC corpus, Umberto-commoncrawl - and examined the output of the first or projection layer[5]. In this way we intended to check the predicting ability of BERT on the masked word, by selecting in turn one content word at a time allowing BERT to use the rest of the sentence as a context to make appropriate predictions. To this aim we ran BERT by masking each content word and some function word, one at a time in order to be able to make a detailed error analysis and parameter evaluation.

The text is made up of 18 sentences, 11 belonging to the newswire domain and 7 sentences belonging to Italian poetry of last century[6]. The English translation is available in the Appendix. We signed every sentence with letter A for those belonging to the poetry domain - 7, and letter B for newswire domain - 11. The newswire sentences are taken from the treebank of Italian – VIT, Venice Italian Treebank – available also under UD repositories. [7]; the poetry set of sentences is taken from publicly available collections of Italian poets of the first half of the nineteenth century which have already undergone specific analysis in previous work [8]. In what follows we make a detailed description of the outcome of the BERT masked word experiment for each word of every sentence analysed. The comments are followed by the lookup result of each content word in the ItWac frequency list to assess their position. The overall results are then reported in separate tables and discussed in detail in the following section.

Sentence 1.B - Oggi ringrazio della cortesia in più occasioni dimostrata a me e ai miei colleghi. 1.Bc Oggi ringrazio della cortesia dimostrata a me e ai miei colleghi in più occasioni. The sentence belongs to the newswire domain: it is computed best in the canonical form, with 5 words over 8 while the non-canonical version has only 3 words predicted correctly – only "più/more", "occasioni/chances" and "miei/my". Cosine values are not particularly high except for "miei/my" the possessive which being in its attributive position has a favourable predictive condition. "Oggi" is wrongly predicted as being a separator with very high value, " s 0.99998". It can be noted that "ringrazio" is partially predicted by "Grazie" in first position but very low value 0.14397. Now the canonical version: Ringrazio (0.0238), più (0.287), occasioni (0.545), dimostrata (0.165), miei (0.882). Interesting to note that the three words predicted in both structural versions have the same cosine values. When we add the remaining 7 sentences, another word is predicted, colleghi (0.076). No connection with frequency values of the missing words: they are all positioned in the high part of the frequency list – excluding "più" and "miei" which are grammatical words and are positioned close to the top. **Frequency List: °-più; °-miei; °-Oggi; °-colleghi; °-occasioni; °-ringrazio; °-dimostrata; °-cortesia**

Sentence 2.A - Lei sola forse il freddo sognatore educherebbe al tenero prodigio. 2.Ac Forse il freddo sognatore educherebbe lei sola al tenero prodigio. The second sentence belongs to the poetry domain. The original non-canonical version has no candidate found in the first 5 positions. This may be due to presence of a rather infrequent

object fronting (the object comes before the subject at the beginning of the sentence) in sentence 2A and 5A;
adjective extraction (the adjective is extracted and fronted from the noun phrase) in sentence 13A and 14A;
PPadjunct preposing from participial clause in sentence 1B and 13A;
lexical verb left extraction (the main verb - untensed non-finite - is positioned before the auxiliary/modal) in sentence 3A;
subject right dislocation (the subject is positioned after the complements) in sentence 3A and 6B;
subject and object fronting (the subject comes before the object and both are positioned before the main verb) in sentence 4A and 5A;
PPspecification extraction from the noun phrase and fronted to the left in sentence 5A;
clitic left dislocation in sentence 8B;
object right dislocation (the object is positioned after the indirect object or the adjuncts) in sentence 10B;
parenthetical insertion (a parenthetical is inserted after the subject before the main verb) in sentence 11B and 16B;
adjective right extraction (the adjective is extracted from the noun phrase and positioned after the noun adjuncts) in sentence 11B and 14A;
PPspecification right stranding - the PPof is stranded to the right out of the noun phrase in sentence 14B;
lexical verb right extraction (the main verb - untensed non-finite - is positioned after the complements) in sentence 12A;
double parenthetical insertions (after the subject and after the verb complex and before the complements) in sentence 15B and 16B;
clitic left dislocation with subject fronted as hanging topic in sentence 18B.

[4]presented in the paper by Loreto Parisi et al. (Parisi et al., 2020)

[5]We produced the whole experiment leveraging the ability of the Huggingface implementation (Wolf et al., 2019)

[6]That these sentences are hard to understand is indirectly confirmed by parsers' accuracy. We comment and analyze in depth all sentences in a paper where parsers of Italian have been used to parse them and have resulted in an accuracy lower than 50%. (see (Delmonte, 2018))

[7]`https://universaldependencies.org/`

[8]see (Delmonte et al., 2007) (Delmonte, 2009)

word like "educherebbe/would+educate" as main verb which only appears listed low only in the Upper List. On the contrary, the canonical form has three words predicted: first "Forse/Maybe ", second word "lei/She", and third word "solo"/alone but with wrong masculine morphology. However, these words are correctly predicted with low cosine values - Forse (0.149), lei (0.0355) solo (0.0145). No version provides useful approximations of the meaning of the missing words even though "freddo/cold" is included in the high portion of the 50000 vocabulary. As to the remaining words, they are still included in the Vocabulary but in the lower portion. It is important to note that the lack of prediction can only be motivated just because by combining not so frequent words in unusual combination has produced metaphors like "cold dreamer", "tender prodigy", in association with a verb like "educate". **Frequency List: °-solo; °-lei; °-Forse; °-freddo; *-tenero; *-prodigio; *-sognatore; **-educherebbe**

Sentence 3.A - Penso a un verde giardino ove con te riprendere può a conversare l'anima fanciulla. 3.Ac Penso a un verde giardino ove l'anima fanciulla può riprendere a conversare con te. The non-canonical version of this sentence has two words correctly predicted, giardino/garden, ove/where and a third word with different morphology, in slot 5, Pensa/Think(3rd+person+singular+present+indicative), rather than Penso(1st+person). In the canonical version we find correctly Penso/think in second slot, and another word is added può/can, the modal auxiliary that is now positioned correctly in front of its main verb "riprendere/restart", which is by itself a very frequent verb. As to cosine values, we have the following low values for the canonical version: Penso (0.085), giardino (0.194), ove (0.146), può (0.0865). The non-canonical version has a lower value for Penso but a higher value for giardino (0.291). In the longer context, the interesting fact is constituted by the substitution of "Pensa" with fino/until in the non-canonical version; while in the canonical version Penso/think is moved to a worse position from second slot to last slot, slot 5 and a lower cosine value (0.06112). As to the non-predicted noun modifier "fanciulla/maid", this is certainly an unusual combination even though the two words are highly frequent. The result of the combination is of course a beautiful metaphor which combines "primavera"/spring with "fanciulla"/maid and the garden. Notice the different position of Penso+1st+pers, with respect to Pensa+3rd+pers which is by far less frequent. Now consider the word conversare/conversing which receives the following list of non-word predicted candidates: erare/?? (0.4455), rare/rare?? (0.16737), lare/?? (0.0549), mare/sea?? (0.0479), scere/?? (0.03124). Apart from RARE and MARE which I don't regard being selected for their current meaning but just for being part of the list of subwords, the remaining segments are all meaningless and bear no semantically useful relation with the masked word CONVERSARE. **Frequency List: °-può; °-ove; °-anima; °-verde; °-Penso; °-riprendere; *-Pensa; *-fanciulla; *-conversare**

Sentence 4.A - Se primavera il mio cuor generoso soffocasti di spasimi sordi. 4.Ac Primavera, se soffocasti il mio cuor generoso di spasimi sordi. In this sentence only the phrase "mio cuor"/my heart is predicted in both structural versions. mio (0.291), cuor (0.394). The word "Primavera", which is the first word in the canonical version, has no close prediction: as happens in all sentences, the prediction is totally missed whenever a content word appears in first position. In the non-canonical version, the word comes second, after the conjunction "Se"/If, which predicts the appearance of an auxiliary BE/HAVE in their correct morphological word form – fossi/were, avessi/had in both cases with first person morphology, but also fosse/were, and the last two: con/with and solo/alone. The version with the addition of the 7 sentences has the worsening effect of introducing a subword in place of con/with, MMAI which I assume derives from the wrongly split SEMMAI/if+ever. The word has been wrongly split because the segment SE is wrongly – at least in the word SEMMAI - regarded as a legitimate segment due to its very high frequency. Again the problem seems the unusual combination of the remaining words which are fairly common, apart from soffocasti/choked which is not included in the frequent nor in the Rare wordform list; and spasmi/spasms which is only included in the Upper List. In other words, it's their metaphorical import that prevents the correct prediction. However, it is the position that produces the worst results: the adjective "sordi/deaf" in predicative position is predicted as a punctuation mark in both structural versions. **Frequency List: °-Se; °-mio; °-cuore; °-primavera; *-generoso; *-Primavera; *-sordi; **-spasmi**

Sentence 5.A - Né l'oblioso incanto dell'ora il ferreo battito concede. 5.Ac Né il ferreo battito dell'ora concede l'oblioso incanto. This sentence is the worst case of the poetry domain lot: it has no word predicted neither in the non-canonical nor in the canonical version. This may be due to the presence of a very infrequent word "obliosi/oblivious". However, we notice the presence of an unusual combination of the attributive metaphoric use of "ferreo/iron-like", a rather unusual word. But of course, it is just the combination of words used to build a powerful metaphor that prevents predictions to take place. It is worthwhile noting that "incanto"/enchantment is substituted by ten candidates semantically loosely related to the domains evoked by the masked word: temporal dimension (rhythm, stepping, passing, proceeding, beat), and a condition of the contemplating mind (silence, rest, meaning, thought, sound). Also another important remark regards the inability to predict the ambiguous word "ora"/hour, homograph with "ora"/now, thus clearly showing that context is the determining factor. **Frequency List: °-ora; °-Né; °-concede; °-incanto; *-battito; **-ferreo; **-oblioso**

Sentence 6.B - Diventa così più acuta la contraddizione. 6.Bc La contraddizione diventa così più acuta. This sentence has different predicted words in the two structural representations, Diventa/Becomes is present in both. Then "così/so" and "più/more" are predicted in the canonical sentence - diventa (0.215), così (0.0439), più (0.559); while in the non-canonical structure only acuta/sharp is predicted, acuta (0.0441), and the cosine value for "Diventa" is lower being in sentence first position. The canonical form has predicted the discourse marker "così/so" positioned in sentence center: not so in the non-canonical structure where we can again assume that it is the position right after the verb at the beginning of the sentence that does not allow the prediction, notwithstanding its high frequency. Now consider the high frequency of "contraddizione" which is not predicted presumably because of its position at the end of the sentence: the first candidate is the subword "mente" with cosine value (0.16536), followed by sensibilità/sensibility, coscienza/conscience, gioia/joy. **Frequency List: °-più; °-così; °-contraddizione; °-acuta; *-Diventa**

Sentence 7.B - Buono invece in complesso il resto. 7.Bc Invece in complesso il resto è buono. No word was predicted in either versions. In order to transform the original non-canonical version in the corresponding canonical one we added the copula "è" that is missing in the original sentence. This is predicted in the canonical version but since it has been added we do not count it for the actual predictive task. All the words are very frequent. As will be clarified further on, whenever the first word of the sentence coincides with a discourse marker or a conjunction the prediction is very close if not equal. This is the case for the canonical form of the sentence starting with "Invece"/Rather, which has the five following best predictions: "Ma"/But, "E"/And, "Però"/However, "Più"/More, "Ed"/And, all belonging to the same grammatical category and in two cases, also to the same semantic type ("Ma", "Però"). Considering the status of the adjective "Buono"/Good which comes in first position in the non-canonical structure and in second position in the canonical one, one can clearly realize the importance of the respective position and the context on the ability of BERT to predict. In the first case, the word coming first position has no left context and there is no similarity, not even at a grammatical level: only conjunctions and verbs are predicted. On the contrary, in the canonical form, "buono" appears as predicate in a copulative structure and the predictions are very close: diverso/different, risolto/resolved, compiuto/achieved, secondario/secondary, positivo/positive. **Frequency List: °-invece; °-resto; °-complesso; *-Buono**

Sentence 8.B - Una decisione importante Ghitti l'ha riservata a dopo le feste. 8.Bc Ghitti ha riservato una decisione importante a dopo le feste. Only one word is predicted in both versions but it is not the same word. The canonical version predicts "importante/important", (0,0605), the non-canonical version predicts "dopo/after", (0.0152). As can be noticed, the cosine values are very low and again the frequency of occurrence of the words contained in the sentence is fairly high - excluding the proper name "Ghitti" which does not exist in the overall frequency list. The unexpected fact is constituted by the inability to predict the auxiliary "ha"/has in the non-canonical structure – as opposed to what happens in the canonical one -, and the association in fourth slot of a non-word like "vamteen", presumably a subword of some kind. The only explanation could be the presence of a past participle with feminine+singular ending which is only allowed by presence of the resumptive clitic "la" needed to construct the Clitic Left Dislocation of the object NP "Una decisione importante". As said above, the canonical version predicts the presence of the auxiliary HAVE in the correct form and also in two additional morphologically possible forms: "aveva"/had+3rd+pers and "avrebbe"/would+have+3rd+pers; final word predicted in the other auxiliary legal form "è"/is. **Frequency List: °-dopo; °-importante; °-decisione; °-riservata; °-feste; ***ukn-Ghitti**

Sentence 9.B - L'importante ora è aprirlo di più. 9.Bc Ora è importante aprirlo di più. This sentence is perhaps too short and only function words are captured by BERT embeddings: ora/now (0.3825) più/more (0.0911). The ambiguous word "ora"/now is better predicted in the non-canonical structure - in first position - for the availability of right context - the canonical version predicts "Ora" in fourth position (0.0844). Again this is not relatable to a frequency problem but just structural problems, with the exception perhaps of the final word "aprirlo" which is only present in the very-low frequency list. In fact, in the canonical version, "aprirlo"/open+it is substituted by cliticized verbs - though semantically unrelated, however, showing that the morphology has been captured correctly. As to "importante"/important, it does not appear in the first five candidates, but it is predicted in sixth position (0.04902). **Frequency List: °-ora; **-aprirlo**

Sentence 10.B - Le sue informazioni darebbero anche agli orientamenti di democrazia laica maggiori spinte. 10.Bc Le sue informazioni darebbero maggiori spinte anche agli orientamenti di democrazia laica. This sentence has the same predicted word "maggiori/major" in both structural representations. As before, the words are all very frequent with the exception of "darebbero/+would+give, which is below the threshold and is only part of the "very+low" List. Now consider the word spinte/boosts: predicted masked words are as follows: certezze/certainties (0.0852), garanzie/guarantees (0.0824), informazioni/information (0.04183), taria/tary (0.04003), opportunità/opportunities (0.0383). The fourth slot contains a subword, in fact a non-word, which is assigned a score higher than the one assigned to "opportunities". The question is that the masked word is not frequent enough to be able to collect the co-occurrences required. As a result, even very low scored embeddings are considered. The non-word gets a slightly better score when the text is considered as a whole with the last 7 sentences added, up to (0.06002), but remains always in fourth position. **Frequency List: °-anche; °-informazioni; °-sue; °-maggiori; °-democrazia; °-orientamenti; °-laica; *-spinte; *-darebbero**

Sentence 11.B - In questo libro Maria Teresa, spiegano alla Mondadori, darà esempi di carità concreti. 11.Bc In questo libro Maria Teresa darà esempi di carità concreti, spiegano alla Mondadori. In this sentence there is a striking difference in prediction between the two structures. The non-canonical version has only two words predicted, "libro/book" and "esempi/examples", libro (0.0242), esempi (0.653). On the contrary, in the canonical version BERT manages to predict four words, "questo/this", "Maria/Mary", "Teresa/Therese", "esempi/examples", questo (0.767), Maria (0.283), Teresa (0.141), esempi (0.734). Strangely enough, the word "libro" does not figure in the first five candidates. Useless to say, the remaining words are all very frequent. The third run with a longer text including the following 7 sentences gives interesting results: "Teresa" now becomes first candidate substituting the previously chosen first candidate "ci"/us. The word "esempi"/examples, predicted as first candidate, in the text is followed by "carità"/charity which is not predicted in both version: in its place, the first candidate is again "esempi", thus certifying that predictions are made one word at a time disregarding the textual context. Now consider the adjective "concreti" which has been dislocated and is disjoined from its head, "esempi". The list of five candidates for the canonical version is the following: "cristiana+fem+sing"/Christian (0.1919), '.' (0.0909), ',' (0.0387), "civile+sing"/civil (0.0383), "esemplare+sing"/exemplar (0.0222). None of the candidates is plural in number as it should be, if the morphology of Italian has to be respected. On the contrary, the first candidate agrees both in number and gender with the preceding word "carità+fem+sing"/charity, which is not to be considered the correct nominal head. The non-canonical version has one punctuation mark less and an additional adjective "pastorale+sing"/pastoral. **Frequency List: °-questo; °-libro; °-esempi; °-carità; °-concreti; °-darà; °-spiegano; °-Mondadori**

Sentence 12.A - Disse che gli hanno il cor di mezzo il petto tolto. 12.Ac Disse che gli hanno tolto il cuore di mezzo il petto. This sentence from the poetry subset has only one word in common "cor/heart" and an additional word predicted in the canonical structure, "tolto/taken+off". The cosine values are all very low, cor-cuore (0.1019), for the non-canonical, and cor-cuore (0.0756), tolto (0.156) in the other structure. Interesting enough, when using the configuration with the whole text, also "mezzo/means" is predicted in second slot. **Frequency List: °-mezzo; °-cuore; °-petto; °-tolto; *-Disse**

Sentence 13.A - I ritrosi pareri e le non pronte e in mezzo a l'eseguire opere impedite. 13.Ac I ritrosi pareri e le opere non pronte e impedite in mezzo a l'eseguire. No prediction found by BERT in the two structural representations - with the exception of "mezzo"/means which however is only appearing in 8th position and not considered in this evlauation. However it is important to note that the previous seven predicted words are in fact only subwords, mostly meaningless, and some having a corresponding identical wordform with a totally different meaning. Here they are: "dotti"/learned+mas+plur, "dotte"/learned+fem+plur, "tente"/meaningless, "sistenti"/meaningless, "sistenza"/meaningless,"difficoltà"/difficulty, "fami"/meaningless. As to their frequency, words are mostly frequent but there are two missing words in the overall frequency lists: "ritrosi/reluctant" and "impedite/hampered". These two words may have been supplemented as subwords but with no useful context for the current analysis. The five candidates appearing are as follows: for "ritrosi" we have - suoi/his+hers, non/not, buoni/good+masc+plur, mal/bad(truncated), loro/their+them+they; and for "impedite" - '.', buone/good+fem+plur, inutili/useless+plur, nuove/new+fem+plur, pubbliche/public+fem+plur. In all of these cases, even if the correct word has not been predicted, the morphology has been matched correctly. **Frequency List: °-mezzo; °-opere; °-pareri; °-eseguire; °-pronte; ***ritrosi; ***impedite**

Sentence 14.A - Un'eco di mature angosce rinverdiva a toccar segni alla carne oscuri di gioia. 14.Ac Un'eco di mature angosce rinverdiva a toccar segni di gioia oscuri alla carne. This is another sentence from poetry domain very hard to tackle and to understand. Both the canonical and the non-canonical analyses have just one word found, "eco/echo" (0.0984). Of course the main verb "rinverdiva" is not amongst the frequent words in the list: in fact, it is missing. The remaining words are frequent but they are organized in a peculiar structural configuration with the declared aim to produce metaphors. No changes or improvements when the sentence is analysed with the canonical version of the text. As we did for example 11, we now consider the discontinuous adjective "oscuri+masc+plur"/obscure and the morphology of the five candidates predicted. In the non-canonical version we have: "pieni+mas+plur"/full (0.5461), "piena+fem+sing"/full (0.0486), "e"/and, ',', "pieno+mas+sing"/full (0.0216). Now the canonical version: "fino"/until (0.1139), "intorno"/around (0.1139), "dentro"/inside (0.1001), "sino"/until (0.0476), "vicino"/close (0.0437). As can be noticed, all of the predicted words for the non-canonical structure are function words and none – with the possible exclusion of the ambiguou "vicino+mas+sing" - is an adjective. The reason for this lack of grammatical match may be due to the presence of the articulated preposition "alle"/to the+fem+plur in the canonical version. In the non-canonical version the word "oscuri" was followed by a preposition "di" which is the most frequent wordform with 65 million occurrences. **Frequency List: °-alla; °-carne; °-gioia; °-segni; °-toccare; °-eco; *-oscuri; *-mature; *-angosce; ***rinverdiva**

Sentence 15.B - Il governo, quindi, pur rinunciando alla maggioranza assoluta, ha voluto, come già nell'IMI, puntare a una privatizzazione graduale. 15.Bc Quindi, il governo ha voluto puntare a una privatizzazione graduale pur rinunciando alla maggioranza assoluta come già nell'IMI. This long sentence belongs to the domain of the news and even in its non-canonical structure, it is more linear and thus more predictable. There are seven words predicted (over ten we masked) in the two versions: governo/government (0.304), maggioranza/majority (0.0377), assoluta/absolute (0.349), ha/has (0.977), voluto/wanted (0.491), puntare/aim (0.0385). The proper name IMI is in the very low list. Strangely enough the function word come/like (0.1925/0.9186) is predicted as first candidate in its non-canonical position, as second position ,but with a much lower cosine measure in canonical position. **Frequency List: °-governo; °-maggioranza; °-voluto; °-assoluta; °-puntare, °-privatizzazione; °-graduale; *-rinunciando; **-IMI**

Sentence 16.B - In una conferenza al Viminale il ministro, quando viene interrogato sul senatore a vita, sulle prime non capisce il nome. 16.Bc In una conferenza al Viminale, quando viene interrogato sul senatore a vita sulle prime il ministro non capisce il nome. There are four words predicted in this long sentence, again in the domain of the news, in the canonical and the non-canonical structures. They are: ministro/minister (0.497), viene (0.795), senatore/senator (0.808), vita/life (0.996). Again, most words are very frequent. An apparent difficulty is constituted by presence of a multiword: "sulle prime/at first" which may be hard to distinguish and differentiate on the basis of the context. In fact, in both structures, "prime" is substituted by riforme/reforms, banche/banks, dimissioni/resignation , pensioni/pensions, cose/things. **Frequency List: °-vita; °-viene: °-nome; °-ministro; °-prime; °-senatore: °-conferenza; °-capisce; *-interrogato; *-Viminale**

Sentence 17.B - Primo intervento da fare, ha detto in questi giorni, è di attuare la riforma. 17.Bc Primo intervento da fare è di attuare la riforma, ha detto in questi giorni. This is another fairly simple sentence which has the major number of predicted words in the whole set in relation to the total number in the sentence. There are six words predicted both in the canonical and the non-canonical version: "fare/do" (0.818), "ha/has" (0.283), questi/these (0.961), giorni/days (0.83), riforma/reform (0.194). The only difference being the slot assigned to riforma/reform, which has first slot in the canonical version and second slot in the non-canonical one, preceded by Costituzione/Constitution. Useless to say, the missing words are all very frequent. **Frequency List: °-fare; °-giorni; °-detto; °-intervento; °-riforma; °-Primo; °-attuare**

Sentence 18.B - Io il privato lo concepisco come un metodo di lavoro, come contratti di lavoro, come modo di gestire insomma. 18.Bc Io concepisco il privato come un metodo di lavoro, come contratti di lavoro, come modo di gestire insomma. In this final sentence again belonging to the newswire domain, there are four words predicted: metodo/method (0.0618), lavoro/work (0.214), lavoro/work (0.214), modo/way (0.794). Again very frequent missing words, apart from "concepisco/surmise" which is the only word present in the Rare-Words list. When analyzed with the canonical version of the text, the word lavoro/work moves from third to first slot, with a slightly improved cosine score. **Frequency List: °-lavoro; °-modo; °-Io; °-contratti; °-privato; °-metodo; °-insomma; °-gestire; ***-concepisco.**

3 Experimental Results and Discussion

The evaluation has been carried out in three different configurations: on a first configuration, part of the sentences, the last 7 – are withheld with the aim to reduce the overall context at sentence level. This is done both for non-canonical and canonical structures. Then the last 7 sentences are added and the cosine values verified to see if predictions have been modified.

We assume that a better form of evaluation should account for gradable differences between predictions in which the actual word is not found but the ones predicted are very "similar". The word "similar" then will need to be better decomposed into its various linguistic aspects and we have devised a graduality which may be turned into scores according to simple linguistic criteria. Similarity may attain morphological, lexical, grammatical, syntactic, semantic criteria. Thus the more the choices are close to the actual meaning of the expected word, the higher the score will be which we assume will be a real value from 0 to 1. Since the final choice is done on the basis of the theoretical assumptions underlying the Distributional Semantic Model we will call Table 1. accordingly.

Linguistic Category	Feature Type	Score
Identical	(first position)	1
Identical	(second position)	0.99
Identical	(third position)	0.97
Identical	(fourth position)	0.95
Same word	different morphology	0.8
Same word	different grammatical category	0.7
Hyponym/ Antonym/ Meronym, Synonym	same morphology same grammatical category	0.6
Hyponym/ Antonym/ Meronym, Synonym	different morphology same grammatical category	0.5
Hyponym/ Antonym/ Meronym, Synonym	different morphology different grammatical category	0.4
Different word	same grammatical category same morphology	0.3
Different word	same grammatical category different morphology	0.2
Different word	different grammatical category	0.1
No word	Punctuation - ukn	0

Table 1: Graded Evaluation Scale for a Linguistically Based Similarity Scoring according to DSM

We applied the scores reported in the table to the whole set of sentences and computed the results in the two tables below. In Table 2. we evaluate the seven sentences from the poetry domain, and in Table 3. the eleven sentences from the newswire domain. We computed three main parameters: in column 2, Number of Words masked with respect to total number of tokens; in columns 3 and 4 we list words correctly predicted with the identical corresponding word respectively in the Non Canonical and in the Canonical sentence structure; then in columns 5 and 6 we list the number of words with frequency values respectively Higher and Lower than a given threshold that we established at 10.000 occurrences. We also considered words that don't appear in the 50000 vocabulary and reported them after a slash: we assume their import should be valued double. Thus for instance, in the Poetry text, we found 5 such words and the total number of Low Frequency Words is increased by 10 points. Finally, in column 7, we reported the result of applying the scoring function described in Table 1.

Sent. No.	No. Mask. Ws.	Non Can. W.s	Can. Ws.	High Fr. Ws.	Low Fr. Ws.	Ling. Eval.
2.A	10/8	0	3	4	3/1	3.76
3.A	14/9	3	4	6	3	6.04
4.A	10/8	2	2	4	4	3.99
5.A	9/6	0	0	4	1/2	2
12.A	11/7	1	2	4	1	3.49
13.A	15/7	0	0	5	0/2	2.4
14.A	14/9	1	1	6	3/1	3.1
totals	83/54	7	12	33	15/6 =27	24.78
ratios	0.65	0.58			0.82	0.46

Table 2: Linguistic Evaluation of Poetry Sentences

Sent. No.	No. Mask. Ws.	Non Can. W.s	Can. Ws.	High Fr. Ws.	Low Fr. Ws.	Ling. Eval.
1.B	14/8	3	5	8	0	5.97
6.B	6/5	2	3	5	0	3.84
7.B	5/4	0	0	3	1	2.4
8.B	10/7	1	2	6	1	2.37
9.B	7/4	2	3	4	1	2.99
10.B	12/9	1	1	7	2	4.79
11.B	15/10	2	4	10	0	6.17
15.B	25/10	7	7	8	2	8.23
16.B	22/10	4	4	8	2	7.2
17.B	15/9	6	6	10	0	7.1
18.B	22/10	4	4	9	0/1	5.7
totals	153/86	31	38	78	9/1=11	56.76
ratios	0.56	0.82			0.14	0.66

Table 3: Linguistic Evaluation of Newswire Sentences

As can be easily noticed by comparing all parameters, poetry and news have opposite values. Quantities measured in column 2 show how the ratio of masked words is higher in poetry than in the news domain – 0.65 vs 0.56 -, the reason being that poetry text makes use of less grammatical or function words, like articles, clitics, prepositions which are highly predictable but are less informative. The first important parameter is the difference in number of masked words identified in Non-Canonical vs Canonical Sentences, and here again as can be easily noticed the newswire domain has a much higher score than the poetry domain – 0.816 vs 0.583. Then the second relevant parameter derived by the proportion of High Frequency words vs Low Frequency words and computed as a ratio between the sum of the absolute number of words plus a doubling of the number of very low frequency words. Here the scores show the opposite relation, Poetry domain has a much higher number of Low Frequency words than Newswire domain – 0.818 vs 0.141. Eventually, the linguistic evaluation of every single masked word on the basis of its cosine measure and the graded scoring scale reported in Table 1. Where we see again a much higher overall score for the Newswire than the Poetry domain – 0.66 vs 0.4589. The conclusion we can safely draw from these data is that the News domain has a higher linguistically and frequency-based evaluated prediction score:

- because it has a much lower number of Low Frequency words
- because it has a higher number of contextually predictable words in Non-canonical structures

In other words, the context is both dependent on word frequency and word structural position. One example is highly representative of the interplay between frequency and context and is the word "Ora", an ambiguous word with two homographs-homophones: one meaning "now", an adverbial contained in sentence n. 9 - the newswire domain; and another meaning "hour", a (temporal) noun, contained in sentence n. 5 - the poetry domain. Only the adverbial is predicted in both structural versions. The noun is contained in a sentence belonging to the poetry domain where the overall context is not supportive for that word predictability. In Figure 1. below we show weighted - by number of masked words - cosine values - by choosing always the value associated with the first candidate - when compared with weighted Linguistic Parameter by listing sentences in descending order according to their score. Correlation evaluation between our Linguistic Parameter and Cosine values is estimated at 0.8705 when computed on absolute values, but it goes down to 0.6349 when using weighted values. News texts have overall higher parameters in both evaluations: the descending trend is however much more linear for linguistic parameters than for the cosine ones.

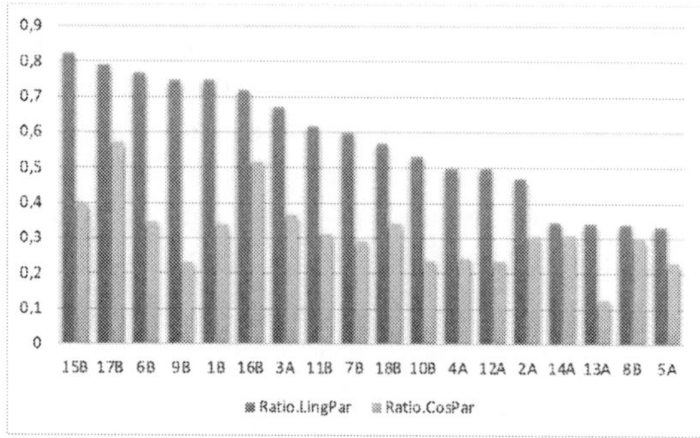

Figure 1: Evaluation by Two Parameters

4 Conclusion

In this paper we have proposed a word predictability parameter based on linguistically motivated information that we have tested in a highly constrained context determined by the combination of three fundamental factors for a sentence meaning understanding perspective on the prediction task represented by BERT masked task: use of infrequent words - as measured against the ItWac frequency list - and their phrase level combination – word poetic usage for metaphors w.r.t possible semantic association -, and their larger sentential context in uncommon syntactic structures – non-canonical structures. In order to be able to evaluate the different impact of the three adversarial factors on masked word prediction, we have included in the dataset a higher number of sentences from newswire domain showing the same structural syntactic properties but lacking both the usage of very infrequent words – with a few exceptions - and their uncommon combination to produce metaphors. Word predictability has then been measured by BERT raw word embeddings and their cosine measure, by masking one content word at a time - and a few function words. Each content word has then been searched in the frequency list made available by the ItWac frequency list. The results have clearly shown the ability of newswire sentences to receive an overall higher word predictability score thanks to the smaller effect of adversarial factors we investigated. The answer to the question: is frequency or context the determining factor for Transformer Language Models to predict the masked word, is both are. The news domain has less infrequent words and less uncommon non-canonical structures than the poetry domain, which is what explains the remarkable difference in final results.

References

Niki Parmar Jakob Uszkoreit Llion Jones Aidan N Gomez Lukasz Kaiser Ashish Vaswani, Noam Shazeer and Illia Polosukhin. 2017. Attention is all you need. In *Advances in Neural Information Processing Systems*, pages 6000–6010.

Rodolfo Delmonte. 2009. *Treebanking in VIT: from Phrase Structure to Dependency Representation*, pages 51–80. IOS Press, Amsterdam.

Rodolfo Delmonte. 2014. A computational approach to poetic structure, rhythm and rhyme. In *Proceedings of CLiC-it - The First Italian Conference on Computational Linguistics*, volume 1, pages 144–150, Pisa, Italy. Pisa University Press.

Rodolfo Delmonte. 2016. Syntactic and lexical complexity in italian noncanonical structures. In *Proceedings of the Workshop on Computational Linguistics for Linguistic Complexity*, pages 67–78, Stroudsburg, PA, USA. ACL.

Rodolfo Delmonte. 2018. Syntax and semantics of italian poetry in the first half of the 20th century. *Umanistica Digitale*, pages 35–66.

Rodolfo Delmonte. 2021. What's wrong with deep learning for meaning understanding. In *Proceedings of the 2nd Italian Workshop on Explainable Artificial Intelligence (XAI.it 2021)*.

Rodolfo Delmonte, Antonella Bristot, and Sara Tonelli. 2007. Vit - venice italian treebank: Syntactic and quantitative features. In *Proc. Sixth International Workshop on Treebanks and Linguistic Theories*, volume 1, pages 43—-54. Nealt Proc. Series.

K. Mahowald, E. Fedorenko, S.T. Piantadosi, and Edward Gibson. 2012. Info/information theory: speakers choose shorter words in predictive contexts. *Cognition*, 126(2):313–318.

Teresa Paccosi, Alessio Palmero Aprosio, and Sara Tonelli. 2022. It is markit that is new: An italian treebank of marked constructions. In *Proceedings of CLiC-It 2021 - Eighth Italian Conference on Computational Linguistics)*.

Loreto Parisi, Simone Francia, and Paolo Magnani. 2020. Umberto: an ital- ian language model trained with whole word masking.

Paolo Pedinotti, Giulia Rambelli, Emmanuele Chersoni, Enrico Santus, Alessandro Lenci, and Philippe Blache. 2021. Did the cat drink the coffee? challenging transformers with generalized event knowledge. In *Proceedings of the 10th Conference on Lexical and Computational Semantics*, pages 1–11, Bangkok, Thailand. Association for Computational Linguistics.

Steven T. Piantadosi, Harry Tily, and Edward Gibson. 2012. The communicative function of ambiguity in language. *Cognition*, 122(3):280–291.

Rocco Tripodi and Stefano Li Pira. 2017. Analysis of italian word embeddingsg.

Thomas Wolf, Lysandre Debut, Victor Sanh, Julien Chaumond, Clement Delangue, Anthony Moi, Pierric Cistac, Tim Rault, Rémi Louf, and Morgan Funtowicz et al. 2019. Huggingface's transformers: State-of-the-art natural language processing.

5 Appendix - English Version of the Canonical and Non-canonical text

1.B Today I thank for the courtesy on several occasions demonstrated to me and my colleagues. 2.A She alone maybe the cold dreamer would educate to the tender prodigy. 3.A I think of a green garden where with you resume can conversing the soul maiden. 4.A If spring my generous heart choked of deaf spasms. 5.A Neither the oblivious enchantment of the hour the iron-like beat grants. 6.B Becomes thus sharper the contradiction. 7.B Good instead overall the rest. 8.B An important decision Ghitti reserved after the holidays. 9.B The important thing is now to open it more. 10.B His information would also give to the guidelines of laique democracy greater boosts. 11.B In this book Maria Teresa, they explain at Mondadori's, will give examples of charities concrete. 12.A Said that they have his heart from inside the chest removed. 13.A The reluctant opinions and not ready and in the midst of executing works hampered. 14.A An echo of mature anguish revverdived to touch signs to the flesh dark of joy. 15.B The government, therefore, though giving up the absolute majority, has wanted, as already in IMI, focusing on a gradual privatization. 16.B At a conference in the Viminale the minister, when he is questioned on the senator to life, at first does not understand the name. 17.B First intervention to do, he said these days, is to implement the reform. 18.B I conceive the private as a work method, as work contracts, as a way to manage in short.

1.Bc Today I thank you for the courtesy demonstrated to me and my colleagues on several occasions. 2.Ac Maybe the cold dreamer educated her alone to the tender prodigy. 3.Ac I think of a green garden where the soul maid can resume conversing with you. 4.Ac Spring if you choked my generous heart of deaf spasms. 5.Ac Neither the iron-like beat of the hour grants the oblivious enchantment. 6.Bc The contradiction becomes thus sharper. 7.Bc Instead, overall the rest is good. 8.Bc Ghitti reserved an important decision after the holidays. 9.Bc Now it's important to open it more. 10.Bc His information would also give greater boosts to the guidelines of laique democracy. 11.Bc In this book Maria Teresa will give concrete examples of charities, they explain at Mondadori's. 12.Ac They said they took off his heart from the chest. 13.Ac The reluctant opinions and not ready works hampered in the middle of executing. 14.Ac An echo of mature anguish revverdressed to touch signs of joy obscure to the flesh. 15.Bc So the government wanted to focus on a gradual privatization while giving up the absolute majority as already in IMI. 16.Bc At a conference in the Viminale, when he is questioned on the senator to life at first the minister does not understand the name. 17.Bc To implement the reform is first intervention to do, he said these days. 18.Bc I conceive the private as a work method, such as work contracts, as a way to manage in short.

Proceedings of ISA-18 Workshop at LREC2022, pages 53–60
Marseille, 20 June 2022

Testing the Annotation Consistency of Hallidayan Transitivity Processes: A Multi-variable Structural Approach

Min Dong[1], Xiaoyan Liu[1], Alex Chengyu Fang[2, 3]
[1]School of Foreign Languages, Beihang University, PR China
[2]Department of Linguistics and Translation, City University of Hong Kong, HKSAR
[3]The Halliday Centre for Intelligent Applications of Language Studies, City University of Hong Kong, HKSAR
{mdong, liuxiaoyan0112}@buaa.edu.cn, acfang@cityu.edu.hk

Abstract

SFL seeks to explain identifiable, observable phenomena of language use in context through the application of a theoretical framework which models language as a functional, meaning making system (Halliday & Matthiessen 2004). Due to the lack of explicit annotation criteria and the divide between conceptual vs. syntactic criteria in practice, it has been a tough job to achieve consistency in the annotation of Hallidayn transitivity processes. The present study proposed that explicit structural and syntactic criteria should be adopted as a basis. Drawing on syntactic and grammatical features as judgement cues, we applied structurally oriented criteria for the annotation of the process categories and participant roles combining a set of interrelated syntactic variables and established the annotation criteria for contextualised circumstantial categories in structural as well as semantic terms. An experiment was carried out to test the usefulness of these annotation criteria, applying percent agreement and Cohen's kappa as measurements of interrater reliability between the two annotators in each of the five pairs. The results verified our assumptions, albeit rather mildly, and, more significantly, offered some first empirical indications about the practical consistency of transitivity analysis in SFL. In the future work, the research team expect to draw on the insights and experience from some of the ISO standards devoted to semantic annotation such as dialogue acts (Bunt et al. 2012) and semantic roles (ISO-24617-4, 2014).

Keywords: annotation consistency, Hallidayan transitivity process, structurally oriented criteria

1. Introduction

Systemic functional linguistics (SFL) founded by Halliday (1967/8), together with American "West-Coast" functionalism represented by Hopper & Thompson (1980), has "moved up" its descriptions of transitivity from the rank of the verb to that of the clause and thus enabled more holistic and explanatory accounts of transitivity. From the vantage point of semantics, significantly, SFL characterises transitivity in functional terms as a lexicogrammatical resource for construing a quantum of change in our experience of the flow of events around us and inside us. As a result, the domain of transitivity is modelled as a configuration of a process (a verb group), participants directly involved in it (nominal groups) and attendant circumstances (adverbs and prepositional phrases). Six process categories are proposed in the grammar of SFL, among which, in terms of relative frequency, material, relational, mental and verbal processes constitute the major types while behavioural and existential processes make up the two minor categories (Matthiessen 1999, 2014). There is a general agreement that transitivity analysis is problematic in practice (O'Donnel et al 2009). The community survey about the annotation practice of transitivity in O'Donnell et al (2009) reveals that the divide between the use of syntactic (based on the syntactic structure of the clause) vs. conceptual (on the basis of the underlying action or event represented by the clause) criteria is widespread throughout the SFL community. The analysts, however, may unconsciously find themselves forced to fall back on purely semantic criteria, particularly when encountered with challenging cases in which lexicogrammatical structures associated with one process type appear to be realising a different one in terms of the meaning being expressed (O'Donnell et al 2009). Explicit statements of annotation criteria of transitivity are needed for determining how each and every clause should be annotated in terms of process configuration, including one of the six processes, the obligatory or optional participants and attendant circumstances.

Despite the fact that the descriptions offered in Halliday's accounts of transitivity are primarily based on semantic criteria, certain key grammatical criteria for transitivity categorisation (such as preferred tense/aspect, and the potential to project) have been elaborated (Halliday 1994: 115-16). Essentially, all possible clausal configurations including subject types, verb forms and complementation patterns need to be taken into account. It seems more practical to view the issue in terms of syntactic variables, which may (or may not) come into play in deciding particular transitivity categories, and which may combine a wide range of judgements. We are thus motivated to propose an approach which draws on a wider array of syntactic variables for automated grammatical analysis from Fang (2007) to establish explicitly stated sets of criteria for the annotation of transitivity. It is expected to be a promising approach to pinning down more precisely than has been the case so far with the kinds of variables that are relevant for particular verbs or groups of verbs (or of verb senses). To test these assumptions, the present study carries out an experiment by giving ten postgraduates a set of explicit annotation guides (to be expounded in Section 2) for their analysis of the component sentences of a news article randomly assigned to each of them.

2. Structurally Oriented Annotation of Hallidayan Transitivity Categories

According to Matthiessen (1999), a principle can be held that the more frequently a process type is selected in text, the more highly elaborated it is systemically in terms of a larger number of verb classes, verbs and thus verb senses that can be assigned to it. Based on Levin's (1993) verb classes, Matthiessen (2014) further reveals that the material process is most highly elaborated in lexis and is followed by the two highly elaborated types of mental and verbal processes; the two least frequent types of behavioural and existential processes are accordingly least elaborated. An exception is found in "relational" process clauses: while they are equally frequent compared with "material" ones, they are far less highly elaborated, attributable to the characteristic that the lexical elaboration is allocated to the participants of the clause rather than to the process verbs. According to such a descending order of the six process types in terms of relative elaboratedness in lexis, a descriptive framework of transitivity is devised below as a basis of the coding criteria in syntactic terms for the annotation of transitivity categories. First of all, Table 1 offers descriptions of each of the transitivity terms in each of the six process types.

Process type	*Process category & Participant role*	*Description*
Material	Material process	creative (event/ thing) & transformative experience
	Actor	the role responsible for bringing about a change
	Goal	the entity that is brought into existence
	Beneficiary	the role who is given goods or for whom a service is performed
	Scope	the role which construes the process itself or the domain over which the process takes place
	Initiator	the role responsible for making the Actor perform an action
Mental	Mental process	cognitive, desiderative, emotive & perceptive experience
	Senser	the conscious role who thinks, perceives, feels or desires something or someone
	Phenomenon	the role that reflects what is thought, perceived, felt or desired
	Inducer	the role that causes the Senser to think, perceive, feel or desire something
Verbal	Verbal process	non-projecting (communicating & targeting) & projecting (imperating & indicating) experience
	Sayer	the role who puts out a signal of symbolic exchange of meaning
	Verbiage	the role which denotes the content or nature of the message itself
	Receiver	the role to whom the message is addressed
	Target	the role usually in the verbal clause of judgement, such as praise, blame, criticism, representing the entity that is the object of judgement by the Sayer
Relational: Attributive	Relational process	circumstantial (causal/comparative/locative/matter), intensive (attributed/ non-attributed) & possessive (benefactive/ non-benefactive) relations
	Carrier	the entity to which the Attribute is ascribed
	Attribute	the class to which the Carrier is attributed
	Attributor	the role that brings about the attribution of the Attribute to the Carrier
Relational: Identifying	Relational process	circumstantial (causal/comparative/locative/matter), intensive (assigned/ non-assigned) & possessive (benefactive/ non-benefactive) relations
	Token	the specific embodiment which is assigned to a more generalisable category of Value in the relational clause of identification
	Value	the more general category which is assigned to a specific realisation of Token in the relational clause of identification
	Assigner	the role which assigns the relationship of identity between the Token and the Value
Behaviroural	Behavioural process	inter-active & intro-active (conscious activity/ physiological) experience
	Behaver	a conscious being inherent in the process of physiological or psychological behaviour
Existential	Existential process	entity & event existence
	Existent	an entity existing in concrete or abstract space, or an event occurring in time

Table 1: Description of process categories and participant roles in the six process types

Halliday (1994) stresses that in order to posit a grammatical category there must be a "lexico-grammatical reflex of the difference [in meaning]". This all clearly suggests that the focus is the lexicogrammar and that the structural configurations are always associated with particular meanings. In line with a corpus-based approach to syntactic analysis, Fang (2007) demonstrates how automated grammar analysis is able to be implemented using AUTASYS (Fang 1996) and Survey Parser (Fang 2006). On this basis, we draw on a range of 20 grammatical and syntactic variables from Fang (2007) as shown in Table 2. The structurally oriented coding criteria for transitivity annotation are derived accordingly.

Process	Transitivity	Verb Complementation Types						Syntactic Functions and Structural Features												
		cop	cxtr	ditr	intr	montr	trans	A: phr	*by*	CO	CS	CT	EX	OD: cl	OD: *ing*	OD: phr	OD: *to*	OI	SU	SU: agent
Material	Material pro		√	√	√	√	√					√			√		√			
	Actor								√										√	
	Goal								√										√	
	Beneficiary																	√	√	
	Scope							√		√						√				
	Initiator																			√
Mental	Mental pro		√			√	√					√		√	√		√			
	Senser								√										√	
	Phenomenon								√										√	
	Inducer																			√
Verbal	Verbal pro		√	√	√	√	√					√		√	√		√			
	Sayer								√										√	
	Verbiage								√										√	
	Receiver																	√	√	
	Target								√										√	
Relational: Attributive	Relational pro	√				√									√		√			
	Carrier																		√	
	Attribute								√		√									
	Attributor																			√
Relational: Identifying	Relational pro	√				√									√		√			
	Token																		√	
	Value								√		√								√	
	Assigner																			√
Behavioural	Behavioural pro				√										√		√			
	Behaver																		√	
Existential	Existenital pro				√								√		√		√			
	Existent																		√	

Table 2: Grammatical and syntactic variables (Fang 2007) associated with configured transitivity categories in each of the six process types

cop – copula verb
cxtr – complex transitive verb
ditr – ditransitive verb
intr – intransitive verb
montr – monotransitive verb
trans – transitive verb
A:phr – verb-preposition-adverbial phrase
by – Prepositional complement of *by*-phrase,
CO – Object complement
CS – Subject complement
CT – Transitive complement
EX – Existential *there* structure
OD – Direct object
OD:*cl* – Finite *that*-clause as object
OD:ing – Non-finite *ing*-clause as object
OD:phr – Verb-noun-object phrase
OD:*to* – Non-finite *to*-infinitive clause as object
OI – Indirect object
SU – Subject
SU:agent – Agentive subject

Concerning circumstance categories, in terms of the frequency and size of prepositions used, as observed in Matthiessen (1999), "location" is both the most frequently used option and also the most highly elaborated, followed by "manner", "cause" and "accompaniment". Interestingly, while "extent" is more frequently used than "matter", it is much less elaborated than the latter, which is possibly related to the fact that "extent" is typically frequently realised by adverbial groups. Table 3 presents a descriptive framework of these circumstantial terms in descending order of lexical elaboration, both conceptually and syntactically. It is important to note that circumstantial elements perform the function of adverbials. The coding criteria for the annotation of circumstantial categories are therefore established in structural as well as semantic terms.

Type	*Subtype*	*Grammatical category*	*Syntactic functions*
Location	Place	PP/ AVP	Adverbial
	Time	PP/ AVP	Adverbial
Manner	Means	PP/ AVP	Adverbial
	Quality	PP/ AVP	Adverbial
	Comparison	PP/ AVP	Adverbial
	Degree	PP/ AVP	Adverbial
Cause	Reason	PP	Adverbial
	Purpose	PP	Adverbial
	Behalf	PP	Adverbial
Accompaniment	Comitative	PP/ AVP	Adverbial
	Additive	PP/ AVP	Adverbial
Extent	Distance	PP/ AVP	Adverbial
	Duration	PP/ AVP	Adverbial
	Frequency	AVP	Adverbial
Matter		PP	Adverbial
Contingency	Condition	PP	Adverbial
	Default	PP	Adverbial
	Concession	PP	Adverbial
Role	Guise	PP	Adverbial
	Product	PP	Adverbial
Angle	Source	PP	Adverbial
	Viewpoint	PP	Adverbial

Table 3: Circumstantial categories in semantic, grammatical and syntactic terms (Halliday & Matthiessen 2004)

3. Experiment on Transitivity Annotation

In this section we describe an experiment carried out on transitivity annotation. It is based on a text of news report which comprises forty sentences in total. Ten postgraduates in the field of linguistics were recruited and assigned into five pairs of two annotators..Each pair were given eight sentences randomly selected from the news report. They were all instructed and trained about the structurally oriented annotation criteria in terms of interrelated grammatical and syntactic variables for the annotation of process categories and participant roles in each of the six process types and attendant circumstantial categories. More specifically, each annotator was instructed to analyse the test sentences according to the following requirements:

1. All directly embedded clausal constituents which perform sentential syntactic functions, whether finite or non-finite, are required to undertake transitivity annotation.
2. All clausal constituents indirectly embedded in nominal, adjectival or prepositional phrases, whether finite or non-finite, should be exempted from transitivity annotation.

In order to determine interannotator agreement between the two coders in each of the five pairs and the general level of agreement among the ten coders with regard to their transitivity annotation of the whole text, two methods of measurement of interrater reliability are deployed in the present study, namely, Percent agreement and Cohen's kappa (McHugh 2012):

Percent agreement. This statistic is calculated by dividing the number of zero difference codings by the number of variables provides a measure of percent agreement between the raters. It is also directly interpretable as the percent of data that are correct. It is typically recommended that 80% agreement as the minimum acceptable interrater agreement.

Cohen's kappa. In view of the limitation of Percent agreement that it does not consider the possibility that raters guessed on scores and may thus overestimate the true agreement among raters, the Kappa was designed to take account of the possibility of random guesses (Cohen 1960). The calculation of Cohen's kappa may be performed according to the following formula:

$$k = \frac{\Pr(a) - \Pr(e)}{1 - \Pr(e)}$$

where *Pr(a)* represents the actual observed agreement, and *Pr(e)* represents the expected chance agreement. Notably the sample size consists of the number of observations made across which raters are compared. Kappa is a form of correlation coefficient based on the *chi*-square table. While correlation coefficients cannot be directly interpreted, a squared correlation coefficient is directly interpretable, namely the amount of variation in the dependent variable that can be explained by the independent variable. The estimate of such variance accounted for is usually obtained by squaring the correlation value. It is by extension of this logic that the calculation of *Pr(e)*, the chance agreement is carried out by squaring the amount of accuracy in the data due to congruence among the raters.

It is noted that Kappa is typically a considerable reduction in the level of congruence compared with percent agreement, and thus it has the limitation that it may lower the estimate of agreement greatly. The greater the expected chance agreement, the lower the resulting value of the Kappa. In addition, it cannot be directly interpreted. However, any Kappa value below 0.60 indicates inadequate agreement among the raters and little confidence should be placed in the study results. Considering the great chance of guessing in semantic annotation like transitivity annotation focused on in this study, and the fact that the ten annotators have been trained on the annotation criteria proposed in structural terms, we are thus motivated to calculate both percent agreement and Kappa.

4. Results and Discussion

Using the two statistical techniques of Percent agreement and Cohen's kappa, Table 4 shows the calculation results of measurement of interrater reliability between the two transitivity annotators in each of the five pairs. As displayed, the scores of Percent agreement indicate that four pairs achieve a fairly adequate agreement between the two annotators in each of them. Pair 4, however, performs as an outlier, far below 80% agreement. A closer look at the Kappa values, however, shows that the interrater reliability accomplished by the two annotators in the five pairs visibly diverge among themselves, constituting a typical cline ranging from "None" and "Weak" at one end to "Moderate" and "Strong" at the other. More interestingly, Pair 3 and Pair 5 both gain notably adequate agreement, namely well above 80% agreement, and accordingly they respectively achieve moderate and strong agreement in terms of Kappa value. This observation might bring additional support for the compatibility and complementarity between the two techniques as discussed in the literature (McHugh 2012).

	Percent	*Kappa*	*Level of Kappa agreement*	*% of reliable data*
Pair 1	0.74	0.41	Weak	about 16%
Pair 2	0.76	0.16	None	about 3%
Pair 3	0.86	0.61	Moderate	about 36%
Pair 4	0.63	0.12	None	about 2%
Pair 5	0.94	0.80	Strong	about 64%

Table 4: Interrater reliability in Percent agreement and Cohen's kappa

With respect to the transitivity annotation of the whole text of the selected news article, it can be suggested that each of the ten annotators made a deliberate choice of an annotation of process categories, participant roles and circumstance types, and that the majority have had a certain amount of correct understanding of the structurally oriented annotation criteria proposed in this study. The detailed information of the distribution of correct ("normal"), incorrect ("abnormal") and incongruent ("normal+ abnormal") scores between the two annotators in each of the five pairs is offered by Table 5. It is observed that the percentage of data that both Annotator A and Annotator B make correct ("normal") judgments on is all above 50% across the five pairs, with Pair 4 obtaining the lowest and Pair 5 the highest.

Pair 1		Annotator B			
		Normal	Abnormal		
Annotator A	Normal	63	15	78	rm1
	Abnormal	15	23	38	rm2
		78	38	116	
		cm1	cm2	n	
Pair 2		Annotator B			
		Normal	Abnormal		
Annotator A	Normal	57	13	70	rm1
	Abnormal	6	4	10	rm2
		63	17	80	
		cm1	cm2	n	
Pair 3		Annotator B			
		Normal	Abnormal		
Annotator A	Normal	48	4	52	rm1
	Abnormal	6	12	18	rm2
		54	16	70	
		cm1	cm2	n	
Pair 4		Annotator B			
		Normal	Abnormal		
Annotator A	Normal	46	22	68	rm1
	Abnormal	10	9	19	rm2
		56	31	87	
		cm1	cm2	n	
Pair 5		Annotator B			
		Normal	Abnormal		
Annotator A	Normal	67	1	68	rm1
	Abnormal	4	13	17	rm2
		71	14	85	
		cm1	cm2	n	

Table 5: Correct, incorrect and incongruent annotations

Now we draw attention to the distribution of the annotations of the six process types and the nine circumstance categories across the three types of interannotator agreement, including both correct ("both normal"), both incorrect ("both abnormal") and correct+incorrect ("normal+ abnormal"), in each of the five pairs. In this way we are enabled to determine to what extent students have learnt annotating these transitivity categories reliably guided by the structurally oriented annotation criteria expounded in Section 2. As shown below, while Table 6 provides the basic information of distribution of the three types of interannotator agreement of the six process types across each of the five pairs, Table 7 presents the parallel distributional information of the nine circumstantial categories.

Pair 1	Material Pro	Relational Pro: Attributive	Relational Pro: Identifying	Mental Pro	Verbal Pro	Existential Pro	*Sub-total*
Both Normal	31.58%	2.63%	2.63%	5.26%	2.63%	0.00%	44.74%
Both Abnormal	15.79%	2.63%	2.63%	2.63%	0.00%	0.00%	23.68%
Normal+Abnormal	18.42%	2.63%	5.26%	0.00%	2.63%	2.63%	31.58%
Total	65.79%	7.89%	10.53%	7.89%	5.26%	2.63%	100.00%
Pair 2	Material Pro	Relational Pro: Attributive	Relational Pro: Identifying	Mental Pro	Verbal Pro	Existential Pro	*Sub-total*
Both Normal	22.22%	18.52%	7.41%	0.00%	14.81%	7.41%	70.37%
Both Abnormal	0.00%	3.70%	0.00%	0.00%	0.00%	0.00%	3.70%
Normal+Abnormal	11.11%	3.70%	3.70%	3.70%	3.70%	0.00%	25.93%
Total	33.33%	25.93%	11.11%	3.70%	18.52%	7.41%	100.00%
Pair 3	Material Pro	Relational Pro: Attributive	Relational Pro: Identifying	Verbal Pro	*Sub-total*		
Both Normal	18.18%	13.64%	0.00%	18.18%	50.00%		
Both Abnormal	18.18%	4.55%	4.55%	4.55%	31.82%		
Normal+Abnormal	4.55%	4.55%	0.00%	9.09%	18.18%		
Total	40.91%	22.73%	4.55%	31.82%	100.00%		
Pair 4	Material Pro	Relational Pro: Attributive	Mental Pro	Verbal Pro	*Sub-total*		
Both Normal	26.32%	0.00%	0.00%	21.05%	47.37%		
Both Abnormal	5.26%	5.26%	5.26%	0.00%	15.79%		
Normal+Abnormal	21.05%	0.00%	0.00%	15.79%	36.84%		
Total	52.63%	5.26%	5.26%	36.84%	100.00%		
Pair 5	Material Pro	Relational Pro: Attributive	Mental Pro	Verbal Pro	Behavioral Pro	*Sub-total*	
Both Normal	37.93%	3.45%	10.34%	27.59%	0.00%	79.31%	
Both Abnormal	3.45%	6.90%	3.45%	0.00%	3.45%	17.24%	
Normal+Abnormal	0.00%	3.45%	0.00%	0.00%	0.00%	3.45%	
Total	41.38%	13.79%	13.79%	27.59%	3.45%	100.00%	

Table 6: Correct, incorrect and incongruent annotations of different processes

Pairwise, it is observable that the two coders in Pair 5 exhibit a high level of correctness and agreement in judgments of the process types concerned, whereas Pair 3, Pair 1 and Pair 4 perform considerably weaker due to a saliently larger proportion of data judged either as both incorrect or as incongruent with one of them being incorrect. More notably, close to Pair 5, the two annotators in Pair 2 also achieve a high level of correctness in their annotations, but they are far more remarkably at odds with each other, which explains their low Kappa value. This finding verifies the usefulness of the instruction of the structurally-oriented coding criteria proposed in this study. It also demonstrates the necessity of addressing the issue of interrater reliability encountered in transitivity annotation due to the lack of more fully explicit annotation criteria in structural rather than semantic terms and the long-standing divide between the use of conceptual as opposed to syntactic criteria in the community. Process-wise, it seems that the problems with annotation of the six process types are evenly distributed across each of the five pairs, regardless of their larger or smaller relative frequency and elaboratedness in lexis. Concerning the annotation of circumstantial categories, however, Table 7 presents a visibly different picture.

Notably, a high level of correctness and agreement in judgments of the five circumstantial categories in Pair 5 is not as saliently exhibited as in Table 6. In addition, the two annotators in Pair 3, perform slightly better than Pair 5 as they achieve a narrowly higher level of correctness and a broadly lower level of incorrectness in their annotations, though exhibiting a larger data of incongruence. This observation may be related to the far smaller number of different types of circumstance to be annotated in Pair 3. Furthermore, compared with the parallel data of annotations of different process types offered in Table 6, while Pair 1 and Pair 4 make a similarly substantially poor performance both in terms of a higher level of incorrectness and of incongruence, Pair 2 unexpectedly achieves a much lower level of correctness and agreement in their annotations of circumstantial categories. This result might suggest the urgency of developing explicit syntactic criteria for transitivity annotation given that the instances where prepositional phrases function as adverbials are often easily confused with those in which they function as qualifiers of nominal or adjectival phrases. Circumstance-wise, quite evidently, the annotation of each of the nine circumstantial categories is problematic at a general level, whether they are of larger or smaller relative frequency and lexical elaboration.

Pair 1	Cir: Location	Cir: Manner	Cir: Cause	Cir: Accompaniment	Cir: Matter	*Sub-Total*			
Both Normal	31.58%	15.79%	0.00%	0.00%	0.00%	47.37%			
Both Abnormal	0.00%	10.53%	0.00%	0.00%	0.00%	10.53%			
Normal+Abnormal	21.05%	5.26%	5.26%	5.26%	5.26%	42.11%			
Total	52.63%	31.58%	5.26%	5.26%	5.26%	100.00%			
Pair 2	Cir: Location	Cir: Manner	Cir: Role	Cir: Matter	Cir: Angle	*Sub-Total*			
Both Normal	28.57%	7.14%	0.00%	0.00%	0.00%	35.71%			
Both Abnormal	7.14%	14.29%	0.00%	0.00%	0.00%	21.43%			
Normal+Abnormal	7.14%	14.29%	7.14%	7.14%	7.14%	42.86%			
Total	42.86%	35.71%	7.14%	7.14%	7.14%	100.00%			
Pair 3	Cir: Location	Cir: Manner	Cir: Angle	*Sub-Total*					
Both Normal	38.46%	7.69%	15.38%	61.54%					
Both Abnormal	7.69%	7.69%	0.00%	15.38%					
Normal+Abnormal	23.08%	0.00%	0.00%	23.08%					
Total	69.23%	15.38%	15.38%	100.00%					
Pair 4	Cir: Location	Cir: Extent	Cir:Manner	Cir: Cause	Cir: Contingency	Cir: Accompaniment	Cir: Matter	Cir: Angle	*Sub-Total*
Both Normal	26.92%	0.00%	3.85%	3.85%	0.00%	0.00%	0.00%	0.00%	34.62%
Both Abnormal	7.69%	0.00%	3.85%	3.85%	0.00%	0.00%	0.00%	3.85%	19.23%
Normal+Abnormal	7.69%	7.69%	7.69%	0.00%	3.85%	3.85%	11.54%	3.85%	46.15%
Total	42.31%	7.69%	15.38%	7.69%	3.85%	3.85%	11.54%	7.69%	100.00%
Pair 5	Cir: Location	Cir: Extent	Cir:Manner	Cir: Cause	Cir: Contingency	*Sub-Total*			
Both Normal	42.86%	7.14%	0.00%	7.14%	0.00%	57.14%			
Both Abnormal	0.00%	7.14%	14.29%	0.00%	7.14%	28.57%			
Normal+Abnormal	7.14%	0.00%	7.14%	0.00%	0.00%	14.29%			
Total	50.00%	14.29%	21.43%	7.14%	7.14%	100.00%			

Table 7 Correct, incorrect and incongruent annotations of different circumstantial categories

5. Conclusion

Tough challenges have been encountered for the task of transitivity annotation due to the stratal blurring of whether transitivity is positioned at the level of semantics or lexico-grammar in SFL. The situation is aggravated by the lack of explicit annotation criteria as well as the divide between conceptual vs. syntactic criteria in practice. To help address these issues, the present study proposed that explicit structural and syntactic criteria should be adopted as a basis to maximize the consistency in annotations that are conceptual and semantic in nature. Drawing on syntactic and grammatical features as judgement cues, we applied structurally oriented criteria for the annotation of the Hallidayan process categories and participant roles combining a set of interrelated syntactic variables and established the annotation criteria for contextualised circumstantial categories in structural as well as semantic terms. The experiment, which was carried out to test the usefulness of these annotation criteria, applied percent agreement and Cohen's kappa as measurements of interrater reliability between the annotators in each of the five pairs. The results verified our assumptions, albeit rather mildly, and, more significantly, offered some first empirical indications about the practical consistency of transitivity analysis in SFL. The results have also produced insights and suggestions for some future work. The research team expect to integrate automated syntactic analysis and manual transitivity annotation to compute the probability of the association between the grammatical and syntactic categories and transitivity categories in preparation for the implementation of automated transitivity analysis. It is also expected to draw on the insights and experience from some of the ISO standards devoted to semantic annotation such as dialogue acts (Bunt et al. 2012) and semantic roles (ISO-24617-4, 2014).

6. Acknowledgements

Research described in this article was partially supported by grants received from Beijing Municipality Planning Office of Philosophy and Social Sciences (Project No 19YYA001) and CityU Strategic Interdisciplinary Research Grant (Project No 7020036).

7. Bibliographical References

Bunt, H, Alexandersson, J, Choe, J W, Fang, A C, Hasida, K, Petukhova, V, Popescu-Belis, A, & Traum, D (2012). *ISO 24617-2:2012 Language resource management – Semantic annotation framework (SemAF) – Part 2: Dialogue acts*. Geneva: The International Organization for Standardization.

Cohen, J. (1960). A coefficient of agreement for nominal scales. *Educational and Psychological Measurement*, 20: 37-46.

Fang, A.C. (1996). AUTASYS: Automatic Tagging and Cross-Tagset Mapping. In S. Greenbaum (Ed.), *Comparing English World Wide: The International Corpus of English*. Oxford: Oxford University Press, pp. 110--124.

Fang, A.C. (2006). Evaluating the Performance of the Survey Parser with the NIST Scheme. In A. Gelbukh (Ed.), *LNCS 3878: Computational Linguistics and Intelligent Text Processing*. Berlin Heidelberg: Springer-Verlag, pp. 168--179.

Fang, A.C. (2007). *English Corpora and Automated Grammatical Analysis*. Beijing: The Commercial Press.

Halliday, M, A, K. (1994). *An Introduction to Functional Grammar*. London: Edward Arnold, 2nd edition.

Halliday, M.A.K. (1967/8). Notes on transitivity and theme in English. *Journal of Linguistics*, 3(1): 37-81, 3(2): 199-244, 4(2): 179-215.

Hopper, P. & Thompson, S.A. (1980). Transitivity in grammar and discourse. *Language*, 56(2): 251-99.

ISO-24617-4. 2014. *Language resource management - Semantic annotation framework (SemAF) - Part 4: Semantic roles* (SemAF-SR). Geneva: International Organization for Standardization.

Levin, B. (1993). *English Verb Classes and Alternations: A Preliminary Investigation*. Chicago: University of Chicago Press.

Matthiessen, C. M. I. M. (1999). The system of transitivity: An exploratory study of text-based profiles. *Functions of Language*, 6(1): 1-51.

Matthiessen, C. M. I. M. (2014). Extending the description of process type within the system of transitivity in delicacy based on Levinian verb classes. *Functions of Language*, 21(2): 139-175.

McHugh, M.L. (2012). Interrater reliability: the kappa statistic. *Biochemia Medica*, 22(3): 276-282.

O'Donnell, M., Zappvigna, M. and Whitelaw, C. (2009) A survey of process type classification over difficult cases. In J. Carys and E. Ventola (Eds.), *From Language to Multimodality: New Developments in the Study of Ideational Meaning*. Bristol: Equinox Publishing, pp. 47--64.

Proceedings of ISA-18 Workshop at LREC2022, pages 61–70
Marseille, 20 June 2022

The place of ISO-Space in Text2Story multilayer annotation scheme

António Leal, Purificação Silvano, Evelin Amorim, Inês Cantante, Fátima Silva
Alípio Jorge, Ricardo Campos
CLUP-Universidade do Porto, INESC TEC
{jleal, msilvano, mhenri}@letras.up.pt, cantante.ines@gmail.com
{evelin.f.amorim, alipio.jorge}@inesctec.pt
ricardo.campos@ipt.pt

Abstract

Reasoning about spatial information is fundamental in natural language to fully understand relationships between entities and/or between events. However, the complexity underlying such reasoning makes it hard to represent formally spatial information. Despite the growing interest on this topic, and the development of some frameworks, many problems persist regarding, for instance, the coverage of a wide variety of linguistic constructions and of languages. In this paper, we present a proposal of integrating ISO-Space into a ISO-based multilayer annotation scheme, designed to annotate news in European Portuguese. This scheme already enables annotation at three levels, temporal, referential and thematic, by combining postulates from ISO 24617-1, 4 and 9. Since the corpus comprises news articles, and spatial information is relevant within this kind of texts, a more detailed account of space was required. The main objective of this paper is to discuss the process of integrating ISO-Space with the existing layers of our annotation scheme, assessing the compatibility of the aforementioned parts of ISO 24617, and the problems posed by the harmonization of the four layers and by some specifications of ISO-Space.

Keywords: ISO-space, multilayer annotation scheme, European Portuguese, news articles corpus.

1. Introduction

The consideration of spatial information, in general, and spatial relations, in particular, is one of the essential functions of natural language. The formal mapping of such information is challenging, notably due to the vastness and diversity of linguistic constructions that materialize them, with the consequent impact on the setting of relations' patterns (Kordjamshidi et al., 2010). However, this knowledge and its computational modelling are fundamental for many applications in computational linguistics and artificial intelligence, for which annotated datasets are essential (Pustejovsky et al., 2019). The existence of such datasets is still limited, with English being the dominant language.

In this context, some models of spatial information extraction have been proposed, working independently or in integration with other information domains (a.o., SpatialML (Mani et al., 2008); Language resource management — Semantic annotation framework: (ISO-24617-7, 2020)). They aim to map the spatial information of a text or other type of information modality in a formal representation that seeks to account for how humans conceptualize and process space in a wide variety of genres and domains (Gritta et al., 2018).

In the context of Text2Story project [1], which aims to extract narratives from news, represent them in intermediate data structures, and make these available to subsequent media production processes, we follow ISO 24617-7 (ISO-24617-7, 2020), which allows for the annotation of static and dynamic locations, and of a wide range of spatial relations. So far, only a few datasets have applied these ISO guidelines for annotating spatial information, none of which are in European Portuguese. We have selected this model because it proposes a framework that allow us to represent properly the spatial relations occurring in our corpus, contributing to a more effective subsequent visualization. Additionally, ISO-Space conforms with the multilayer semantic annotation scheme that combines and harmonizes three parts of ISO 24617-1/4/9, and that we have already designed (Silvano et al., 2021) to represent time and events, semantic roles, and referential information. This new model also promotes the balance between the amount of needed information to extract narratives and the load of the annotation process.

All in all, this paper aims to:

- put forward a multilayer annotation model;
- describe the integration of the spatial information and the procedures necessary for its harmonization with the existing scheme;
- identify some problems related to the harmonization process, and pointers to overcome them.

The remainder of the paper is organized as follows. Section 2 is dedicated to presenting some previous work about spatial annotation. Section 3 presents Text2Story ISO-based annotation framework, starting with the description of the harmonization of the temporal, referential and thematic layers 3.1 and proceeding to the description of the integration of the spatial layer 3.2. Section 3.3 explains some of the problems of combining ISO-Space to parts 1, 4, 9 of ISO 24617 and of applying it to the annotation of Portuguese data.

[1] https://text2story.inesctec.pt

Finally, some concluding remarks and future work are provided in Section 4.

2. Related work

During the past few years, there have been some new proposals for modeling spatial information, based on different theoretical, and domain-specific, approaches, which have advanced the state-of-art. Mani et al. (2008), for instance, propose SpatialML, an annotation scheme for marking up named and nominal references to places in natural language with geo-coordinates, whenever possible, and relationships among places in terms of a region calculus. Kordjamshidi et al. (2010) describe the task of spatial role labeling, which is language-independent, to identify and classify spatial arguments of spatial expressions in a sentence, and the mapping of the spatial relations established in natural language to formal representations by means of machine learning.

One of the best known and most comprehensive proposals is *Language resource management — Semantic annotation framework (SemAF) — Part 7: Spatial information (ISO-Space) Standard ISO/IEC TR 24617-7* (ISO-24617-7, 2020). ISO-Space, which has been under development for several years – one of the first papers to introduce was Pustejovsky et al. (2011) - aims at postulating "normative specifications not only for spatial information, but also for information content in motion and various other types of event in language" (ISO-24617-7, 2020), thus, enabling static and dynamic spatial annotations. The first edition, published in 2014, was revised in 2020 to conform with ISO 24617-6 (ISO-24617-6, 2016), incorporating some changes proposed along the years (for instance, Lee (2016)), and restoring the original proposal by Pustejovsky et al. (2012) and Pustejovsky and Yocum (2013), regarding event-paths (Pustejovsky et al., 2019).

There are, however, only a few studies and tasks that actually apply ISO-Space to corpus annotation. Some of those have been carried out during the process of building the standard, and they have been useful to identify some issues and to come up with solutions for them. For instance, Pustejovsky and Yocum (2013) describe the motion sub-corpus of ISO-SpaceBank with 50 entries from a travel blog, and its pilot annotation revealed some problems, which have led to the inclusion of further specifications in the standard. SpaceEval task (Pustejovsky et al., 2015) goes one step further aiming at automatic extraction of spatial information by means of supervised and semi-supervised machine learning systems. The evaluation results show that recognition of spatial entities and of *MOVELINK* are more easily achieved than of recognition of spatial relations between spatial entities. Since ISO-Space is an international standard directed to a wide range of languages, Lee et al. (2011) apply a first draft of ISO-Space to datasets from three typologically different languages, English (inflectional analytic), Korean (agglutinative) and Chinese (isolating), to ascertain its descriptive suitability. The version that was applied was considered largely suitable to describe spatial information, even though some modifications were required to deal with language specificities.

Other studies have demonstrated ISO-Space's scope and expressivity. On the one hand, the model can be used to represent spatial information in textual data, be they narratives (Pustejovsky and Yocum, 2013) or captions of images (Pustejovsky and Yocum, 2014) or even scene descriptions (Gaizauskas and Alrashid, 2019), and there are plans to transfer such annotations to three dimensions environments facilitating the reconstruction of scenes from text (Henlein et al., 2020). On the other hand, in terms of language coverage, although ISO-Space (ISO-24617-7, 2020) refers that the specification language for spatial annotation concerns English, and that its applicability to other languages is missing, Estarrona and Aldezabal (2018) discuss the viability of applying it to a Basque corpus. Despite the fact that the two languages differ, namely concerning prepositions, which in Basque, an agglutinative language like Korean, are postpositions, and that some adaptations are required, the authors conclude that this standard is adequate to codify spatial information in Basque.

Regardless of what has been accomplished, the reality is that ISO-Space, in particular the last edition from 2020, is not yet widely used in corpus annotations and/ or in applications (like, for instance, ISO-TimeXL). According to Henlein et al. (2020), the reasons that explain why such situation is happening with this and other linguistic models for spatial information could be the model's complexity, and the lack of annotated datasets and of automated taggers. With our work, we intend to: (i) demonstrate that the ISO-Space is not so complex that it cannot be applied to a dataset from other language than English and that it cannot be integrated into a multilayer annotation scheme with models from other parts of ISO 24617; (ii) alleviate the shortage of annotated corpus in European Portuguese.

3. Text2Story annotation scheme

3.1. Temporal, referential and thematic layers

In order to extract the relevant information from our dataset, composed of news articles, we developed an interoperable multilayer semantic annotation that harmonizes three parts of the standard *Language resource management-Semantic annotation framework*: Part 1- Time and events (ISO-24617-1, 2012), Part 4- Semantic roles (ISO-24617-4, 2014) and Part 9- Referential annotation framework (ISO-24617-9, 2019) (Silvano et al., 2021). This task presented some obstacles, but we were able to overcome difficulties, with a constant work of annotation, revision and correction as proposed by MATTER's (Pustejovsky and Stubbs, 2012) subcycle, MAMA. This methodology allowed us to solve problems and incongruities that were identified along the way. Furthermore, the use of BRAT (Stenetorp et al., 2012) as an annotation tool made it possible to update the scheme almost incrementally, maintaining, therefore, some of its parts, while erasing superfluous ones.

The first step was to model the types of structures as entity structures and link structures. The entity structures comprise events, times and participants, while the link structures incorporate the following links: *temporal, aspectual, subordination, objectal* and *semantic role*. Our model enables the annotation of an intricate network of relationships, because the different entity structures can be related among them by different types of link structures. For each structure type, subtypes were selected from the aforementioned parts of ISO-24617, rendering an annotation scheme with three layers: temporal, referential and thematic (semantic role labeling).

The temporal layer, based on ISO-24617-1, contains temporal information, and reconstructs the temporal sequencing of events, through the use of temporal links (*TLinks*). Despite following the standard, our scheme leaves out some tags and links that we considered unnecessary for the project's goal, that is, the construction of narratives' visualizations extracted from news [2]. Thus, we adopted the tags for events (*EVENT*) and times (*TIMEX3*). The former is used to mark eventualities, in the form of verbs, nominalizations, adjectives, pronouns, predicative constructions or prepositional complements. The remaining information about the eventualities is given by the following attributes: *class, part of speech, tense, aspect, verb form, mood, modality* and *polarity*. These attributes have the same values that were established for the Italian, in ISO-24617-1, with the exception of *mood*, to which we added the value *future*, and *modality*, complemented with the European Portuguese modal verbs *dever* (*must*), *poder* (*can*), *ter de* (*have to*) e *ser capaz de* (*be able to*). Regarding *TIMEX3* tag, we decided to keep the annotation scheme very simple, maintaining only two tags, relative to *type* (*date, time, duration, set*) and *value*, which refers to a specific value, manually inserted by the annotator, and two attributes, *temporal function*, to indicate that the *TIMEX3* expression corresponds to the *publication time*, and *anchor time*. Lastly, the extraction of the events timeline is accomplished by means of temporal links (*TLinks*), which represent relations between the events, events and times and between times. The aspectual and subordination links (*ALink* and *Slink*, respectively) encompass the pertinent aspectual and subordination information as proposed by ISO-24617-1.

The second layer refers to the identification and annotation of referential expressions, which, in Text2Story project, are represented by named entities referring to participants in the narrative. Although overall ISO-24617-9 is followed, considering that the scheme is multilayer, in order to avoid repetitive information and an overly complex annotation work, we have selected only the relevant tags for our purposes. For the discourse entity structures, the attribute *lexical head* has the values *noun* or *pronoun*. For the referential expression structures, the attributes for *domain* and *involvement* were integrated. The former introduces information about *individuation*, with the values *set, individual or mass*, retrieved from ISO-24617-9, and *types*, with values taken from several named entity classification typologies (PER (person), ORG (organization), LOC (location), OBJ (object), NAT (nature), OTHER). The *involvement* specifies the involvement of the participants in the event, and has the values *0, 1,* >1, *all* or *undefined*, which were stipulated by us. Finally, with the purpose of representing nominal anaphora's mechanisms, we use the *objectal links* provided by ISO-24617-9, to identify the following relations: *objectal identity, part of, member of* and *referential disjunction*.

The third annotation layer is relative to semantic role labeling, and is grounded on ISO-24617-4. In this case, we integrated in our framework thematic relations between event structures and participant structures.

3.2. Spatial layer

This section describes the process of adding a spatial layer using ISO 24617-7 to the annotation scheme described previously.

In a nutshell, ISO-Space, in accordance with the general principles of ISO 24617-6 (ISO-24617-6, 2016), proposes the use of a set of entity structures, and a set of link structures, with attributes and values, which are employed to annotate spatial information. In ISO-Space, entity structures comprise participants, eventualities, and measures. Participant structures include two kinds of entities: (i) locational entities, such as places, paths (roads, rivers, etc.) and event-paths (motional trajectories), and (ii) non-locational entities that are involved in spatial relations. Eventuality structures include motion (i.e., events describing the displacement of an entity, or the change in some property or conformation of an object), and non-motion events. Measure structures provide quantitative information regarding some dimension of spatial entities or regarding some relation between spatial entities. As for link structures, they consist of four types: (i) qualitative spatial links, which express static relations between regions; (ii) orientational links, which express the spatial disposition or direction of an object; (iii) movement links, which relate an entity that moves to the trajectory that is being followed by that entity in the course of a motion event; and (iv) measure links, which connect an object to its measure. Measure structures and eventuality structures are always anchored in markables, i.e., word/expressions occurring in the

[2]For a more detailed account about the choices and their justification related to the annotation scheme described in this subsection, see Silvano et al. (2021).

text. However, participant structures are not always anchored in markables. In fact, ISO-Space (2020 version) proposes the use of "non-consuming" tags, i.e., tags without a markable, namely in the case of the entity structure *event-path*. As for link structures, they relate participant structures with each other.

From this ISO, we chose the following tags, attributes, and links: (i) for entities: *place, path, non-locational spatial entity, spatial relation, motion and non-motional eventualities* and *measure*, leaving out *event-path*; (ii) for links: *qualitative spatial link, movement link*, and *measure link*, leaving out *orientational link*.

Starting with entities, the *non-locational spatial entity* is subsumed, in our annotation scheme, into the entity structure *participant*, which has several attributes for the tag *type* (cf. section 3.1; e.g. PER, ORG). There was no need to formally introduce the notion of *non-locational spatial entity* in the existing annotation scheme. Although *place* tag was already in the list of attributes of the tag *type* of the entity structure *participant*, according to ISO 24617-7 one needed to distinguish the different types of places. The solution that we implemented included, in the list of attributes of the tag *type* of *participant structure*, the attributes of *place type* stipulated by ISO 24617-7 that were relevant to annotate the news articles. The restricted set of attributes for *place type* that we decided to add to the list of participants *type* already present in our annotation scheme is the following: *Pl_water*, *Pl_celestial*, *Pl_mountain*, *Pl_civil*, *Pl_country*, *Pl_mount_range*, *Pl_capital*, *Pl_region*, and *Pl_state*. In fact, we merged participant structures types proposed by ISO 24617-7 with tags that were already part of our annotation scheme, and that came from ISO 24617-9. Example (1) illustrates a locative participant structure.

(1) o bairro da Pasteleira Nova
the neighbourhood of-the Pasteleira Nova
the Pasteleira Nova neighbourhood
participant: lexicalHead=noun; individuationDomain=individual; type=plCivil; involvement=1

As for *paths*, the option was not to give any attribute of the ISO 24617-7 and simply to insert *path* also as an attribute of the tag *type* of participants. Overall, the already existing participant entity structures were enriched with the specification of different types of locative participants. There was no need to create new entity structures for locative participants.

Motions and *non-motional eventualities* were also easily included in our annotation scheme, as there were already entity structures for events. Therefore, besides the existing tags and attributes of the event structure defined by ISO24617-1 (cf. figure 1), we only added to the entity structure *event* the attribute *motion* with the tags *motion_literal, motion_fictive, motion_intrChange* (inherited from the attribute *motionSense* of the tag *motion* in ISO 24617-7) and *non-motion*. These attributes allow us to distinguish changes in the location of the *Figure* (*motion_literal*) and changes in the *Figure*'s configuration (*motion_intrChange*), both of them corresponding to event-type situations, from most cases of fictive motion (*motion_fictive*), which correspond to state-like eventualities. So, the different kinds of motion that are envisaged by ISO 24617-7 can be properly identified (as literal, fictive, or intrinsic change) and be opposed to all non-motional eventualities. We do not use any of the remaining attributes of the *motion* tag in ISO 24617-7 (for instance, *motionType* or *motionClass*), because such level of detailed information is not pertinent to our project's purposes, at least for the time being. Hence, for instance, all eventualities that receive the tag *motion* are interpreted as if there was a *motionClass=move*, that is, that specific eventuality is associated to a trajectory (or *event-path*) (being the subeventive structure underspecified; cf.(Pustejovsky, 2017)). Example (2) illustrates an event structure.

(2) os camponeses saíam das lavras
the peasants were leaving from-the fields
The peasants were leaving the fields
saíam: event: class=state; eventType=state; pos=verb; tense=past; aspect=progressive; polarity=pos; movement=motionLiteral

Finally, in order to encompass all sorts of spatial information, it was required to add two entity structures to our annotation scheme: *spatial relations*, and *measures*. *Measures* was introduced to deal with measurement relations, most of them corresponding to distances. Following ISO 24617-7, the markables that are identified as measures are further manually annotated with information regarding *measure value*, *measure unit* and *measure modification* (whenever required). Example (3) represents a measure structure.

(3) uma faixa de proteção inferior a 250 metros
a band of protection inferior to 250 meters
a protection zone under 250 meters
inferior a 250 metros: value=250; unit=metro; mod=inferior a

Spatial relations is associated with preposition and adverb-like markables. As defined by ISO 24617-7, this relation connects a *Figure* to a location or trajectory. *Spatial relation* in our annotation scheme only uses the tag *sRelation type*, with only two values: *topological* and *path defining*. Other values that are proposed by ISO 24617-7, namely *directional* and *topo-Directional*, appear to be unnecessary for different reasons. Regarding *Directional* value, it seems to be residual in the news texts that constitute our corpus. In fact, in the analysed news texts, there were no examples of directional prepositions, such as *em frente de* (*in front of*), which justifies our option of not using *directional spatial relations*, nor *orientational links*, for now. In our corpus, *spatial relations* are mainly of the *topological* type, performing a vague location, which typically corresponds to *disjunction of tangential proper part* and *non-tangential proper part.* With respect to *topo-Directional*, this *sRelation type* does not correspond to any specific preposition or adverb in European Portuguese. The English preposition *on*, which codifies this relation, in European Portuguese is translated as *em*, which subsumes English prepositions *in* and *on*.

The *topological* value uses the nine attributes proposed by ISO 24617-7: *disconnected; externally connected; partial overlap; equal; tangential proper part; tangential proper part inverse; non-tangential proper part; non-tangential proper part inverse*; and *disjunction of tangential proper part* and *non-tangential proper part.* Nevertheless, the utility of using *tangential proper part inverse* or *non-tangential proper part inverse* is debatable, as the annotator can establish the relation from a participant structure A (the *Figure*) to a participant structure B (the *Ground*), or the other way round.

As for *path defining* value, we use the three attributes put forward by ISO 24617-7: *start, end* and *mids*. However, and this is a relevant adaptation of ISO 24617-7 to our annotation scheme, we have also merged the *goal defining* value with the attributes of the *path defining* value, so the tag *path defining* effectively has four attributes. The rationale for this option is related, for instance, to the fact that there is a frequently used preposition in European Portuguese, *para*, which can easily exhibit two readings: a mere directional reading (that can be translated by *towards*), and a goal reading (equivalent to English *to*). Accordingly, the preposition *para* can occur with both readings and, in most cases, the choice between the two is context-dependent. In other words, the goal preposition *para* easily allows also non-culminating readings, i.e., of canceling the event's culmination, when the Figure reaches the intended destination (Leal et al., 2018), contrary to other prepositions, such as *a* (*to*) and *até* (*up to*). Hence, in the presence of a sentence with *para*, it is easier for the annotator to mark this preposition with a *path-defining* value, with either the attribute *end*, or *goal-defining*. Example 4 represents a spatial relation structure.

(4) os camponeses saíam das lavras
the peasants were leaving from-the fields
The peasants were leaving the fields
d(as): spatialRelation: pathDefining=start

An important difference between our annotation scheme and ISO 24617-7 is the absence of *event-path* in the entity structures. In fact, there is a basic incompatibility problem between ISO 24617-7 and our annotation scheme: the former proposes entity structures that do not correspond to markables, whereas the latter presupposes that all entity structures are always linked to markables in the text. In order to overcome this major incompatibility, and to be able to accommodate the notion of *event-path* within our annotation scheme, since *event-paths* have triggers that correspond to motion verbs, we use those verbs as markables for building event structures and we associate to those event structures the relevant links. We do not include, in these event structures, any of the attributes of the *event-path* tag, namely *eventPath start, eventPath end*, or *eventPath mids*, and, instead, we resort to link structures to fill in this information. Adopting this solution means not discarding completely the notion of *event-path*. In fact, we make use of some of the information codified in its attributes to represent the spatial information present in our corpus.

The main reason not to include non-consuming tags, and just annotate lexical material concerns limitations of BRAT, the annotation tool that we use. Although this may not be the most valid reason, the following is more compelling. As mentioned before, the current proposal aims at integrating a spatial layer into a multilayer annotation scheme, which harmonizes parts 1, 4 and 9 of ISO 24617. In all of these parts, tags have always markables. So, if we wanted ISO-Space to fit the existing annotation scheme, we had to exclude non-consuming tags, at least at this stage of the project.

As far as the link structures are concerned, we deemed it best to use only three types: *qualitative spatial link, movement link*, and *measure link.* Since the information captured by the *orientational link* was not necessary to annotate our corpus, we discard it. The *qualitative spatial link* uses only two required attributes - *Figure* and *Ground.* The *relType* attribute, which is also required, is already present in the *spatial relation* structure. Accordingly, after the annotation of a markable with a *spatial relation* structure with a *topological* value, the annotator must connect that structure with a participant structure or an event structure by means of a *Figure* link, and with a (locative) participant structure by means of a *Ground* link. Example (5) illustrates the qualitative spatial links.

(5) Um homem de 20 anos foi detido pela PSP no bairro da Pasteleira Nova
A man of 20 years was arrested by-the PSP in-the neighbourhood of-the Pasteleira Nova
A 20-year-old man has been arrested by the PSP in the Pasteleira Nova neighbourhood.
QSLINK-Ground=n(o), o bairro da Pasteleira Nova
QSLINK-Figure=n(o), detido

The *movement link* was substantially adapted because, as mentioned earlier, *event-paths* are not part of our annotation scheme. Therefore, we took the *moveLink* trigger as the markable from where different relations that correspond to different attributes of the tag *moveLink* are established. So, in the presence of an event structure tagged as *motion*, the annotator must connect that event structure: (i) to a participant structure by means of the *Figure* link (corresponding to the *moveLink figure*), (ii) to a spatial relation structure by means of the *spatialRelation* link, and (iii) to a (locative) participant structure with a *targetSpatialRelation* link (corresponding to the *moveLink ground*). These two links (*spatialRelation* link and *targetSpatialRelation* link) are not in ISO 24617-7. We added them to deal with the problem of not having the non-consuming tag *event-path*. The solution that we envisioned includes the following: the combination of (i) a markable that is a motion event with (ii) a participant that is a *Figure* of that event, (iii) a *spatial relation* that defines the initial, medial or final part of a trajectory, or just the direction of the motion, and (iv) the *Ground* of the spatial relation. Therefore, it is the combination of a motion event structure with a directional spatial relation and its *Ground* that functions as a substitute of the *event-path* notion of ISO 24617-7. Once again, this approach allow us to keep part of the information represented by this entity structure. In (6), we exemplify this solution.

(6) os camponeses saíam das lavras
the peasants were leaving from-the fields
The peasants were leaving the fields.
moveLink: figure=saíam, os camponeses moveLink: spatialRelation=saíam, d(as) moveLink: targetSpatialRelation= saíam, as lavras

Finally, the measure link uses the *relType* attributes (*distance, length, width, height* and *generalDimension*) and it connects an event structure or a participant structure to a measure structure by a *Ground* link (following ISO 24617-7, as "entities to which the measure value applies"). Example (7) shows how this annotation is performed.

(7) uma faixa de proteção inferior a 250 metros
a band of protection inferior to 250 meters.
A protection zone under 250 meters.
MLINK-Width=inferior a 250 metros, uma faixa de proteção

Figure 1 illustrates our annotation scheme.
In what follows, we show how Text2Story annotation scheme can be applied to represent the interpretation of example (8).

(8) Um homem de 20 anos foi detido pela PSP no [3] bairro da Pasteleira Nova
A man of 20 years was arrested by-the PSP in-the neighbourhood of-the Pasteleira Nova
A 20-year-old man has been arrested by the PSP in the Pasteleira Nova neighbourhood.

[3]In this example, the preposition *em* contracts with the definite article, as it happens frequently in Portuguese

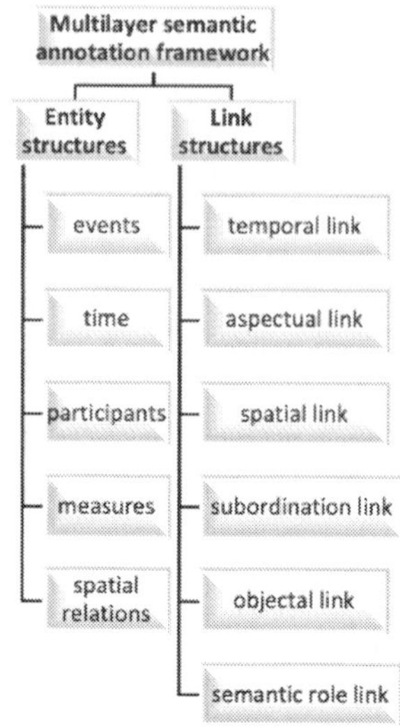

Figure 1: Text2Story multilayer annotation scheme.

STRUCTURES
um homem de 20 anos: participant: lexicalHead=noun; individuationDomain=individual; type=per; involvement=1
a PSP: participant: lexicalHead=noun; individuationDomain=individual; type=org; involvement=1
o bairro da Pasteleira Nova: participant: lexicalHead=noun; individuationDomain=individual; type=plCivil; involvement=1
detido: event: class=occurrence; eventType=transition; pos=verb; tense=past; aspect=perfective; polarity=pos; movement=nonMotion
n: spatialRelation: topological=disjunction-TTP-NTTP

LINKS
QSLINK-ground=n, o bairro da Pasteleira Nova
QSLINK-figure=n, detido
SR-patient=detido, um homem
SR-agent=detido, a PSP

From Example 8, it is possible to build a Discourse Representation Structure (DRS) as depicted in Figure 2. The event is described as a First Order Logic formula. The participants and spatial relations are represented as constants. Using this kind of notation makes it possible to reason over the events formulas, which is useful, for instance, to infer new relations between such elements. The Brat2Viz tool (Amorim et al., 2021) employed DRS as an intermediate language to aid in building a visual representation of the narrative components. The input of this tool is a human annotation text file, then a corresponding DRS is generated, and finally, a visual representation of the annotation is produced.

```
» EVENTS
# T2 (detido) -> a
# FOL: exists a.(relationRole(qsfigure,T2) &
relationRole(patient,T2) & relationRole(agent,T2) &
event(a))
# DRS: ([a],[relationRole(qsfigure,T2),
relationRole(patient,T2), relationRole(agent,T2), event(a)])

» ACTORS
# T1 -> Um homem de 20 anos
# T3 -> a PSP
# T5 -> o bairro da Pasteleira Nova

» SPATIAL-RELATION
# T4 -> n

» RELATIONS
# T4 - qsground - T5
# T4 - qsfigure - T2
# T2 - patient - T1
# T2 - agent - T3
```

Figure 2: DRS text built from the annotation of example 8

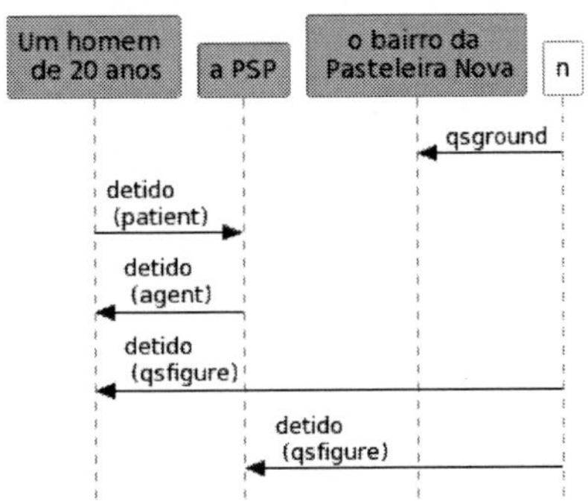

Figure 3: Message Sequence Chart for example (8)

Brat2Viz uses the Message Sequence Chart (MSC) diagram to represent the annotations, as in Figure 3.

Currently, in Text2Story project, the only options for the visualization of the annotation are either (MSC), or knowledge graphs (KG). A foreseen follow-up of this project is the improvement of visualization methods, namely with Venn diagrams and flowcharts. Both will put the events as the narrative element to follow in a timeline. In an MSC, participants are the elements in a timeline of events, and in a KG there is no timeline. Arranging the events in sequence to follow in a diagram also helps the reader to get a better perception of their relative position in the timeline.

At the moment, we are mainly concerned with defining a sound and comprehensive annotation scheme that can deal with the semantic content of news texts in a way that can be used in the development of visualization algorithms. As we are finishing up the annotation scheme, no inter-annotator agreement tasks were performed yet.

To sum up, the introduction of a spatial annotation level in our annotation scheme involved, in addition to the inclusion of some spatial-specific entity structures and link structures, the modification of pre-existing entity structures: (i) the participant structure attribute *type* was enriched with a value *path*, which corresponds to the notion of spatial entity *path* in ISO-Space, and with most of the values of the *placeType* attribute of the tag *place* of ISO-space; (ii) event structures were enriched with the attribute *motionSense* from the *motion* tag of ISO-Space. Simultaneously, the integration of the spatial layer enabled the removal of some (redundant) semantic role links, those that bear spatial nature: *location, initialLocation, finalLocation, path* and *distance*. In fact, as expected, spatial annotation was substantially improved with the replacement of locative semantic roles with spatial-specific annotation. For instance, there is now the possibility of expressing different relations that were previously included in the semantic role of *finalLocation*. They can now be marked as *end* or *goalDefining*, which gives rise to different entailments concerning the Figure's location at the end of the event. Additionally, measure structures and links can be utilized for a better characterization of participants: the semantic role link *amount* can was replaced by measure structures and links, with more information concerning *type, value* and *modification*, and with the possibility of being used not only to link a participant to an event, but also to describe a participant (cf. example (3) and (7)).

3.3. Some problems

In this section, we pinpoint some shortcomings of the implementation of ISO-Space to our annotation scheme.

As already stated, some problems arose when trying to combine ISO 24617-7 with our annotation scheme, which resulted from the harmonization of parts 1, 4 and 9 of ISO 24617. One of the major problems that we encountered was the incompatibility between the existence of "non-consuming" tags in ISO 24617-7 and our project's principle of annotating only lexical material occurring in text (also a principle of parts 1, 4 and 9 of ISO 24617), evidenced by the *event-path* issue that we discussed before. A similar issue is related to a very frequent structure in our corpus exemplified in (9).

(9) O caso deu-se na freguesia de Refogos de Basto, concelho de Cabeceiras de Basto, distrito de Braga.
The case happened-itself in-the parish of Refogos de Basto, municipality of Cabeceiras de Basto, district of Braga.
The case took place in the parish of Refogos de Basto, municipality of Cabeceiras de Basto, district of Braga.

In order to conduct spatial annotation, the annotator tags the spatial location of *the case* in a place called *Regofos de Basto*. That spatial location is expressed by the preposition *em (in)*, heading the PP *na freguesia de Refogos de Basto*. The journalist adds further information about that place, as it is often done when the place in question is not part of the speakers "common knowledge". Typically, the journalist expands the sentence with appositive modifiers locating it in a bigger (and more well-known) location. In some cases, those appositive phrases correspond to PPs headed by *em* (*in*). However, in most cases, as in (9), the preposition is absent (*concelho de Cabeceiras de Basto* and *distrito de Braga*). This poses a challenge to our annotation scheme, because a preposition (or an adverb) is obligatory to mark the spatial relation. The solution that we implemented was the following. Firstly, as our annotation scheme has different levels of annotation, and since one of those levels is the referential level, we can connect *na freguesia de Refogos de Basto*, annotated as a participant of the type *placeCivil*, to the participant *concelho de Cabeceiras de Basto*, also a participant of the type *placeCivil*, by means of a *partOf* objectal relation. The same sort of connection can be established between the participant *concelho de Cabeceiras de Basto* and the participant *distrito de Braga*, of the type *placeCivil*, as well. Secondly, since all cases of locations without preposition correspond to places that are a part of other locations, we decided to insert an inference rule in the DRS, which acts as an intermediate language to generate visualizations (cf. section 3.3). This inference rule (cf. (10)) states that whenever two locative participants are connected by a *partOf* relation, there is a topological spatial relation with the value *IN* (as defined by ISO 24617-7) that takes the first location in the text as its *Figure* and the second location as its *Ground*.

(10)

$$\forall x \forall y (LOCATION\, x \wedge LOCATION\, y \\ \wedge PART\_OF\, x, y) \rightarrow \exists z \\ (SPATIAL - RELATION\_IN\, z \wedge FIGURE\, x, y \\ \wedge GROUND\, y, z)$$

In the process of harmonizing the different parts of ISO 24617, we have also observed some incongruities when we compare the parts of ISO 24617 that we used in our framework. We have already referred to one of them: the existence of non-consuming tags in ISO-Space, namely the *event-path* tag, contrary to happens in the other relevant parts. There are also some differences between the aforementioned parts of ISO 24617 regarding the level of granularity required to annotate the same type of entities, namely eventualities. As a matter of fact, ISO 24617-1 has only three values for the attribute *type* of event structure: *state*, *process*, and *transition*. However, in ISO-Space, the attribute *motionClass* of the *motion* tag has several values (*move*, *moveExternal*, *moveInternal*, *leave*, *reach*, *cross*, *detach*, *hit*, *follow*, *deviate*, and *stay*), which are related to the different subevent structures, and their consequences regarding the location of the *Figure*. Motion events are not the only ones exhibiting subevent structure, so it would maybe be congruent if ISO 24617-1 also contemplated a similar proposal of subeventive analysis for non-motion eventualities.

A final remark concerning ISO-Space more practical matters. This document could benefit (in clarity) if more definitions and examples were given regarding attributes and values. In fact, the scarcity of examples, together with the fact that they are all in English, poses some challenges when one tries to use it in the annotation of texts in languages that differ from English in distinct (and, sometimes, understudied) aspects.

4. Conclusion and Future Work

Representing and extracting information from texts is a challenging task. In our project, we aim to create visualizations from information extracted from news texts. To do so, we initially designed a multilayer annotation scheme comprising three levels of annotation (times and events, participants, and semantic roles) combining three parts of ISO SemAF (ISO-24617-1; ISO-24617-4; and ISO-24617-9). In this paper, we describe the efforts of improving our annotation scheme with spatial information by adding a fourth layer of annotation that uses ISO-Space (ISO-24617-7, 2020). To achieve a coherent annotation architecture, we had to select tags, attributes and values from ISO-Space that were relevant to the project's purposes, and to insert them into the pre-existing annotation scheme. This required not only adapting some of the proposals of ISO-Space, but also deleting and/or adjusting some of the tags/attributes of the first version of our annotation scheme.

Despite the fact that we discarded at this stage some of the ISO-Space tags and attributes (eg. type of motion), because either our dataset or annotation scheme did not require them, or because we needed to alleviate the annotation load within a four layer framework, overall the annotation as is performs in a satisfactory manner, being able to represent the pertinent information from our dataset.

In the future, it is our intention to validate Text2Story annotation scheme by using inter-annotator agreement and by generating different types of visualizations from narratives. Furthermore, more spatial information will be considered to enable the mapping of the locations referred in the texts to maps. This task will require adding more attributes to the *placeType*, such as *place latLong*. We will also conduct a detailed study about the specificities of European Portuguese regarding the expression of spatial information and assess to what extent ISO-Space can account for their representation. Since we recognize that the expressive power of ISO-Space goes beyond the annotation of news texts to extract where actions happen, we plan as well to expand the initial corpus of Text2Story project to encompass pre-processed texts that include a large array of spatial relations (for instance, texts depicting places, or travel descriptions), which will allow us to test all potentialities of ISO-Space.

5. Acknowledgements

This research is funded by the ERDF – European Regional Development Fund through the North

Portugal Regional Operational Programme (NORTE 2020), under the PORTUGAL 2020 and by National Funds through the Portuguese funding agency, FCT - Fundação para a Ciência e a Tecnologia within project PTDC/CCI-COM/31857/2017 (NORTE-01-0145-FEDER-03185).

6. Bibliographical References

Amorim, E., Ribeiro, A., Cantante, I., Jorge, A., Santana, B., Nunes, S., Silvano, M. d. P., Leal, A., and Campos, R. (2021). Brat2viz: a tool and pipeline for visualizing narratives from annotated texts. In *Proceedings of Text2Story-Fourth Workshop on Narrative Extraction From Texts held in conjunction with the 43rd European Conference on Information Retrieval (ECIR 2021)*.

Estarrona, A. and Aldezabal, I. (2018). Towards a Spatial Annotation Scheme for Basque based on ISO-Space. In Francesco Mambrini, et al., editors, *Proceedings of the Second Workshop on Corpus-Based Research in the Humanities (CRH-2)*, pages 13–21. Gerastree Proceedings, GTP 1, Dept. of Geoinformation, TU Wien.

Gaizauskas, R. and Alrashid, T. (2019). SceneML: A Proposal for Annotating Scenes in Narrative Text. In Harry Bunt, editor, *Proceedings of the 15th Joint ACL - ISO Workshop on Interoperable Semantic Annotation (ISA-15)*, pages 13–21.

Gritta, M., Pilehvar, M. T., and Collier, N. (2018). Which Melbourne? Augmenting Geocoding with Maps. In *Proceedings of the 56th Annual Meeting of the Association for Computational Linguistics (Volume 1: Long Papers)*, pages 1285–1296, Melbourne, Australia, July. Association for Computational Linguistics.

Henlein, A., Abrami, G., Kett, A., and Mehler, A. (2020). Transfer of ISOSpace into a 3D Environment for Annotations and Applications. In *16th Joint ACL - ISO Workshop on Interoperable Semantic Annotation PROCEEDINGS*, pages 32–35, Marseille, May. European Language Resources Association.

ISO-24617-1. (2012). Language resource management- semantic annotation framework (semaf) - part 1: Time and events (semaf-time, iso-timeml). Standard, Geneva, CH.

ISO-24617-4. (2014). Language resource management- semantic annotation framework (semaf) - part 4: Semantic roles (semaf-sr). Standard, Geneva, CH.

ISO-24617-6. (2016). Language resource management- semantic annotation framework (semaf) - part 6:principles of semantic annotation (semaf principles). Standard, Geneva, CH.

ISO-24617-7. (2020). Language resource management-semantic annotation framework (semaf) - part 7: Spatial information. Standard, Geneva, CH.

ISO-24617-9. (2019). Language resource management- semantic annotation framework (semaf) - - part 9: Reference annotation framework (raf). Standard, Geneva, CH.

Kordjamshidi, P., Van Otterlo, M., and Moens, M.-F. (2010). Spatial Role Labeling: Task Definition and Annotation Scheme. In *Proceedings of the Seventh International Conference on Language Resources and Evaluation (LREC'10)*, Valletta, Malta, May. European Language Resources Association (ELRA).

Leal, A., Oliveira, F., and Silvano, P. (2018). Movimento ascendente e descendente em português europeu: os casos dos verbos subir e descer. In *Para Óscar Lopes: Estudos de Linguística*, pages 99–114. Afrontamento.

Lee, K., Fang, A. C., and Pustejovsky, J. (2011). Multilingual verification of the annotation scheme iso-space. In *2011 IEEE Fifth International Conference on Semantic Computing*, pages 449–458.

Lee, K. (2016). An abstract syntax for ISO-Space with its ¡moveLink¿ reformulated. In Harry Bunt, editor, *Proceedings of the LREC 2016 Workshop, 12th Joint ACL–ISO Workshop on Interoperable Semantic Annotation (isa-12)*, pages 28–37. Association for Computational Linguistics.

Mani, I., Hitzeman, J., Richer, J., Harris, D., Quimby, R., and Wellner, B. (2008). SpatialML: Annotation Scheme, Corpora, and Tools. In *Proceedings of the Sixth International Conference on Language Resources and Evaluation (LREC'08)*, Marrakech, Morocco, May. European Language Resources Association (ELRA).

Pustejovsky, J. and Stubbs, A. (2012). *Natural Language Annotation for Machine Learning - a Guide to Corpus-Building for Applications*. O'Reilly.

Pustejovsky, J. and Yocum, Z. (2013). Capturing motion in iso-spacebank. In *ACL 2013*.

Pustejovsky, J. and Yocum, Z. (2014). Image Annotation with ISO-Space: Distinguishing Content from Structure. In *Proceedings of the Ninth International Conference on Language Resources and Evaluation (LREC'14)*, pages 426–431, Reykjavik, Iceland, May. European Language Resources Association (ELRA).

Pustejovsky, J., Moszkowics, J., and Verhagen, M. (2011). ISO-Space: The Annotation of Spatial Information in Language. In *Proceedings of the Sixth Joint ISO - ACL SIGSEM Workshop on Interoperable Semantic Annotation*, pages 1–9. Association for Computational Linguistics.

Pustejovsky, J., Moszkowics, J., and Verhagen, M. (2012). The current status of ISO-Space. In Harry Bunt, editor, *Proceedings of the Seventh Joint ACL–ISO Workshop on Interoperable Semantic Annotation (ISA-7), SRSL3 Workshop on Semantic Representation for Spoken Language, and I2MRT Workshop on Multimodal Resources and Tools*, pages 23–30.

Pustejovsky, J., Kordjamshidi, P., Moens, M.-F., Levine, A., Dworman, S., and Yocum, Z. (2015). SemEval-2015 Task 8: SpaceEval. In *Proceedings of the 9th International Workshop on Semantic Evaluation (SemEval 2015)*, pages 884–894, Denver, Colorado, June. Association for Computational Linguistics.

Pustejovsky, J., Lee, K., and Bunt, H. (2019). The Semantics of ISO-Space. In Harry Bunt, editor, *Proceedings of the Fifteenth Joint ACL - ISO Workshop on Interoperable Semantic Annotation (ISA-15)*, pages 46–53.

Pustejovsky, J., (2017). *ISO-Space: Annotating Static and Dynamic Spatial Information*, pages 989–1024. Springer Netherlands, Dordrecht.

Silvano, P., Leal, A., Silva, F., Cantante, I., Oliveira, F., and Jorge, A. (2021). Developing a multilayer semantic annotation scheme based on ISO standards for the visualization of a newswire corpus. In *Proceedings of the 17th Joint ACL - ISO Workshop on Interoperable Semantic Annotation*, pages 1–13, Groningen, The Netherlands (online), June. Association for Computational Linguistics.

Stenetorp, P., Pyysalo, S., Topić, G., Ohta, T., Ananiadou, S., and Tsujii, J. (2012). Brat: a Web-based Tool for NLP-Assisted Text Annotation. In *Proceedings of the Demonstrations at the 13th Conference of the European Chapter of the Association for Computational Linguistics*, pages 102–107, Avignon, France, April. Association for Computational Linguistics.

Proceedings of ISA-18 Workshop at LREC2022, pages 71–75
Marseille, 20 June 2022

Do machines dream of artificial agreement?

Anna Lindahl
Språkbanken Text
University of Gothenburg
Sweden
anna.lindahl@svenska.gu.se

Abstract

In this paper the (assumed) inconsistency between F1-scores and annotator agreement measures is discussed. This is exemplified in five corpora from the field of argumentation mining. High agreement is important in most annotation tasks and also often deemed important for an annotated dataset to be useful for machine learning. However, depending on the annotation task, achieving high agreement is not always easy. This is especially true in the field of argumentation mining, because argumentation can be complex as well as implicit. There are also many different models of argumentation, which can be seen in the increasing number of argumentation annotated corpora. Many of these reach moderate agreement but are still used in machine learning tasks, reaching high F1-score. In this paper we describe five corpora, in particular how they have been created and used, to see how they have handled disagreement. We find that agreement can be raised post-production, but that more discussion regarding evaluating and calculating agreement is needed. We conclude that standardisation of the models and the evaluation methods could help such discussions.

Keywords: annotation, inter-annotator agreement, argumentation mining, machine learning

1. Introduction

Most tasks in natural language processing require datasets annotated with some information, preferably of high quality, to learn from. The quality of such datasets is often measured by how well the annotators agree on the phenomenon being annotated: an inter-annotator agreement (IAA). The intuition behind this is that if a certain number of people agree upon something then the annotations represent some knowledge which can deemed more reliable, and thus it will be easier for a machine-learning algorithm to learn from the data.

However, in many tasks reaching high IAA is difficult, especially in more complex and possibly more subjective areas. In the field of argumentation mining, which aims to automatically identify and analyze argumentation, this is especially true. Many datasets annotated with argumentation report lower IAA than other tasks in natural language processing. This raises the question of what do with datasets in which the agreement is lower, can this be solved and will they still be useful?

In argumentation mining, there are several examples of corpora which have an IAA on the lower side, but still have been proven useful (that is good results[1]) in machine learning tasks. These results might also indicate that the current measurements of agreement might not be suitable for our tasks and that the agreement measures themselves can be difficult to interpret, something which has been discussed in Artstein and Poesio (2008).

Therefore, in this paper we describe some of these argumentation corpora, in order to explore how the agreement in these corpora has been tackled or how the (assumed) inconsistency can be explained. These corpora where selected as they are all within the same task in argumentation mining and all report moderate agreement but high F1-scores.

First, we give the field of argumentation mining a short introduction. Then, the argumentation corpora are described followed by discussion.

2. Argumentation mining & annotation

Argumentation mining is a relatively young field which aims to develop methods and datasets for automatically identifying argumentation. This is a challenging task, as argumentation can be complex and often implicit. How to annotate argumentation is also a challenge in itself, because argumentation does not have a unified definition which can be applied in all cases or an agreed upon way of modelling it (Van Eemeren et al., 2019; Habernal and Gurevych, 2017).

Nonetheless, the argumentation mining process is often described similarly – first identify the argumentative text, then the argumentation components such as claims and premises. After this step, relations between components and the arguments themselves can be annotated (for example attack or support) (Palau and Moens, 2009; Peldszus and Stede, 2013; Stab and Gurevych, 2017). There are also approaches focusing on argument quality (El Baff et al., 2018) or inferences in argumentation (Visser et al., 2018).

The agreement is often calculated using Cohen's κ, Fleiss' κ or Krippendorff's α, all of them measuring agreement (disagreement) by taking into account agreement (or disagreement) by chance. Values below 0 indicates agreement less than the chance agreement, and 1 indicates perfect agreement. Values be-

[1] What is "good" machine learning results can of course also be up for discussion but we leave that for another paper.

tween 0–1 are usually interpreted using the Landis & Koch scale, which says that results between 0.41–0.60 are moderate and 0.61–0.80 are substantial. As discussed in Artstein and Poesio (2008), the suitability of these measurements for linguistic annotation is not always clear. Duthie et al. (2016) raise the issue of using Cohen's κ when evaluating argumentation, and suggest the CASS-κ technique, however this has not been widely adopted.

The variety in how argumentation is modelled means there is also a great variety in how argumentation is annotated and how it is evaluated (see for example Lawrence and Reed (2020) or Habernal and Gurevych (2017)). This can make it difficult to compare results and datasets, even within similar tasks.

In this paper we focus on corpora annotated with the argumentation components claims and premises, but as we shall see there are variations of how to describe these components. There are also other examples of moderate IAA and higher machine learning results in other areas of argumentation mining Ajjour et al. (2017; Boltužić and Šnajder (2014).

3. Corpora annotated with claims and premises

In this section we will describe examples of argumentation annotated datasets. For each dataset, we will describe the data, annotation scheme and evaluation. Then, the results from a machine learning experiment using the same corpus as training data will be described. The datasets are also described in table 1.

A relatively early (with respect to the field of argumentation mining) argumentation annotated corpus was created by (Rosenthal and McKeown, 2012). This corpus consists of 4,000 sentences, half taken from blogposts from LiveJournal and half from discussions from Wikipedia debate forums. These sentences were annotated, without context, for presence of an opinionated claim. The definition of a claim was that "a claim is a statement that is a belief that can be justified". Two annotators annotated 2,000 sentences from each source, and the agreement is reported as 0.5 Cohen's κ for 633 blogpost sentences and 0.56 Cohen's κ for 997 Wikipedia sentences. The final gold standard was created by the annotators discussing and resolving all their disagreements. The final corpus has a ratio of 60–40% claims–non-claims for the blogposts and 64–36% for Wikipedia.

(Rosenthal and McKeown, 2012) then use logistic regression together with various features such as part of speech, sentiment and punctuation. They run experiments on both balanced and unbalanced versions of the two corpora. The best results on a balanced, combined, version of the corpus is 68.8% accuracy. Interestingly, when training on one domain and applying it to the other, the highest accuracy is achieved, between 74–76% for balanced, and 75–83% for unbalanced datasets.

(Teruel et al., 2018) perform an annotation study in which two annotators annotate major claims, claims and premises, and relations (attack or support) between them, in 7 judgments from the European Court of Human Rights (28,000 words). In their annotation study, they present a methodology for improving annotation guidelines. They loosely follow Toulmin (2003) when defining their components, adapting them according to Stab and Gurevych (2015). They define major claim as: "a general statement expressing the author's stance with respect to the topic under discussion", claim as: "a controversial statement whose acceptance depends on premises that support or attack it" and premise as: "reasons given by the author for supporting or attacking the claims"

While they find that annotators agree whether a sentence contains a span which represents an argumentation component or not (0.77–0.84 Cohen's κ), they agree less on which component is in the span (0.48–0.56 Cohen's κ). The corpus contained 3.0% major claims, 18.2% claims, 26.6% premises and 52.2% non-argumentative components. Noting that there is high disagreement in the major claim category, the authors merge these categories. This increases the agreement to 0.51–0.64 Cohen's κ.

There is no report on how the gold standard was created, but they report that using the system developed by Eger et al. (2017), the automatic classifier makes more mistakes in the categories in which humans disagree more. The corpus is also used for classification by Frau et al. (2019), who report that they use a version of the corpus with only claims and premises. They use a BiLSTM architecture with attention for two tasks: in a paragraph, detect which tokens are part of a claim or not, and likewise, in a paragraph, detect claims and premises. For the first task, they reach an F1-score of 0.82 and the latter 0.68.

In (Haddadan et al., 2019), a corpus of transcripts from US presidential debates between 1960–2016 is presented. The corpus consists of 6601 turns of dialogue, made up of about 34,000 sentences. The debates are annotated with claims and premises, where examples of claims are policies advocated for, judgments about other parties and candidates, stances on controversial subjects or opinions on issues, and premises are "are assertions made by the debaters for supporting their claims (i.e., reasons or justifications)". Three non-expert annotators annotated the debates, and the IAA was determined on a subset of 19 debates which were annotated by all three annotators. IAA was 0.57 κ[2] for sentences containing an argumentation component or not, and 0.4 κ for argumentation components. In order to create a gold-standard, two expert annotators annotated a subset of 6 debates. When resolving disagreement between the non-expert annotators, the annotator which had the highest agreement with the experts were chosen. The resulting corpus has 16,087 claims and

[2]The kind of κ is not reported.

13,434 premises.

This corpus was then used for two classification tasks – argumentation detection and argumentation component detection. The best results for both tasks came from using an LSTM, 0.84 for the first task and 0.67 F1 for the second.

(Schaefer and Stede, 2020) annotate 300 tweet-reply pairs, where the first tweet is seen as a context to the tweet which replies to it. The tweets are in German and all contain the German word for climate. The tweets were annotated with claim and evidence. A claim is described as a standpoint to a topic being discussed, while evidence is a statement which is used to support a standpoint. There were two annotators, and they reached an IAA of 0.55 Cohen's kappa for if a tweet contained a claim and 0.44 for if a tweet contained an evidence. They found that 14% of the tweets contained no argumentation component, 27% contained one argumentation component and 59% more than one component. Of the ones that contained one component, claim was the dominating component. How the gold standard is created is not reported, but the corpus is used for classification. Using different models, they achieve an F1-score of 0.82 for determining if a tweet contains an argument component, and 0.82 and 0.67 for if a tweet contained a claim or a premise, respectively. When classifying spans in tweets in a sequence labelling approach, the F1 for argumentation is 0.72, 0.59 for claims and 0.75 for evidence. Despite evidence having the lowest IAA, the sequence labeling approach worked best for that category.

(Wührl and Klinger, 2021) also annotate tweets, but in English and in the biomedical domain. Their corpus consists of 1200 tweets collected based on keywords from the medical domain. They annotate claims in the tweets following Stab and Gurevych (2017), describing claims as the central component of an argument in which the arguer expresses their conclusion. The claims are further annotated as explicit or implicit. Two annotators annotated the tweets, with 100 of the tweets being annotated by both annotators. The IAA was 0.56 κ for claim or not claim, and 0.48 κ for claims as implicit or explicit. About 44% of the tweets contained a claim.

There is no mention of how the gold standard was produced, but the corpus is used for claim classification. The best macro F1 results are reached with logistic regression for claims–non-claims and is 0.73 for explicit and implicit claims, or no claim, the macro F1 is 0.54 using a pipeline approach. They also report using their twitter corpus as training data and test it on a persuasive essays corpus (Stab and Gurevych, 2017), reaching 0.83 for the claims class.

4. Discussion and Outlook

As we have seen there are several ways the annotation and evaluation of argumentation components can be carried out, as well as machine learning applications. There are also different strategies in solving disagreement.

Most of the above studies revised their annotation and discussed the guidelines in order to increase the agreement and three of the mentioned studies took measures in order to increase the IAA after the annotation. (Rosenthal and McKeown, 2012) had their annotators solve their disagreement between themselves, which resulted in good machine-learning results. Likewise, (Haddadan et al., 2019) solved the disagreement using expert annotators, also reporting good machine learning results. However, while we can assume the expert annotators to be more in agreement with each other (Bayerl and Paul, 2011), we do not know by how much.

(Teruel et al., 2018) merge their annotation categories and increase their IAA, but not to a substantial level. Still, their machine learning results show that their corpus can be used for learning. Finally, for the two last studies we are not told how a gold standard was reached, but the machine learning task show that it is possible to learn from the data. Indeed, all studies described above show that it is possible to either solve disagreement in data or to learn from it anyway.

However, as previously mentioned, the measures of agreement can be difficult to interpret. But if we assume that the mentioned datasets all have not good agreement, we can think of a few, not mutually exclusive, explanations for the good machine learning results:

1. The corpus has been curated in such a way that the agreement has been raised.
2. What the machine-learning learns does not correspond to the original intention of the annotation.
3. The agreement measure is not representative of the "true" agreement.
4. High agreement is not needed in order to learn the task.

We have seen that 1. is indeed possible. Number 2 as an explanation could be due to anything between an unbalanced dataset (although all mentioned datasets here are fairly balanced.) to the machine learning algorithm picking up spurious cues (which relates to the whole field of blackbox nlp, see for example Niven and Kao (2019)). Number 3 would mean that there is agreement in the data which is not captured by the chosen IAA measure or that the scale for judging the IAA is not suitable. As previously stated, the suitability and interpretability of the different agreement measures has been discussed. However, they are still widely used as measure of quality, instead of for example percentage agreement. Perhaps, if the goal is to use the dataset for machine learning, the machine learning results could be included in evaluating the quality of a dataset.

Author	Size	IAA	F1-score
(Rosenthal and McKeown, 2012)	4,000 sent.	0.5–0.55 Cκ (subset)	68–80% accuracy (No F1 reported)
(Teruel et al., 2018)	28,000 words	arg sent.: 0.78–0.88 Cκ arg comp.: 0.48–0.56 Cκ	claim detection: 0.841 arg comp.: 0.704 (Frau et al., 2019)
(Haddadan et al., 2019)	34,013 sent.	arg. sent.: 0.57 κ arg. comp.: 0.4 κ	arg: 0.84 arg comp.: 0.67
(Schaefer and Stede, 2020)	300 tweets	claims: 0.55 Cκ evidence 0.37 Cκ	arg: 0.82 F1 claim detection: 0.82 premise detection: 0.67
(Wührl and Klinger, 2021)	1,200 tweets	claims: 0.56 Cκ explicit or implicit: 0.48 Cκ (subset)	claims: 0.70 non-claims: 0.76

Table 1: Argumentation corpora with moderate IAA.

Number 4 ties in to discussions in Uma et al. (2021) which discuss scenarios where there might be more that one possible interpretation of a gold label and how to learn from that. As two of the datasets provide the raw annotations, approaches mentioned Uma et al. (2021) would be also be a potential future research. Number 4 also raises the question of whether there is a lower limit of an IAA for the data to be useful.

All of above the explanations open up for more studies, but especially calls for more discussion of IAA in relation to machine learning results, such as the discussion in (Teruel et al., 2018).

To conclude, we have seen that it is possible to achieve good results on classification tasks even with lower IAA. This raises several interesting questions, such as what do the machine algorithm learn from or what is a sufficient IAA, but also highlights the need for discussing these issues. In particular, it calls for more discussion regarding agreement, how to calculate it and how to use it. It also shows the need for standardisation in many of the aspects in argumentation mining – the annotation, evaluation and use of datasets.

5. Bibliographical References

Ajjour, Y., Chen, W.-F., Kiesel, J., Wachsmuth, H., and Stein, B. (2017). Unit segmentation of argumentative texts. In *Proceedings of the 4th Workshop on Argument Mining*, pages 118–128, Copenhagen, Denmark, September. Association for Computational Linguistics.

Artstein, R. and Poesio, M. (2008). Inter-coder agreement for computational linguistics. *Computational linguistics*, 34(4):555–596.

Bayerl, P. S. and Paul, K. I. (2011). What determines inter-coder agreement in manual annotations? A meta-analytic investigation. *Computational Linguistics*, 37(4):699–725.

Boltužić, F. and Šnajder, J. (2014). Back up your stance: Recognizing arguments in online discussions. In *Proceedings of the First Workshop on Argumentation Mining*, pages 49–58.

Duthie, R., Lawrence, J., Budzynska, K., and Reed, C. (2016). The cass technique for evaluating the performance of argument mining. In *Proceedings of the Third Workshop on Argument Mining (ArgMining2016)*, pages 40–49.

Eger, S., Daxenberger, J., and Gurevych, I. (2017). Neural end-to-end learning for computational argumentation mining. In *Proceedings of ACL 2017 (Volume 1: Long Papers)*, pages 11–22, Vancouver. ACL.

El Baff, R., Wachsmuth, H., Al Khatib, K., and Stein, B. (2018). Challenge or empower: Revisiting argumentation quality in a news editorial corpus. In *Proceedings of the 22nd Conference on Computational Natural Language Learning*, pages 454–464.

Frau, J., Teruel, M., Alemany, L. A., and Villata, S. (2019). Different flavors of attention networks for argument mining. In *The Thirty-Second International Flairs Conference*.

Habernal, I. and Gurevych, I. (2017). Argumentation mining in user-generated web discourse. *Computational Linguistics*, 4(1).

Lawrence, J. and Reed, C. (2020). Argument mining: A survey. *Computational Linguistics*, 45(4):765–818.

Niven, T. and Kao, H.-Y. (2019). Probing neural network comprehension of natural language arguments. In *Proceedings of the 57th Annual Meeting of the Association for Computational Linguistics*, pages 4658–4664, Florence, Italy, July. Association for Computational Linguistics.

Palau, R. M. and Moens, M.-F. (2009). Argumentation mining: the detection, classification and structure of arguments in text. In *Proceedings of ICAIL 2009*, page 98, Barcelona. ACM Press.

Peldszus, A. and Stede, M. (2013). From argument diagrams to argumentation mining in texts: A survey.

Int. J. Cogn. Inform. Nat. Intell., 7(1):1–31.

Stab, C. and Gurevych, I. (2015). Guidelines for annotating argumentation structures in persuasive essays. *Ubiquitous Knowledge Processing Lab (UKP Lab) Computer Science Department, Technische Universität Darmstadt.*

Stab, C. and Gurevych, I. (2017). Parsing argumentation structures in persuasive essays. *Computational Linguistics*, 43(3):619–659.

Toulmin, S. E. (2003). *The uses of argument.* Cambridge university press.

Uma, A. N., Fornaciari, T., Hovy, D., Paun, S., Plank, B., and Poesio, M. (2021). Learning from disagreement: A survey. *Journal of Artificial Intelligence Research*, 72:1385–1470.

Van Eemeren, F. H., Grootendorst, R., and Kruiger, T. (2019). Handbook of argumentation theory. In *Handbook of Argumentation Theory*. De Gruyter Mouton.

Visser, J., John, L., Jean, W., and Chris, R. (2018). Revisiting computational models of argument schemes: Classification, annotation, comparison. In *Proceedings of the 7th International Conference on Computational Models of Argument (COMMA 2018).*

6. Language Resource References

Haddadan, Shohreh and Cabrio, Elena and Villata, Serena. (2019). *Yes, we can! Mining Arguments in 50 Years of US Presidential Campaign Debates*. ACL.

Rosenthal, Sara and McKeown, Kathy. (2012). *Detecting Opinionated Claims in Online Discussions.*

Schaefer, Robin and Stede, Manfred. (2020). *Annotation and detection of arguments in tweets.*

Teruel, Milagro and Cardellino, Cristian and Cardellino, Fernando and Alonso Alemany, Laura and Villata, Serena. (2018). *Increasing Argument Annotation Reproducibility by Using Inter-annotator Agreement to Improve Guidelines.* ELRA.

Wührl, Amelie and Klinger, Roman. (2021). *Claim Detection in Biomedical Twitter Posts.* Association for Computational Linguistics.

Proceedings of ISA-18 Workshop at LREC2022, pages 76–80
Marseille, 20 June 2022

CroaTPAS: A Survey-based Evaluation

Costanza Marini
[1]University of Pavia, [2]University of Bergamo
[1]University of Pavia, Dipartimento di Studi Umanistici, Strada Nuova 65, 27100 Pavia
[2]University of Bergamo, Dipartimento di Lingue, Letterature e Culture Moderne, via Salvecchio 19, 24129 Bergamo

costanza.marini@unibg.it

Abstract

The Croatian Typed Predicate Argument Structures resource (CroaTPAS, Marini and Ježek, 2019) is a Croatian/English bilingual digital dictionary of corpus-derived verb valency structures, whose argument slots have been annotated with Semantic Types labels following the CPA methodology (Hanks, 2013). CroaTPAS is tailor-made to represent verb polysemy and currently contains 180 Croatian verbs for a total of 683 different verbs senses. In order to evaluate the resource both in terms of identified Croatian verb senses, and of the English descriptions explaining them, an online survey based on a multiple-choice sense disambiguation task was devised, pilot tested and distributed among respondents following a snowball sampling methodology. Answers from 30 respondents were collected and compared against a yardstick set of answers in line with CroaTPAS's sense distinctions. Jaccard similarity index was used as a measure of agreement. Since the multiple-choice items respondents answered to were based on a representative selection of CroaTPAS verbs, they allowed for a generalization of the results to the whole of the resource.

Keywords: Croatian, pattern, survey

1. Introduction

CroaTPAS (Marini and Ježek, 2019) is a Croatian/English bilingual digital dictionary focusing on representing verb polysemy. It currently contains the semantically annotated corpus-derived verb valency structures of a selection of 180 Croatian verbs, which will be made freely available online by the end of 2022.

In order to evaluate the overall goodness of the resource, both in terms of adequacy of the identified Croatian verb senses, and of the English descriptions explaining them, an online survey mainly consisting of a multiple-choice sense disambiguation task was devised, pilot tested and later distributed among candidate respondents using a snowball sampling methodology.

The items respondents were presented with contained a selection of verbs deemed representative of the whole resource, thus allowing for a generalization of the results to the whole of CroaTPAS.

2. The resource

The Croatian Typed Predicate Argument Structures resource (CroaTPAS, Marini and Ježek, 2019) is a digital lexicographic resource containing a collection of corpus-derived Croatian verb valency structures, whose argument slots have been manually annotated with a hierarchy of semantic labels called System of Semantic Types (Ježek 2019).

Like its Italian sister project T-PAS (Ježek et al., 2014), CroaTPAS is primarily conceived for representing verb polysemy, since each semantically typed verb argument structure in its inventory – henceforth called *pattern* – corresponds to a different verb sense. In its inventory, the resource currently contains 180 Croatian verbs, for a total of 683 different patterns.

2.1 Generative Lexicon Theory

According to Generative Lexicon Theory, which is the shared theoretical framework both resources rely on (Pustejovsky, 1995; Pustejovsky and Ježek, 2008), verb meaning is conceived as "contextually generated" by the interaction between the semantics of the verb and that of its arguments (Figure 1).

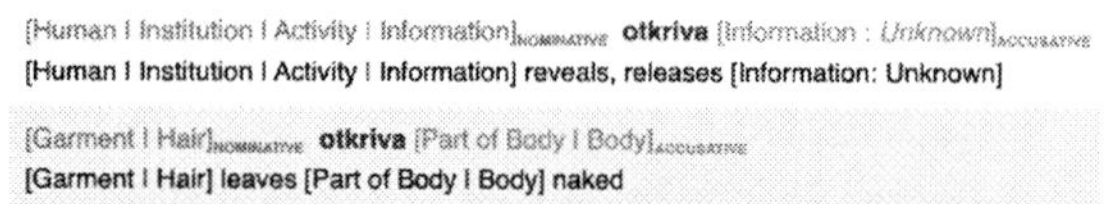

Figure 1: CroaTPAS patterns encoding two of the meanings of the verb otkrivati (Eng. 'to reveal')

For instance, all the corpus lines linked to the first pattern of the Croatian verb *otkrivati* (Eng. 'to reveal') above contain direct objects that may be classified as unknown pieces of [Information], thus generating the meaning of "releasing that information". On the other hand, all the corpus lines containing a [Garment] or [Hair] as subject and a direct object typed as [Part of Body] or [Body] generate the meaning of "leaving that body part naked".

2.2 CPA Methodology

The resource methodology is a customized version of Corpus Pattern Analysis (Hanks, 2013), a lexicographic methodology resting on the idea that meaning should be mapped onto its prototypical contexts of use.

CPA usually requires the following four steps: 1) 250 corpus lines are randomly sampled for each verb from a reference corpus, in this case, the Croatian Web as Corpus (Ljubešić and Klubička, 2014), a web-crawled reference corpus of standard Croatian containing 1.2 billion tokens; 2) the different verb senses are identified by the lexicographer; 3) pattern strings are created in a pattern editing environment labelling argument slots with the appropriate Semantic Types and, finally, 4) numbers are assigned to the corpus lines exemplifying each identified pattern, so that each semantically tagged valency structure is justified by corpus evidence.

In CroaTPAS, underneath each pattern string, users will also be presented with an English definition of the verb meaning portrayed above, as you can see in Figure 1. These definitions go by the name of "sense descriptions" and contain the same Semantic Types used in the corresponding pattern string. They were written in English in order to make CroaTPAS a bilingual online resource available to Croatian language learners.

3. The survey

To evaluate the overall goodness of both the identified verb senses stored in CroaTPAS, and the English sense descriptions elucidating them, it was decided to administer an online multiple-choice questionnaire aimed at native speakers of Croatian with a good command of the English language, as well as to individuals with native-like Croatian proficiency.

In the multiple-choice section of the survey, respondents had to carry out a verb sense disambiguation task on a selection of 91 corpus examples with GDEX values (Kilgarriff et al. 2008) higher than 0.8 extracted from the Croatian Web as Corpus via the Sketch Engine (Kilgarriff et al. 2014). GDEX is an algorithm able to identify Good Dictionary EXamples by assigning corpus sentences a score ranging from 0 to 1 based on their lexical and syntactic complexity.

Each example featured one of the recorded verb senses of the CroaTPAS verb under scrutiny and was followed by English alternative sense explanations to choose from, corresponding to the array of English sense descriptions available in CroaTPAS underneath the patterns of that specific verb. Here is an example of multiple-choice item.

(0) Kako *podnijeti* ljetne vrućine, a osjećati se ugodno?[1]

o [Human | Human Group] can stand, endures [Anything: Negative]
o [Human | Institution] submits, files [Document | Request | Offer]

Before starting data collection, the questionnaire was briefly piloted by a group of two respondents, whose feedback contributed to improving the survey (see § 3.3).

As for the sampling method, the choice fell upon *snowball sampling* (Johnstone Young 2016: 169, Dörnyei 2007: 98), which consists in contacting a small group of good candidate participants, who are then asked to generate a chain reaction forwarding the survey to other appropriate candidate participants among their contacts. Given this choice of method, the evaluation survey was presented as a Google Form, i.e., a free online survey which can be built using Google Suite and easily forwarded via link.

All instructions were given in English to ensure that respondents did realize the need to be proficient not only in Croatian but also in English to be able to carry out the verb sense disambiguation task that constitutes the main bulk of the survey.

It was also decided not to mention the name of the resource in any part of the survey, nor to go into technical details when it comes to verb polysemy, so as not to distract respondents from the task at hand.

Special attention was devoted to thanking and reassuring respondents of the confidentiality and anonymity of their answers, as well as of the availability of the author to answer any possible question concerning the project. To comply with the ethical principle of informed consent, respondents were explicitly asked to submit the form only if they accepted that their anonymous answers were going to be used for research purposes

[1] "How to *endure* summer heat and feel comfortable?"

3.1 Background Information

In light of the fact that asking for demographic information at the start of a questionnaire can be off-putting (Fife-Schaw 2006), background questions were asked after the multiple-choice section. Questions included both open questions, multiple-choice items, and three sentence completion items involving semantic differential scales (Dörnyei 2007: 105). Two of the latter were designed to let respondents complete statements concerning their language proficiency in English and Croatian by marking a 5-step continuum between two polar adjectives, namely *basic* and *excellent*, in order "to elicit a more meaningful answer than a simple question" (*ibidem*, 107).

3.2 Verb Selection

Out of the 180 verbs in CroaTPAS, 32 were excluded since they only feature one sense and could thus not be used in a sense disambiguation task such as the one devised for the survey. To provide respondents with corpus examples from a representative selection of CroaTPAS verbs, the 148 remaining entries were divided by pattern number as well as aspect, and percentages were subsequently calculated for each verb class.

To guarantee a verb selection representative of the whole resource, we decided to keep the percentages fixed and determine how many verbs would have to be chosen for each class given an arbitrary total of 20 verbs. Given their paucity, three biaspectual verbs were included by default in the poll to guarantee their evaluation. Table 1 provides a complete overview of the final selection of verbs included in the survey after pilot testing it.

3.3 Pilot testing

Following Johnstone Young (2016: 176), the questionnaire was piloted before beginning with data collection. The pilot group included two respondents, who were asked to complete the draft survey and reflect on its design, the wording of items and the clarity of the example sentences. The items from the background information section were deemed clear and able to capture the background of both respondents.

Both appreciated the presence of a non-binary gender option, and both agreed that asking for participants who had either a native or "a native-like proficiency of Croatian" was a good way to include not only foreigners, but also Serbian, Bosnian and Montenegrin native speakers.

The most important amendment made after the pilot testing phase was eliminating all multiple-choice items based on verbs with 7 and 11 senses, since both participants found that skimming through multiple-choice lists containing that many senses took too hard a toll on their attention levels. Moreover, since the survey was deemed quite long, it was decided to remove the items for one of the 5-pattern imperfective verbs, too.

The following Table offers an overview of the final 19 verbs included in CroaTPAS's evaluation survey after pilot testing, corresponding to a total of 91 items.

Perfective	N	verbs
2P	2	podnijeti, prekinuti
3P	2	isključiti, sletjeti
4P	2	otkriti, ubiti
5P	1	prodati
6P	1	popiti
Imperfective	**N**	**verbs**
2P	2	gostiti, željeti
3P	2	čitati, kupovati
4P	2	osnovati, slati
5P	1	voziti
6P	1	žderati
Biaspectual	**N**	**verbs**
2P	1	informirati
3P	1	napredovati
5P	1	kontrolirati

Table 1: The final selection of verbs included in CroaTPAS's evaluation survey after pilot testing

Following the respondents' feedback, several of the sentences included in the multiple-choice items were also discarded and replaced with shorter and simpler sentences. Despite their high GDEX scores, in fact, these sentences were identified as problematic since they either contained anaphoric pronouns pointing at referents outside sentence limits, thus taking away the readers' focus from verb meaning, or were deemed syntactically too complex, for example by featuring the verb under scrutiny only at the end of the sentence.

4. Results

In a period of approximately 2 months, we were able to collect answers from 30 respondents, which was deemed a reasonable sample to carry out the evaluation on.

4.1 Respondent Sample

The average age of our 30 respondents is 35.4 years: 12 (40%) are in their 20s, 7 (23.3%) in their 30s, 7 (23.3%) in their 40s, 3 (10%) in their 50s and one (3.3%) in her 60s. Gender-wise, 20 respondents identify as female, 9 as male and 1 as non-binary.

As for educational level, 83.3% of the participants in the study has attended or is currently attending university, while 16.7% holds a secondary school diploma. Of the university-trained respondents, those who decided to specify their field of interest, 87% have a Humanities background (Croatian language and literature, Linguistics, Foreign Languages, Social studies, Political Sciences, Theatre) and 13% Hard sciences (IT, Engineering and Chemistry).

All respondents except one consider Croatian as one of their native languages. All of them grew up in either Croatia or Bosnia and Herzegovina except for four, who were either born in or moved to an English-speaking country quite early on. Two of these four respondents still live abroad (included the only non-native speaker of Croatian), while the rest lives in Croatia.

4.2 Jaccard Index of Similarity

For what concerns the multiple-choice section of the survey, each of the respondents' answer sheets was compared against a yardstick set of answers in line with CroaTPAS's sense distinctions. To provide a measure of how similar each of the 30 survey answers was to the yardstick, we calculated the Jaccard index of similarity.

The Jaccard similarity between two sets A and B is defined as "the ratio of the number of elements in the intersection of A and B over the number of elements in the union of A and B" (Zumel and Mount 2014: 184).

Given that respondents were presented with 91 multiple-choice items, each of the 30 survey answer sheets was assigned a similarity score ranging from 0 to 91 depending on the number of multiple-choice answers in line with the answers from CroaTPAS's yardstick answer sheet. That number was then divided by 91 and multiplied by 100, thus returning a normalised Jaccard index expressing the similarity score (%) between each collected answer sheet and CroaTPAS's annotation.

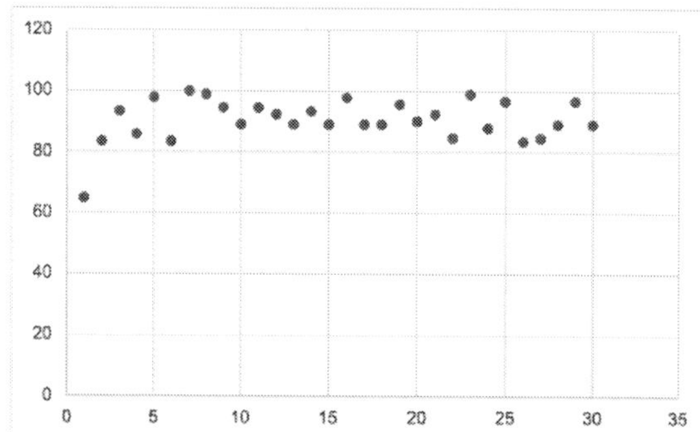

Figure 2: Dispersion plot of the similarity scores (%) of the 30 survey answers sheets against CroaTPAS's yardstick

As you can see from the dispersion plot above, all survey answer sheets but one range between 100% and 83.51% similarity. The only answer sheet scoring a lower similarity value (64.84%) was identified by Rosner's Test[2] as a possible outlier both at 5% and 1% significance and subsequently discarded.

Therefore, since the mean similarity score of the remaining 29 survey answer sheets stands at 91.36% (± 5.12) and data sets with a normalised Jaccard similarity above 85% can be considered highly stable (Zumel & Mount 2014: 184), we can conclude that the collected survey answers form a proper cluster showing a high level of agreement with the yardstick answer representative of CroaTPAS's sense distinctions.

4.3 Similarity Scores and Polysemy

After assessing the overall similarity scores of the collected survey answer sheets with the yardstick, we decided to group together the individual multiple-choice answers in five classes (2P, 3P, 4P, 5P and 6P) according to the degree of polysemy (two, three, four, five or six senses) expressed by the verb they portray and then calculate five new sets of similarity scores comparing them to the five corresponding

[2] Rosner's Test was run using the statistical software ProUCL 5.0

groups of yardstick answers representing the sense distinctions made in CroaTPAS.

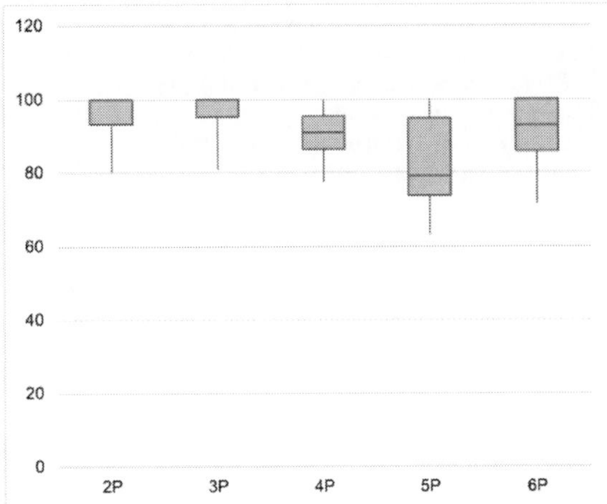

Figure 3: Box plots showing the different distribution of similarity scores (%) in survey answers referring to verbs with a different degree of polysemy

As you can see from the box plot in Figure 3, the similarity score of the survey answers does vary according to the number of senses expressed by the verbs they refer to. Participants tend to be more in line with the yardstick answers when it comes to less polysemous verbs, scoring a mean similarity value of 95.5% (± 5.94) in the 2P answer class and 95.89% (± 5.2) similarity in the 3P answer class. On the other hand, when the verb is more polysemous, the mean similarity scores of the answers decrease slightly to 91.38% (± 6.8) for answers to items containing verbs with four senses, 83.3% (±11.43) for answers to items on five-sense verbs and 91.13% (± 8.89) for those to items containing six-sense verbs.

Bearing in mind that mean similarity scores for all answer classes remain higher than 80%, thus showing a high level of agreement with the yardstick annotation regardless of verb polysemy, we might venture at tracing this difference back to the fact that disambiguating meanings when given more options is more demanding than when one is given fewer options to choose from.

4.4 Similarity Scores and Gender

To provide further support to CroaTPAS's evaluation, we divided the similarity scores of the survey answers by gender. Given that only one respondent identified as non-binary, only two similarity score distributions were compared, namely the one corresponding to the answers given by female respondents (19) and the other corresponding to the answers given by male participants (9). Two box plots were drawn for to provide a graphical representation of each population (Figure 4).

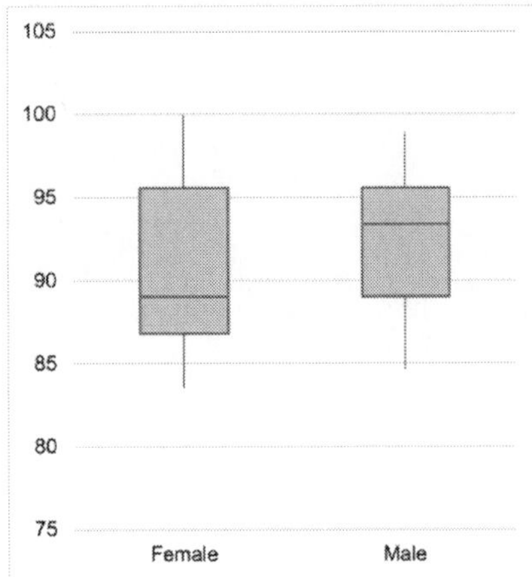

Figure 4: Box plots showing the different distribution of similarity scores (%) in survey answers by gender

As you can see, the two box plots are quite similar: the mean similarity score for survey answers provided by women respondents is 90.80 % (± 5.46), while the mean similarity score of male respondents 92.80 % (± 4.60). However, to assess the possible presence of a statistically significant gender bias, we ran a t-Test for two independent means, after making sure that both populations qualify as normally distributed using the Kolmogorov-Smirnov Test of Normality.

As it turns out, there is no significant difference for gender between the two populations, since the computed t-value is 1.02785, which is lower than 2.0555, the critical value for 26 degrees of freedom and 10% level of significance (5% in each tail).

4.5 Similarity Scores and English Level

As in the case of gender, it was decided to investigate the possible influence of the English language proficiency on the recorded similarity scores. This was the reason why participants were asked to rate their level of English in the first place.

The box plots in Figure 5 show the different distribution of similarity scores according to the different levels of English language skills respondents declare to possess. Only one participant gave themselves 1/5 on the semantic differential scale provided in the online survey and was thus discarded. Having already excluded the outlier, the remaining 28 respondents distribute on three distinct self-assessed language levels: 5 on level 3, 12 on level 4 and 11 on level 5. The mean similarity scores for the three levels are all quite high, standing at 92.53% (± 5.46), 91.21% (± 5.62) and 91.71% (± 4.46), respectively.

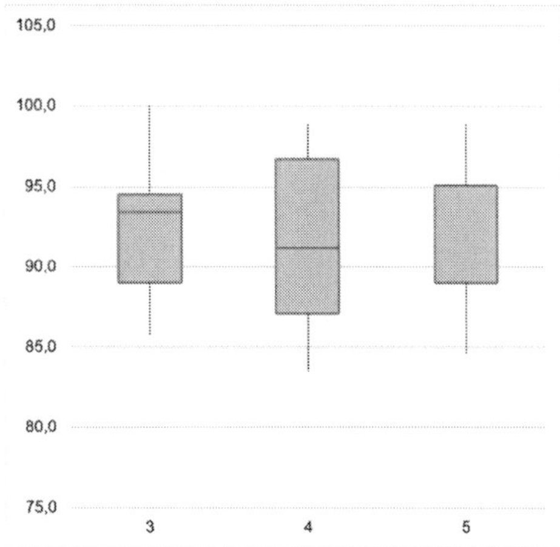

Figure 5: Box plots showing the different distribution of similarity scores (%) by self-assessed level of English

After ascertaining that all populations qualify as normally distributed, t-Tests were run between the similarity scores associated to levels 3 and 4, levels 3 and 5 and levels 5 and 4, which returned the following t-values: 0.44395, 0.31856 and 0.23454. The corresponding critical values of t for 15, 14 and 21 degrees of freedom at 10% level of significance (5% in each tail) are 2.1314, 3.1448 and 2.0796.

Since in all three cases, computed t-values are well below the corresponding critical values, we can conclude there is no statistically significant influence in terms of the self-assessed English language skills possessed by respondents on their sense-disambiguation task results.

This may either mean that asking respondents to self-evaluate their English language proficiency is not a good indicator of their actual English knowledge or that the English sense descriptions provided as multiple-choice options in the sense-disambiguation section of the survey were sufficiently clear to guarantee an effective meaning disambiguation regardless of the respondents' English language skills.

5. Conclusions

In conclusion, the attempt at evaluating the CroaTPAS resource generalising on the results of an online multiple-choice Google Form survey devised on a selection of verbs representative of the whole resource gave very good results.

In a period of approximately two months, 30 answer sheets were collected through a snowball sampling methodology. To provide an agreement metric between the respondents' answers and CroaTPAS's verb sense distinctions, the participants' answers were compared against a yardstick set of answers in line with CroaTPAS and a normalised Jaccard index of similarity was subsequently calculated.

After discarding one respondent, the mean similarity score of the remaining 29 was calculated at 91.36% (± 5.12). Since data sets with a Jaccard similarity above 85% can be considered highly stable (Zumel & Mount 2014: 184), the collected survey answers qualify as a single cluster with a high level of agreement with CroaTPAS's annotation of sense distinctions.

The distribution of similarity scores is not found to vary depending on gender nor on the respondents' English language skills.

6. Bibliographical References

Dörnyei, Z. (2007). *Research Methods in Applied Linguistics: Quantitative, Qualitative and Mixed Methodologies*. Oxford: Oxford University Press.

Hanks, P. (2013). *Lexical Analysis: Norms and Exploitations*. Cambridge: The MIT Press.

Fife-Schaw, C. (2006). Questionnaire Design. In Breakwell, G. M. et al. *Research Methods in Psychology* (3rd ed.). London: Sage.

Ježek, E., Magnini, B., Feltracco, A., Bianchini, A., and Popescu, O. (2014). T-PAS: A resource of Typed Predicate Argument Structures for linguistic analysis and semantic processing. In *Proceedings of the 9th conference on International Language Resources and Evaluation (LREC)*. Reykjavik, Iceland.

Ježek, E. (2019). Sweetening Ontologies Cont'd: Aligning bottom-up with top-down ontologies. In *Proceedings of CREOL 2019*. Graz, Austria.

Johnstone Young, T. (2016). Questionnaires and Surveys. In Zhu, H. (Ed.) Research Methods in Intercultural Communication : A Practical Guide, 165-181.

Kilgarriff, A., Husák, M., McAdam, K., Rundell, M., and Rychlý, P. (2008). GDEX: automatically finding good dictionary examples in a corpus. *Proceedings of the 13th EURALEX International Congress*. Barcelona, Spain.

Kilgarriff, A., Baisa, V., Busta, J., Jakubícek, M., Kovár, V., Michelfeit, J., Rychlý, P., & Suchomel, V. (2014). The Sketch Engine: ten years on. *Lexicography*, 1(1), 7-36.

Ljubešić, N. and F. Klubička (2014). {bs, hr, sr} WaC – web corpora of Bosnian, Croatian and Serbian. In *Proceedings of the 9th Web as Corpus Workshop*.

Marini, C. and Ježek, E. (2019). CROATPAS: Resource of Corpus-derived Typed Predicate Argument Structures for Croatian. In *Proceedings of the 6th Italian Conference on Computational Linguistics (CLiC-it)*. Bari, Italy.

Pustejovsky, J. (1995). *The Generative Lexicon*. Cambridge: The MIT Press.

Pustejovsky, J. and Ježek, E. (2008). Semantic Coercion in Language: Beyond Distributional Analysis. *Italian Journal of Linguistics*, 20: 181-214.

Zumel, N., and Mount, J. (2014). *Practical data science with R*. Shelter Island, NY: Manning Publications Co.

Proceedings of ISA-18 Workshop at LREC2022, pages 81–85
Marseille, 20 June 2022

Simplifying Semantic Annotations of SMCalFlow

Joram Meron
Telepathy Labs GmbH
36 Militärstrasse, Zurich, Switzerland
joram.meron@telepathy.ai

Abstract

SMCalFlow (Semantic Machines et al., 2020) is a large corpus of semantically detailed annotations of task-oriented natural dialogues. The annotations use a dataflow approach, in which the annotations are programs which represent user requests. Despite the availability, size and richness of this annotated corpus, it has seen only very limited use in dialogue systems research work, at least in part due to the difficulty in understanding and using the annotations. To address these difficulties, this paper suggests a simplification of the SMCalFlow annotations, as well as releases code needed to inspect the execution of the annotated dataflow programs, which should allow researchers of dialogue systems an easy entry point to experiment with various dataflow based implementations and annotations.

Keywords: Semantic annotation, dialogue, dataflow

1. Introduction

As in many other natural language processing tasks, dialogue systems have achieved impressive advances due to the use of machine learning techniques. These techniques typically require large amounts of high quality annotated data in order to ensure that the resulting models will be able to generalize correctly to unseen input. Since the models used by dialogue systems need to also learn the effect of previous turns in the dialogue context (as opposed to models which operate on isolated sentences), even larger amounts of training data are needed.

Training data for dialogue systems typically includes the natural language utterances of the user ("request") and agent ("answer"), as well as some structured data representing the state of the dialogue after the turn (including any additional actions affected by the agent). While the user input can be collected from naive users (e.g. using crowd sourcing platforms), the agent response (both natural language and structured data) need skilled annotators which have been trained specifically for the task.

Due to these difficulties, the number , and size, of available datasets for training dialogue systems has been very limited - a few hundreds or thousands of dialogues only, limiting the type of models which can be used. MultiWOZ (Budzianowski et al., 2018), with 10K dialogues and 70K turns was until recently the largest available set, and is being widely used in many research works.

More recently, SMCalFlow (Semantic Machines et al., 2020) was released, comprising of more than 40K dialogues (totalling more than 155K turns) of natural (non-scripted) task-oriented user-agent interactions in several domains (calendar events, weather, places and people), with semantically rich annotation.

The Dialogues were collected via a Wizard-of-Oz process. At each turn, a crowdworker acting as the user was presented with a dialogue as context and asked to append a new utterance. An annotator acting as the agent labelled the utterance, and then selected a natural-language response from a set of candidates produced by the language generation model. Annotators were provided with detailed guidelines containing example annotations and information about available library functions.

Despite the size of this dataset, and the high level of detail given by the annotations, it was not adopted by the dialogue systems research community. The assumption in this paper is that this is the result, at least in part, of the difficulty in understanding and using this dataset by the research community. This difficulty is due to two factors: 1) The annotation scheme is complex, and lacks sufficient documentation to explain it, and 2) tools to inspect and verify that the annotations are correct.

This paper addresses these difficulties by 1) suggesting a simplified annotation scheme, which, hopefully is easier to understand, and 2) releasing the necessary code to inspect the annotation results. It is hoped that with these contributions, the research community will be encourage to explore and exploit potential of this rich dataset.

2. Dataflow Dialogues

SMCalFlow uses dataflow (DF) computational graphs, composed of a rich set of both general and application specific functions (see figures 1 and 4), to represent the user requests as rich compositional (hierarchical) expressions. These computational graphs can be executed, which results in manipulating the computational graphs, generating an answer (possibly an error message), and optionally producing some side effects through API's to external services (e.g. updating the user's calendar appointments on an external database). The prominent features of this paradigm are:

- The dialogue history is represented as a set of graphs, where each computational graph typically represents one user turn.
- It has a *refer* operation to search over the current and previous computational graphs (as well as external resources) which allows easy look-up and re-use of graph nodes which occurred previously in the dialogue.
- It has a *revise* operation which allows modification and reuse of previous computations
- It has an exception mechanism which allows convenient interaction with the user (e.g. asking for missing information, and resuming the computation once the information is supplied).

These features correspond to essential phenomena in natural conversations (referring to previous turns, modifying previous requests, reacting to wrong information, etc.), which allows the system to effectively handle these kinds of user requests.

3. Simplifying SMCalFlow

In this work, a simplified annotation is presented, with the motivation to reduce the effort on the annotator/reader, without increasing the learning effort for the machine translation models used to convert the users' natural language requests to the target annotation format.
As described below, this simplification requires some additional logic to be implemented in the execution engine, as well as in the individual functions, but this additional logic is typically trivial.
The starting point of this work is SMCalFlow, with its original annotation style. Because of its size, and the limited resources available in this work, manual modification of individual annotations were not feasible. Instead, the modifications had to be done fully automatically, using a programmatic solution to do the conversion. The consequences of this decision are:

- The new annotations are still tied to the original ones, so some of the design decisions made by the original annotators are difficult to change (as opposed to the case where the new annotation would start from scratch).
- Specifically, any mistakes or anomalies in the original annotations are carried over to the simplified annotations.
- An automatic conversion mechanism had to be created and configured to convert the annotations correctly.

While DF is not inherently complicated, finding a good design is a challenging task. A novel aspect of this challenge is the need for the design to function correctly within the DF paradigm (e.g. use the *refer* and *revise* operators). Indeed, one of the motivations of this work is the hope that the community can suggest interesting new designs, which can serve as templates for further applications.

3.1. Simplification Mechanism

The simplification was performed by implementing a set of tree transformation rules, which convert specified sub-trees of the original expressions into simplified sub-trees. The transformation code is part of the release, and can be used to replicate the work reported here.
The simplification is applied to the whole dataset, resulting in a simplified dataset, which can then be fed into the exact same machine translation training and evaluation pipeline used in the original paper.
For convenience, the simplified format uses Python style expressions (as opposed to the Lisp style S-expressions in the original dataset), as this format is generally more familiar (the released system itself is written in Python).

3.2. Simplification Approach

The design principles for the simplifications were:

1. Retain only necessary information
2. Avoid explicit logical steps
3. Move logic from the annotation to the implementation of the individual functions
4. Group and reuse repeating sequences of functions
5. Relax strict type constraints
6. Reduce unnecessary compositions

Practically this means: Try to omit any information which can be *deterministically* inferred - keep only information which can not be inferred. Specifically, logical steps which can be inferred from context, are moved from the annotation into the implementation of the functions. For example:

- Explicit type casts which are clear from the context can be omitted.
- When needed information is missing in the user input, but can be inferred from the computation, the simplified annotation should leave the inference of the missing information to the function implementation.
- The simplified annotation tries to avoid fragments of the original annotation which serve only "formal" purposes, and instead tries to style the annotation to be closer to a more natural/comprehensible description of the user requests (and in general be closer to the surface form of the user request, as can be seen in the examples).

Below are examples of original vs. simplified annotations.

```
(Yield
  :output (DeleteCommitEventWrapper
    :event (DeletePreflightEventWrapper
      :id (:id
        (singleton
          (:results
            (FindEventWrapperWithDefaults
              :constraint (EventOnDate
                :date (Tomorrow)
                :event (Constraint[Event]
                  :attendees (AttendeeListHasRecipient
                    :recipient (FindManager
                      :recipient (Execute
                        :intension (refer
                          (extensionConstraint
                            (RecipientWithNameLike
                              :constraint (Constraint[Recipient])
                              :name #(PersonName "John"))))))))))))))))
```

Figure 1: Example 1 - original annotation

```
DeleteEvent(
  AND(
    starts_at(
      Tomorrow()),
    with_attendee(
      FindManager(#John))))
```

Figure 2: Example 1 - simplified annotation

3.2.1. Example 1

The user's request is:
`"Delete the meeting with John's supervisor tomorrow".`
Figures 1 and 2 show the original and simplified annotations for this request. Figure 3 show the annotations as computational graphs.
This example illustrates a few of the simplification ideas:

- Computational steps which always appear together are bundled into one step: *'DeletePreflightEventWrapper'* and *'DeleteCommitEventWrapper'* correspond to two sub steps of the act of deleting an event. Here, they are simplify by combining them into one step *'DeleteEvent'*.

- Relax strict type constraints in the annotation. In the original annotation, *'DeletePreflightEventWrapper'* can accept only an integer input (representing the unique id of the event to be deleted). In the simplified version, the implementation of the *'DeletePreflightEventWrapper'* can handle additional types of input, by calling the necessary type conversion, i.e.: if the input is an *'Event'* type, then extract its *'Event.id'* value, and if the input is a set of events, then additionally invoke a call to the *'singleton'* function.

- Avoid explicit logical steps. In the original annotation, the process of searching for a person is an explicit part of the annotation (see the input to the *'FindManager'* function). In the simplified annotation, this logic is added to the implementation of *'FindManager'* , so the annotation can be simply *'FindManager(John)*.

- Avoid unnecessary compositions and annotations which serve only "formal" purpose. In the original annotation, *'RecipientWithNameLike'* implements a compositional pattern, where one of the inputs is an empty constraint, which is dropped in the simplified annotation (in this case, the whole surrounding block is also removed).

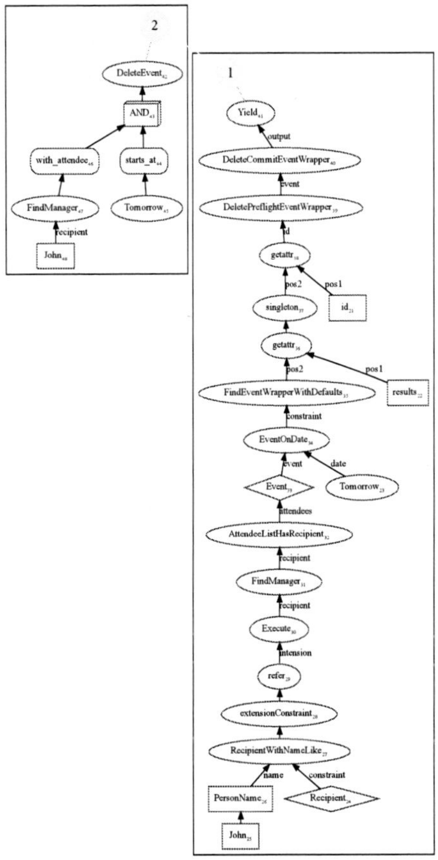

Figure 3: Example 1 - original and simplified annotations shown as graphs

3.2.2. Example 2

The user's request is:
`"I want John, Emily, John's supervisor and Bob to attend".`
Figures 4 and 5 show the original and simplified annotations for this request.
This example illustrates some simplification ideas:

- Simplification of the assignment construct, avoiding unnecessary assignments (which are used only once) - in this example, variable *x1* is used only once, so it is substituted directly into the main expression.

- Reducing the use of compositions, in favour of flatter expressions. In this example, instead of

```
(let
  (x0
    (Execute
      :intension (refer
        (extensionConstraint
          (RecipientWithNameLike
            :constraint (Constraint[Recipient])
            :name #(PersonName "John"))))))
  (Yield
    :output (Execute
      :intension (ReviseConstraint
        :rootLocation (roleConstraint #(Path "output"))
        :oldLocation (Constraint[Constraint[Event]])
        :new (Constraint[Event]
          :attendees (andConstraint
            (andConstraint
              (andConstraint
                (AttendeeListHasRecipient
                  :recipient x0)
                (AttendeeListHasRecipient
                  :recipient (Execute
                    :intension (refer
                      (extensionConstraint
                        (RecipientWithNameLike
                          :constraint (Constraint[Recipient])
                          :name #(PersonName "Emily")))))))
              (AttendeeListHasRecipient
                :recipient (FindManager
                  :recipient x0)))
            (AttendeeListHasRecipient
              :recipient (Execute
                :intension (refer
                  (extensionConstraint
                    (RecipientWithNameLike
                      :constraint (Constraint[Recipient])
                      :name #(PersonName "Bob"))))))))))))
```

Figure 4: Example 2 - original annotation

```
do(
    Let(
        x0,
         refer(
            Recipient?(#John))),
    ModifyEventRequest(
       AND(
          with_attendee(#Bob),
           with_attendee(
             FindManager($x0)),
           with_attendee($x0),
           with_attendee(#Emily))))
```

Figure 5: Example 2 - simplified annotation

chaining constraints using *'andConstraint'*, the simplified annotation uses a flat *'AND'* construct.

3.3. Executing Simplified Annotations

At execution time, an additional step transforms the simplified annotation to a fully executable expression. This is done, again, by implementing tree transformation rules (for each function), which can add deterministically inferable missing information/steps (e.g. casting input to the right type, or performing other conversions/functions based on input type).

This step could be viewed, in principle, as the inverse of the dataset simplification step, but in practice the run-time transformation of the simplified annotation is often quite different from the original annotation, due to different design decisions and function implementations.

Figure 6 shows the result of transformation and execution of the simplified annotation for example dialogue 1 above. The transformed graph is clearly different from the original annotation's graph.

	Program Length
Original Annotation	(11, 37, 58)
Simplified Annotation	(2, 11, 20)

Table 1: Program length of the two annotation styles. Length is measured as number of seq2seq target tokens, when translating user request to annotation. Showing (.25, .50, .75) quantiles over the entire dataset.

	1k	3k	10k	33k
Original	30.2±3.6	41.8±7.9	55.7±7.0	72.8
Simplified	35.9±4.2	47.7±7.0	62.1±1.9	73.8

Table 2: Translation accuracy (exact match) as function of training data size, showing average and std. (in percent) over 7 randomly selected samples per size.

3.4. Simplification Results

Since the original code to execute SMCalFlow was not released (and documentation not supplied), it is impossible to verify that the suggested simplifications implement/execute the exact same logic (in fact this was one of the motivations for this paper). It can only be left to the readers to inspect the simplified annotations and the code and draw their own conclusions.

Qualitative evaluation confirmed correct execution of a sample of expressions, but further work is needed to obtain more significant quantitative evaluation.

Table 1 shows the results of a comparison of the annotation lengths of the original and simplified annotations, confirming that the simplification does make the annotation significantly shorter.

The example annotations shown above should show that the simplified annotations are not just significantly shorter, but are also significantly simpler to understand, which should reduce annotation efforts when creating new training data.

Table 2 shows that the simplification did not reduce (and maybe increased) the accuracy of machine translation of natural language user requests to dataflow expressions. Refinement of the simplification rules may result in further improvements.

4. Further Work

The work presented in this paper is still in progress, trying to improve the simplified annotation format and the automatic simplification.

Accordingly, the implementation of the executable functions will continue to evolve, to be able to correctly execute modified annotation formats.

While the automatic simplification covers all of the dataset, the implementation of functions has concentrated mostly (but not exclusively) on turns dealing with the calendar domain (which is the most complex domain in this dataset).

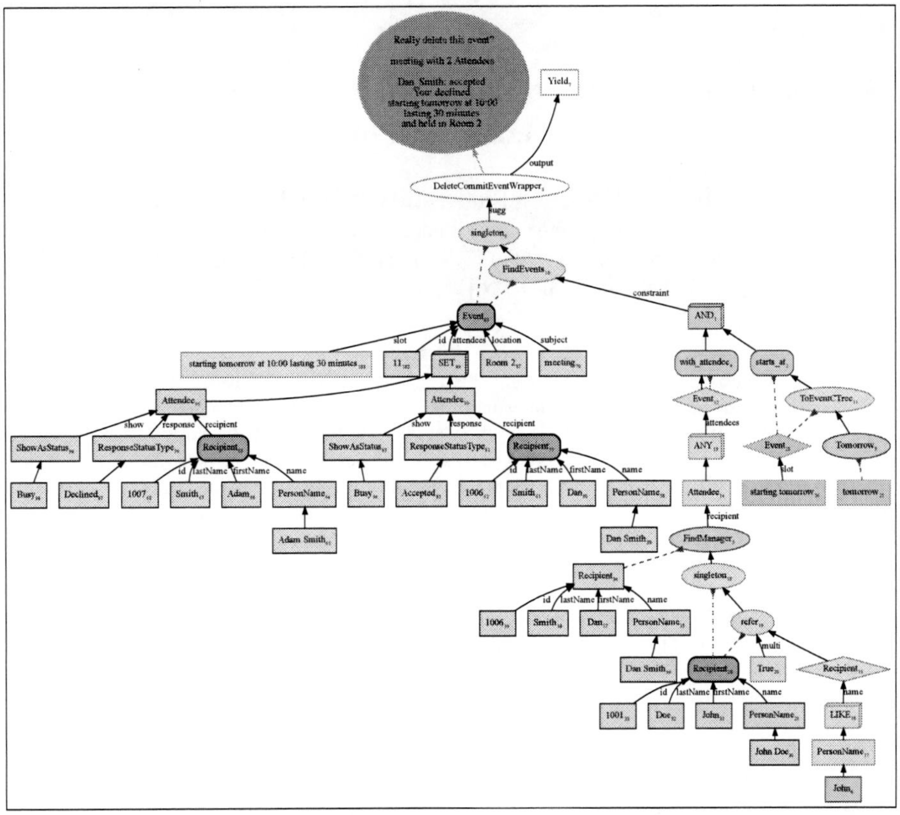

Figure 6: The result of transforming and evaluating the simplified annotation for the request *"Delete the meeting with John's supervisor tomorrow"*. Nodes from the simplified annotation are shown in gray. Yellow nodes indicate nodes added automatically by expansion logic, green nodes indicate information extracted from external DB (the result of searching for John and his manager, and for the event matching the requested constraints). Blue dashed lines indicate execution results (some nodes are omitted to reduce clutter).

Further ideas and work on the simplified annotation definition (and transformation process) from the community are encouraged. With the released code, researchers should be able to experiment with new ideas and share them with the community.
Additional areas of interest may include:

- Evaluation: in addition to the exact-match metric for translation accuracy, other metrics can be used, such as comparison of execution results, graph structure similarity, etc.

- Using the graph structure: the graph structure (at different points of the execution) can be used by prediction models.

- Different design patterns which are beneficial to specific parts of the system. For example, the execution of a computation graph could emit various types of information which would then be useful for subsequent prediction models.

5. Conclusion

A simplification of the SMCalFlow annotations has been presented. Some simplification principles have been suggested, and an automatic conversion tool has been implemented. Examples have been given to show that the simplified annotations are significantly shorter, as well as easier to understand, than the original annotations.
The code for reproducing this work [1] allows to run annotation simplification as well as executing these annotations to inspect and verify they satisfy user requests, and should lower the barrier of entry into Dataflow dialogue design for interested researchers, allowing them to experiment with new ideas.

6. Bibliographical References

Budzianowski, P., Wen, T.-H., Tseng, B.-H., Casanueva, I., Ultes, S., Ramadan, O., and Gašić, M. (2018). MultiWOZ - a large-scale multi-domain Wizard-of-Oz dataset for task-oriented dialogue modelling. In *Proceedings of the 2018 Conference on Empirical Methods in Natural Language Processing*, Brussels, Belgium.

Semantic Machines et al. (2020). Task-oriented dialogue as dataflow synthesis. *Transactions of the Association for Computational Linguistics*, 8:556–571.

[1] https://github.com/telepathylabsai/OpenDF

Proceedings of ISA-18 Workshop at LREC2022, pages 86–94
Marseille, 20 June 2022

Multilingual Reference Annotation: A Case between English and Mandarin Chinese

Joanna Ut-Seong Sio, Luis Morgado da Costa
Palacký University Olomouc, The Czech Republic
Katedra asijských studií FF UP, tř. Svobody 26, 779 00 Olomouc
joannautseong.sio@upol.cz, lmorgado.dacosta@gmail.com

Abstract

This paper presents the on-going effort to annotate a cross-lingual corpus on nominal referring expressions in English and Mandarin Chinese. The annotation includes referential forms and referential (information) statuses. We adopt the RefLex annotation scheme (Baumann and Riester, 2012) for the classification of referential statuses. The data focus of this paper is restricted to [*the*-X] phrases in English (where X stands for any nominal) and their translation equivalents in Mandarin Chinese. The original English and translated Mandarin versions of 'The Adventure of the Dancing Men' and 'The Adventure of Speckled Band' from the Sherlock Holmes series were annotated. It contains 1090 instances of [*the*-X] phrases in English. Our study uncovers the following: (i) bare nouns are the most common Mandarin translation for [*the*-X] phrases in English, followed by demonstrative phrases, with the exception that when the noun phrase refers to locations/places, in such cases, demonstrative phrases are almost never used; (ii) [*the*-X] phrases in English are more likely to be translated as demonstrative phrases in Mandarin if they have the referential status of 'given' (previously mentioned) or 'given-displaced'(antecedent of an expression occurs earlier than the previous five clauses). In these Mandarin demonstrative phrases, the proximal demonstrative is more often used and it is almost exclusively used for 'given' while the distal demonstrative can be used for both 'given' and 'given-displaced'.

Keywords: referential status, referring expressions, noun phrases, definiteness, English, Mandarin Chinese

1. Introduction

1.1. Reference and referential statuses

In linguistic communication, noun phrases (e.g., *a cat, the song, that professor*) are prototypically used to refer to entities. This referring relationship is called reference. Coherence in discourse depends crucially on using an appropriate referential expression for introducing, referring, and re-introducing an entity after a long pause. This is an easy task for any competent speaker, but such knowledge is notoriously difficult to make explicit.

To pick the right referring expression is to correctly map referential forms (noun phrases) to discourse contexts. Referring expressions can be definite (e.g., *the cat, that cat, it*) or indefinite (e.g., *a cat*). Definite expressions are used to refer to identifiable entities. The former is a grammatical category and the latter a cognitive category. Identifiability can be understood as a speaker's assessment of whether a particular discourse referent is already stored in the hearer's mind or not (Lambrecht, 1996). Entities can be identifiable in different discourse contexts (Christophersen, 1939; Hawkins, 1978; Lyons, 1999). They could be identifiable from previous mentions (e.g., *I bought a shirt yesterday. The shirt was blue.*), shared general knowledge (e.g., *the sun*), association (e.g., *I bought a shirt yesterday, but the sleeves were too long.*), or being unique in the speech environments (e.g., *Please close the window.*), to name a few. Indefinite expressions are used to introduce new and non-identifiable entities (e.g., *I saw a cat yesterday*, where the particular cat cannot be identified and/or its identity is not relevant for the discourse).

These discourse contexts (e.g., previous mentions, shared knowledge, new/non-identifiable, etc.) can be understood as the relevant entity having different referential statuses and will cause the speaker to select a particular referential form to refer to it (Baumann and Riester, 2012).[1]

Reference is an essential and yet unsolved problem in Natural Language Processing (NLP) and this limits the reach of various applications (e.g., parsing, machine translation, language generation and information retrieval). A better understanding of the mapping between referential forms and referential statuses would have a tremendous impact in all NLP tasks that deal with language understanding or generation.

1.2. Expression of definiteness in English and Mandarin Chinese

Different languages can have different inventories of referring expressions. In languages like English, articles (*the, a/an*) provide one way of distinguishing definite and indefinite NPs. In article-less languages (e.g., Chinese and Slavic), there are more interpretative ambiguities of surface forms and word order might also play a role. It has been proposed that the Mandarin equiva-

[1]Different referential statuses are often cast in terms of accessibility, which can be understood as a property of memory representation, with some information being more privileged/accessible/salient/prominent (Arnold and Zerkle, 2019). It is usually framed as a continuum from low to high (Gundel et al., 1993).

lents of [*the*-X] phrases in English can be a bare noun, which is ambiguous between a definite and an indefinite reading (Cheng and Sybesma, 1999) or a nominal containing a demonstrative (a demonstrative phrase) (Chen, 2004). An example of 'the dog' with a bare noun as an equivalent is given in (1); an example of 'the dog' with a demonstrative phrase as an equivalent is given in (2).

(1) 狗 要 過 馬路。
gǒu yào guò mǎlù
dog needs cross road

'The dog needs to cross the road' (Cheng and Sybesma, 1999)

(2) 有 一 個 獵人 養著 一 隻 狗，
yǒu yī gè lièrén yǎng-zhe yī zhī gǒu,
have one CL hunter keep-ASP one CL dog.
這 隻 狗 很 懂事。
zhè zhī gǒu hěn dǒngshì
this CL dog very intelligent

'There was a hunter who had a dog, the dog was very intelligent.' (Chen, 2004)

Demonstratives in Mandarin have been claimed to share some of the functions of the definite article in English (Chen, 2004). A comparison of the original English version of *Alice in Wonderland* and its Mandarin translations shows that demonstratives used in the Mandarin versions outnumber those in the English text, up to 3 times more in one translated version (Lu et al., 2018). This suggests the usage of the Mandarin demonstratives are less restricted than the English ones.

1.3. Goal of the paper

The annotation effort reported in this paper serves several goals: (i) to map [*the*-X] phrases in English to its equivalents in Mandarin; (ii) to map referential information statuses to referential forms within each language; (iii) to test and revise the RefLex annotation scheme (Baumann and Riester, 2012) using both English and Mandarin data.

As discussed earlier on, Mandarin bare nouns can be definite (Cheng and Sybesma, 1999) and demonstrative-containing phrases in Mandarin are always definite. We are particularly interested in finding out whether these two kinds of referring expressions are indeed the Mandarin translation equivalents of [*the*-X] phrases in English, as suggested in the literature, and if so, what the distribution is like with respect to the different referential information statuses.

The rest of this paper is structured as follows. In Section 2 we will describe the methodology of our analysis. Section 3 discusses the key findings of the annotation effort. Section 4 concludes and points to new directions for future studies. Sections 5 and 6 include some notes on the release of the tagged data and all necessary acknowledgments respectively.

2. Methodology

2.1. The Data

This project is currently using texts from the NTU Multilingual Corpus (Tan and Bond, 2014) – an open corpus with parallel data in multiple languages containing, among other genres, the full canon of Sherlock Holmes, by Sir Arthur Conan Doyle. The work presented in this paper is based on the annotation of two full short stories: *The Adventure of the Specked Band* (Conan Doyle, 1892) and *The Dancing Men* (Conan Doyle, 1905).

The English version of the *The Adventure of the Specked Band* short story contains 599 sentences and 11,741 words. Its Mandarin translation contains 620 sentences and 12,444 words. The English version of the *The Dancing Men* short story contains 666 sentences and 12,602 words. Its Mandarin translation contains 606 sentences and 11,339 words.

Short stories made an excellent data source for this project since its nature required the use of text suitable to analyze discourse structure. This means that we could not use use corpora comprised only of single sentences or text snippets since many discourse features are only present in longer narratives. At the same time, in order to future-proof our project and plan for future analyses that may require us to trace entities across their entire discourse life, we needed to find narratives that were not too long.

In addition, we were happy to choose the NTU Multilingual Corpus because it was readily available under an open license, allowing us to openly share all new layers of annotation we produce. Furthermore, both short stories chosen for this project have had a substantial amount of annotation and analysis from previous projects including sense-tagging using the Princeton Wordnet for English (Fellbaum, 1998) and the Chinese Open Wordnet for Mandarin (Wang and Bond, 2013). Even though we are not currently making full use of this layer of annotation, we believe that the information made available through sense tagging (e.g., relations of hyponymy and hypernymy across different discourse entities) will be of great valuable for the future directions of this project. Finally, the fact that the NTU Multilingual Corpus contains not only more short stories, but also parallel translations of some of these stories in other languages (including Japanese, Dutch, German, Indonesian and Italian) made this corpus extremely interesting to support the study of multilingual and cross-lingual referential analysis.

2.2. Expanding IMI: a Multilingual Semantic Annotation Environment

An important step of the methodology of this project was to decide on an annotation system to support our current and future goals within this project. While there were no shortage of options – e.g., Slate (Kummerfeld, 2019) or SALTO (Burchardt et al., 2006) have both been used as annotation benches for the RefLex Scheme –, we ended up choosing to expand IMI – a multilingual semantic annotation environment (Bond et al., 2015)[2]. Despite each annotation system having their strengths, our decision to use IMI was based on the fact that it was an online, open-source project specifically designed for multilingual semantic annotation – able to enrich a corpus with multiple layers of morphosyntactic and semantic information, as well as interfaces to manage cross-lingual links between sentences, concepts and words.

IMI was originally designed for sense tagging, using Open Multilingual Wordnet (Bond and Foster, 2013). It provides multiple layers of annotation that include lemmatization, POS tagging, sense tagging, sentiment annotation and interlingual-mapping. It is developed in Python and SQLite, and supports both concurrent annotation (i.e., multiple taggers tagging the same data at the same time), as well as parallel tagging (i.e., multiple taggers tagging the same set of data in parallel, using multiple databases). This annotation tool has been tested for a wide selection of languages, including English, Mandarin, Japanese and Indonesian. Finally, its flexibility and ease of customization had been proven by the development of multiple project-specific layers of annotation including: sentiment analysis (Bond et al., 2016), grammatical error analysis (Winder et al., 2017), and semantic role labeling (Choi, 2019).

Another strong motivation to use IMI was the fact that this system was designed to develop the NTU Multilingual Corpus (Tan and Bond, 2014) – the open corpus used for this project. This means that the short stories tagged in the context of this project were already in the required format to be used with this annotation system.

Within the context of this project we developed a new annotation interface within IMI which we named 'The RefLex Corpus Tagger' (see Figure 1). This interface allows the use of any custom tagset, which can be organized in different classes/types of tags. Tagsets can be language specific or shared across all languages. The system allows the tagset to grow incrementally, which is ideal for projects of exploratory nature such as this one. In future iterations, new tags can be easily added to the interface without jeopardizing the integrity of the data.

The annotation process is done sentence by sentence (but the tool also provides annotators with access to the full text, for reference). To add a new annotation, annotators can select a single word or any number of words (contiguous or non-contiguous) – referred as *chunks* within the system. Multiple tags can be provided for the same *chunk*, allowing the adoption of flexible tagset of varied classes/types. Finally, total and partial overlap of *chunks* are also allowed within the tagging system – which was an essential feature to allow the independent annotation of embedded phrases within larger phrases.

2.3. Annotation Schema

Currently, the RefLex Corpus Tagger has two separate tagsets: one for English and one for Mandarin. Each tagset is divided in different layers of annotation. The English tagset has three such layers: NP Structure (referential forms), Referential Status and Modification. The Mandarin tagset has an additional layer – i.e., Semantic Class –, totaling four layers. For each *chunk* created within a sentence, annotators had to select one value for each layer, which is selected from a predefined dropdown box (see Figure 2 for the interface of the Mandarin Chinese Tagger and Figure 3 for a full list of available tags, English and Mandarin Chinese combined).

The inventories of referential forms are different in English and in Mandarin. In this study, we only focus on [*the*-X] phrases in English (e.g., *the boys*), this also includes [*the*-numeral-X] phrases (e.g., *the three boys*) and [*the*-numeral] (e.g., *the three*) phrases, though the last two types only constitute 3% of the total, see Table 1. For Mandarin, we include a full range of possible referential forms (see Figure 3). It should be noted that the NP structure includes only the functional elements within a noun phrase. Elements such as modifiers do not affect the classification. For example, a modified bare noun in Mandarin is still considered a bare noun.

Regarding referential statuses, we annotate using the RefLex Scheme (Baumann and Riester, 2012). RefLex provides a fine-grained classification scheme to annotate texts on two levels, referential and lexical. On the referential level, the scheme provides a list of contexts for the use of referring and non-referring expressions. These contexts are distinguished based on referential statuses (e.g., different kinds of anaphoric contexts and discourse-new contexts). The lexical level provides explicit evaluation of the degree of relatedness of lexical expressions (e.g., hypernym). In this paper, we only focus on the referential level. We plan to deal with the lexical level at a later stage of the project, by exploiting the existing sense annotations available through the NTU Multilingual Corpus and consider a fuller range of lexical relations provided by wordnets.

The tags used for the referential level are as follow: **given-sit**: an expression whose referent is immediately present in the text-external context; **given**: an expression whose referent mentioned in previous discourse context; **given-displaced**: an expression whose referent is mentioned in the previous discourse context earlier than 5 clauses before; **cataphor**: an expression whose referent is established only in the subsequent text; **bridging**: a non-coreferential anaphoric expression which is dependent on a unique referent established in a previously introduced scenario; **bridging-contained**: a non-coreferential anaphoric expression that is anchored to an embedded phrase; **unused**: a discourse-new expression which is unique; **new**: an expression denoting a discourse-new and non-uniquely identifiable referent;

In addition to our main interests, referential forms (NP structure) and referential statuses, we have also included the layers of annotation indicating whether the

[2]https://github.com/bond-lab/IMI

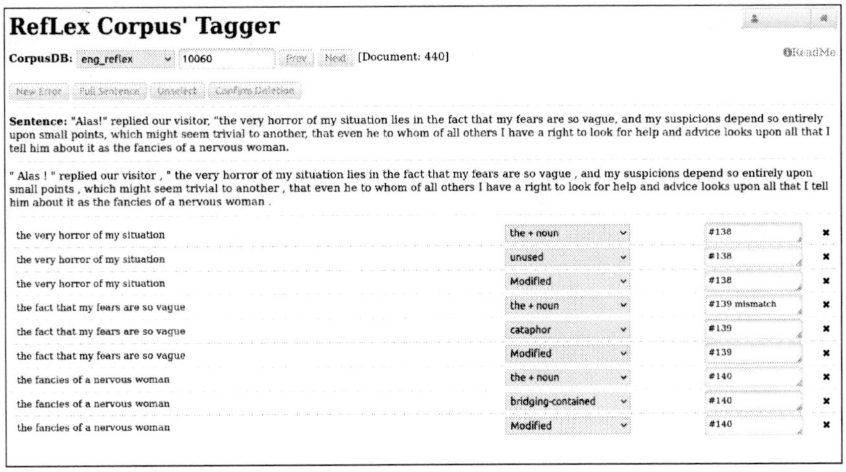

Figure 1: New IMI annotation layer developed: the IMI RefLex Tagger (English)

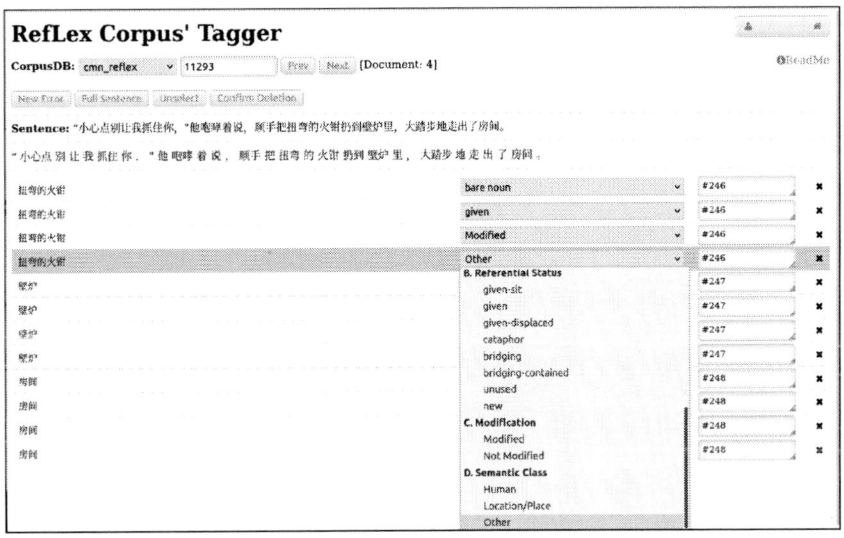

Figure 2: IMI RefLex Tagger (Mandarin Chinese): view of dropdown box with flexible tagging schema

noun phrase is modified and some information regarding the semantic class of the noun, whether it refers to human, location, or others. For a simple illustration, an English example is given below:

(3) I met a man yesterday. [The man] told me a story.

The annotated nominal is 'the man'. The NP structure will be 'the + noun'; the referential status tag is 'given'. The referring expression is 'not modified'.

These layers of annotation allow for a fine-grained analysis of the use and distribution of referential statuses. In this analysis, we will provide a summary of how these layers of annotation relate with each other. However, in the interest of scope, it will be impossible to cover all available relations between layers. Concerning semantic classes, in particular, we will only be able to discuss key relations that concern 'location/place'. A detailed analysis of other semantic classes will be left as future work.

2.4. Annotation Process

Annotation was conducted in two stages, by two trained taggers fluent in both English and Mandarin Chinese. The data was first tagged by a single annotator who worked with an early version of the tagging schema. Once the tagging schema was revised and expanded, the data was re-tagged by a second annotator.

The annotation process also included multiple discussions with both authors of this paper, which guided the annotation process, clarified any doubts and made final decisions in difficult or ambiguous cases. The annotation process was also aided by a series of automatic checks (written in Python) that flagged inconsistencies in the data annotation.

A. NP Structure (English)
- the + noun
- the + numeral + noun
- the + numeral

A. NP Structure (Mandarin)
- Ø
- pronoun
- proper names (bare)
- bare noun
- classifier + noun
- one + classifier + noun
- any other numeral + classifier + noun
- dem
- dem + noun
- dem + (one) + classifier
- dem + any other numeral + classifier
- dem + (one) + classifier + noun
- dem + any other numeral + classifier + noun

B. Referential Status (English and Mandarin)
- given-sit
- given
- given-displaced
- cataphor
- bridging
- bridging-contained
- unused
- new

C. Modification (English and Mandarin)
- Modified
- Not Modified

D. Semantic Class (Mandarin)
- Human
- Location/Place
- Other

Figure 3: IMI RefLex Tagger tagset

In total, the annotation of the two short stories took a total of 200 hours to complete (divided among the two annotators).

3. Discussion of Results

The tagging process resulted in 1090 [*the*-X] nominal phrases tagged for English and their Mandarin counterparts. As can be seen in Table 1, the overwhelming majority of [*the*-X] nominal phrases in these two short stories were of the form 'the + noun' (i.e., without the use of numerals). This means that we do not currently have enough data to fully discuss if the use of numerals has a measurable impact in the use of referential expressions.

Out of all English nominal phrases, 46% were modified in some way. This includes mostly adjectival modification and relative clauses. For comparison, only 38% of the Mandarin Chinese translations were modified.

NP Structure	Freq.
the + noun	**0.97**
the + numeral + noun	0.02
the + numeral	0.01
Total (n=1090)	1.00

Table 1: English by NP Structure

The most common Mandarin translation for [*the*-X] phrases in English are bare nouns (64%), followed by demonstrative phrases (including different kinds in the list, and adding up to 17%) – see Table 2. It is expected that bare nouns and demonstrative phrases are the most common equivalents for the English simple definite [*the*-X], as has been suggested in the literature. The new and interesting finding is that the use of bare nouns is much more common (almost 4 times more) than the use of demonstrative phrases.

Even though Chen (2004) proposes that demonstrative phrases in Mandarin can be semantic equivalents of [*the*-X] phrases in English, he also mentions some differences. Consider the following scenario. A and B enter A's house. B is aware that A has a baby but the baby is not in sight. A can say:

(4) 安靜 點兒， 別 把 孩子 吵醒 了。
ānjing diǎnr, bié bǎ háizi chǎo-xǐng le.
quiet bit, don't BA baby wake-up SFP.

'Be quiet. Don't wake up the baby.'(Chen, 2004)

The translation of 'the baby' in 4 is *háizi*, a bare noun. The use of a demonstrative phrase will be inappropriate in this case as the baby is not in sight. Visibility seems to be a condition that governs the use of the demonstratives in some situations. It is also not possible to use demonstratives in Mandarin to translate phrases like 'the sun', as it is globally unique. These semantic restrictions on the use of the Mandarin demonstratives might explain why the percentage of demonstrative phrases as the translation equivalents of [*the*-X] phrases is much lower than that of bare nouns.

Another interesting find worth mentioning from Table 2 is the fact that about 10% of [*the*-X] phrases in English are completely missing from the Mandarin translation (shown as '—missing—'). We are currently not equipped to discuss exactly when this can happen, but our findings suggest that dropping a reference in the translation may be related to the referential status of the original expressions. Table 3 shows that English expressions missing Mandarin counterparts were mostly tagged as 'unused', 'given' or 'cataphor'. A fuller study including these expressions' permanence in the discourse could shed further light into this topic.

Table 4 and Table 5 show the distribution of referential statuses across the tagged English and Mandarin nominal expressions. The information provided in these tables is not unexpected. While it is possible to see a broad parallelism in the overall referential statuses of

NP Structure	Freq.
bare noun	0.64
dem + (one) + classifier + noun	**0.14**
—missing—	0.10
one + classifier + noun	0.06
dem + noun	**0.02**
any other numeral + classifier + noun	0.01
pronoun	0.01
classifier + noun	0.01
dem + any other numeral + classifier + noun	**0.01**
Ø	0.01
proper names (bare)	0.00
dem + any other numeral + classifier	**0.00**
Total (n=1090)	1.00

Table 2: Mandarin by NP Structure

Referential Status	Freq.
unused	**0.36**
given	**0.19**
cataphor	**0.17**
given-sit	0.12
given-displaced	0.06
bridging	0.06
bridging-contained	0.04
Total (n=108)	1.00

Table 3: English referential statuses for missing Mandarin translations

the tagged nominal expressions, we can also observe small discrepancies across these classes (e.g., slightly higher values for 'given' expressions in Mandarin, or slightly higher 'unused' expressions in English). These discrepancies can be explained in part by the fact that some expressions were missing in the Mandarin translations, as already discussed, but also by how normal translation practices of literary texts do not always follow a strict literal translation method, and often change slightly the focus and even the flow of information.

Referential Status	Freq.
given	0.30
given-sit	0.20
unused	0.19
given-displaced	0.10
bridging	0.09
bridging-contained	0.07
cataphor	0.04
Total (n=1090)	1.00

Table 4: English referential statuses across all nominal expressions

One of the main goals of this paper was to map referential information statuses to referential forms. Figure 4 shows a summary of this mapping by providing the top two NP structures for each referential status in the Mandarin text. The categories 'given' and 'given-displaced'

Referential Status	Freq.
given	0.36
given-sit	0.20
unused	0.15
—missing—	0.10
given-displaced	0.10
bridging	0.07
bridging-contained	0.03
cataphor	0.01
Total (n=1090)	1.00

Table 5: Mandarin referential statuses across all nominal expressions

have the highest percentage of demonstrative phrases (29% and 31% respectively) while the overall average is 17% only. The use of the demonstratives in 'given-displaced' contexts can be understood as a way to re-introduced/activate a referent that has been mentioned not too recently (the threshold is set at 5 clauses before in RefLex). If the use of the demonstratives in Mandarin is used as a way to reactivate a certain referent, it can then be understood why in 'given-sit' and 'bridging-contained' the percentages are low. In these contexts, the referent is in the immediate text-external context in the former, and anchored to an element in the embedded phrase (linguistically very proximal) in the latter.

A deeper analysis of demonstrative phrases in Mandarin shows an interesting distribution between proximal and distal usages. Out of the 185 tokens of demonstrative phrases in the Mandarin tagset (which are translations of [*the*-X]), proximal demonstratives are more frequent: 59% (n=109) phrases use the proximal demonstrative 這 *zhè* and 41% (n=76) phrases use the distal demonstrative 那 *nà*.

When we look at their distribution with respect to referential statuses, a clearer difference emerges. Out of the 109 tokens of the proximal demonstrative *zhè*, 89% are 'given' (an expression whose referent is mentioned in previous discourse) – see Table 6. On the other hand, out of the 76 tokens of the distal demonstrative *nà*, 41% are 'given' while 42% are 'given-displaced' (an expression whose referent is mentioned in the previous discourse context earlier than 5 clauses before) – see Table 7. Both 'given' and 'given-displaced' are anaphoric in nature. They differ in that the former is used for recent mentions (fewer than 5 clauses) and the latter is for distant mentions (more than 5 clauses). The proximal demonstrative *zhè* is overwhelmingly used for recently mentioned antecedents. The distal demonstrative *nà* can be used for both, recent mentions or earlier mentions.[3]

Our data does not have noun phrases under the cate-

[3]Chen (2004) suggests that the proximity of *zhè* makes it a better anaphoric device than the distal *nà* in referring to an antecedent recently introduced into discourse.

Referential Status	Freq.
given	0.89
given-sit	0.06
given-displaced	0.04
unused	0.02
Total (n=109)	1.00

Table 6: Mandarin referential statuses across proximal (这, zhè) demonstrative nominal expressions

Referential Status	Freq.
given-displaced	0.42
given	0.41
unused	0.07
bridging	0.05
given-sit	0.04
bridging-contained	0.01
Total (n=76)	1.00

Table 7: Mandarin referential statuses across distal (那, nà) demonstrative nominal expressions

gory 'new'. This is expected as generally only indefinite noun phrases are used to refer to new entities, and for this study, we are only looking at [*the*-X] phrases in English and its Mandarin equivalents.

unused
- bare noun — 81%
- one + classifier + noun — 8%

given
- bare noun — 56%
- dem + (one) + classifier + noun — 29%

given-sit
- bare noun — 83%
- one + classifier + noun — 10%

bridging
- bare noun — 92%
- dem + (one) + classifier + noun — 5%

given-displaced
- bare noun — 63%
- dem + (one) + classifier + noun — 31%

bridging-contained
- bare noun — 97%
- dem + any other numeral + classifier + noun — 3%

cataphor
- bare noun — 75%
- dem + any other numeral + classifier + noun — 25%

Figure 4: Top two Mandarin NP structures per referential status

When the semantic class of the noun is 'location/place', the percentage of Mandarin demonstrative phrases as the translation equivalents of English [*the*-X] phrases is very low. Among the 140 tokens of 'location/place' noun phrases, only 4% of the tokens are translated with a demonstrative (see Table 8). This could be related to the issue of discourse persistent/prominence. Entities that are 'props' rather than regular participants in discourse are often marked differently in discourse. Quoting Recasens et al. (2013): 'not all discourse entities are created equal. Some lead long lives and appear in a variety of discourse contexts (coreferents), whereas others never escape their birthplaces, dying out after just one mention (singletons).' Hopper (1986) observes that in Malay, the absence of the classifier in an NP correlates with the entity having a short 'discourse persistence' (or 'thematic importance' in Givón (1984), referring to the importance of a referent in discourse). This could be the reason why in Mandarin, the demonstrative is almost never used when translating 'location/places' from English because locations/places very often have low discourse persistent/prominence. As discussed earlier on, the categories 'given' and 'given-displaced' have a high percentage of demonstrative phrases, around 30% in average. Among NPs tagged as 'location/place' in the two categories, the percentage of NP forms using demonstratives were much lower than the average – only 8%.

NP Structure	Freq.
bare noun	0.89
dem + (one) + classifier + noun	0.04
one + classifier + noun	0.04
proper names (bare)	0.01
pronoun	0.01
Total (n=140)	1.00

Table 8: Mandarin NP type for NPs tagged as Location/Place

Referential Status	Freq.
given-sit	0.49
given	0.18
given-displaced	0.17
unused	0.14
bridging	0.01
bridging-contained	0.01
Total (n=140)	1.00

Table 9: Mandarin NP Ref-Status Mapping for NPs tagged as Location/Place

4. Conclusion and Future Work

In this study, even though we have only tagged [*the*-X] phrases in English and their Mandarin equivalents, we have been able to detect patterns that are interesting for the study of reference. In tracking the Mandarin translation equivalents for English [*the*-X] phrases, we observe that Mandarin bare nouns are the most common Mandarin translation, followed by demonstrative phrases, with the exception that when the noun phrase refers to locations/places. In fact, when the noun phrase refers to locations/places demonstrative phrases are almost never used. We show that [*the*-X] phrases in English are more likely to be translated as demonstrative phrases in Mandarin if they have the referential status of 'given' (previously mentioned) or 'given-displaced'(antecedent of an expression occurs earlier than the previous five clauses). Finally, we also show evidence for a clear functional difference between the Mandarin proximal demonstrative and the distal demonstrative: the Mandarin proximal demonstrative appears more frequently and is almost exclusively used to refer to referents with recent antecedents (fewer than 5 clauses before) while the Mandarin distal demonstrative can be used for both recent and distant referents.

This study is very limited in scope, we only look at [*the*-X] phrases in English and their Mandarin equivalents. However, even maintaining its scope, there are still ways to expand our analysis, for example, adding more tagging categories. We would like to add 'shell nouns' as one of the semantic classes. Shell nouns are nouns that conceptually encapsulate complex pieces of information (Schmid, 2018), such as *fact, reason, problem, position, fact*, etc. Similar to semantically empty nouns for 'fellow' or 'person' in Mandarin, when unmodified, we expect such nouns to be less likely to appear bare due to the lack of semantic content. Instead, a demonstrative will be expected.[4] We would also like to add the tags for proximal and distal demonstratives since our discussion of results has shown this to be a dimension worthy of further exploration.

To expand the scope in the future, we want to include other English phrases and their Mandarin equivalents using more parallel texts, ideally also including other genres. Furthermore, we would like to track the referential forms referring to specific referents throughout the whole discourse. This would allow us to study the relationship between fluctuation in salience/accessibility and referential forms in a referent's discourse life.

In addition to expanding our project's depth of analysis through new layers of annotation, we would also like to better exploit the multilingual nature of the dataset we used. The NTU Multilingual Corpus includes sense-tagged translations of shorts stories and of texts in other genres for Japanese, Italian, and Indonesian. Adopting a widely multilingual research agenda looking into mapping referential statuses to structural forms, abandoning English-centric analyses, could help gain new insights on the distinction between general trends and language specific features of referential analysis.

Finally, another important area we believe worth pursuing is the further development of the IMI RefLex Tagger. While it serves its current purpose, the annotation interface could still be improved further, especially in the cross-lingual link of expressions in two languages (which is currently done manually), and also in the ability to tag both languages side by side (which currently has to be emulated by opening two browser windows).

[4]This is motivated by some preliminary work done with manual annotation between English and Mandarin text. We found that there is a higher chance for relatively semantically empty nouns, e.g., *fellow*, *fact*, etc. to be translated in Mandarin with a demonstrative (Sio and Juan, 2019).

5. Release Notes

The raw text and all annotations produced as part of this corpus will be released under a Creative Commons Attribution 4.0 International License (CC BY 4.0)[5]. This data will be deposited in the following GitHub repository: https://github.com/lmorgadodacosta/multilingual-referential-annotation-corpus.

6. Acknowledgements

We would like to thank Belinda Juan and Jaroslav Tecl for helping us to annotate data. The research described here is supported by the European Regional Development Fund - Project 'Sinophone Borderlands - Interaction at the Edges' CZ.02.1.01/0.0/0.0/16_019/0000791 and by the European Union's Horizon 2020 research and innovation programme under the Marie Skłodowska-Curie grant agreement H2020-MSCA-IF-2020 CHILL – No.101028782.

7. Bibliographical References

Arnold, J. E. and Zerkle, S. A. (2019). Why do people produce pronouns? pragmatic selection vs. rational models. *Language, Cognition and Neuroscience*, 34(9):1152–1175.

Baumann, S. and Riester, A. (2012). Referential and lexical givenness: Semantic, prosodic and cognitive aspects. *Prosody and meaning*, 25:119–162.

Bond, F. and Foster, R. (2013). Linking and extending an Open Multilingual Wordnet. In *51st Annual Meeting of the Association for Computational Linguistics: ACL-2013, Sofia*, pages 1352–1362.

Bond, F., Morgado da Costa, L., and Le, T. A. (2015). IMI – A multilingual semantic annotation environment. In *Proceedings of the 53rd Annual Meeting of the Association for Computational Linguistics and the 7th International Joint Conference on Natural Language Processing of the Asian Federation of Natural Language Processing, System Demonstrations (ACL 2015)*, pages 7–12, Beijing, China.

Bond, F., Ohkuma, T., Da Costa, L. M., Miura, Y., Chen, R., Kuribayashi, T., and Wang, W. (2016). A multilingual sentiment corpus for chinese, english and japanese. In *6th Emotion and Sentiment Analysis Workshop (at LREC 2016)*.

Burchardt, A., Erk, K., Frank, A., Kowalski, A., Pado, S., and Pinkal, M. (2006). Salto-a versatile multi-level annotation tool. In *LREC*, pages 517–520. European Language Resource Association.

Chen, P. (2004). Identifiability and definiteness in chinese.

[5]https://creativecommons.org/licenses/by/4.0/

Cheng, L. L.-S. and Sybesma, R. (1999). Bare and not-so-bare nouns and the structure of np. *Linguistic Inquiry*, 30(4):509–542.

Choi, H. Y. J. (2019). A corpus based analysis of-kan and-i in Indonesian. Master's thesis, Nanyang Technological University, Singapore.

Christophersen, P. (1939). The articles: A study of their theory and use in english.

Conan Doyle, A. (1892). *The Adventures of Sherlock Holmes*. George Newnes, London.

Conan Doyle, A. (1905). *The Return of Sherlock Homes*. George Newnes, London.

Christiane Fellbaum, editor. (1998). *WordNet: An Electronic Lexical Database*. MIT Press, Cambridge, MA.

Givón, T. (1984). The pragmatics of referentiality. *Georgetown University round table on language and linguistics*, pages 120–138.

Gundel, J. K., Hedberg, N., and Zacharski, R. (1993). Cognitive status and the form of referring expressions in discourse. *Language*, pages 274–307.

Hawkins, J. A. (1978). Definiteness and indefiniteness. atlantic highlands.

Hopper, P. J. (1986). Some discourse functions of classifiers in malay. *Noun classes and categorization*, 7:309–325.

Kummerfeld, J. K. (2019). SLATE: A super-lightweight annotation tool for experts. In *Proceedings of the 57th Annual Meeting of the Association for Computational Linguistics: System Demonstrations*, pages 7–12, Florence, Italy, July. Association for Computational Linguistics.

Lambrecht, K. (1996). *Information structure and sentence form: Topic, focus, and the mental representations of discourse referents*, volume 71. Cambridge university press.

Lu, W., Verhagen, A., and Su, I. (2018). A multiple-parallel-text approach for viewpoint research across languages. *Expressive minds and artistic creations: Studies in cognitive poetics*.

Lyons, C. (1999). *Definiteness*. Cambridge University Press.

Recasens, M., Danescu-Niculescu-Mizil, C., and Jurafsky, D. (2013). Linguistic models for analyzing and detecting biased language. In *Proceedings of the 51st Annual Meeting of the Association for Computational Linguistics (Volume 1: Long Papers)*, pages 1650–1659.

Schmid, H.-J. (2018). Shell nouns in english-a personal roundup. *Caplletra. Revista Internacional de Filologia*, (64):109–128.

Sio, J. U.-S. and Juan, L.-T. B. (2019). Investigate the differences between chinese bare nouns and demonstrative phrases using parallel texts. *Presented at the Annual Conference on Asian Studies (ACAS), Olomouc, the Czech Republic*.

Tan, L. and Bond, F. (2014). NTU-MC toolkit: Annotating a linguistically diverse corpus. In *Proceedings of COLING 2014, the 25th International Conference on Computational Linguistics: System Demonstrations*, page 86–89, Dublin.

Wang, S. and Bond, F. (2013). Building the Chinese Open Wordnet (COW): Starting from core synsets. In *Proceedings of the 11th Workshop on Asian Language Resources, a Workshop at IJCNLP-2013*, pages 10–18, Nagoya.

Winder, R. V. P., MacKinnon, J., Li, S. Y., Lin, B., Heah, C., Morgado da Costa, L., Kuribayashi, T., and Bond, F. (2017). NTUCLE: Developing a corpus of learner English to provide writing support for engineering students. In *Proceedings of the 4th Workshop on NLP Techniques for Educational Applications (NLPTEA 2017)*, Taipei, Taiwan.

Proceedings of ISA-18 Workshop at LREC2022, pages 95–101
Marseille, 20 June 2022

Graph Querying for Semantic Annotations

Maxime Amblard, Bruno Guillaume, Siyana Pavlova, Guy Perrier
Université de Lorraine, CNRS, Inria, LORIA, F-54000 Nancy, France
{firstname.lastname}@loria.fr

Abstract

This paper presents how the online tool GREW-MATCH can be used to make queries and visualise data from existing semantically annotated corpora. A dedicated syntax is available to construct simple to complex queries and execute them against a corpus. Such queries give transverse views of the annotated data, these views can help for checking the consistency of annotations in one corpus or across several corpora. GREW-MATCH can then be seen as an error mining tool: when inconsistencies are detected, it helps finding the sentences which should be fixed. Finally, GREW-MATCH can also be used as a side tool to assist annotation tasks helping to find annotation examples in existing corpora to be compared to the data to be annotated.

Keywords: Graph matching, Semantic annotations, Error mining, Abstract Meaning Representation, Parallel Meaning Bank

1. Semantic annotations as graphs

There are a huge number of proposals in the literature to describe the formal representations of the semantics of natural language texts. This diversity can be due to several factors; the main one being different linguistic theories used in the modeling. We also observe differences in terms of levels of annotations or with a specific focus on some level.

Most of these representations use the notions of objects as *entities* and *events*. They describe semantic relations between these objects. Of course, many propositions go further and propose other mechanisms to deal with temporal aspects or to describe the scope or the restriction linked to the logical interpretation of determiners as quantifiers; but we can consider that semantic relations between entities and/or events are a kind of minimal common denominator of the these proposals.

The mathematical notion of graphs is well-adapted to describe such kind of objects and we propose here to consider insofar as possible semantic annotations as graphs. In our context, we consider labeled graphs, where nodes are decorated with flat features structures and edges are associated with specific labels.

In this paper, three semantic annotation frameworks are considered: Abstract Meaning Representation (AMR), Discourse Representation Structure (DRS), as they are used in the Parallel Meaning Bank (PMB), and QuantML. The freely available annotated data for these three frameworks are now available in the GREW-MATCH[1] tool. In the following, we briefly review these frameworks and illustrate how the tool facilitates annotation while making it more consistent.

Apart from tools specific to the different formalisms, we can cite Cohen et al. (2021) which also proposed a generic framework based on graph visualisation adapted to several semantic frameworks. However, the tool is more focused on single graph visualisation and with manipulation features. It does not propose complex queries with negative application patterns or the clustering feature we describe here for GREW-MATCH.

1.1. AMR

The Abstract Meaning Representation (AMR) (Banarescu et al., 2013) is a proposal whose focus is the predicate argument structure, using PropBank (Palmer et al., 2005) as an inventory of semantic concepts.

As shown in Figure 1, we interpret an AMR annotation as a graph in the following way:

- each concept (like *fox* or *know-02* is a node with a feature name `concept`;
- each value (like *1*) is a node with a feature name `value`;
- each semantic relation, with prefix ":" in Penman notation is an edge, typed with the relation name.

In GREW-MATCH, two freely available AMR English corpora can be queried: The Little Prince Corpus version 3.0[2] (1,562 sentences) and BioAMR Corpus version 3.0[3] (6,952 sentences).

1.2. DRS in the PMB

There are several presentations of the DRS structures. In this paper we focus on the one used in the Parallel Meaning Bank (PMB) (Abzianidze et al., 2017)[4], version 4.0.0, released in October 2021. As in the AMR case, the predicate-argument structure is described with typed entities and typed semantic relations which can be converted into a graph representation. In addition, the box notation is used to describe the discourse relations and other constructions for which a notion of

[1] `http://semantics.grew.fr`

[2] `https://amr.isi.edu/download/amr-bank-struct-v3.0.txt`

[3] `https://amr.isi.edu/download/2018-01-25/amr-release-bio-v3.0.txt`

[4] `http://pmb.let.rug.nl/`

```
(r / resemble-01
  :ARG1 (y / you)
  :ARG2 (f / fox
    :poss (i / i))
  :time (k / know-02
    :ARG0 i
    :ARG1 f
    :ord (o / ordinal-entity :value 1)))
```

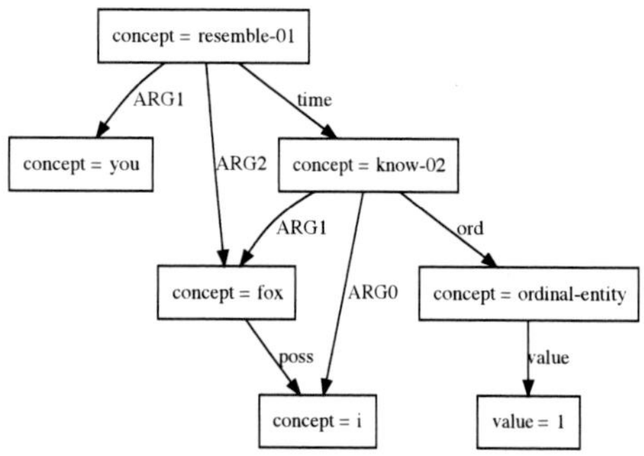

Figure 1: AMR annotation in Penman notation and its interpretation as graph of the sentence [lpp_1943.1161] *You are like my fox when I first knew him.*

scope is needed (like quantifiers or negation). The box notation requires a specific encoding into the graph structure. Following the Bos' proposal (Bos, 2021b; Bos, 2021a), each box is drawn as a new node. Moreover, the embedding of a semantic node in a box is marked with a link which is drawn with a dotted line and labelled with the relation name **in** in the figures.

```
                    NEGATION -1
be.v.01             Theme 15 Co-Theme +1
prime_number.n.01
```

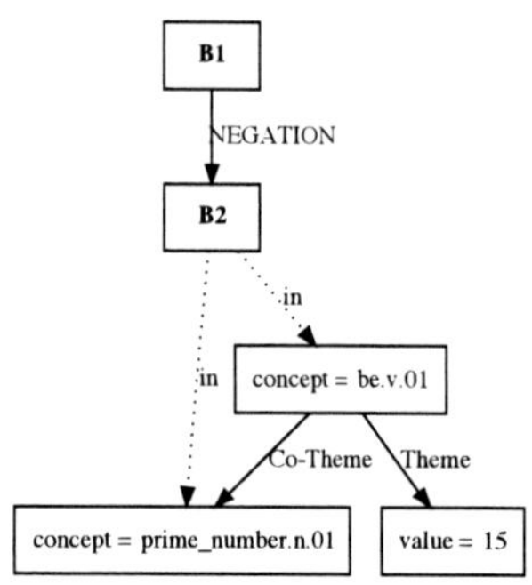

Figure 2: PMB annotation in SBN (Simplified Box Notation) and its interpretation as graph of the sentence [p52/d2324] *Fifteen is not a prime number.*

Figure 2 shows an example of the a DRS annotation from the PMB and its representation as a graph. In GREW-MATCH, the gold data of the PMB is available (10,715 sentences in English, 2,844 in German, 1,686 in Italian and 1,467 in Dutch).

1.3. QuantML

QuantML (Bunt et al., 2018; Bunt, 2020) is another semantic annotation with a focus on quantification. There is currently no annotated corpus in QuantML but a few annotations are proposed in the Guidelines part of the technical report (Bunt, 2020). Again, the so-called *Concrete syntax* of examples from the guidelines are converted into graphs.
An example of the graph associated to the concrete level of a QuantML annotation is shown on Figure 3. These graphs are richer: they use a skeleton with predicate/argument structure, but information about definiteness, distributivity or scope constraint is also given. Features structures are used to describe different semantic aspects both on nodes and edges. Scoping constraint between different arguments of the same predicate can be expressed (red edge **equal** in the figure).

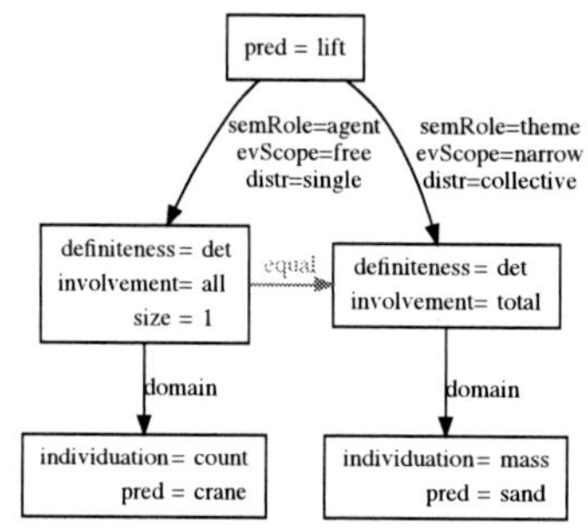

Figure 3: QuantML graph of the sentence [A10] *The crane lifted all the sand*

In Amblard et al. (2021), we have participated in the ISA-17 shared task and proposed such annotations for 7 English sentences (with two alternative annotations for an ambiguous sentence). In GREW-MATCH, these annotations are available together with the 11 English examples[5] of the guidelines in Bunt (2020).

2. The GREW-MATCH tool

In some previous works (Bonfante et al., 2018), we have proposed to consider the representation of linguistic structures as graphs and to promote the well-studied computational model of Graph Rewriting to describe transformations of these structures. In this framework, complex transformations can be encoded as a sequence of elementary and local transformations. The local steps are graph rewriting rules, composed of a pattern (describing the part of the graph to be modified) and a sequence of commands (describing in which way the graph is changed). The GREW (Guillaume, 2021) tool is an implementation of this framework.
A mechanism of graph matching is used in GREW to detect when a rule can be applied to a graph. But

[5]for five of them, we have detected annotation errors (see an example in section 4 and we give both the original version and the fixed version.

we have observed that this mechanism can be used on its own as a way to query a graph or a collection of graphs. This querying aspect give birth to a new tool, called GREW-MATCH, a web-based interface to express queries on annotated corpora and to visualise the occurrences returned by the query.

A screenshot of the tool applied to AMR example is shown in Figure 4. The visualisation of semantic structures uses the Graphviz tool[6].

Theoretically, graph matching is an NP-complete problem but in the present context, matching is done on a set of small graphs (one graph per sentence) and then the complexity is not an issue and most of the graph requests can be executed very quickly. We have made a few experiments on larger graphs (around 20,000 nodes) and then the complexity strongly relies of the shape of the pattern. If a pattern has a tree structure, the matching is easing and linear in the size of the graph; for general patterns, there is no generic efficient algorithm and some heuristics will be needed.

2.1. The query language

We briefly describe here the main aspects of queries in GREW-MATCH, we let the reader go to the GREW documentation pages for more details. The main part of a query is introduced by the keyword `pattern` which describes the set of nodes and edges that should be matched in the host graph. For nodes and edges, several constraints can be expressed. More general constraints can also be expressed, for example the fact different nodes share the same feature value. Given a corpus and a basic request (introduced by the keyword `pattern`), we can further refine the query by adding negative application patterns (introduced by the keyword `without`). Each negative application pattern is a constraint that filters out the occurrences returned by the basic pattern according to additional constraints.

As an example, the following pattern with one basic pattern (first line) and two negative application patterns (last two lines). It shows the syntax to express: find all the concept nodes in the corpus where the concept is `say-01` but such that there are no outgoing edges labelled **ARG0** from this node (note that the identifier `N` is used to refer to the same node) and such that there are no incoming edges labelled **ARG0-of** on this node. An example of a graph returned by this pattern is given in section 3 below.

```
pattern { N [concept = "say-01"] }
without { N -[ARG0]-> A0 }
without { A0 -[ARG0-of]-> N }
```

Another feature which has been proved useful in GREW-MATCH is the ability to cluster the results given by a complex request. The user can chose a clustering key (like the feature of one of the nodes of the basic pattern), the set of occurrences is clustered according to value of this feature (see example in the next section).

The clustering can also be done following a sub-pattern: considering a pattern P and a sub-pattern P', all occurrences of P are clustered in two subsets P_{yes} and P_{no} depending on whether P' is also satisfied by the considered occurrence. For instance, we can observe how coordination is annotated with the pattern P: `pattern { N [concept = "and"] }` and the sub-pattern `N -[op1]-> X`, to see if the concept `and` appears with or without an **op1** outgoing edge. On The Little Prince, there are 215 occurrences in P_{yes} and 127 in P_{no}. With the same P and the sub-pattern `N -[op2]-> X`, the occurrences are 240 in P_{yes} and 102 in P_{no}. This shows that "unary" coordination (sentence beginning with the word *and* are not consistently annotated: the unique conjoint is sometimes annotated **op1** and sometimes **op2**.

3. Linguistic observations on semantic annotations

We list here a few examples of requests which can be used to make observations on the annotated corpora.

Concepts linked to a given verb. With the following request and a clustering on `N.concept`

```
pattern { N [concept = re"make-.*"]; }
```

we obtained the distribution of the usage of the concepts. On The Little Prince Corpus, the concepts returned are `make-02` (18), `make-01` (17), `make-05` (1), `make-06` (1) and `make-up-07` (1).

Realisation of an argument of a predicate. In The Little Prince Corpus, the most frequent predicate is `say-01` (234 occurrences). According to PropBank, this predicate has 4 core arguments: **ARG0** (*Sayer*), **ARG1** (*Utterance*), **ARG2** (*Hearer*) and **ARG3** (*Attributive*). With a few requests on GREW-MATCH, we can observe how often the different arguments are realised of not. For **ARG0**, the following request gives the 6 occurrences of the predicate without the *Sayer*. Note that we have to take care both of the **ARG0** outgoing edges (line 2) but also to the **ARG0-of** incoming edges (line 3) (without the last line, 9 occurrences would be wrongly reported).

```
pattern { N [concept = "say-01"] }
without { N -[ARG0]-> A0 }
without { A0 -[ARG0-of]-> N }
```

An example of one of the six occurrences is shown in Figure 5.

Observation of distributions in the data. Graph querying is also available through scripts which produces statistics about the number of occurrences in corpora. With the following pattern, and a clustering following the label of the edge named `e`, we can observe the distribution of relations between two "concept" nodes (see Figure 6).

[6] https://graphviz.org/

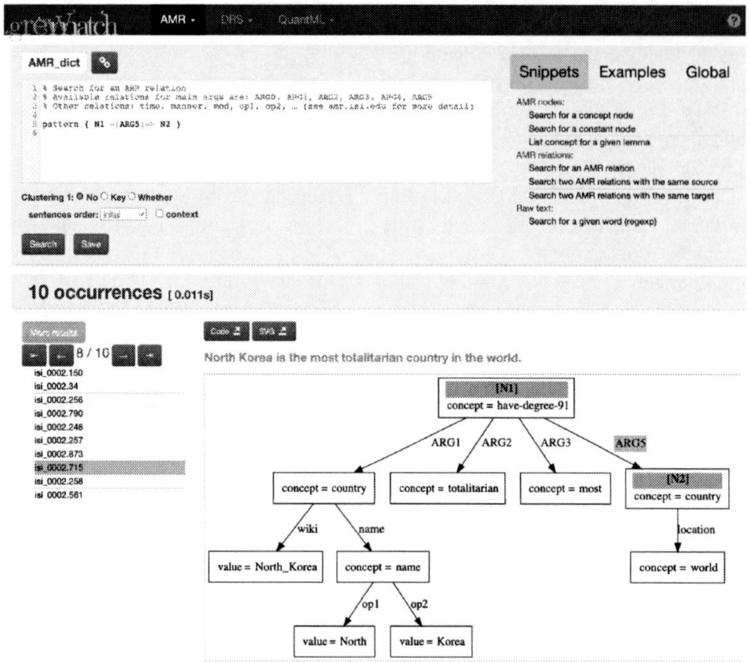

Figure 4: The GREW-MATCH tool

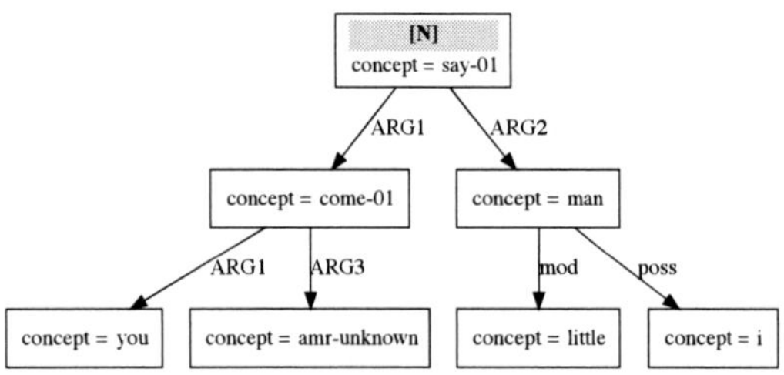

Figure 5: AMR annotation of the sentence *"My little man, where do you come from?.*

```
pattern {
  M [concept]; N [concept];
  e: M -> N
}
```

With the encoding of boxes we have described above, it is possible to request for specific configurations of boxes. The next pattern corresponds to two nested negations.

```
pattern {
  B1 -[NEGATION]-> B2;
  B2 -[NEGATION]-> B3
}
```

With this query, in Figure 7, we can observe a perfect illustration of the encoding of universal quantification through a double negation.[7]

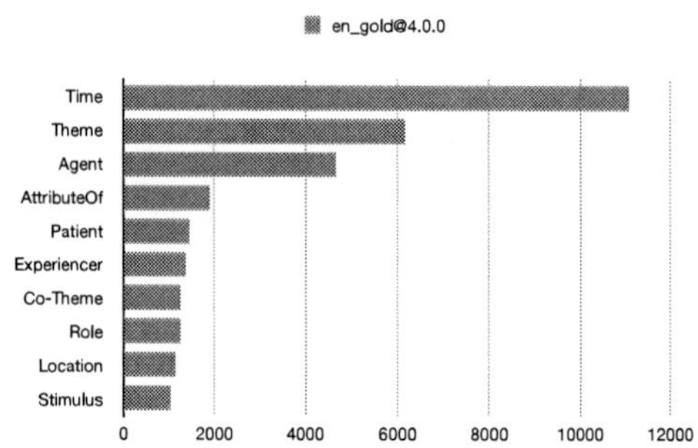

Figure 6: distribution of the ten most frequent semantic relations between two "concept" nodes

Global graph structure. More general queries about the graph structure allow for instance to check for cyclic structures.

```
global { is_cyclic }
```

The AMR guidelines say "Approximately 0.3% of AMRs are legitimately cyclic"[8]. But, with the query above, we can report the ratio of cyclic structures in AMR corpora: more than 3% in The Little Prince Corpus and almost 6.9% in the BioAMR corpus.
On the gold data of the PMB, cyclic structure are rare: there are 34 cyclic structures in English (among 10,715 sentences) and 1 in German (in 2,844 sentences). There are no examples in Italian or Dutch data.

[7] In PMB, TPR stands for *temporal precedence*.

[8] `https://github.com/amrisi/amr-guidelines/blob/master/amr.md`

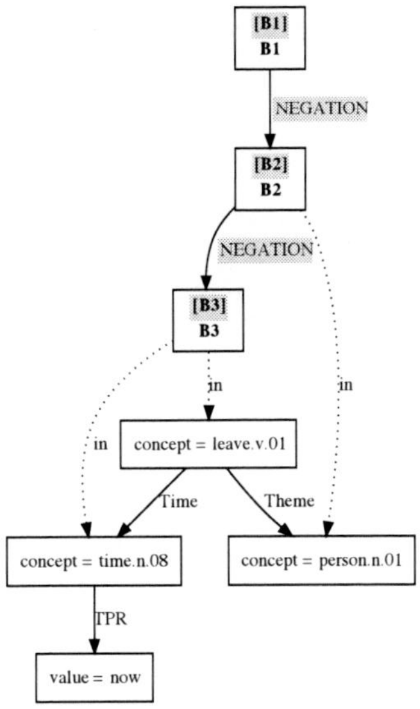

Figure 7: Double negation encoding for the sentence `[p18/d1454]` *Everybody left.*

4. Error mining

GREW-MATCH can be used to detect inconsistencies in the annotations. A query is designed to express a constraint which should be respected by all the annotated structures. Such a query is supposed to return an empty set of occurrences. If it is not the case, we can observe the exceptions given. These can be annotation errors or if the annotation is legitimate, the query should be refined to take into account these cases. It also helps to find missing information in the guidelines where some cases are not recorded.
We give below a few examples of such usage of GREW-MATCH for inconsistencies detection.
In AMR structures, according to the guidelines, each named entity, is annotated with a node whose concept expresses the kind of entity (*Person*, *City*...) and with two outgoing edges labeled **name** and **wiki**. With the following pattern, we can search for nodes with an outgoing edge **name** and without an **wiki** edge, and spot inconsistent annotations.

```
pattern { M -[name]-> N }
without { M -[wiki]-> * }
```

This pattern returns one occurrence in the data from the AMR Annotation Dictionary[9] where the city name *New Orleans* is not associated with its wikipedia page. We can also report that the BioAMR Corpus is not consistently annotated in this respect: 95% of **name** edges appear without a **wiki** edge.
On the PMB, we can use the following pattern to observe structures where the same entity (node E) is both the **Agent** and the **Patient** of the same predicate P.

```
pattern {
  P -[Agent]-> E;
  P -[Patient]-> E;
}
```

On the English gold data (10,715 sentences), 20 occurrences are returned. In 15 cases, the pattern is legitimate (sentences with *himself, herself*...) but the 5 remaining cases are annotation errors: for instance, `[p60/d0784]`*Betty killed her mother.* or `[p62/d1397]`*He was seduced by Tom.* (see Figure 8 for this last sentence).

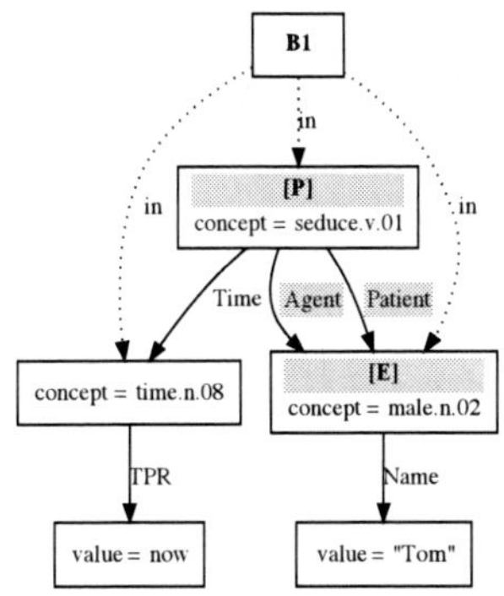

Figure 8: PMB annotation of the sentence `[p62/d1397]` *He was seduced by Tom.*

With the pattern already given in section 3 for double negation, we retrieve also the example given in Figure 9 where the structure is not the one expected. The two internal boxes should be at the same level and not embedded as in the figure. In fact, in the clause notation of the PMB (the original notation from which the SBN notation is extracted), the sentence is correctly annotated. We have indeed found a bug in the conversion process for the SBN notation which has been reported to the PMB maintainers.
On QuantML, the number of available annotated sentences is really tiny: 11 sentences in the TiCC report and 7 sentences in Amblard et al. (2021). Hence, sentences can be checked one by one without using queries; nevertheless, having a graph visualisation of this annotation was useful. When working on the ISA-17 shared task, we started producing the graphs for the examples in the guidelines and we discovered some inconsistencies. In Figure 10, we present the wrong graph of one example and the corrected version of the same annotation.

5. Conclusion

Semantic structures are often complex and represent several different levels of information in the same structure. It is then very useful to provide graphical visualisation in order to assist the humans who have to work with these data, either as annotators or as users. With the GREW-MATCH tool, we propose to use the mathematical model of graphs as a common way to

[9] `https://www.isi.edu/~ulf/amr/lib/amr-dict.html`, consulted on 2022/03/31

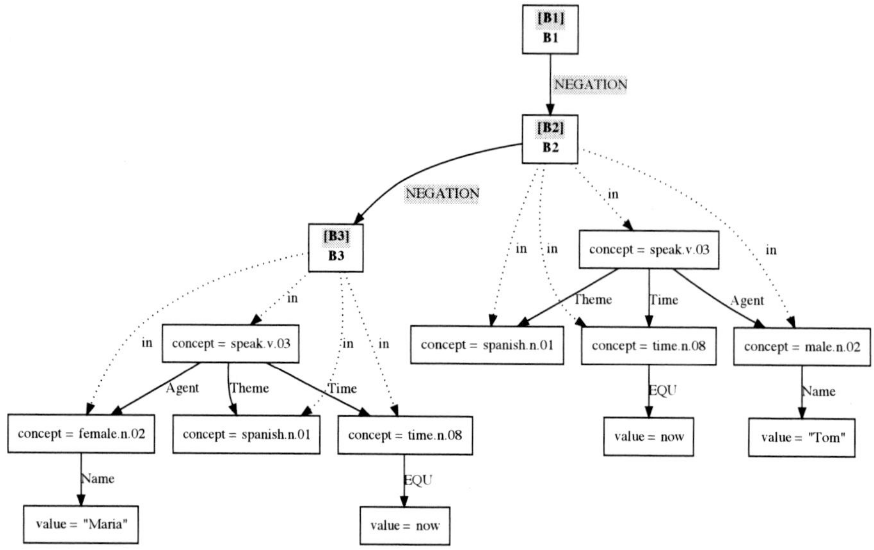

Figure 9: SBN annotation in the PMB of the German sentence [p38/d2263] *Weder Tom noch Maria sprechen Spanisch* (*'Neither Tom nor Mary speaks Spanish.'*).

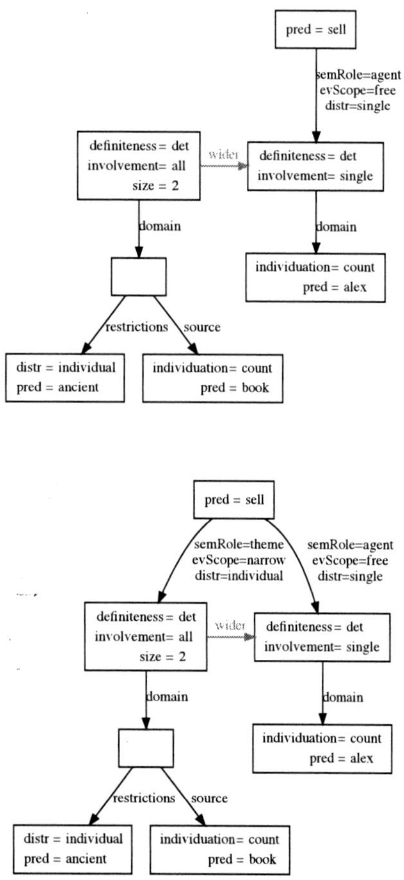

Figure 10: QuantML annotation of the sentence [A7] *Alex sold the two ancient books* in the TiCC report (top) and the corrected annotation (bottom).

represent the semantically annotated data in various frameworks. Doing this, we have the possibility to visualise the annotations but also to use the graph query languages provided to make request on corpora of annotated sentences.

Querying graphs with GREW-MATCH has been useful to make linguistic observations on the data or to check the consistency of the data and the conformity with the guidelines. When inconsistencies are reported, it helps finding how the data or the guidelines (or some other tool) should be improved. GREW-MATCH can also be used as a side-tool when doing annotation, which helps finding similar examples in the already annotated data and thus helps annotators to take consistent decisions for similar constructions. We would like to recommend to use the methodology presented in this paper, based on graph visualisation and graph querying as a non regression evaluation tool for any framework.

In future work, we plan to consider other semantic annotations frameworks like UCCA (Abend and Rappoport, 2013) or DMRS (Copestake, 2009) for instance for which a graph based visualisation and querying would probably be useful as well.

6. Acknowledgements

This work was partially supported by the ANR fund (ANR-20-THIA-0010-01) We would like to thanks Clara Serruau for her preliminary work on the subject and the reviewers for thier comments and suggestions.

7. Bibliographical References

Abend, O. and Rappoport, A. (2013). Universal Conceptual Cognitive Annotation (UCCA). In *Proceedings of the 51st Annual Meeting of the Association for Computational Linguistics (Volume 1: Long Papers)*, pages 228–238, Sofia, Bulgaria, August. Association for Computational Linguistics.

Abzianidze, L., Bjerva, J., Evang, K., Haagsma, H., van Noord, R., Ludmann, P., Nguyen, D.-D., and Bos, J. (2017). The Parallel Meaning Bank: Towards a Multilingual Corpus of Translations Annotated with Compositional Meaning Representations. In *15th Conference of the European Chapter of the Association for Computational Linguistics, Volume 2, Short Papers*, pages 242 – 247, Valencia, Spain, April.

Amblard, M., Fort, K., Guillaume, B., de Groote, P., Li, C., Ludmann, P., Musiol, M., Pavlova, S., Perrier, G., and Pogodalla, S. (2021). The Annotators Did Not Agree on Some of the Guidelines Examples. In *ISA 2021 - 17th Workshop on Interoperable Semantic Annotation*, Groningen/Virtuel, Netherlands, June.

Banarescu, L., Bonial, C., Cai, S., Georgescu, M., Griffitt, K., Hermjakob, U., Knight, K., Koehn, P., Palmer, M., and Schneider, N. (2013). Abstract meaning representation for sembanking. In *Proceedings of the 7th Linguistic Annotation Workshop and Interoperability with Discourse*, pages 178–186.

Bonfante, G., Guillaume, B., and Perrier, G. (2018). *Application of Graph Rewriting to Natural Language Processing*, volume 1 of *Logic, Linguistics and Computer Science Set*. ISTE Wiley, April.

Bos, J. (2021a). Quantification Annotation in Discourse Representation Theory. In *ISA 2021 - 17th Workshop on Interoperable Semantic Annotation*, Groningen/Virtuel, Netherlands, June.

Bos, J. (2021b). Variable-free discourse representation structures. `https://semanticsarchive.net/Archive/jQzMzJlY/compact.pdf`.

Bunt, H., Pustejovsky, J., and Lee, K. (2018). Towards an ISO standard for the annotation of quantification. In *Proceedings of the Eleventh International Conference on Language Resources and Evaluation (LREC 2018)*, Miyazaki, Japan, May. European Language Resources Association (ELRA).

Bunt, H. (2020). Semantic annotation of quantification in natural language. Technical report, TiCC Technical Report 2020-2. Tilburg Center for Cognition and Communication and Department of Cognitive Science and Artificial Intelligence, Tilburg University.

Cohen, J., Cohen, R., Toledo, E., and Buys, J. (2021). RepGraph: Visualising and analysing meaning representation graphs. In *Proceedings of the 2021 Conference on Empirical Methods in Natural Language Processing: System Demonstrations*, pages 79–86, Online and Punta Cana, Dominican Republic, November. Association for Computational Linguistics.

Copestake, A. (2009). Invited talk: Slacker semantics: Why superficiality, dependency and avoidance of commitment can be the right way to go. In *Proceedings of the 12th Conference of the European Chapter of the ACL (EACL 2009)*, pages 1–9, Athens, Greece, March. Association for Computational Linguistics.

Guillaume, B. (2021). Graph Matching and Graph Rewriting: GREW tools for corpus exploration, maintenance and conversion. In *EACL 2021 - 16th conference of the European Chapter of the Association for Computational Linguistics*, Kiev/Online, Ukraine, April.

Palmer, M., Gildea, D., and Kingsbury, P. (2005). The Proposition Bank: An annotated corpus of semantic roles. *Computational Linguistics*, 31(1):71–106.

Proceedings of ISA-18 Workshop at LREC2022, pages 102–109
Marseille, 20 June 2022

Intuitive and Formal Transparency in Semantic Annotation Schemes

Harry Bunt
Tilburg University
harry.bunt@tilburguniversity.edu

Abstract

This paper explores the application of the notion of *transparency* to annotation schemes, understood as the properties that make it easy for potential users to see the scope of the scheme, the main concepts used in annotations, and the ways these concepts are interrelated. Based on an analysis of annotation schemes in the ISO Semantic Annotation Framework, it is argued that the way these schemes make use of 'metamodels' is not optimal, since these models are often not entirely clear and not directly related to the formal specification of the scheme. It is shown that by formalizing the relation between metamodels and annotations, both can benefit and can be made simpler, and the annotation scheme becomes intuitively more transparent.

Keywords: semantic annotation, annotation methodology, metamodels, annotation schema design, ISO standard

1. Introduction

Interoperable semantic annotation has been a concern of the International Organization for Standardization ISO for the last 15-20 years. After a number of exploratory and feasibility studies such as Ide & Romary (2001), Bunt & Romary (2002), Bunt et al. (2005) and Ide & Pustejovsky (2010) the development of a suite of annotation standards was launched, in particular the Semantic Annotation Framework (SemAF), ISO 24617. In view of the complexity of semantic annotation, and taking into account the differences in maturity of approaches to various aspects of semantic analysis, as well as the lack of consensual approaches to some areas of semantics, it was decided to design SemAF as a suite of separate standards for the annotation of different aspects of semantic content.

The first standard in this suite, ISO 24617 Part 1, published in 2012, was a revamped version of the TimeML annotation scheme (Pustejovsky et al., 2003), which was a *de facto* standard for the annotation of temporal information. This standard is therefore informally known as 'ISO-TimeML'. Similarly, Part 2, also published in 2012, was a streamlined version of the existing DIT++ annotation scheme for dialogue act annotation (Bunt, 2009).

During the revamping of TimeML and the streamlining of DIT++, certain methodological aspects of the design of linguistic annotation schemes in general and semantic annotation schemes in particular, crystallized out. Discussions on the details of representing annotation of temporal information as XML expressions made it clear that annotation standards should not be established at the level of representation formats, but at a more abstract level, focusing on the use of standardized *concepts*. This insight came hand in hand with embracing the notion of *data categories*, as specifications of concept definitions according to well-defined terminological standards, to be documented not only in individual standards but also in a global *data category registry* (DCR, Broeder et al., 2010).

The Linguistic Annotation Framework (Ide & Romary, 2004; ISO 24612) captures some of the fundamental insights about linguistic annotation that emerged in the process, such as the importance of stand-off annotation and the distinction between annotations and representations. *Annotations* capture linguistic information about certain stretches of primary data, irrespective of a particular representation format; *representations* describe annotations in a particular format, such as XML. ISO standards should thus be specified at the level of annotations, rather than representations.

The distinction between annotations and representations is one of the cornerstones of the principles of semantic annotation formulated by Bunt (2010; 2014), and laid down in the methodological standard ISO 24617-6 (2016), which aims at securing the quality and methodological consistency of further SemAF parts. The annotation/representation distinction is implemented in this standard in requiring SemAF standards to have a 3-level architecture consisting of an abstract syntax, a concrete syntax, and a semantics, as displayed in Fig. 1. In this architecture, a concrete syntax for a given abstract syntax (plus semantics) is required to be *complete* and *unambiguous*. Completeness means that every well-formed annotation structure defined by the abstract syntax has a representation that encodes it; unambiguity means that every representation encodes exactly one structure of the abstract syntax. A representation format with these properties is called *ideal*. Due to the properties of completeness and unambiguity, all ideal representation formats for a given abstract syntax are semantically equivalent.

In addition to the three levels of this architecture, a tradition in the formulation of ISO standards for language resources is the presentation of a 'metamodel' as a visual view of the types of concepts involved in annotations. Figure 1 shows this architecture in a

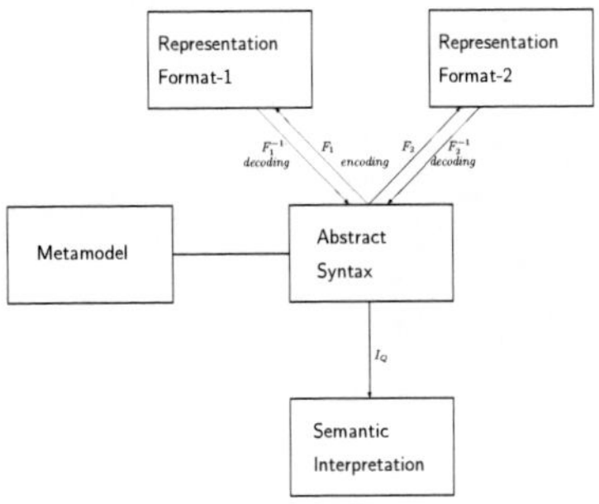

Figure 1: Architecture of SemAF standards.

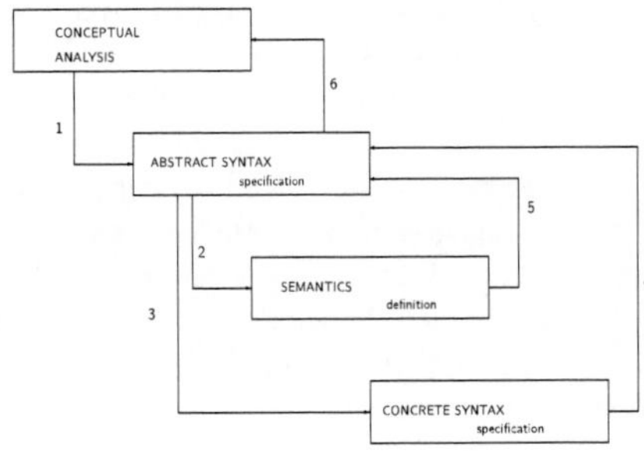

Figure 2: CASCADES development process.

schematic fashion, with two alternative representation formats specified by two different concrete syntax specifications.

Metamodels have often played an important role in developing SemAF parts, in making the scope of an annotation scheme explicit, and indicating its main concepts to be used in annotations, and their interrelations. From a methodological point of view, a question that remains, however, is what exactly is the status of the metamodel. Figure 1 shows the metamodel as somewhat hanging loose, not really connected with the ingredients of the formal specification of an annotation scheme. Is it just an easily interpretable pretty picture?

The paper proposes an answer to this question. It does so by showing that there can be a tight connection between a metamodel and actual annotations, and that such a coupling makes the annotation scheme intuitively transparant for its users. This notion of transparency is given a formal basis by defining a relation of 'instantiation' between metamodels and annotations. The simplicity of this relation largely determines the transparency of the annotation scheme. Formal transparency as the basis of intuitive transparency. This will be illustrated by several SemAF metamodels and in particular by showing how the aim of transparency helps to simplify both the metamodel and the annotations in the standard under development for quantification phenomena.

This paper is organised as follows. Section 2 discusses the development of annotation schemes in the ISO Semantic Annotation Framework and the role of metamodels in the process. Section 3 discusses the notion of transparency applied to metamodels. Section 4 develops the idea that annotations can be viewed as instances of a metamodel, formalizing the notion of a metamodel as a graphical structure and showing how XML annotations can be mapped to that format. The metamodel and annotations of QuantML (ISO WD 24617-12) are used to illustrate this. Section 5 discusses the advantages of treating annotations as instances of a metamodel, and concludes by considering the methodological consequences of this idea.

2. Metamodels in SemAF

2.1. The CASCADES development process

For the development of the individual SemAF parts, a process methodology has been developed called CASCADES (**C**onceptual analysis, **A**bstract syntax, **S**emantics, and **C**oncrete syntax for **A**nnotation **DES**ign) (Bunt, 2015) which has been included in the methodological standard ISO 24617 Part 6, Principles. Figure 2 shows the steps in this process, starting with a conceptual analysis phase and ending in the specification of a concrete syntax.

The CASCADES model derives its usefulness in the first place from enabling a systematic design process, in which due attention is given to the conceptual and semantic choices on which more superficial decisions such as the choice of particular XML attributes and values should be based. Second, the model provides methodological support by means of procedures for how to make the step from one level of decision-making to the next, in particular for (1) how to construct an abstract syntax given a metamodel (step 1 in Fig. 2); (2) how to define a formal semantics for a given abstract syntax (step 2); and (3) how to map an abstract syntax to an XML-based concrete syntax.

Realistic design processes require feedback loops. Figure 2 shows three such loops. First, the specification of an abstract syntax is a way to formalise the conceptual analysis in the initial stage of the process. This formalisation may very well clarify or alter some aspects of the initial analysis; CASCADES step 6 is for feeding the results of the formalisation back into the conceptual analysis. Second, the specification of a concrete syntax, defining a specific representation format, may by virtue of its concreteness motivate adaptations in the underlying abstract syntax; step 4 is for this feedback in the design process. Third, since the definition of a semantics for an abstract syntax is the best way to find inadequacies in the latter, this may be fed back into the abstract syntax specification (step 5). And finally, the latter two feedback loops may well be combined: if the feedback in step 4 has resulted in a revised specification of the abstract syntax, them this will require adaptations to be made in the semantics (step 2), which may be fed back again into the abstract syntax specification (step 5). This cycle $\langle 2; 5\rangle$ may be repeated until the abstract syntax and its semantics are satisfactory and stable, at which point the annotation language is considered to be semantically adequate. The concrete syntax should now be adapted to this abstract syntax (step 3) - which in turn may have consequences that should be fed back (step 4). In fact, the 'outer cycle' $\langle 3; 4\rangle$ does not make much sense to perform if not combined with the 'inner cycle' $\langle 2; 5\rangle$, resulting together in the feedback loop (1):

(1) $\langle 4; \langle 2; 5\rangle^*; 3\rangle^*$

This feedback loop is particularly important not only for systematically developing a consistent design, starting from scratch with of conceptual analysis, but also for being applied to a pre-existing representation format, in order to detect semantic deficiencies, or to develop an annotation language that better meets the requirements of the ISO Linguistic Annotation Framework and the requirements of semantic adequacy.

3. Transparency in Metamodels

An annotation scheme is intuitively more transparent if presented with a metamodel that is conceptually clear and informative. Conceptual clarity can be achieved by using a relatively small number of well-defined concepts. In several SemAF documents, such as ISO 24617-2 and ISO WD 24617-12, a metamodel is presented together with a discussion of basic concepts in order to support this aspect of the model's clarity. Informativeness means that the metamodel gives a good indication of the concepts that make up annotations according to this scheme.

Figure 3, for example, shows the metamodel for reference annotation in ISO 24617-9 (2019). This metamodel indicates that (1) referring expressions are anchored to segments in the primary data; (2) such expressions refer to entities that play a role in a discourse ('discourse entities'); and (3) that two kinds of relations are distinguished: relations between referring expressions ('lexical relations', like synonymy) and relations between discourse entities ('objectal relations', like identity).

Its simplicity makes this metamodel exemplary in its clarity, but it is not very informative: it hardly provides any information about the concepts that go into annotations according to this annotation scheme. Moreover, a critical look at the metamodel raises various questions: What is the significance of the frame around the top

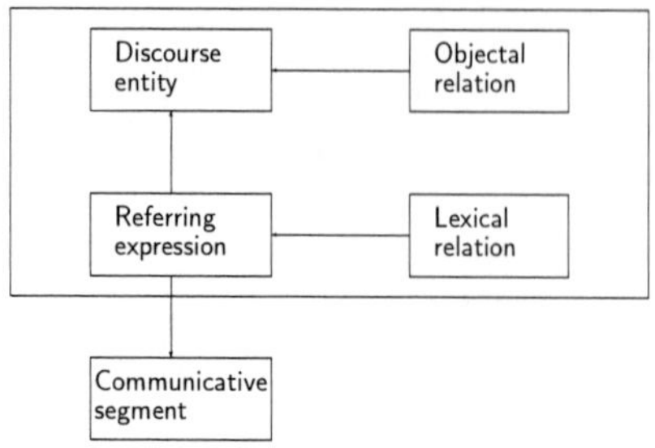

Figure 3: Metamodel for coreference annotation (ISO 24617-9).

four boxes? What do the arrows from objectal relations and lexical relations to discourse entities and referring expressions signify? Do the arrows from referring eXpressions to discourse entities and communicative segments have the same significance? Altogether, this metamodel does not contribute much to making the Reference Annotation Schema (ISO 24617-9) transparent to its users.

Figure 4 shows the metamodel underlying QuantML annotations, as proposed in ISO WD 24617-12, i.e. Part 12 of the SemAF suite, which is currently under development. Arrows with multiple heads indicate the possibility of multiple linking (like for the participation in events) or an attribute having multiple values (like for the reference domain of a quantification being defined by a source domain and multiple modifiers). This metamodel contains all and only those concepts of which instances may occur in QuantML annotations. In the next section, we formalize the relation between this metamodel and the annotations that it supports.

4. Annotations as Metamodel Instances

This section explores the idea that annotations can be regarded as instances of the metamodel. This idea is based on the observation that a metamodel provides information about relevant combinations of concepts. For example, the QuantML metamodel in Fig. 4 says that a set of participants may be involved in a set of events in a variety of ways, characterized by five concepts: distributivity, semantic role, event scope, polarity, and exhaustiveness. The annotation of a given item of primary data, such as the sentence *"Only three of the fifty-two students protested"* will for example say that there is a participant set of three students, taken from the reference domain consisting of 52 students, individually involved as Agents, with positive polarity, and exhaustively (none of the other students protested). The annotation thus combines instances of the concepts in the metamodel. The annotation of this sentence represented in QuantML/XML format is shown in (7) below. This representation has a straightforward mapping to a graphical representation in terms of com-

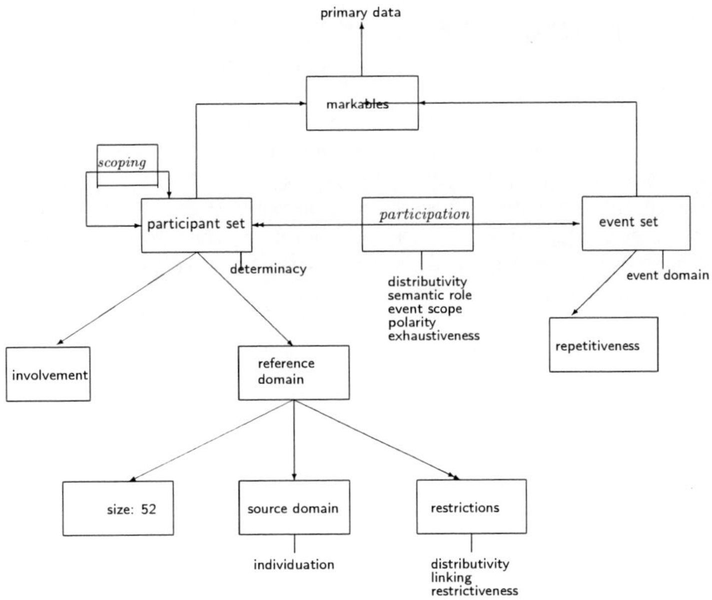

Figure 4: Metamodel for quantification annotation (ISO WD 24617-12:2021)

ponents of the metamodel. Boxed entities in the latter representation correspond to XML elements, and strings associated with boxes correspond to (string) values of attributes within such elements; arrows from boxes to boxes indicate attributes with structured values. Double-headed arrows indicate the possible multiplicity of relata (such as multiple sets of participants involved in certain events) To further explore the formal relation between metamodels and annotations, we first formalize the graphical representation of metamodels used in Fig. 4 and subsequently introduce the notion of 'instance' of such a graph.

4.1. Metamodels as M-Graphs

First, inspecting the metamodel shown in Fig. 4, we note that there are four types of ingredients:

(2) Metamodel ingredients:

1. boxes containing structured concepts (such as participant sets and reference domains), source domains. Some of these are linked to markables, others are not;
2. boxes containing unstructured objects (such as size, involvement, and repetitiveness; these are not linked to markables);
3. structured labeled relations (such as participation, scoping);
4. unlabeled arrows emanating from boxes of type 1 and connecting these to boxes of type 2.

These types of ingredients can be formally defined as follows:

(3)
1. An M-Box is a quadruple ⟨markable, element type, simple concept list, complex concept list ⟩.
2. A simple concept list is a list of concepts of which the instances are unstructured entities.
3. A complex concept list is a list of concepts of which the instances are structured entities (represented by M-Boxes that are pointed to).
4. An M-link is a triple ⟨M-Box, M-label, M-Box⟩.
5. An M-label is a triple ⟨label-name, simple concept list⟩.

A Metamodel Graph (M-Graph) is a collection of M-boxes and M-links. Metamodels of the form of Fig. 4 can be formalized as M-graphs using the following mapping relation.

(5) Mapping metamodel diagrams to M-Graphs:

1. Boxes containing structured concepts are mapped to M-Boxes.
2. Boxes containing unstructured objects are mapped to elements in the simple concept list of the M-Box at the tail of the arrow to such boxes.
3. Structured labeled relations are mapped to M-links with the same label name.
4. Unlabeled arrows connecting two boxes with structured concepts are mapped to elements in the complex concept list of the M-Box at the tail.

Using these formal definitions and mappings to M-Graphs, the QuantML metamodel can be formally

(4) QuantML metamodel as M-graph:
$M_{QuantML}$ =
{ ⟨markable, event set, [repetitiveness, event domain]⟩,
⟨markable, participant set, [determinacy, involvement, reference domain]⟩,
⟨markable, reference domain, [size, source domain, restrictions]⟩,
⟨markable, source domain, [individuation]⟩,
⟨⟨markable, event set, [repetitiveness, event domain]⟩,
⟨participation, [distributivity, semantic role, event scope, polarity, exhaustiveness]⟩,
⟨markable, participant set, [determinacy, involvement, reference domain]⟩⟩,
⟨⟨markable, participant set, [determinacy, involvement, reference domain]⟩,
⟨scoping, [argument scope]⟩,
⟨markable, participant set, [determinacy, involvement, reference domain]⟩⟩ }

specified as the M-Graph in (9).

It may be noted that the status of the ingredients in the QuantML metamodel is in some cases not entirely clear. Concepts like determinacy, polarity, and exhaustiveness are clearly unstructured, but for concepts like involvement, markables, and size it isn't obvious whether they are structured or unstructured. The 'restrictions' concept is clearly one with internal structure, so why does the metamodel not say anything about that? Why are some boxes with structured concepts linked to markables, others not? The formalization of metamodels as M-Graphs helps to make these issues explicit and resolve them. It may be noted here that by identifying M-Boxes with diagram boxes containing structured concepts, as in (5), every box in this diagram should either be linked to a markable or should contain an unstructured concept. This is not the case: the boxes 'source domain' and 'restrictions' contain structured objects but are not linked to markables. Moreover, the concepts of 'involvement', 'size', and 'repetitiveness' are in fact structured, which is not indicated in the metamodel, and which requires them to also be linked to markables. We will return to these issues below.

4.2. MI-Graphs

Just as metamodels, represented graphically in terms of boxes connected by labelled and unlabelled arrows, can be formalized as M-Graphs, similarly annotations can be represented graphically in much the same way, which can be formalized as 'instances' of M-Graphs. Such instances are called 'MI-Graphs', and are formally defined as follows.

A Model Instantiation Graph (MI-Graph) is a collection of nodes connected by labeled structured edges, called MI-links, and labeled unstructured edges. Nodes have the form of boxes, called MI-boxes, which consist of a name (like 'participant set'), a markable, a list of attribute-value pairs, and zero or more directed edges labeled by attribute names (like 'size' and 'domain') which point to other boxes. Formally, an MI-Graph is a collection of MI-boxes and MI-links such that all MI-boxes are linked to one or more other MI-boxes, and all MI-links connect two MI-boxes. The following definitions formalize the notions of MI-box and MI-link.

(6) **Definition.** An MI-Graph is an instance of an M-Graph, i.e.:

- An MI-Box is a quadruple ⟨m, e, AV, AMI⟩, where m is a markable, e is an element type of the M-Graph (such as 'event set'), AV is a list of instances of unstructured concepts, and AM is a list of instances of structured concepts, labeled with names of attributes that have structured values.
- An MI-label is a pair ⟨label-name, AV⟩, with AV as above.
- An MI-link is a triple ⟨MI-Box, MI-label, MI-Box⟩.

4.3. Annotations as MI-Graphs

Example (7) shows the QuantML annotation of "Only three of the fifty-two students protested" in XML.

(7) **Primary data:**
"Only three of the fifty-two students protested."
Segmentation:
m1 = three of the fifty-two students, m2 = the fifty-two students, m3 = students, m4 = protested.
Annotation in QuantML/XML:
<event xml:id="e1" target="#m4" pred="protest"
<entity xml:id="x1" target="#m1" domain="#x2" involvement="#n1" determinacy="indet" size= "52"/>
<refDomain xml:id="x2" target="#m2" source="#x3" restrs=""/>
<sourceDomain xml:id="x3" target="m3" individuation="count" pred="student"/>
<numPred xml:id="n1" numRel="equal" num="3"/>
<event xml:id="e1" target="m4" pred="protest"/>
<participation event="e1" participant="x1" semRole="agent" distr="individual" eventScope= "narrow" exhaustiveness= "exhaustive" polarity= "positive"/>

The corresponding MI-Graph is not easily obtained from this representation, since the latter includes the specification of the reference domain size as a property of the participant set, whereas in the metamodel it is a property of the reference domain. This suggests a lack of transparency in the annotation scheme. To remedy this, the simplest solution is to move the @size attribute from <event> elements (corresponding to participant sets) to <refDomain> elements.

The XML representation can be converted into an MI-Graph by applying the function F_{XG}, defined in (8). This function takes a QuantML/XML annotation structure A_X as a parameter and converts its constituent XML elements into MI-Boxes and MI-Links.

(8)
1. $F_{XG}(A_X$, <entity xml:id="x" target="#m" involvement="#xi" domain="#y" determinacy="d"/>) = ⟨m, participant set, [⟨'d'⟩], [⟨involvement, $F_{XG}(A_X$,#xi)⟩, ⟨domain, $F_{XG}(A_X$,#y)⟩]⟩
2. For any identifier of the form $\#z$, $F_{XG}(A_X$, $\#z$) = the result of applying F_{XG} to the A_X-element with xml:id="z".
3. For any constant c, $F_{XG}(A_X$, c) = c.
4. $F_{XG}(A_X$, <event xml:id="e" target="#m" pred="P" rep="#r"/>) = ⟨m, event set, [⟨$F_{XG}(A_X$,#r)⟩, ⟨domain, $F_{XG}(A_X$,P)⟩]⟩
5. $F_{XG}(A_X$, <participation event="#e" participant="#x" semRole=A distr="individual" exhaustiveness="exhaustive" polarity= "positive"/>) = ⟨$F_{XG}(A_X$,#e), ⟨participation, [$F_{XG}(A_X$, A), individual, exhaustive, positive]⟩, $F_{XG}(A_X$,#x)⟩
6. $F_{XG}(A_X$, <numPred xml:id="n" target="#m" numRel="R" num="#k"/>) = ⟨m, numPred, [⟨$F_{XG}(A_X$,R)⟩, ⟨nu, $F_{XG}(A_X$,#k)⟩]⟩
7. And so on.

Similarly, the inverse function F_{GX} converts an MI-Graph into a QuantML/XML annotation structure.

The MI-Graph corresponding to the QuantML/XML representation in (7) is shown in (9), in which the annotations of involvement (participant set size "three") and reference domain size ("fifty-two") have for the sake of readability been simplified to numbers.

(9) Annotation (8) as MI-graph:
{ ⟨m4, event set, [protest]⟩,
⟨m1, participant set, [indeterminate, 3, 52], [⟨domain, F_{XG}(#x2)]⟩,
⟨m2, reference domain, [], [source domain, F_{XG}(#x3)]⟩,
⟨m3, source domain, [count, student]⟩,
⟨⟨m4, event set, [protest]⟩,
⟨participation, [individual, agent, narrow, positive, exhaustive]⟩,
⟨m1, participant set, [indeterminate, 3, 52], [⟨domain, F_{XG}(#x2)]⟩,
⟨scoping, [argument scope]⟩ } }

After applying the recursively embedded calls to F_{XG}, and using the visualization meethod of M-Graphs that is behind the diagram in Fig. 4 the MI-Graph in (7) can be rendered graphically as shown in Fig. 5. Comparing this representation with the metamodel in Fig. 4, we can see clearly that the QuantML metamodel is optimally 'transparent' in the sense of giving users of the annotation scheme an immediate impression of the annotations that the scheme supports. The relative simplicity of the graphical representation as a metamodel instantiation graph is rather surprising, given the complexity of quantification phenomena in natural language. The graphical representations of annotations can also be viewed as better human-readable than the XML-representations. As the conversion function F_XG makes explicit, XML expressions can be automatically converted to this graphical format, which opens a possibility for easy inspection of QuantML annotations.

5. Discussion and Conclusions

The formalization of metamodels as M-Graphs, and the notion of instantiating an M-Graph to represent annotations, is useful for defining metamodels with greater precision and to see that a metamodel is an abstraction of individual annotations. In that sense, the metamodel is maximally informative, and maximally transparent. While formalizing the informal box-and-arrow representation of the QuantML metamodel as an M-Graph, we encountered several issues that the metamodel did not address properly.

First, as noted in section 4.1, every non-relational box is intended to correspond to a structured concept, characterized by a number of features.[1] The fact that some of these concepts are linked to a markable while others are not, suggests that some of them are expressed in the primary data while others are not. This is not really the case: involvement, size, source domain, domain restrictions, and repetitiveness are all expressed in the data. Specifications of size and repetitiveness are possibly complex quantitative predicates, like *slightly more than 12 ounces, between 40 and 45*; involvement specification can also use such predicates, as well as vague predicates like *not much, just a few, quite a lot* and proportional indications like *nearly all, by*

[1]In terms of the QuantML abstract syntax, not considered in this paper, every non-relational box corresponds to a so-called 'entity structure' and every relational box to a 'link structure'. Entity structures by definition contain semantic information about a stretch of primary data, and are thus always linked to a markable,

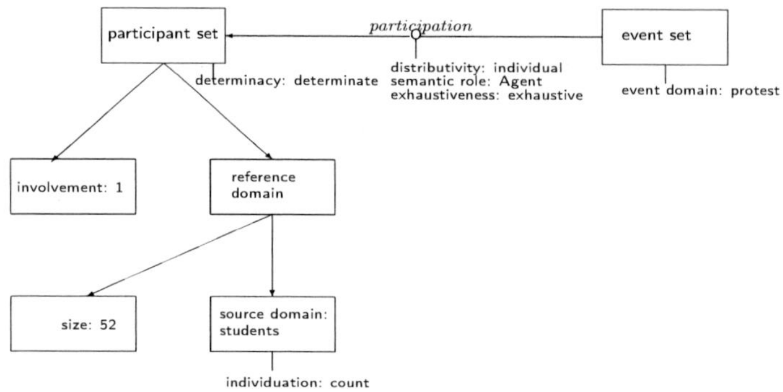

Figure 5: QuantML annotation as instantiation of the metamodel .

far most. The QuantML metamodel is deliberately unspecific about how much detail such structures should be covered in its annotations, imagining that annotation scheme plug-ins, possibly based on the ISO standard for annotating measurable quantitative information (ISO 2417-9XX), could be added on for this purpose. Where this is a viable strategy remains to be seen.

Second, another deliberate choice in the metamodel concerns the lack of detail about of reference domain restrictions. Such restrictions can take a variety of forms natural language, such as adjectives, nouns, relative clauses, prepositional phrases, and possessive phrases. Each of these forms comes with slightly different semantic structures, and it would clutter up the metamodel to make these all explicit. This could perhaps be resolved by specifying one or more separate sub-metamodels for the various forms of restriction.

From a methodological point of view, the explorations in this paper shed new light on the relation between metamodels and annnotation representations, as depicted in Fig. 5, and on the role of this relation in the CASCADES development process depicted in Fig. 2. Conceptually, the metamodel of an annotation scheme is closely related to the abstract syntax specification, as the CASCADES model in Fig. 2 also suggests, but in this paper we have shown that the metamodel can also be tightly coupled with a particular annotation representation format through the notion of instantiation. This is shown in Fig. 6. For the CASCADES design model, it suggests that it may be useful to add a step where a forward jump is made from metamodel specification to the establishment of an annotation representation format, and a backward jump in the opposite direction - this is shown in Figure 7.

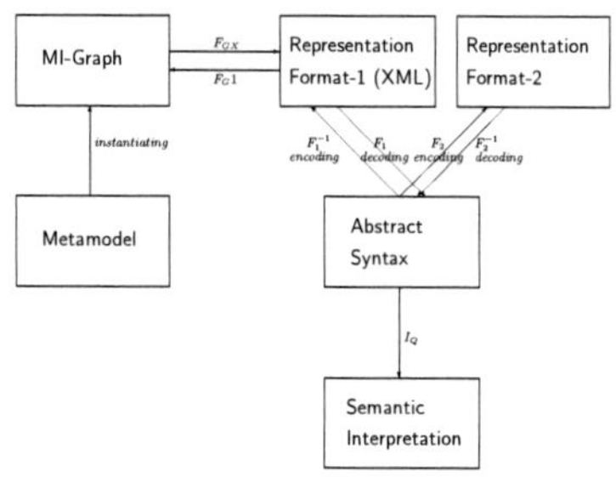

Figure 6: Architecture of SemAF standards with metamodel instantiation.

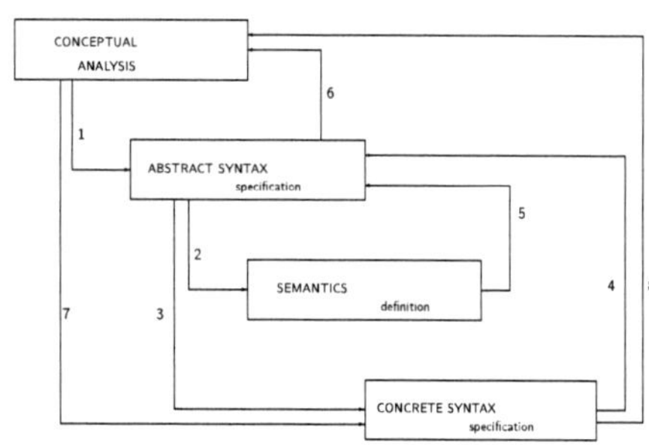

Figure 7: CASCADES development process with metamodel instantiation.

6. References

Broeder, D., M. Kemps-Snijders, D. Uytvanck, M. Windhouwer, P. Wittenburg, and C. Zinn (2010). A data cataegory registry and component-based metadata framework. In *Proceedings of LREC 2010*. ELRA, Paris.

Bunt, H. (2009a). A framework for dialogue act specification. In R. C. D. Heylen, C. Pelachaud and D. Traum (Eds.), *Proceedings of EDAMLAAMAS Workshop "Towards a Standard Markup Language for Embodied Dialogue Acts, Budapest*, pp. 36–36.

Bunt, H. (2015). On the principles of semantic annotation. In *Proceedings 11th Joint ACL-ISO Workshop on Interoperable Semantic Annotation (ISA-*

11), London, pp. 1–13.

Bunt, H., M. Kipp, M. Maybury, and W. Wahlster (2005). Fusion and coordination for multimodal interactive information presentation. In O. Stock and M. Zancanaro (Eds.), *Multimodal Intelligent Information Presentation*, pp. 325–339. Dordrecht: Springer.

Bunt, H. and L. Romary (2004). Standardization in Multimodal Content Representation: Some methodological issues. In *Proceedings of LREC 2004*, Lisbon, pp. 2219–2222. Paris: ELRA.

Bunt, H. and A. Shiffrin (2006). Methodologial aspects of semantic annotation. In *Proceedings of the 5th International Conference on Language Resources and Evaluation (LREC 2006), Genova, Italy*, Paris. ELRA.

Ide, N. and J. Pustejovsky (2010). What does interoperability mean, anyway? toward an operational definition of interoperability. In *Proceedings of the Second International Conference on Global Interoperability for Language Resources (ICGL 2010)*, Hong Kong.

Ide, N. and L. Romary (2001). Standards for language resources. In *Proceedings of the IRCS Workshop on Linguistic Databases*, Philapdelphia.

Ide, N. and L. Romary (2004). International Standard for a Linguistic Annotation Framework. *Natural Language Engineering 10*, 211–225.

ISO (2009). *24612:2009, Language Resource Management - Linguistic Annotation Framework (LAF)*. International Organisation for Standardisation ISO, Geneva.

ISO (2012). *ISO 24617-1: 2012, Language Resource Management - Semantic Annotation Framework (SemAF) - Part 1: Time and events*. Geneva: International Organisation for Standardisation ISO.

ISO (2014). *ISO 24617-4: 2014, Language Resource Management - Semantic Annotation Framework (SemAF) - Part 4: Semantic roles*. Geneva: International Organisation for Standardisation ISO.

ISO (2015). *ISO 24617-6:2015, Language Resource Management - Semantic Annotation Framework (SemAF) - Part 6: Principles of semantic annotation*. Geneva: International Organisation for Standardisation ISO.

ISO (2019a). *ISO 24617-9:2019, Language Resource Management - Semantic Annotation Framework (SemAF) - Part 9: Reference annotation framework (RAF)*. Geneva: International Organisation for Standardisation ISO.

ISO (2019b). *ISO/WD 24617-12:2019, Language Resource Management: Semantic Annotation Framework (SemAF) - Part 12: Quantification*. Geneva.: International Standard. International Organisation for Standardisation ISO.

ISO (2021, November). *ISO/WD 24617-12: 2021, Language Resource Management - Semantic Annotation Framework (SemAF) - Part 12: Quantification (Second Draft)*. Geneva: International Organisation for Standardisation ISO.

Petukhova, V. and H. Bunt (2008). LIRICS semantic role annotation: design and evaluation of a set of data categories. In *Proceedings of the Sixth International Conference on Language Resources and Evaluation (LREC 2008)*, Marrakech, Morocco. ELRA, Paris.

Pustejovsky, J., H. Bunt, and K. Lee (2010). ISO-TimeML. In *Proceedings of the 7th International Conference on Language Resources and Evaluation (LREC 2010)*, Malta. ELDA, Paris.

Pustejovsky, J., J. Castano, R. Ingria, R. Gaizauskas, G. Katz, R. Saurí, and A. Setzer (2003, January). TimeML: Robust Specification of Event and Temporal Expressions in Text. In *Proceedings of the Fifth International Workshop on Computational Semantics (IWCS-5)*, Tilburg, Netherlands, pp. 337–353.

Proceedings of ISA-18 Workshop at LREC2022, pages 110–117
Marseille, 20 June 2022

How much of UCCA can be predicted from AMR?

Siyana Pavlova, Maxime Amblard, Bruno Guillaume
Université de Lorraine, CNRS, Inria, LORIA, F-54000 Nancy, France
{firstname.lastname}@loria.fr

Abstract

In this paper, we consider two of the currently popular semantic frameworks: Abstract Meaning Representation (AMR) - a more abstract framework, and Universal Conceptual Cognitive Annotation (UCCA) - an anchored framework. We use a corpus-based approach to build two graph rewriting systems, a deterministic and a non-deterministic one, from the former to the latter framework. We present their evaluation and a number of ambiguities that we discovered while building our rules. Finally, we provide a discussion and some future work directions in relation to comparing semantic frameworks of different flavors.

Keywords: Semantic Framework, Graph Rewriting, Abstract Meaning Representation, Universal Conceptual Cognitive Annotation

1. Introduction and Motivation

A number of frameworks for semantic annotation have been proposed in the past decades. As each puts the main focus on a different aspect of semantics, each is fit for its purpose, has its set of adopters and there is no one framework that is better than the rest. As a result, semantically annotated data, which is not easy to come by in the first place and is laborious and time-consuming to produce manually, is scattered across different frameworks. It would be useful if we can transform annotations from one framework into another, thus making more data available in various frameworks.

In the current work, we focus on the comparison between two of the existing semantic frameworks, with different relations to anchoring - one anchored and one more abstract - and an experiment we carried out to see how much of the former can be predicted from the latter. These frameworks are Universal Conceptual Cognitive Annotation (UCCA) (Abend and Rappoport, 2013) and Abstract Meaning Representation (AMR) (Banarescu et al., 2013).

In section 2, we give an overview of the two frameworks that we consider in this work as well as the shared task from which the data we use comes from. In section 3, we describe the Graph Rewriting experiment we carried out to transform AMR graphs into UCCA-like structures. Then section 4 describes how our graph rewriting system was evaluated and reports our results and observations. In section 5 we present some of the ambiguous cases we discovered when building out rewriting systems. Finally, in section 6, we provide a broader discussion on some of the points stemming from this experiment and some future work directions.

2. Background

Our choice of frameworks is grounded in the current popularity of the two we are considering - AMR is often discussed in the community, with proposals for potential enhancements in many of the semantic workshops and conferences, and UCCA has increasingly been gaining traction in the past years, with more data being made available continuously and proposals for extension layers being made too.

Additionally, AMR and UCCA are two of the frameworks that were part of the 2019 and 2020 Meaning Representation Parsing (MRP) shared tasks (Oepen et al., 2019; Oepen et al., 2020) thanks to which there is parallel annotated data for the two, even though only a small amount (87 sentences from the WSJ corpus) is freely available.

2.1. AMR

AMR was introduced in 2013. Broadly speaking, it represents "who did what to whom" in a sentence. AMR abstracts from the surface representation of a sentence and is what (Koller et al., 2019) describe as a flavor 2 semantic framework, where the "flavor" of a framework stands for correspondence between surface level tokens and graph nodes. In flavor 2 frameworks, such as AMR, there is no direct correspondence between the two - not all tokens are present as nodes in the graph and not all graph nodes correspond to tokens. Thus, sentences that are different on the surface, but have the same basic meaning are represented by the same AMR. For example, the AMR in Figure 1 is the representation of the sentence "*The girl made adjustments to the machine.*", but also of the sentences "*The girl adjusted the machine.*" and "*The machine was adjusted by the girl.*" as shown in the official AMR specifications[1] .

AMR relies heavily on predicate-argument structure and makes extensive use of PropBank predicates (Palmer et al., 2005), trying to maximize their use whenever possible in sentences. Predicates are used

[1] `https://github.com/amrisi/amr-guidelines/` (at the time of writing, this link points to version 1.2.6 of the specifications)

```
(a / adjust-01
   :ARG0 (b / girl)
   :ARG1 (m / machine))
```

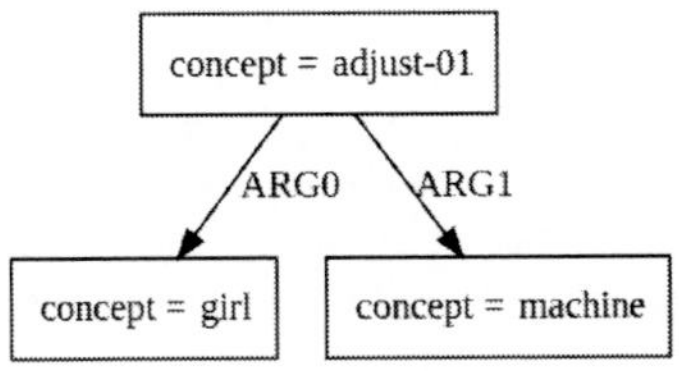

Figure 1: AMR annotation of the sentences "*The girl made adjustments to the machine.*", "*The girl adjusted the machine.*" and "*The machine was adjusted by the girl.*" in Penman format (top) and as a graph (bottom).

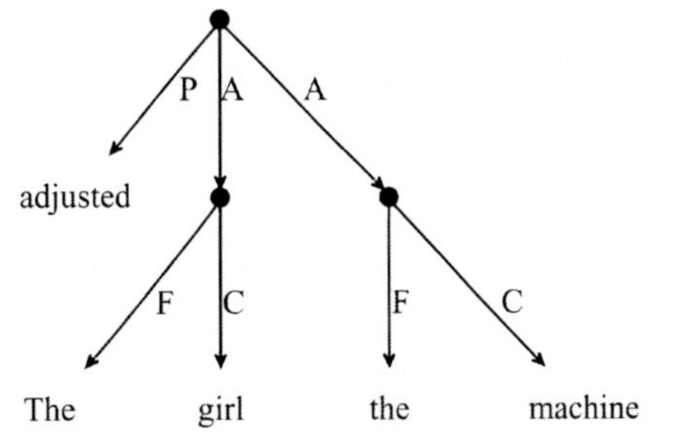

$[\mathtt{The}_{F}\ \mathtt{girl}_{C}]_{A}\ \mathtt{adjusted}_{P}\ [\mathtt{the}_{F}\ \mathtt{machine}_{C}]_{A}$

Figure 2: UCCA annotation of the sentence "*The girl adjusted the machine.*" as a graph (top) and in textual format (bottom).

not only to annotate the verbs in a sentence, but also the nouns and adjectives whenever possible. As seen with the example from Figure 1, the noun *adjustment* and the verb *adjust* are both annotated with the PropBank predicate `adjust-01`. The arguments of PropBank predicates appear as core roles in AMR graphs. In addition, non-core roles such as `location`, `time`, `purpose`, etc. form the rest of the AMR relations.

In terms of graph features, AMR graphs are directed acyclic graphs (DAGs) and singly-rooted. The acyclicity and single-rootedness come at the cost of using inverse relations. Any role, core or non-core, can be reversed by adding `-of` to its name and changing the direction of the relation. Apart from avoiding cycles, inverse roles also serve to highlight the *focus* of a sentence by making sure that the central concept is the root of the AMR graph.

The AMR Bank is a manually-produced corpus of AMR annotations in English. Only a portion of it (namely the Little Prince corpus and the BioAMR corpus) are freely available. The rest of the AMR Bank can be obtained by a (paid) license from the Linguistics Data Consortium. AMR was designed with English in mind and does not aim to be a universal semantic representation framework. That being said, there have been attempts to use the framework for other languages, notably Chinese, in the Chinese AMR (CAMR) Bank[2].

While powerful in its ability to abstract from surface representation, there are a number of phenomena that the framework does not cover - tense, plurality, definiteness, scope, to name some of the more prominent ones. Some of these issues have been addressed: (Bos, 2020) proposes an extension to deal with scope in AMR, while (Donatelli et al., 2018) proposes to augment AMR with tense and aspect. However, to the best of our knowledge, no corpora exist that use the proposed extensions yet.

[2]`https://www.cs.brandeis.edu/~clp/camr/camr.html`

2.2. UCCA

UCCA was introduced in 2013 as well, but has gained more traction in recent years - a number of extension layers have been proposed and the number of available annotated datasets has been increasing.

Following (Koller et al., 2019)'s flavor classification, UCCA is a flavor 1 framework, i.e. an *anchored* framework - each token (or a group of tokens in the case of named entities, such as proper names and dates) corresponds to a leaf node in the graph, but additional nodes are present in the graph too. UCCA organises processes (actions) and states into *scenes*, where the central process or state, its participants, temporal and adverbial information are labeled. Each of these may expand into its own subgraph where elaborations, quantifiers, function and relation words are labeled. A sentence may give rise to multiple scenes and these can be labeled as well. UCCA offers 14 relation types in total. It allows for re-entrances via the so-called "remote" edges. As with AMR, UCCA graphs are also singly-rooted DAGs.

Figure 2 shows the UCCA annotation of the sentence "*The girl adjusted the machine*". The process `P` at the center of the scene is *adjusted*. That scene includes two participants `A`, which are internally annotated further, with the central concept (*girl, machine*) receiving the label `C` and the function word *the* - `F`.

As the name suggests, UCCA is designed to be a *universal* semantics framework, i.e. it aims to work across languages as opposed to being designed with a specific language in mind. Indeed, the currently available UCCA datasets span across English, French, German and Hebrew.

A number of extension layers have been proposed for UCCA, such as adding semantic roles (Shalev et al., 2019; Prange et al., 2019a), co-reference (Prange et al., 2019b) and implicit arguments (Cui and Hershcovich, 2020). However, while small proof of concept datasets exist for some of these, there is no parallel corpus between any of the UCCA extension layers and other semantic frameworks, such as AMR. Therefore, for this study we concentrate on the foundational layer of UCCA.

2.3. MRP

The MRP 2019 and 2020 Shared Tasks are parsing tasks, that have sentences annotated in a number of semantic frameworks. AMR, UCCA, DM: DELPH-IN MRS Bi-Lexical Dependencies (DM), Prague Semantic Dependencies (PSD) and Elementary Dependency Structures (EDS) were part of the 2019 task. The 2020 task drops DM and PSD in favour of Prague Tectogrammatical Graphs (PTG) and Discourse Representation Graphs (DRG). All the sentences in these datasets are in English. Both tasks use the same portion of the WSJ corpus in the freely available sample[3] of annotations and so for the purposes of comparing AMR and UCCA, they are equivalent. The sample contains an overlap of 87 annotated sentences for both AMR and UCCA, which we have used for this study.

An evaluation tool, *mtool*[4], was introduced for these tasks as well and is what we make use of for our evaluation.

It must be noted that the UCCA graphs are not entirely consistent with the UCCA guidelines[5]. There are a few small structural differences, which can easily be adjusted, but our analysis, especially when discussing the *mtool* evaluation scores, will be misleading without highlighting these differences. These are (1) punctuation is not annotated in the guidelines, but is in the MRP dataset and (2) the root node from the UCCA guidelines would not be the same as the one in the MRP dataset.

The MRP graphs for AMR are generally consistent with the AMR specifications. With that being said, we have discovered on error in the annotations. The AMR specifications state that "to represent conjunction, AMR uses concepts `and`, `or`, `contrast-01`, `either`, and `neither`, along with `:opx` relations". We note that sentence `#20003008` has not been annotated in the best possible way because the annotation uses `and` plus `:polarity -` (see Figure 5) when `neither` is available and arguably a more appropriate option.

3. Experiments

3.1. Data and Data Processing

As mentioned in subsection 2.3, we use the freely available sample of annotations from the MRP 2019 and 2020 Shared Tasks. The corpus has 87 sentences that overlap between UCCA and AMR. We use the first 17 sentences (called the train set hereupon), which constitute 20% of the corpus, to construct the rules for our graph rewriting system. The remaining 70 sentences are our test set, used for evaluation.

The data in the shared task is provided both in `JSON` and in `DOT` format. `PDF` files with the graphs generated from the DOT files are also provided. We used the aforementioned `DOT` files to produce images of the two graphs (AMR and UCCA) for each sentence alongside each other. The AMR graphs were then manually adjusted so that property-value pairs were turned into edges and nodes, as in many cases the values directly corresponded to UCCA nodes and made it more straightforward to draw parallels between the two representations. For example, for sentence `#20003007` (Figure 3a), the property-value pair `polarity -` of node `#0`, was transformed to an edge `polarity` from node `#0` to a new node with label `-` and given the next available ID number (`#5`). Comparing that with the UCCA graph of the same sentence in Figure 3b, we can see these new node and edge directly correspond to node `#2` labeled `no` and its incoming `D` edge.

We used these modified pictorial representations of the graphs to make our first observations. For each sentence, we manually identified the corresponding (overlapping) subgraphs between the AMR graph and the UCCA graph. As a rule, we marked subgraphs as sets of predicates along with their arguments and any properties of the arguments (e.g. `opN`, `year`, `month`). Furthermore, clearly identifiable direct transformations between relations were marked. For example, in the example in Figure 3, `time` and `polarity` can be directly linked to `T` and `D` respectively[6]. Through this we made some initial observations about the most probable correspondents for each AMR relation. We also noted some observations about the differences in the generic structure of the graphs. UCCA graphs, unsurprisingly, tend to have more nodes than AMR graphs. In AMR, predicates are parent nodes of their arguments, whereas in UCCA, participants in a scene appear as siblings of the process or state that is at the center of that scene.

3.2. Graph Rewriting

We use GREW[7] for graph rewriting (Guillaume, 2021; Bonfante et al., 2018) from AMR to an UCCA-like structure. GREW allows us to define rules that match patterns in a graph and apply commands to transform the matched part of the graph.

We design two sets of rules. **R1** is our initial set of rules, which serves as a base line system with a direct and deterministic set of rules. We then build **R2** - an extended set of rules that tries to cover some of

[3] `http://svn.nlpl.eu/mrp/2019/public/sample.tgz`

[4] `https://github.com/cfmrp/mtool`

[5] `https://github.com/UniversalConceptualCognitiveAnnotation/docs/releases`) (at the time of writing this link points to v2.1 of the guidelines

[6] The coloured pictures for the 17 sentences along with the code and data for the experiments are available at `https://gitlab.inria.fr/semagramme-public-projects/resources/amr2ucca`

[7] `https://grew.fr/`

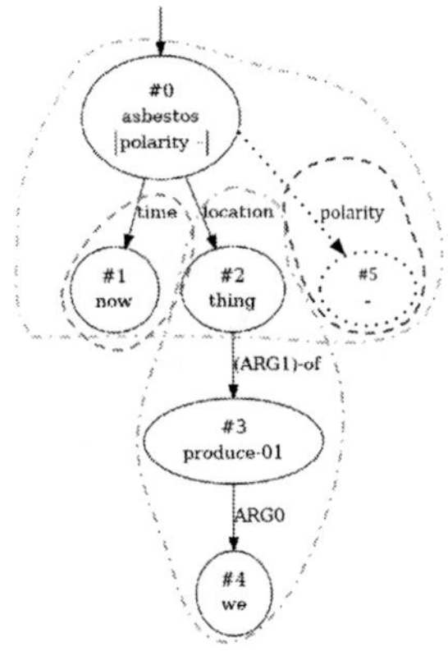

(a) AMR with property-value pair `polarity -` extracted as an edge and a node.

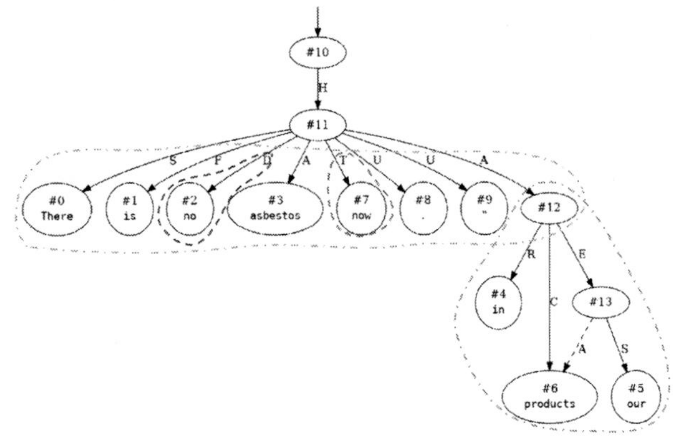

(b) UCCA

Figure 3: AMR and UCCA annotations of the sentence *"There is no asbestos in our products now.""* `[#20003007]` with corresponding subgraphs circled in matching colours.

the identified problems with **R1**, namely (a) more complex structures and (b) ambiguous transformations, for which we use a non-deterministic set of rules.

3.2.1. Initial set of rules - R1

We built a set of rules **R1** based on our initial observations. **R1** was constructed such that any core and non-core AMR relation was rewritten to its most probable correspondent based on the observation of the train set. Additionally, the AMR root (usually a predicate) was "pushed down" to the level of its arguments. Inverse relations were not dealt with separately at this stage. *mtool* runs only if all edges in a graph are valid relations from the framework being tested. Therefore, to be able to apply it on the produced graphs, we added a back-off rule, `ensure_ucca_edges`, that rewrites any remaining non-UCCA edges to `A` (participant). We chose `A` since this was the most frequent relation in the UCCA train set and the relations affected by this rule were mostly `ARGx-of` relations, where `x` is the argument number. This also ensures that if there are any relations in the test set that were not present in our train set, they will still be transformed into a valid UCCA relation.

Figure 4a shows one of the rules in R1, `time_to_T` which matches a pair of nodes that are linked via the AMR relation `time` and the edge itself. If such a pattern is found, the rule deletes the `time` relation and adds a `T` relation from the parent to the child. In Figure 4b, highlighted in green, we can see the part of the graph for sentence `#20003008` of the corpus that has been matched by this rule. In Figure 4c, we see the resulting subgraph after the rewriting.

`time_to_T` is one of the 16 rules that constitute **R1**. The first rule, `push_root_down`, is applied once at the start. It puts the sentence in a parallel scene (`H`) in order to comply with the dataset structure. Other rules are then iterated as much as possible. Finally the back-off rule rewrites any remaining non-UCCA edges to `A`.

3.2.2. Extended set of rules - R2

Next, we constructed **R2** - an extension of **R1**, following a more systematic approach. Each of the AMR relations, along with special AMR nodes (e.g. `have-org-role-91`) present in the corpus[8] was explored further and either (a) rules were written that account for each of the occurrences of that structure or (b) a conclusion was reached that a specific structure is too ambiguous to rewrite in a decisive manner.

R2 contains 44 rules, which, aside from treating the relations from **R1**, also treat more complex constructions such as conjunction and some special nodes such as `date-entity`. Furthermore, for two pairs of rules, (`time_to_T`, `time_to_D`) and (`quant_to_D`, `quant_to_Q`), we apply a non-deterministic GREW strategy. This means that whenever faced with a choice between multiple ways to rewrite a relation, the system produces a graph for each possible option and the rest of the rules are applied to each of these, resulting in multiple outputs for a single input graph.

4. Evaluation

We use *mtool* for the initial evaluation of **R1** and **R2**, so that our results are comparable to the systems that participated in the MRP 2019 and 2020 tasks. We report the results in Table 1. We use *mtool*'s `mrp` setting for

[8]There are 27 relations in the first 17 sentences of the corpus: `ARG0`, `ARG1`, `ARG2`, `ARG3`, `ARG4`, `ARG4`, `day`, `month`, `year`, `domain`, `mod`, `name`, `time`, `prep-in`, `location`, `op1`, `op2`, `op3`, `quant`, `purpose`, `decade`, `part`, `duration`, `unit`, `polarity`, `topic`, `manner`, `age` and `poss`, `consist-of`, and seven reversed relations: `ARG0-of`, `ARG1-of`, `ARG2-of`, `quant-of`, `polarity-of`, `part-of`. Though, arguably, `mod` can be considered as the reverse relation `domain-of`.

```
rule time_to_T {
    pattern {
        e: X -[time]-> Y;
    }
    commands {
        del_edge e;
        add_edge X -[T]-> Y;
    }
}
```

(a)

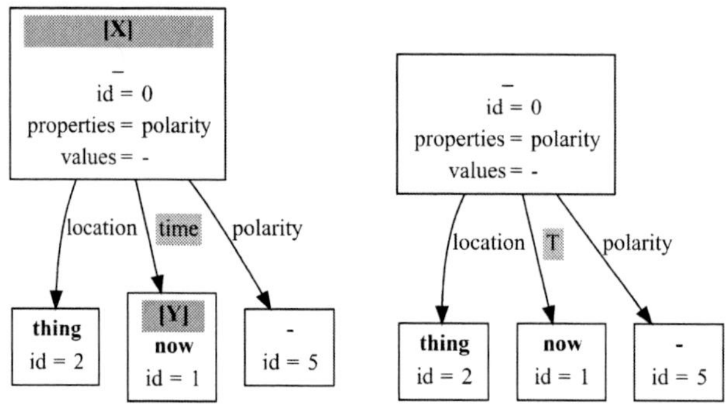

(b) (c)

Figure 4: The rule `time_to_T` (a), the subgraph of the sentence *"There is no asbestos in our products now.""* `[#20003007]` that it matches (b) and the resulting subgraph after rewriting (c).

`--score` which, for UCCA graphs, counts the number of anchors, edges, attributes (which in UCCA account for remote edges) and top nodes to compute precision, recall and F1-score.

In Table 1, we present the precision, recall and F1-score for both the train and the test set. Since for **R2**, we have multiple output graphs per sentence, the scores presented there are the macro-average, i.e. for each sentence, we compute the average value for each metric across all outputs for that sentence, and then average that value across sentences. For the train set, we get 4.05 output graphs per sentence on average, and for the test set, 2.67.

While the results are low as such, it is still important to note that they double for our train set and increase significantly for our test set. It is interesting to note that with the exception of precision for **R2**, our scores are higher on the test set than on the train set. This seems surprising, as one normally expects the opposite to be true. However, with such a small dataset, it is difficult to say whether this is a valid trend or simply due to a non-uniform train-test split.

It must be noted, however, that despite giving us a basis to compare our results to those obtained during the MRP tasks, *mtool* may not be well-suited to evaluate our experiments. To get a better idea of how well our system performs with respect to our goals, we evaluate again with a number of modifications to the UCCA gold data.

To comply with the official UCCA guidelines (see subsection 2.3), we evaluate against an updated version of the dataset, where all the punctuation edges (`U`) have been removed.

AMR annotations do not include anchors. Therefore, without a mapping between the AMR graph and the raw text, we know that producing any would be a guessing game. However, *mtool* takes them into consideration when evaluating UCCA graphs, giving each anchor an equal weight as any edge or node. Thus, anchors constitute a large part of the "points" given at evaluation and our system is bound to get lower score because of this. To get a better idea of how well our system does only on nodes and edges, we run an additional evaluation without taking anchors into consideration.

Finally, we put these two modifications together and evaluate the graphs without punctuation and without anchors.

Table 2 shows the results of these evaluations. As with the **R2** scores in Table 1, the **R2** scores here are macro-averages as well. As expected, we get higher scores when punctuation, anchors or both are removed. As seen with the unmodified evaluation, with the exception of precision for **R2**, we get higher scores on the test set. The **R2** scores on the train set are significantly higher than those of **R1** and higher, but by a smaller margin for the test set.

Since with the non-deterministic set of rules, we get a number of output graphs, which differ in at least one edge label from each other, we know that there is one that is closest to the UCCA representation and one that is farthest from it. In Table 3, we show again the macro-average of the F1-score of **R2** and its modifications on the train set and test set, alongside the average of the minimum and the average of the maximum scores for each sentence. In most of the cases, we observe a difference between 0.01 and 0.02 on either side of the macro-average.

Even though higher than those of **R1**, the results of **R2** are still rather low. This is partially due to features of UCCA that cannot be predicted from the AMR only, as we have seen with anchors. However, it is also largely due to ambiguities in the transformation task. We show some examples of these in section 5. These ambiguities stem from the fact that, as one of the six AMR slogans states, we cannot read off a unique English sentence from an AMR[9]. Thus, producing an UCCA-like representation from AMR is more simi-

[9] `https://github.com/amrisi/amr-guidelines/blob/master/amr.md#amr-slogans`

	Train			Test		
	Precision	Recall	F1-score	Precision	Recall	F1-score
R1	0.128	0.037	0.057	0.173	0.055	0.083
R2	0.249	0.079	0.119	0.239	0.091	0.131

Table 1: Results for *mtool* evaluation of **R1** and **R2**.

	Train			Test		
	Precision	Recall	F1-score	Precision	Recall	F1-score
R1 - No punct	0.128	0.040	0.061	0.179	0.062	0.092
R1 - No anchors	0.128	0.058	0.080	0.173	0.088	0.117
R1 - No punct + no anchors	0.128	0.063	0.084	0.179	0.097	0.126
R2 - No punct	**0.280**	0.100	0.147	**0.255**	0.108	0.151
R2 - No anchors	0.249	0.126	0.167	0.239	0.147	0.181
R2 - No punct + no anchors	**0.280**	**0.155**	**0.198**	**0.255**	**0.173**	**0.204**

Table 2: Results for *mtool* evaluation of the modifications.

lar to a generation task. The ambiguities that we describe in section 5 can be addressed by adding more non-deterministic rules to the system. This will ensure that we produce a correct graph, but it is not possible to determine which one of the multiple ones produced it is. As the number of output graphs grows exponentially for each non-deterministic rule applied, the task becomes even harder, the more non-deterministic rules we add. This shows that the input graph does not contain enough information to let us compute the correct structure in a deterministic manner.

5. Ambiguities

In this section, we would like to highlight some of the ambiguities that stem from the structural differences of the two frameworks, that we encountered while exploring the train set.

Figure 5 shows the AMR of sentence #20003008 of the MRP corpus. This is an interesting example for a number of reasons that we have outlined below.

Proper names. In AMR, the structure for annotating a proper names is

```
(e / entity-type
    :name (n / name
        :op1 "..."
        ...
        :opN "...")
```

where *entity-type* is the type of the entity whose name is used, such as person, city, book[10] and :op1 – :opN point to each of the tokens in the proper name. In the example in Figure 5, we have two such subgraphs - one for *Kent cigarettes* and one for *Lorillard*, which is a *company*. On the surface, however, these are realised in different ways - for *Kent cigarettes* the entity type cigarette is realised along with the name, while

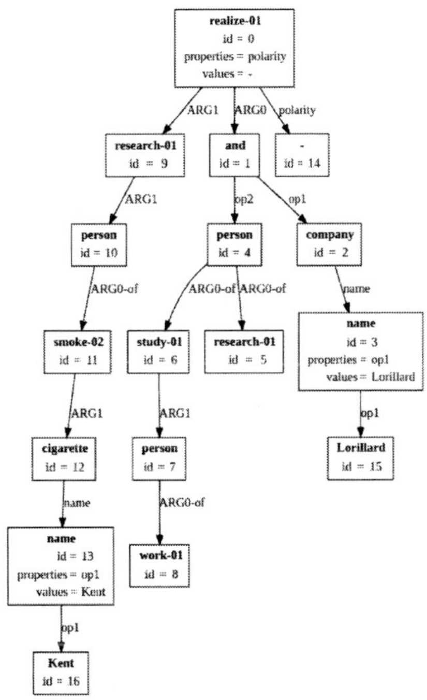

Figure 5: AMR of the sentence *"Neither Lorillard nor the researchers who studied the workers were aware of any research on smokers of Kent cigarettes."* [#20003008].

for *Lorillard* only the name is present[11]. Thus, in the UCCA representation, the subgraphs for these two instances will have different structures too. It is therefore

[10] An exhaustive list of entity types available in AMR can be found in the AMR specifications.

[11] Interestingly, this suggests that the AMR graph relies either on context (previous sentences mentioning that Lorillard is a company) or world knowledge. The latter seems to be true for proper names in AMR in general, especially taking into consideration we often include a :wiki relation when a Wikipedia article for that entity is available.

	Train F1-scores			Test F1-scores		
	Min	Avg	Max	Min	Avg	Max
R2	0.107	0.119	0.137	0.121	0.131	0.138
R2 - No punct	0.132	0.147	0.167	0.143	0.151	0.159
R2 - No anchors	0.150	0.167	0.191	0.168	0.181	0.192
R2 - No punct + no anchors	0.179	0.198	0.225	0.193	0.204	0.215

Table 3: Minimum, average and maximum F1-scores across train and test set for **R2** and its modifications.

not possible, from AMR only, without access to the surface realisation of the sentence, to decide whether the entity type should be included in the UCCA representation or not.

Nouns that invoke predicates. Another interesting case is that of AMR's nouns that invoke predicates. In the example from Figure 5, we have three such nouns - *researchers*, *workers* and *smokers*. In the AMR graph they are all realised as

```
(p / person
    :ARGx-of (p2 / PB predicate))
```

where *PB predicate* is the relevant PropBank predicate and *x* is the relevant argument number, so e.g. *a smoker* is annotated as *a person who smokes*. This can be addressed by our system by making use of GREW's lexicons. However, this structure too, is ambiguous. Apart from the three annotations of the three nouns, we have the same structure once more in the example sentence.

```
(p / person
    :ARG0-of (s / study-01))
```

Here, however, this does not stand for the noun *student*, but for *[...] who studied*.

Negation. In UCCA, depending on the surface realisation of the sentence, negation can be syntactical (such as *no asbestos* in sentence `#20003007`), but also morphological (such as *nonexecutive* in sentence `#20001001`). In AMR, negation is marked as `:polarity -` in both of these cases.

have-org-role-91. Sentences `#20001001`, `#20001002` and `#20003005` all use the special `have-org-role-91` AMR role and the same structure when speaking about the organisational roles of specific people. The surface realisations, however, are very different from each other in all three cases - *"Pierre Vinken [...] will join the board as a nonexecutive director"*, *"Mr. Vinken is chairman of Elsevier N.V."*, *"A Lorillard spokeswoman"*.

6. Conclusion

In this paper we presented a corpus-driven experiment to transform AMR annotations into UCCA-like representations, the evaluation of our experiment and some of the ambiguous cases we discovered through it. Here we present some of the discussion points stemming from our work and further study directions.

Our work can also be viewed as a case study of seeing how much of an anchored (flavor 1) semantic framework can be predicted from a more abstract (flavor 2) one and what it is that is missing from the latter in order to produce the former. The difficulties in transformation we encountered were largely due to the difference in flavor of the frameworks. UCCA is grounded in surface. As we have seen in section 5, many of the ambiguities would be easier to address if there was a link between AMR and surface as well. This would also help us with predicting where features that are not present in AMR, such as function words, should go in the UCCA-like graph. It would be interesting to see if similar ambiguities arise from comparing other pairs of flavor 1 and 2 frameworks in a similar manner.

In section 4, we saw that there were a number of adjustments we had to make to the gold dataset in order to get a better idea of how our system performs on the task we set to tackle. Further ones could be made still (such as removing function words). This suggest that *mtool* may not be the most appropriate tool to do such an evaluation. If more experiments in predicting flavor 1 from flavor 2 frameworks (and vice-versa) were to be carried out, there will be the need to design a more appropriate metric to evaluate this kind of task.

Finally, we consider an orthogonal to our task, but equally important issue. Our choice of frameworks was based on the current popularity of the frameworks, but also on the availability of parallel data. Being limited by the second constraint, highlights once again the need for larger and freely available parallel corpora across various semantic frameworks. The availability of a common corpus would greatly enhance corpus-driven comparison across the features and expressive power of various frameworks. Furthermore, whenever a new framework or framework extension is proposed, there would already be a resource that would allow the study of said framework (or extension) with respect to existing ones. Finally, currently the majority of semantically annotated data exists only in English. It would be beneficial if more multi-lingual projects such as the Parallel Meaning Bank (Abzianidze et al., 2017) existed, ideally with datasets that are parallel both across frameworks and languages.

7. Acknowledgements

Part of this work has been funded by the *Agence Nationale de la Recherche* (ANR, fr: National Agency for Research), grant number ANR-20-THIA-0010-01. We would like to thank the anonymous reviewers for the time taken to review this paper and provide useful feedback.

8. Bibliographical References

Abend, O. and Rappoport, A. (2013). Universal conceptual cognitive annotation (ucca). In *Proceedings of the 51st Annual Meeting of the Association for Computational Linguistics (Volume 1: Long Papers)*, pages 228–238.

Abzianidze, L., Bjerva, J., Evang, K., Haagsma, H., van Noord, R., Ludmann, P., Nguyen, D.-D., and Bos, J. (2017). The Parallel Meaning Bank: Towards a multilingual corpus of translations annotated with compositional meaning representations. In *Proceedings of the 15th Conference of the European Chapter of the Association for Computational Linguistics: Volume 2, Short Papers*, pages 242–247, Valencia, Spain, April. Association for Computational Linguistics.

Banarescu, L., Bonial, C., Cai, S., Georgescu, M., Griffitt, K., Hermjakob, U., Knight, K., Koehn, P., Palmer, M., and Schneider, N. (2013). Abstract meaning representation for sembanking. In *Proceedings of the 7th linguistic annotation workshop and interoperability with discourse*, pages 178–186.

Bonfante, G., Guillaume, B., and Perrier, G. (2018). *Application of Graph Rewriting to Natural Language Processing*. Wiley Online Library.

Bos, J. (2020). Separating argument structure from logical structure in AMR. In *Proceedings of the Second International Workshop on Designing Meaning Representations*, pages 13–20, Barcelona Spain (online), December. Association for Computational Linguistics.

Cui, R. and Hershcovich, D. (2020). Refining implicit argument annotation for UCCA. In *Proceedings of the Second International Workshop on Designing Meaning Representations*, pages 41–52, Barcelona Spain (online), December. Association for Computational Linguistics.

Donatelli, L., Regan, M., Croft, W., and Schneider, N. (2018). Annotation of tense and aspect semantics for sentential AMR. In *Proceedings of the Joint Workshop on Linguistic Annotation, Multiword Expressions and Constructions (LAW-MWE-CxG-2018)*, pages 96–108, Santa Fe, New Mexico, USA, August. Association for Computational Linguistics.

Guillaume, B. (2021). Graph matching and graph rewriting: GREW tools for corpus exploration, maintenance and conversion. In *Proceedings of the 16th Conference of the European Chapter of the Association for Computational Linguistics: System Demonstrations*, pages 168–175, Online, April. Association for Computational Linguistics.

Koller, A., Oepen, S., and Sun, W. (2019). Graph-based meaning representations: Design and processing. In *Proceedings of the 57th Annual Meeting of the Association for Computational Linguistics: Tutorial Abstracts*, pages 6–11, Florence, Italy, July. Association for Computational Linguistics.

Oepen, S., Abend, O., Hajic, J., Hershcovich, D., Kuhlmann, M., O'Gorman, T., Xue, N., Chun, J., Straka, M., and Uresova, Z. (2019). MRP 2019: Cross-framework meaning representation parsing. In *Proceedings of the Shared Task on Cross-Framework Meaning Representation Parsing at the 2019 Conference on Natural Language Learning*, pages 1–27, Hong Kong, November. Association for Computational Linguistics.

Oepen, S., Abend, O., Abzianidze, L., Bos, J., Hajic, J., Hershcovich, D., Li, B., O'Gorman, T., Xue, N., and Zeman, D. (2020). MRP 2020: The second shared task on cross-framework and cross-lingual meaning representation parsing. In *Proceedings of the CoNLL 2020 Shared Task: Cross-Framework Meaning Representation Parsing*, pages 1–22, Online, November. Association for Computational Linguistics.

Palmer, M., Gildea, D., and Kingsbury, P. (2005). The Proposition Bank: An annotated corpus of semantic roles. *Computational Linguistics*, 31(1):71–106.

Prange, J., Schneider, N., and Abend, O. (2019a). Made for each other: Broad-coverage semantic structures meet preposition supersenses. In *Proceedings of the 23rd Conference on Computational Natural Language Learning (CoNLL)*, pages 174–185, Hong Kong, China, November. Association for Computational Linguistics.

Prange, J., Schneider, N., and Abend, O. (2019b). Semantically constrained multilayer annotation: The case of coreference. In *Proceedings of the First International Workshop on Designing Meaning Representations*, pages 164–176, Florence, Italy, August. Association for Computational Linguistics.

Shalev, A., Hwang, J. D., Schneider, N., Srikumar, V., Abend, O., and Rappoport, A. (2019). Preparing SNACS for subjects and objects. In *Proceedings of the First International Workshop on Designing Meaning Representations*, pages 141–147, Florence, Italy, August. Association for Computational Linguistics.

Proceedings of ISA-18 Workshop at LREC2022, pages 118–126
Marseille, 20 June 2022

Towards Practical Semantic Interoperability in NLP Platforms

Julian Moreno-Schneider[1], Remi Calizzano[1], Florian Kintzel[1], Georg Rehm[1], Dimitrios Galanis[2], Ian Roberts[3]

[1] Deutsches Forschungszentrum für Künstliche Intelligenz GmbH (DFKI), Germany – firstname.lastname@dfki.de • [2] ILSP, R. C. "Athena", Greece – galanisd@athenarc.gr • [3] University of Sheffield, UK – i.roberts@dcs.shef.ac.uk

Abstract

Interoperability is a necessity for the development of complex tasks that require the interconnection of several NLP services. This article presents the approaches that were adopted in three scenarios to address their respective interoperability issues. The first scenario describes the creation of a common REST API for a specific platform, the second scenario presents the interconnection of several platforms via mapping of different representation formats and the third scenario shows the complexities of interoperability through semantic schema mapping or automatic translation.

Keywords: Semantic Parsing, Semantic Mapping, NLP Platforms Interoperability

1 Introduction

For a long time, the development of NLP infrastructures or platforms that provide a larger number of NLP services was not practically feasible. In recent years this has changed with the appearance of new technologies, especially containerisation and microservices. The main advantage of these technologies is that they enable individual development as well as easy deployment and execution of NLP services, thus facilitating their re-use into one's own computing system/environment. However, individual development of tools especially when distributed among *different* organisations gives rise to interoperability (Rehm et al., 2020b) issues, e. g., the services are developed without a common data model (exchange format), with different technologies and APIs (gRPC, REST) etc. In short, the services cannot be easily combined. Achieving interoperability becomes more complex the greater the number of individual services involved.

For a further analysis of interoperability challenges encountered and potential methods of mitigation we look at three scenarios of different complexity. From simple to more challenging, these are:

- The first interoperability scenario is the situation where the services to be developed use the same format to carry out the processing and annotation of texts. An example of this type of interoperability is the European Language Grid (ELG), where a specific API has been defined that must be used by all the services that want to integrate into and be interoperable within the ELG infrastructure (see Section 2 for more details).
- In the second interoperability scenario we have two different platforms in which the services use different formats (regardless of the semantic schemas). For example, one service might use JSON as its input and output format, and another service might use XML. Interoperability between these two services (and possibly between the two platforms) can be achieved through the transformation of one format into the other, for which there are quite a few tools (SHACL[1], XSLT[2], etc.).
- In the third and most complex interoperability scenario, two services, from the same platform or from different platforms, use the same format as input and output, but the semantic schema they use is fundamentally different, i. e., the semantic information text documents are annotated with differs from one service to another. This difference not only implies that they can annotate different information, but even if they do annotate the same information, for example, an entity such as Berlin, one service uses an `ENTITY` tag and another services uses the tag `ENT` (see Listing 1). In addition, the different services can also use different categorisations to classify such entities, i. e., one service annotates Berlin as `CITY` while the other annotates it as `LOCATION`.

This article presents the work carried out so far to address the three interoperability scenarios mentioned above. The interoperability mechanisms developed in the European Language Grid (ELG) platform[3] to make its heterogeneous and growing set of tools and services compatible (common API specification) and interconnectable (Python SDK) are described in Section 2. The interoperability mechanisms implemented in the QURATOR[4] and SPEAKER[5] projects (in addition to

[1] https://www.w3.org/TR/shacl/
[2] https://www.w3schools.com/xml/xsl_intro.asp
[3] https://www.european-language-grid.eu
[4] https://qurator.ai
[5] https://www.speaker.fraunhofer.de

```
<?xml version="1.0" encoding="utf-8"?>
<text>
<Annotation_1>
  I was living in <ENTITY class="CITY">
    Berlin</ENTITY> last year
</Annotation_1>
<Annotation_2>
  I was living in <ENT class="LOCATION">
    Berlin</ENT> last year
</Annotation_2>
</text>
```

Listing 1: Example of annotations made by two services using the same format and different semantic schema

Lynx[6]) to mainly cover scenario 2, and minimally scenario 3 (Workflow Manager) are presented in Section 3. The proposed solution to solve scenario 3 as generically as possible is introduced in Section 4. Section 5 presents related work. Finally, Section 6 concludes the article and sketches directions for future work.

2 Interoperability through common API Specification (Scenario 1)

The European Language Grid (ELG) platform addresses interoperability by forcing the NLP services to use a predefined format. This corresponds to the first interoperability scenario described in Section 1.

2.1 Introduction to ELG

The ELG platform aims to offer multiple services that will support and boost the Language Technologies (LT) sector and activities in Europe, see Rehm et al. (2020a) for a short overview and Rehm (2022) for an exhaustive description that covers all the details.

Its primary goal is to provide a scalable system dedicated to the distribution and deployment of Language Resources and Technologies (LRT).[7] ELG offers access to thousands of commercial and non-commercial LTs and ancillary data LRs for all European languages and more. These include processing and generation services, tools, applications for written and spoken language, models, corpora, lexicons, ontologies, term lists, computational grammars, etc. Moreover, resources integrated in the ELG cloud infrastructure are directly deployable and/or downloadable.

ELG aims to act as a living observatory of LT, consolidating existing and legacy tools, services, LRs, and information about them, as well as newly emerging ones.

2.2 ELG Language Technology Services

Among the more than 12,000 resources available, at the time of writing the ELG catalogue counts more than 800 functional services deployed in the ELG infrastructure. Figure 1 shows an overview of the ELG platform architecture. An ELG service is a LT tool running inside the ELG Kubernetes cluster and takes the form of a Docker image exposing an ELG-compatible endpoint. An ELG service has to be compatible with the specifications (see Section 2.3) defined by the ELG team which aim to facilitate the deployment of the services but also standardise the LT tools. Currently, ELG supports the integration of tools/services that fall into one of the following broad categories:

- Information Extraction (IE) & text analysis: Services that take text input and produce standoff *annotations* over that text.
- Text-to-text: Services (most notably Machine Translation, but also summarisation, anonymisation, etc.) that take text and return new text that is derived from the input
- Text classification: Services that take text input and classify it somehow (e. g., language identification, "fake news" detection, etc.)
- Speech recognition: Services that accept audio and return a text transcription
- Text-to-speech: Services that take text and return audio

These broad categories cover the vast majority of NLP tasks and the respective specification can be easily extended if required.

2.3 Internal LT Service API Specification

ELG services are accessible from outside the ELG cluster via the LT execution server as shown in Figure 1. The communication between the LT execution server and each NLP/LT service is done using an internal application programming interface called Internal LT Service API. The respective specification details the API that the LT tool containers need to implement in order to be runnable as functional services within the ELG infrastructure. It consists of three request messages and four response messages that ELG functional services have to use as input and output of the LT tool. The three request messages are: Text request, Structured text request, and Audio request. The four response messages are: Annotations response, Classification response, Texts response, and Audio response. These seven messages have been created having two constraints in mind: being permissive to cover as many NLP use cases as possible and being specific to force similar message structures for similar services. They are described in detail in the ELG documentation.[8] Table 1 shows the number of services per service category presented in the previous section with, for each service category, the request and response messages used.

[6]https://lynx-project.eu

[7]https://live.european-language-grid.eu/catalogue

[8]https://european-language-grid.readthedocs.io/en/stable/all/A3_API/LTInternalAPI.html

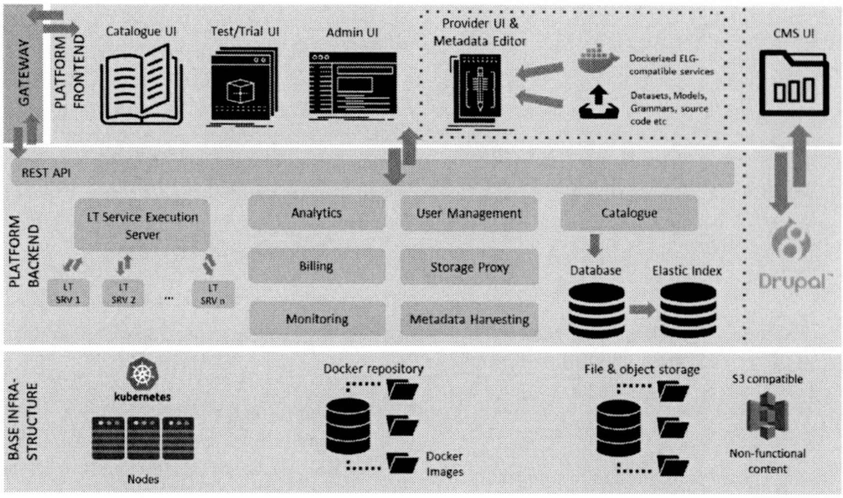

Figure 1: Architecture of the European Language Grid (ELG)

Category	No. of Services	Request Message	Response Message
IE & text analysis	273	Text	Annotations
Text-to-text	405	Text	Texts
Text classification	31	Text	Classification
Speech recognition	35	Audio	Texts
Text-to-speech	23	Text	Audio

Table 1: Number of ELG services per service category with the request and response type of messages used

```
from elg import Service

# initialise LT service using its ID
lt = Service.from_id(17471)
# call LT service
result = lt("I was living in Berlin last
    year.")
print(result) # print the Annotations
    response message returned by the
    service
```

Listing 2: Calling an ELG service using Python

2.4 Calling ELG Services using the Python SDK

The ELG Python SDK provides access to most ELG functionalities through Python.[9] Among its other functionalities, the Python SDK enables users to call functional services available in ELG.

The `Service` class of the Python SDK corresponds to an ELG functional service, and can be initialised using the identifier of the service. As users need to be authenticated to use ELG services, a login step is necessary. A service that is initialised in Python can be called easily. Listing 2 shows the code for calling a named entity recogniser[10]. The Python SDK handles the creation of the input message, the update of the identification token, the communication with the API exposed by the LT execution server, etc.

2.5 Combining ELG Services

ELG provides access to a large variety of heterogeneous services from information extraction to text-to-speech generation (see Section 2). However, thanks to the internal LT service API specification, all the ELG services use the same message structures. Those specifications facilitate the combination of services, i. e., allows to determine if two services are compatible (can run one after the other without conversion) and, if not, it facilitates the required mapping. In the vast majority of cases, text-to-speech services returning an audio response can be used as input of a service accepting an audio request. This is also true for the texts response messages which can likely be converted into text request messages. The rare cases where the conversion is not possible happen when one of the fields that accepts arbitrary content of the response message is not empty. For the services returning an annotations or a classification response, the output cannot easily be converted into an input message for another service. These services are often used last. For the ELG services, the combination of the following categories is theoretically feasible based on the type of messages used (see Table 1): Text-to-text or Speech recognition with IE & text analysis, Text classification, or Text-to-speech, and Text-to-speech with Speech recognition.

The automatic conversion of an audio or a texts response to respectively an audio or a text request is done

[9]https://gitlab.com/european-language-grid/platform/python-client

[10]Cogito Discover Named Entity Recognizer, https://live.european-language-grid.eu/catalogue/tool-service/17471

```python
from elg import Pipeline

# initialise the pipeline using LT
    services IDs
pipeline = Pipeline.from_ids([9183,
    4842])
# call the LT services
results = pipeline("I was living in
    Berlin last year.")
print(results[-1]) # print the Audio
    response message containing the
    audio of the sentence translated in
    German
```

Listing 3: Combining ELG services using the Python SDK and the Pipeline class

using a logical mapping between the fields of each message. For example, the `content` field of the texts response is mapped to the `content` field of the text request. Again, this mapping is possible thanks to the specifications defined by the ELG team. This mapping is not perfect and only the conversion of certain types of messages is possible.

The Python SDK introduced in Section 2.4 provides a `Pipeline` class to make it easy for users to interoperate ELG services. Listing 3 shows how to use the `Pipeline` class to run a machine translation service[11] following by a text-to-speech service[12]. This pipeline returns the German audio of an English sentence by combining two services automatically.

More example combinations using the `Pipeline` class of the Python SDK can be found in Annex A.

3 Intra-Platform Interoperability through Format Mapping (Scenario 2)

As presented in the introduction, interoperability scenario 2 occurs when two (or more) services (from the same or different platforms) use different formats (JSON, XML, RDF, etc.) for input and/or output of the information processed/to be processed.

The distinctive feature of this scenario is that the number of formats is limited, which allows the manual implementation of interoperability between all of them. This means that format conversions are accomplished through manually defined rules for each conversion step. In the following, we present all the implementations made to achieve interoperability in this scenario through a workflow manager (Moreno-Schneider et al., 2020).

[11]HelsinkiNLP – OPUS-MT (eng-gmw): English-German machine translation https://live.european-language-grid.eu/catalogue/tool-service/9183

[12]MaryTTS – German male (dfki-pavoque-neutral-hsmm) https://live.european-language-grid.eu/catalogue/tool-service/4842

3.1 Supported Platforms

The first format considered for integration has been the format used in the Lynx platform (Moreno-Schneider et al., 2021), a domain-specific platform for the generation and use of a Legal Knowledge Graph used and populated through various NLP services (Named Entity Recognition, Summarisation, Machine Translation, etc.), which were integrated and combined through a workflow manager developed in the project (based on Camunda[13]). We decided to use the Lynx format as the first one to be integrated into our workflow manager for a simple reason: the Lynx project used an internal Linked Data information format also based on NIF (Hellmann et al., 2013), which simplifies its integration into our format.

The second format integrated is the one used in the ELG platform (described in Section 2).

The third format is the one developed in the project SPEAKER[14], a platform for speech assistants for the German language, so the interaction with the platform is limited to short interactions (dialogues). The project has developed an API that defines input and output messages and their content, including internal services that should not be consulted externally.

3.2 Format Mapping

There is a very large number of formats to represent text (e. g., TXT, XML, JSON, RDF, etc.), which makes it impossible to develop all potentially necessary converters to cover all possible mappings between formats (TXT→XML, TXT→XML, RDF→JSON, etc.); note, though, that all of these different formats can potentially include a sheer endless number of specific individual approaches how to represent text.

To address this problem we decided to use an intermediate unified format, so that we do not need converters for each format-pairs, but only for the format-pairs including the intermediate unified format. We simplify the necessary work to scale the interoperability solution in future scenarios with new or different formats.

Considering that we are processing text semantically, the unified format we use not only allows easy handling of semantic information, but has been specifically defined for this purpose, i. e., Resource Description Framework (RDF[15]). RDF is used in Linked Data to represent semantic information, especially for ontologies and knowledge bases.

In order to better understand this conversion, we are going to use an XML example document (shown in Listing 4) annotated with two named entities (`Berlin` and `New York`). This document is converted into an RDF document containing exactly the same information (shown in Listing 5).

In the example, we can see that URIs (Unified Resource Identifier) are assigned to each annotation, i. e.,

[13]https://camunda.com

[14]https://www.speaker.fraunhofer.de

[15]https://www.w3.org/RDF/

```xml
<?xml version="1.0"?>
<text>
  I was living in <ENTITY class="
    LOCATION">Berlin</ENTITY> last year,
     but then I moved to <ENTITY class="
    LOCATION">New York</ENTITY>.
</text>
```

Listing 4: Example XML document annotated with semantic information (named entities)

piece of information (whole text, annotation, etc.). The two named entities in the example are converted into specific annotations, http://ex/#char=16,21 and http://ex/#char=54,61, which are completed with semantic information (properties and values). This annotation generation process has been manually defined for the specific XML format.

Furthermore, crucially, in the RDF format there is a lot more explicit information that was not directly present in the XML version, such as *beginIndex* and *endIndex*. This helps the inference of information in semantic systems, such as knowledge bases or graphs.

3.3 Workflow Manager

Our workflow manager is currently primarily used in the scenario of digital content curation (Bourgonje et al., 2017; Bourgonje et al., 2016) but its development was started with regard to the legal domain (Moreno-Schneider and Rehm, 2018; Rehm et al., 2019). One of its main objectives is the management of containerised tools, which need to interact with each other in a flexible and efficient way, even if they have been designed and developed independently. That forces the need for interoperability mechanisms because the services use different formats. Regarding the communication between components, for the moment, the workflow manager allows the usage of REST API (Richardson et al., 2013) and gRPC (Giretti, 2022) based services.

The workflow manager uses a unified intermediate format to represent information internally, and it uses RDF together with NIF (Hellmann et al., 2013). Besides, the different formats that are currently supported for translation in the workflow manager are:

- **Lynx Document:** This document has been defined and implemented in the Lynx project (Moreno-Schneider et al., 2021) based on Linked Data and NIF (Hellmann et al., 2013) whose main objective is the semantic representation of documents and information in the legal domain. This document can be represented in any Linked Data format, such as RDF, JSON-LD or XML.
- **ELG API Specification:** The specification made in ELG has been described in Section 2.3. As mentioned, messages in ELG use JSON format.
- **SPEAKER API:** The API defined in SPEAKER is focused on virtual assistants and not so much on actual language processing, although part of the specification can be adapted (`DialogueRequest` and `DialogueReponse`). The messages in SPEAKER are defined in the Protobuf (Varda, 2008) files using the gRPC protocol.

4 Semantic Interoperability between NLP Services (Scenario 3)

The last scenario pursues the interoperability of NLP services that use different semantic schemas. The term semantic schema refers to the way information is annotated in a document and to what semantic information it is related, i. e., how it is represented in a document that a word is a named entity and of what type.[16]

4.1 Semantic Interoperability Challenge

In scenario 1, we showed the possibility to perform a semantic mapping between the ELG services that are compatible (see Section 2.5). This is possible because all ELG services use the same limited set of messages, which is why we can define rules to map the fields of two different messages. However, in the context presented in the second scenario where the services are from different platforms, it is not possible to define rules as there are theoretically as many rules as the number of pairs of services because each service uses its own semantic schema.

This issue also applies to some ELG services, because as explained in Section 2.3, the ELG messages although based on a common format specification, this specification does not enforce a specific semantic schema for the annotations.

For example, the annotation types used in the `annotations` field of the Annotations response message[17] can differ from one service to another, and we find the same difference in the semantic schemas presented in Listing 1 where the two different annotation types `CITY` or `LOCATION` are used to represent the same entity.

Because of the various semantic schemas used by NLP services, which also are not formally described or documented it is impossible to create universal rules to semantically map messages from the same or different platforms using a different semantic schema.

4.2 Manual Semantic Mapping

The first solution to this problem used by the workflow manager consists of manually creating mappings for each pair of services. In practice, we create a correspondence between the fields of the output of the first service and the fields of the input of the second service. This solution works only when the number of services

[16]In UIMA, the semantic schema is called a typesystem.

[17]https://european-language-grid.readthedocs.io/en/stable/all/A3_API/LTInternalAPI.html#annotations-response

```
@prefix rdf:    <http://www.w3.org/1999/02/22-rdf-syntax-ns#> .
@prefix xsd:    <http://www.w3.org/2001/XMLSchema#> .
@prefix itsrdf: <http://www.w3.org/2005/11/its/rdf#> .
@prefix nif:    <http://persistence.uni-leipzig.org/nlp2rdf/ontologies/nif-core#> .
@prefix rdfs:   <http://www.w3.org/2000/01/rdf-schema#> .
@prefix geo:  <http://www.w3.org/2003/01/geo/wgs84_pos/> .
<http://ex/#char=0,62>
        a                      nif:RFC5147String , nif:String , nif:Context ;
        nif:beginIndex         "0"^^xsd:nonNegativeInteger ;
        nif:endIndex           "62"^^xsd:nonNegativeInteger ;
        nif:isString           "I was living in Berlin last year, but then I moved to New York."^^xsd:string .
<http://ex/#char=16,21>
        a                    nif:RFC5147String , nif:String ;
        nif:anchorOf         "Berlin"^^xsd:string ;
        nif:beginIndex       "16"^^xsd:nonNegativeInteger ;
        nif:endIndex         "21"^^xsd:nonNegativeInteger ;
        nif:referenceContext  <http://ex/#char=0,62> ;
        itsrdf:taClassRef  <http://dbpedia.org/ontology/Location> .
<http://ex/#char=54,61>
        a                      nif:RFC5147String , nif:String ;
        nif:anchorOf           "New York\"^^xsd:string ;
        nif:beginIndex         "54"^^xsd:nonNegativeInteger ;
        nif:endIndex           "61"^^xsd:nonNegativeInteger ;
        itsrdf:taClassRef      <http://dbpedia.org/ontology/Location> ;
        nif:referenceContext  <http://ex/#char=0,62> .
```

Listing 5: Example RDF document using semantic NIF annotations

is rather limited which is the case for scenario 2, for example. However when the number of services is getting bigger the manual solution is no longer viable.

4.3 Automatic Semantic Mapping

A second approach is to make use of recent advances in machine learning and NLP to create a mapping for each couple of services automatically. The idea is to create the mapping rule once so that we do not have to recreate it each time two services are combined to not increase inference time. Here, we assume that the semantic schemas of the services are known in advance. This task can be called automatic semantic mapping rule generation and consists of finding the mapping rule between the semantic schemas of two NLP services. This mapping rule could be used afterwards to interoperate the two services by converting the first service's semantic schema to the semantic schema of the second service.

The mapping rule can take multiple formats like, for example, a Python method that takes the message from the first service as input and returns the same message with a different semantic schema compatible with the second service. We made preliminary experiments with GPT-3 using the OpenAI playground[18] with the `text-davinci-002` model. We tested various prompts and parameters to see if it is possible to generate automatically a Python method that maps two semantic schemas. Our preliminary results are promising because in some of the experiments we have been able to show that this is indeed possible. Listing 6 presents an example in which GPT-3 created a Python method capable to convert a simple semantic schema into another one. However, the model shows its limitations when it comes to mapping complex semantic schemas as shown in Listing 7. We performed these experiments only to demonstrate that advanced NLP models can be used to perform automatic semantic mapping rule generation and can potentially solve, or contribute to solving, the semantic interoperability challenge. We will explore and evaluate various automatic mapping methods with larger experiments in future work.

[18]https://beta.openai.com/playground/

5 Related Work

5.1 NLP Platforms Semantic Schemas

Beyond the platforms we used for our experiments, there are more and more AI platforms offering NLP services via APIs such as HuggingFace (Wolf et al., 2020), Google Cloud Platform[19] (GCP), or OpenAI[20], or via tools such as NLTK (Bird et al., 2009), Spacy[21] or Stanza (Qi et al., 2020). We can divide these platforms into two categories. First, those with a limited number of services like GCP, OpenAI, and Stanza which only offer their services, and second the platforms like HuggingFace and Spacy where there is a wide variety of models and where it is possible to add more. In both categories, the platforms have defined one or more semantic schemas that the services need to use. HuggingFace has, for example, the no-

[19]https://cloud.google.com/natural-language
[20]https://openai.com/api/
[21]https://spacy.io

```
"""
Python method that converts
[{"translation_text": "This is a plain
    text sentence."}]
to
{"type":"text", "content":"This is a
    plain text sentence."}
"""

def convert_to_text(translation_response
    ):
    return {"type": "text", "content":
    translation_response[0]["
    translation_text"]}
```

Listing 6: Example Python method generated by GPT-3 to convert a semantic schema into another. Only the docstring (text in green) is provided and the Python code is generated by the model. The generated Python method is valid and correctly converts the first semantic schema to the second one.

```
"""
Python method that converts
<?xml version="1.0" encoding="utf-8"?><
    text>I was living in <ENTITY class="
    LOCATION">Berlin</ENTITY> last year,
     but then I moved to <ENTITY class="
    LOCATION">New York</ENTITY>.</text>
to
{"response":{"type":"annotations","
    annotations":{"Place":[{"start":16,"
    end":22,"features":{"Lemma":"Berlin
    "}},{"start":54,"end":62,"features
    ":{"Lemma":"New York"}}]}}}
"""

import json
import xml.etree.ElementTree as ET

def convert_xml_to_json(xml_string):
    root = ET.fromstring(xml_string)
    annotations = []
    for child in root:
        if child.tag == "text":
            text = child.text
        elif child.tag == "ENTITY":
            annotations.append({"start":
     child.attrib["start"], "end": child
    .attrib["end"], "features": {"Lemma"
    : child.text}})
    return {"response": {"type": "
    annotations", "annotations": {"Place
    ": annotations}, "text": text}}
```

Listing 7: Example Python method generated by GPT-3 to convert a semantic schema into another. Only the docstring (text in green) is provided and the Python code is generated by the model. The generated Python method is valid Python code but does not correctly convert the XML string to the JSON one.

tion of pipeline (different from the `Pipeline` concept presented in Section 2.5). There are 17 task-specific pipelines and each of these pipelines uses its own semantic schema and message formats. For each pipeline, it is possible to use a multitude of services (called models in the HuggingFace ecosystem) as long as the service is compatible with the semantic scheme of the pipeline. A similar mechanism exists for Spacy which allows the use of different models as long as they respect the conventions imposed by the platform. All these platforms use a semantic approach similar to ELG (Section 2) and each platform has its own common API. However, all these APIs use different semantic schemas and there is no joint standard semantic schema used by these NLP platforms.

5.2 Semantic Interoperability Strategies

We only found a few works on the interoperability of NLP services. Rizzo and Troncy (2012) created a framework which unifies ten NER and disambiguation extraction tools by creating a common ontology. The different semantic schemas are manually mapped to the common ontology. Eckart de Castilho et al. (2019) combine three text annotation repositories (PubAnnotation, LAPPS Grid, and INCEpTION) in order to create one unique corpus. They show the challenges of the interoperability of different annotation types.

We can also look at the interoperability of web services in general. Nagarajan et al. (2006) and Nagarajan et al. (2007), and Sheth et al. (2008) provide three similar data interoperability strategies. Nagarajan et al. (2007) explain the different types of heterogeneities that exist in web services. The syntactic and semantic heterogeneities described in the paper correspond to a difference in the semantic schemas, and the structural and model heterogeneities correspond to the format difference. The authors propose to use a pre-defined mapping to overcome these issues. Nagarajan et al. (2006) and Sheth et al. (2008) propose two other methods, using WSDL-S[22] or XSLT[23] respectively to map the input and output to a common ontology and vice versa. These techniques are specific to web services but show that rule-based mapping is generally used to perform semantic interoperability.

We did not find any related work on automatic semantic mapping solutions.

6 Conclusions and Future Work

We propose an approach to achieve semantic interoperability in NLP services in the most generic way possible. To reach this goal, three scenarios with distinct interoperability needs are described, for which different interoperability solutions have been created.

- For scenario 1, a single format has been defined for all the services, so that they all use the same format and are directly interconnectable.

[22] https://www.w3.org/Submission/WSDL-S/

[23] https://en.wikipedia.org/wiki/XSLT

- In scenario 2, the NLP services use different formats, so a manual mapping between formats has been carried out. This mapping has been done manually because the number of services is limited. This solution does not scale.
- Scenario 3 addresses the problem of semantic mapping, that is, services use different semantic schemas to represent information. Our first solution is to also use manually defined rules, but as mentioned above, this is not scalable or generalisable. Therefore, in this scenario we introduce a novel approach: the automation of the mapping process, i. e., automatic semantic mapping. This method aims to achieve the automatic generation of mapping or conversion rules between different semantic formats without human intervention.

The first experiments with a language model (GPT-3) are promising, but also show their limitations. In terms of future work, we will focus mainly on the development of methods that allow us to successfully implement this automatic mapping.

7 Acknowledgements

This work has received funding from the German Federal Ministry of Education and Research through the project QURATOR (no. 03WKDA1A), from the German Federal Ministry for Economic Affairs and Energy through the project SPEAKER (no. 01MK19011) and from the EU's Horizon 2020 research and innovation programme through the project European Language Grid (no. 825627).

8 Bibliographical References

Bird, S., Klein, E., and Loper, E. (2009). *Natural Language Processing with Python*. O'Reilly Media, Inc., 1st edition.

Bourgonje, P., Schneider, J. M., Rehm, G., and Sasaki, F. (2016). Processing Document Collections to Automatically Extract Linked Data: Semantic Storytelling Technologies for Smart Curation Workflows. In Aldo Gangemi et al., editors, *Proc. of the 2nd Int. Workshop on NLG and the Sem. Web (WebNLG 2016)*, pages 13–16, Edinburgh. ACL.

Bourgonje, P., Schneider, J. M., and Rehm, G. (2017). Domain-specific Entity Spotting: Curation Technologies for Digital Humanities and Text Analytics. In Nils Reiter et al., editors, *CUTE Workshop 2017 – CRETA Unshared Task zu Entitätenreferenzen. Workshop bei DHd2017*, Berne, CH.

Eckart de Castilho, R., Ide, N., Kim, J.-D., Klie, J.-C., and Suderman, K. (2019). Towards cross-platform interoperability for machine-assisted text annotation. volume 17, page e19.

Giretti, A., (2022). *Understanding the gRPC Specification*, pages 85–102. Apress, Berkeley, CA.

Hellmann, S., Lehmann, J., Auer, S., and Brümmer, M. (2013). Integrating NLP using Linked Data. In *12th Int. Semantic Web Conf.*, Sydney, Australia.

Moreno-Schneider, J. and Rehm, G. (2018). Towards a Workflow Manager for Curation Technologies in the Legal Domain. In Georg Rehm, et al., editors, *Proceedings of the LREC 2018 Workshop on Language Resources and Technologies for the Legal Knowledge Graph*, pages 30–35, Miyazaki, Japan.

Moreno-Schneider, J., Bourgonje, P., Kintzel, F., and Rehm, G. (2020). A Workflow Manager for Complex NLP and Content Curation Pipelines. In Georg Rehm, et al., editors, *Proc. of the 1st Int. Workshop on Language Technology Platforms (IWLTP 2020)*, pages 73–80, Marseille, France. 16 May 2020.

Moreno-Schneider, J., Rehm, G., Montiel-Ponsoda, E., Rodríguez-Doncel, V., Martín-Chozas, P., Navas-Loro, M., Kaltenböck, M., Revenko, A., Karampatakis, S., Sageder, C., Gracia, J., Maganza, F., Kernerman, I., Lonke, D., Lagzdins, A., Gil, J. B., Verhoeven, P., Diaz, E. G., and Ballesteros, P. B. (2021). Lynx: A Knowledge-based AI Service Platform for Content Processing, Enrichment and Analysis for the Legal Domain. *Information Systems*, page 101966. Special Issue on Managing, Mining and Learning in the Legal Data Domain.

Nagarajan, M., Verma, K., Sheth, A. P., Miller, J., and Lathem, J. (2006). Semantic interoperability of web services-challenges and experiences. In *2006 IEEE International Conference on Web Services (ICWS'06)*, pages 373–382. IEEE.

Nagarajan, M., Verma, K., Sheth, A., and Miller, J. (2007). Ontology driven data mediation in web services. volume 4, pages 104–126.

Qi, P., Zhang, Y., Zhang, Y., Bolton, J., and Manning, C. D. (2020). Stanza: A python natural language processing toolkit for many human languages. In *Proc. of the 58th Annual Meeting of the ACL: System Demonstrations*, pages 101–108, Online. ACL.

Rehm, G., Moreno-Schneider, J., Gracia, J., Revenko, A., Mireles, V., Khvalchik, M., Kernerman, I., Lagzdins, A., Pinnis, M., Vasilevskis, A., Leitner, E., Milde, J., and enhorn, P. W. (2019). Developing and Orchestrating a Portfolio of Natural Legal Language Processing and Document Curation Services. In Nikolaos Aletras, et al., editors, *Proc. of Workshop on Natural Legal Language Processing (NLLP 2019)*, pages 55–66, Minneapolis, USA. Co-located with NAACL 2019. 7 June 2019.

Rehm, G., Berger, M., Elsholz, E., Hegele, S., Kintzel, F., Marheinecke, K., Piperidis, S., Deligiannis, M., Galanis, D., Gkirtzou, K., Labropoulou, P., Bontcheva, K., Jones, D., Roberts, I., Hajic, J., Hamrlová, J., Kačena, L., Choukri, K., Arranz, V., Vasiļjevs, A., Anvari, O., Lagzdiņš, A., Meļņika, J., Backfried, G., Dikici, E., Janosik, M., Prinz, K., Prinz, C., Stampler, S., Thomas-Aniola, D., Pérez, J. M. G., Silva, A. G., Berrío, C., Germann, U., Renals, S., and Klejch, O. (2020a). European Language Grid: An Overview. In Nicoletta Calzolari, et al., editors, *Proceedings of the 12th Language Resources and Evaluation Conference (LREC 2020)*, pages 3359–3373, Marseille, France. ELRA.

Rehm, G., Galanis, D., Labropoulou, P., Piperidis, S., Welß, M., Usbeck, R., Köhler, J., Deligiannis, M., Gkirtzou, K., Fischer, J., Chiarcos, C., Feldhus, N., Moreno-Schneider, J., Kintzel, F., Montiel, E., Doncel, V. R., McCrae, J. P., Laqua, D., Theile, I. P., Dittmar, C., Bontcheva, K., Roberts, I., Vasiljevs, A., and Lagzdiņš, A. (2020b). Towards an Interoperable Ecosystem of AI and LT Platforms: A Roadmap for the Implementation of Different Levels of Interoperability. In Georg Rehm, et al., editors, *Proc. of the 1st Int. Workshop on Language Technology Platforms (IWLTP 2020)*, pages 96–107, Marseille, France. 16 May 2020.

Georg Rehm, editor. (2022). *European Language Grid: A Language Technology Platform for Multilingual Europe*. Cognitive Technologies. Springer. Forthcoming.

Richardson, L., Amundsen, M., and Ruby, S. (2013). *RESTful Web APIs*. O'Reilly Media, Inc.

Rizzo, G. and Troncy, R. (2012). NERD: A framework for unifying named entity recognition and disambiguation extraction tools. In *Proceedings of the Demonstrations at the 13th Conference of the European Chapter of the Association for Computational Linguistics*, pages 73–76, Avignon, France. Association for Computational Linguistics.

Sheth, A. P., Gomadam, K., and Ranabahu, A. H. (2008). Semantics enhanced services: Meteor-s, sawsdl and sa-rest. *Bulletin of the Technical Committee on Data Engineering*, 31(3):8.

Varda, K. (2008). Protocol buffers: Google's data interchange format. Technical report, Google.

Wolf, T., Debut, L., Sanh, V., Chaumond, J., Delangue, C., Moi, A., Cistac, P., Rault, T., Louf, R., Funtowicz, M., Davison, J., Shleifer, S., von Platen, P., Ma, C., Jernite, Y., Plu, J., Xu, C., Scao, T. L., Gugger, S., Drame, M., Lhoest, Q., and Rush, A. M. (2020). Transformers: State-of-the-art natural language processing. In *Proc. of EMNLP 2020: System Demonstrations*, pages 38–45, Online. ACL.

Appendix

A ELG Python SDK: More Examples

```
from elg import Pipeline

pipeline = Pipeline.from_ids([9395,
    9385])
results = pipeline(request_input="
    audio.mp3", request_types=["audio
    ", "text"])
print(results[-1]) # Sentiment
    Analysis response: {type='
    annotations' features={'OVERALL':
     '71.3'}}
```

Listing 8: Combining ELG services using the Python SDK and Pipeline class. We combine an ASR service and an English sentiment analysis service

```
from elg import Pipeline

pipeline = Pipeline.from_ids([9212,
    18092])
results = pipeline(
    LONG_ENGLISH_ARTICLE)
print(results[-1]) # summary of the
    English article in Ukrainian
```

Listing 9: Combining ELG services using the Python SDK and Pipeline class. We combine an English summariser and a Ukrainian to English MT service

B Parameters (GPT-3 Experiments)

```
engine="text-davinci-002",
prompt="\"\"\"\nPython method that
    converts\n[{\"translation_text\":
     \"This is a plain text sentence
    .\"}] \nto \n{\"type\":\"text\",
    \"content\":\"This is a plain
    text sentence.\"}\n\"\"\"\n\n",
temperature=0,
max_tokens=105,
top_p=0,
frequency_penalty=0,
presence_penalty=0
```

Listing 10: Parameters used in the OpenAI playground for Listing 6

```
engine="text-davinci-002",
prompt="\"\"\"\nPython method that
    converts\n<?xml version=\"1.0\"
    encoding=\"utf-8\"?><text>I was
    living in <ENTITY class=\"
    LOCATION\">Berlin</ENTITY> last
    year, but then I moved to <ENTITY
     class=\"LOCATION\">New York</
    ENTITY>.</text>\nto \n{\"response
    \":{\"type\":\"annotations\",\"
    annotations\":{\"Place\":[{\"
    start\":16,\"end\":22,\"features
    \":{\"Lemma\":\"Berlin\"}},{\"
    start\":54,\"end\":62,\"features
    \":{\"Lemma\":\"New York\"}}]}}}\
    n\"\"\"\n\n",
temperature=0,
max_tokens=150,
top_p=0,
frequency_penalty=0,
presence_penalty=0
```

Listing 11: Parameters used in the OpenAI playground for Listing 7

Proceedings of ISA-18 Workshop at LREC2022, pages 127–132
Marseille, 20 June 2022

Annotating Japanese Numeral Expressions for a Logical and Pragmatic Inference Dataset

Kana Koyano[1], Hitomi Yanaka[2], Koji Mineshima[3], Daisuke Bekki[1]
[1]Ochanomizu University, [2]The University of Tokyo, [3]Keio University
{2-1-1 Otsuka, Bunkyo-ku; 7-3-1, Hongo, Bunkyo-ku; 2-15-45, Mita, Minato-ku}, Tokyo, Japan
{koyano.kana, bekki}@is.ocha.ac.jp, hyanaka@is.s.u-tokyo.ac.jp, minesima@abelard.flet.keio.ac.jp

Abstract

Numeral expressions in Japanese are characterized by the flexibility of quantifier positions and the variety of numeral suffixes. However, little work has been done to build annotated corpora focusing on these features and datasets for testing the understanding of Japanese numeral expressions. In this study, we build a corpus that annotates each numeral expression in an existing phrase structure-based Japanese treebank with its usage and numeral suffix types. We also construct an inference test set for numerical expressions based on this annotated corpus. In this test set, we particularly pay attention to inferences where the correct label differs between logical entailment and implicature and those contexts such as negations and conditionals where the entailment labels can be reversed. The baseline experiment with Japanese BERT models shows that our inference test set poses challenges for inference involving various types of numeral expressions.

Keywords: numeral expressions, Japanese, natural language inference, entailment, implicature

1. Introduction

For example, the English sentence "There are three students" can be expressed in Japanese at least in the following three ways.

(1) 学生が　3人　いる
Gakusei-ga san-nin iru
student(s)-NOM three-CLS be-PRS
'There are three students.'

(2) 3人の　学生が　いる
San-nin-no gakusei-ga iru
three-CLS-GEN student(s)-NOM be-PRS
'There are three students.'

(3) 3名の　学生が　いる
San-mei-no gakusei-ga iru
three-CLS-GEN student(s)-NOM be-PRS
'There are three students.'

In (1) and (2), "3人" (*three people*) appears in different positions.

In (2) and (3), the suffix (i.e. classifier) for person is different ("3人" and "3名," respectively). The variety of quantifier positions and numeral suffixes is an important feature of the Japanese language. However, little work has been done to build a corpus focusing on these features or a dataset to test the understanding of Japanese numeral expressions.

Natural Language Inference (NLI) is the semantic task of determining whether the hypothesis is true, false, or neither, when the premises are all true. It is considered one of the core knowledge underlying natural language understanding. Recently, not only semantic modes of reasoning, but also pragmatic modes of reasoning have been explored in the field of natural language processing (Jeretic et al., 2020). These two modes of inferences correspond to *entailment* and *implicature*, which have been discussed in the linguistic literature (Levinson, 1983; Horn, 1989; Levinson, 2000). For example, consider the following premise–hypothesis pair.

(4) 男性が　道端に　4人　座って いた
Dansei-ga mitibata-ni yo-nin suwatte ita
men-NOM street-LOC four-CLS sit-PROG be-PST
'Four men were sitting on the street.'

(5) 男性が　道端に　5人　座って いた
Dansei-ga mitibata-ni go-nin suwatte ita
men-NOM street-LOC five-CLS sit-PROG be-PST
'Five men were sitting on the street.'

We use different labels (*logical label* and *pragmatic label*) for the judgments based on entailment and implicature, respectively, because they may differ on the same premise–hypothesis pair: the logical label for this inference is NEUTRAL, whereas the pragmatic label is CONTRADICTION. The latter is so because, along with Grice's maxim of quantity, if the speaker knew that five people were sitting there, they would say so, and the fact that they dared to say (4) implies that there is no fifth person. In other words, in entailment, inferences are made only from the semantic information contained in the premises and hypothesis. In implicature, however, the assumption that normal conversation proceeds according to the *co-operative principle* gives rise to information not semantically included in the utterance, considering the context and the speaker's intention, as suggested in Grice's maxims of conversation (Levinson, 1983; Grice, 1989).

In this study, we construct a Japanese corpus in which numeral expressions are annotated regarding the classification of syntactic patterns and the usage of numeral expressions. We use sentences containing numeral expressions extracted from the NINJAL Parsed Corpus of Modern Japanese (NPCMJ) (NINJAL, 2016), which is a phrase structure-based treebank for Japanese. Furthermore, we construct an inference test set for numeral expressions based on this corpus, which reports two modes of judgments, entailment and implicature for each premises-hypothesis pair.

In this paper, we report on the design of the corpus and inference test set as well as the evaluation results of a baseline experiment. The constructed dataset will be made publicly available in a research-usable format[1].

2. Related Work

Regarding the study of NLI focusing on English numeral expressions, (Naik et al., 2018) presents an inference dataset that contains 7,596 premise–hypothesis pairs, with 2,532 in each gold label (entailment, neutral, and contradiction). However, a recent study (Liu et al., 2019) has pointed out that the majority of problems (about 82% of the total) in this dataset can be solved using a few heuristic rules, which is due to the fact that the inference of numeral expressions is constructed using a simple template.

Jeretic et al. (2020) provided an English NLI dataset that focuses on the distinction between logical entailment, presupposition, and implicature. It also contains inference problems for scalar implicature triggered by numeral expressions. However, it is automatically constructed from templates and thus the sentences are relatively simple.

Cui et al. (2022) examined the extent to which multilingual pre-trained language models capture the behavior of generalized quantifiers including various types of numeral expressions in English. Their experiments showed that quantifiers cause performance drops for NLI and question answering models. We can say that numeral expressions pose an important challenge to the study of NLI and other tasks for natural language understanding. Our corpus and inference dataset focusing on numeral expressions in Japanese contribute further insight on how pre-trained language models work.

Previous Japanese inference datasets include JSeM (Kawazoe et al., 2017), the formal semantics test set (the Japanese version of FraCaS); JSNLI (Yoshikoshi et al., 2020), the Japanese version of English SNLI (Bowman et al., 2015); JSICK (Yanaka and Mineshima, 2021b), the Japanese version of English SICK(Marelli et al., 2014); and a crowdsourced dataset from real text, reputation, a travel information website (Hayashibe, 2020), and other sources. However, in these datasets, the syntactic and semantic diversity of Japanese numeral expressions is not fully taken into account. Narisawa et al. (2013) investigated cases where numeral expressions are problematic in Japanese NLI and implemented a module for normalizing numeral expressions. They classify premise–hypothesis pairs containing numeral expressions into seven categories and describe the process required to correctly determine the entailment relation, but they do not consider the difference between the two inference types (namely, entailment and implicature), which may give rise to different judgements according to the classification of numeral expressions and numeral suffixes.

Given these considerations, in our study, we first annotate numeral expressions in a Japanese corpus containing real Japanese texts and classify them according to their usages and the difference in numeral suffixes. By using the annotated corpus, we create an inference dataset involving numeral expressions annotated with entailment and implicature labels.

3. Syntax and Semantics of Japanese Numeral Expressions

3.1. Classification of numeral suffixes

According to Iida (2021), numeral suffixes are classified into three categories: sortal suffixes, unit-forming suffixes, and measure suffixes. In addition, some words have an ordinal number suffix (Okutsu, 1996), which expresses order within a time line or sequence. Thus, in this study, we propose a taxonomy that extends the three types of numeral suffixes in Iida (2021) with ordinal number suffix. Examples of each type of numeral suffix are shown in Table 1.

Table 1: Examples and the number of occurrences of each type of numeral suffix

Type	Example	Occurrence
sortal suffixes	人, 頭, 冊, 枚	56
unit-forming suffixes	瓶, 箱, 袋, パック, 切れ	13
measure suffixes	リットル, 円, バイト	74
ordinal number suffixes	月, 日, 番, 位	107

The classification of some numeral suffixes is not uniquely determined by their surface forms but depends on the context and usage. For example, "階" (*floor*) in "会議室は建物の3階にある" (*the conference room is on the third floor of the building*) is an ordinal number suffix, while "階" (*floor*) in "ここから3階のぼったところに会議室がある" (*there is a conference room three floors up from here*) is a measure suffix. The former refers to a specific location of the conference room, while the latter refers to the number of floors to go up. Note that, in the latter, the conference room is not necessarily located on the third floor.

3.2. Position of occurrence of numeral expressions

Encyclopedia of Japanese (EJ) (Yazawa, 1988) classified the syntactic patterns containing numeral expressions into four categories: *Q no NC*, *N no QC*, *NCQ*, and *NQC*, where *Q*, *N*, *C* stand for a numeral together

[1]https://github.com/KanaKoyano/numeral-expressions-corpus

with a classifier, a common noun, and a case marker, respectively. Iwata (2013) added two categories to the classification of EJ, *predicate* type and *De* type. In this study, we extended the classification by adding the following types, the examples of which are shown in Table 2.

***QV*:** *Q* semantically modifies the verb *V*.

***NvCQ*:** *Q* is a predicate on the event noun phrase *Nv*.

***N dropout*:** The so-called pronominal usage in which *no N* of *Q no NC* is omitted.

***QtQ*:** A time expression and a numeral expression are adjacent, such as in "1時間(で)500円" (*500 yen for 1 hour*) and "1ヶ月に1回" (*once a month*).

***idiom*:** Idiomatic and conventional usages.

***(Q)*:** A numeral expression enclosed within a bracket.

Table 2: Example and the number of occurrences of each position of numeral expressions

Type	Example	Occurrences
Q no NC	3人の学生が来た	31
N no QC	学生の3人が来た	11
NCQ	学生が3人来た	53
NQC	学生3人が来た	11
predicate	来た学生は3人だ	1
De	学生が3人で来た	7
QV	東京に3回行った	74
NvCQ	渡米したことは2回ある	6
N dropout	3人はお金を払った	24
QtQ	1時間500円かかる	3
idiom	1人暮らし, 8人兄弟	14
(Q)	（1998年）	15

3.3. Usage of numeral expressions

In addition to the usage of the numeral expression *Q* studied by Iwata (2013), the present study adds three new usage categories of *Q* by modifying the noun *N* and four more usage categories of *Q* by modifying the verb *V*. In addition, we add the usage of the expression *Q* by modifying *Nv* and idiomatic usage. In summary, we classify each numeral expression according to ten usage categories. The usage classifications and their examples are shown in Table 3.

4. Semantic Annotation of Numeral Expressions

In this study, 250 numeral expressions of sentences extracted from the NPCMJ were annotated by a graduate student with a background in linguistics.

Table 3: Example and the number of occurrences of each usage of numeral expression

Type	Example	Occurrence
Q represents the category information of *N*	3人の学生 (three students)	60
Q represents the number of elements that constitutes *N*	5人の集団 (a group of 5 people)	8
Q represents part of the elements that constitutes *N*	集団の1人 (one person from the group)	7
Q represents an attribute or characteristic of *N*	50歳の男性 (50 years old man)	64
Q for the number of times *V* has taken place	2回来る (come twice)	1
Q for the period in which *V* took place	3日滞在する (stay for 3 days)	21
Q representing the time that *V* took place	9時に来る (come at 9:00)	57
Q for characteristics of *V*	2%上昇する (increase by 2%)	13
Q to qualify *Nv*	渡航歴は2回 (two trips)	5
idiom	1人暮らし (living alone)	14

Table 4: Occurrences of upward/downward monotone inference

upward monotone	downward monotone
1173	118

Semantic annotation We assigned <num> tags to the numeral expressions that appeared in sentences, and made annotations for the classification of numeral suffixes, position of occurrence, and usage of numeral expression, as described in Section 3. When multiple numeral expressions appeared in a sentence, we marked the target expression with the <num> tag. The number of occurrences of each type of numeral suffixes, each position of numeral expression, and each usage in the corpus are shown in Table 1, Table 2, and Table 3, respectively.

5. Inference Test Set of Numeral Expressions

5.1. Data creation

We create an inference test set from a corpus of numeral expressions. We use each sentence in the corpus for a premise sentence T. The hypothesis sentence was created using the sentence annotated in Section 4. We select the clause that does not change the meaning of the numeral expression tagged with <num> as in (6), change the numeral, and add a quantifier modifier, as in (7).

(6) 仙台都市圏（広域行政圏）の
Sendai-tosi-ken（Kouiki-gyousei-ken）-no
推計人口は　約<num>151万人</num>
suikei-zinkoo-wa yaku-151man-nin
で...
de...
Sendai-metropolitan-area (greater-administrative-area)-GEN estimated-population-NOM approximately-1.51-million-CLS be-cont
'The estimated population of the Sendai metropolitan area (greater administrative area)

Table 5: Examples of the inference test set

premise T and hypotheses H_- and H_+	gold labels (T, H_-) logical	(T, H_-) pragmatic	(T, H_+) logical	(T, H_+) pragmatic
T: 前回１９９７年の税率アップ時を参考にすれば、昨年１２月～３月の駆け込み需要で前年比１％の売り上げ増が見込まれる半面、ことし４月以降は４～５％程度の落ち込みが予想される (If the previous tax rate increase in 1997 is used as a reference, a 1% year-on-year increase in sales is expected from December to March of last year due to rush demand, while a 4-5% decline is expected from April of this year.) H_-: 前回の税率アップは１９９６年より後だった (The last tax rate increase was later than 1996.) H_+: 前回の税率アップは１９９８年より後だった (The last tax rate increase was later than 1998.)	ENTAILMENT	ENTAILMENT	CONTRADICTION	CONTRADICTION
T: 勿論、私ひとりで四升呑みほしたわけでは無い (Of course, I didn't finish all four bottles by myself.) H_-: 勿論、私ひとりで三升以上呑みほしたわけでは無い (Of course, I didn't finish more than three bottles by myself.) H_+: 勿論、私ひとりで五升以上呑みほしたわけでは無い (Of course, I didn't finish more than five bottles by myself.)	NEUTRAL	NEUTRAL	ENTAILMENT	ENTAILMENT
T: あの頃は、100ドルを円に両替すれば、12000円になりました (Back then, if you exchanged $100 into yen, it became 12,000 yen.) H_-: あの頃は、50ドル以上を円に両替すれば、12000円になりました (Back then, if you exchanged more than $50 into yen, it became 12,000 yen.) H_+: あの頃は、150ドル以上を円に両替すれば、12000円になりました (Back then, if you exchanged more than $150 into yen, it became 12,000 yen.)	NEUTRAL	NEUTRAL	ENTAILMENT	ENTAILMENT

Table 6: Results of baseline experiments using Japanese BERT (accuracies of correct responses)

training	logical label				pragmatic label			
	all	ENTAILMENT	CONTRADICTION	NEUTRAL	all	ENTAILMENT	CONTRADICTION	NEUTRAL
JSICK	32.22%	70.83%	10.61%	17.74%	30.83%	70.90%	9.62%	16.67%
JSNLI	41.21%	70.83%	35.52%	5.66%	44.46%	70.67%	35.23%	6.67%

Table 7: Inference test set statistics

	ENTAILMENT	CONTRADICTION	NEUTRAL
logical label	432	594	165
pragmatic label	433	738	120

is approximately 1.51 million, and . . . '

(7) 仙台都市圏の 推計人口は
Sendai-tosi-ken-no suikei-zinkoo-wa
160万人 以上 である
160man-nin izyoo dearu
Sendai-metropolitan-area-GEN estimated-population-NOM 1.6-million-CLS over be-PRS
'The estimated population of the Sendai metropolitan area is over 1.6 million'

We rephrase numerals in a premise sentence T with both a lower number (H_-) and a higher number (H_+) and create two premise–hypothesis pairs (T, H_-) and (T, H_+) from T.

As in (6), when a modifier such as "約" (*approximately*) is added to a numeral expression, all judgment labels would become NEUTRAL if the hypothesis sentence is created with too small a number. In such cases, the numbers in a hypothesis sentence were modified so that the pragmatic label becomes as CONTRADICTION while preserving its naturalness. In cases where adding a modifier would result in making an unnatural sentence as in (7), we changed the word order of a sentence while maintaining its original meaning in creating a hypothesis sentence.

In this study, we did not use sentences involving idiomatic usage because changing the number or adding a modifier of such sentences would make the rephrased sentences unnatural.

5.2. Monotonicity inference

We also create inference problems involving the so-called monotonicity inference triggered by numeral expressions. If M is a more specific concept (subconcept) of N, then a sentence $\varphi(M)$ involving M usually entails a sentence $\varphi(N)$ involving N. We call such inference *upward monotone* inference. In the case of numeral expressions, for example, "200人" (*200 people*) refers to a subconcept of "100人" (*100 people*), so if the sentence *There are 200 people in the hall* is true, then the sentence *There are 100 people in the hall* is also true. However, if numeral expressions are embedded in *downward monotonic* contexts such as negations and conditionals, the entailment relation is inverted. Here a sentence containing the more general concept $\varphi(N)$ entails a sentence containing a more specific concept $\varphi(M)$. For example, the sentence *There were not 100 people in the hall* entails the sentence *There were not 200 people in the hall.*

The first example in Table 5 is a premise-hypothesis pair in an upward monotone context. The second and third examples are premise-hypothesis pairs in a downward monotone context involving negation and conditionals, respectively. Table 4 shows the number of occurrences of upward and downward monotone inference. At present, the number of downward monotone inference is small, reflecting the fact that expressions that trigger this type of inference is rare in the corpus. It is left for future work to annotate more examples of downward monotone inferences involving numeral expressions.

5.3. Inference test set

The inference test set created in this study contains 1,291 premise–hypothesis pairs. One annotator assigned logical (entailment) and pragmatic (implicature) labels to each pair in the inference test set.

The statistics of the inference test set are shown in Table 7 and examples of premise and hypothesis sentences are shown in Table 5. We can see that the numbers of CONTRADICTION and NEUTRAL judgments for logical and pragmatic labels are different because some of those that are NEUTRAL for logical labels are CONTRADICTION for pragmatic labels.

5.4. Baseline experiments

To evaluate the extent to which current standard pretrained language models can handle inferences that require an understanding of numeral expressions, we conducted an evaluation experiment using Japanese BERT (Devlin et al., 2019) as a baseline model. In the experiment, we used two standard Japanese NLI datasets to finetune BERT models on the NLI task: Japanese SICK datasets (JSICK, 5,000 pairs) (Yanaka and Mineshima, 2021a) and Japanese SNLI datasets (JSNLI, 530,000 pairs) (Yoshikoshi et al., 2020).

Table 6 shows the evaluation results of the NLI model. Overall, the accuracies to the Japanese BERT tend to be higher for models trained on JSNLI than for those trained on JSICK, but both were below 50%. In particular, the accuracy for ENTAILMENT was over 60%, while the accuracies for CONTRADICTION and NEUTRAL were both below 40%, suggesting a tendency to predict ENTAILMENT when the model is trained on an existing dataset. As for the difference in training data, the accuracy for CONTRADICTION was higher for both logical label and pragmatic label when JSNLI was used than when JSICK was used, which might be due to the larger number of training data used for JSNLI.

Table 8 shows the accuracies for each position of occurrence of the numeral expressions. The results show that the performance on inference examples involving numeral expressions of *De* types was low. One possible reason for the low performance is that numeral expressions of *De* types might be not frequently appear in general, including the training data. Thus models struggled with predicting correct labels for inferences involving numeral expressions of *De* types.

Table 8: Accuracies for each position of occurrence

Type	logical label		pragmatic label	
	JSICK	JSNLI	JSICK	JSNLI
Q no NC	29.70%	35.76%	24.85%	36.97%
N no QC	28.79%	40.91%	25.76%	39.39%
NCQ	32.00%	44.33%	31.00%	48.33%
NQC	31.82%	48.48%	33.33%	53.03%
predicate	0.00%	25.00%	0.00%	25.00%
De	28.21%	43.59%	23.08%	41.03%
QV	32.39%	39.95%	33.10%	44.68%
NvCQ	27.27%	59.09%	27.27%	45.45%
N dropout	39.23%	38.46%	36.92%	45.38%
QtQ	33.33%	33.33%	20.00%	40.00%
(Q)	34.43%	42.62%	31.15%	42.62%

6. Conclusion

In this study, we constructed a Japanese corpus of numeral expressions as well as semantic annotations including the classification of numeral suffixes and their usage. We also created a logical and pragmatic inference test set from the corpus of numeral expressions. As a baseline experiment, we evaluated Japanese BERT on our inference test set. The experiment showed that our inference test set for numeral expressions constructed is challenging enough for the current standard NLI models. When constructing the annotated corpus for numeral expressions and the inference dataset, we focused on the characteristics of Japanese, such as the flexibility of quantifier positions and the diversity of numeral suffixes. Future work remains to annotate and analyze more semantically complex phenomena, i.e., those phenomena that have been studied in the previous analysis of quantification in English (Bunt, 2020), including the scope of quantification, definiteness, and the distributive/collective distinction in Japanese numeral expressions. We will also continue to expand our numeral expression corpus and inference dataset as well as analyze the current NLI models on our inference dataset.

Acknowledgments

We thank the five anonymous reviewers for their helpful comments and feedback. This work was partially supported by JST CREST Grant Number JPMJCR20D2, Japan, and JST PRESTO Grant Number JPMJPR21C8, Japan.

References

Bowman, S. R., Angeli, G., Potts, C., and Manning, C. D. (2015). A large annotated corpus for learning natural language inference. In *Proceedings of the 2015 Conference on Empirical Methods in Natural Language Processing*, pages 632–642.

Bunt, H. (2020). Annotation of quantification: The current state of ISO 24617-12. In *Proceedings of the 16th Joint ACL - ISO Workshop on Interoperable Semantic Annotation*, pages 1–12, Marseille, May. European Language Resources Association.

Cui, R., Hershcovich, D., and Søgaard, A. (2022). Generalized quantifiers as a source of error in multilingual NLU benchmarks. In *Proc. of NAACL*.

Devlin, J., Chang, M.-W., Lee, K., and Toutanova, K. (2019). BERT: Pre-training of deep bidirectional transformers for language understanding. In *Proceedings of the 2019 Conference of the North American Chapter of the Association for Computational Linguistics: Human Language Technologies, Volume 1 (Long and Short Papers)*.

Grice, P. (1989). *Studies in the Way of Words*. Harvard University Press.

Hayashibe, Y. (2020). Japanese realistic textual entailment corpus. In *Proceedings of the 12th Language Resources and Evaluation Conference*, pages 6827–6834.

Horn, L. R. (1989). *A Natural History of Negation*. University of Chicago Press.

Iida, T. (2021). Japanese semantics and the mass/count distinction. In Chungmin Lee, et al., editors, *Numeral Classifiers and Classifier Languages*. Routledge, London.

Iwata, K. (2013). *Nihongo Suuryo Hyoogen no Shoso (Aspects of Japanese Numeral Expressions)*. Kuroshio.

Jeretic, P., Warstadt, A., Bhooshan, S., and Williams, A. (2020). Are natural language inference models IMPPRESsive? Learning IMPlicature and PRESupposition. In *Proceedings of the 58th Annual Meeting of the Association for Computational Linguistics*, pages 8690–8705, Online, July. Association for Computational Linguistics.

Kawazoe, A., Tanaka, R., Mineshima, K., and Bekki, D. (2017). An inference problem set for evaluating semantic theories and semantic processing systems for japanese. In *New Frontiers in Artificial Intelligence*, pages 58–65.

Levinson, S. C. (1983). *Pragmatics*. Cambridge University Press.

Levinson, S. C. (2000). *Presumptive Meanings: The Theory of Generalized Conversational Implicature*. MIT press.

Liu, N. F., Schwartz, R., and Smith, N. A. (2019). Inoculation by fine-tuning: A method for analyzing challenge datasets. In *Proceedings of the 2019 Conference of the North American Chapter of the Association for Computational Linguistics: Human Language Technologies, Volume 1 (Long and Short Papers)*, pages 2171–2179, Minneapolis, Minnesota, June. Association for Computational Linguistics.

Marelli, M., Menini, S., Baroni, M., Bentivogli, L., Bernardi, R., and Zamparelli, R. (2014). A SICK cure for the evaluation of compositional distributional semantic models. In *Proceedings of the Ninth International Conference on Language Resources and Evaluation (LREC'14)*, pages 216–223.

Naik, A., Ravichander, A., Sadeh, N., Rose, C., and Neubig, G. (2018). Stress test evaluation for natural language inference. In *Proceedings of the 27th International Conference on Computational Linguistics*, pages 2340–2353, Santa Fe, New Mexico, USA, August. Association for Computational Linguistics.

Narisawa, K., Watanabe, Y., Mizuno, J., Okazaki, N., and Inui, K. (2013). Is a 204 cm man tall or small? acquisition of numerical common sense from the web. In *Proceedings of the 51st Annual Meeting of the Association for Computational Linguistics (Volume 1: Long Papers)*, pages 382–391, Sofia, Bulgaria, August. Association for Computational Linguistics.

Okutsu, K. (1996). *Syuui Nihon-Bupoo-Ron*. Hitsuji Shobo.

Yanaka, H. and Mineshima, K. (2021a). Assessing the generalization capacity of pre-trained language models through Japanese adversarial natural language inference. In *Proceedings of the Fourth BlackboxNLP Workshop on Analyzing and Interpreting Neural Networks for NLP*, pages 337–349, Punta Cana, Dominican Republic, November. Association for Computational Linguistics.

Yanaka, H. and Mineshima, K. (2021b). JSICK: Japanese constructive inference and similarity dataset construction (in Japanese). In *The Thirty-fifth Annual Meeting of Japanese Society for Artificial Intelligence*.

Yazawa, M. (1988). Suuryo no Hyougen (Expression of quantity). In Haruhiko Kindaichi, et al., editors, *Nihongo Hyakka Daijiten (Encyclopedia of Japanese)*. Taishukan Shobo.

Yoshikoshi, T., Kawahara, D., and Sadao, K. (2020). Multilingualization of natural language inference datasets using machine translation (in Japanese). In *The 244th Meeting of Natural Language Processing*.

7. Language Resource References

NINJAL. (2016). *NINJAL Parsed Corpus of Modern Japanese. (Version 1.0)*.

Proceedings of ISA-18 Workshop at LREC2022, pages 133–141
Marseille, 20 June 2022

Annotating complex words to investigate the semantics of derivational processes

Rossella Varvara, Justine Salvadori, Richard Huyghe
University of Fribourg
{firstname.lastname}@unifr.ch

Abstract

In this paper, we present and test an annotation scheme designed to analyse the semantic properties of derived nouns in context. Aiming at a general semantic comparison of morphological processes, we use a descriptive model that seeks to capture semantic regularities among lexemes and affixes, rather than match occurrences to word sense inventories. We annotate two distinct features of target words: the ontological type of the entity they denote and their semantic relationship with the word they derive from. As illustrated through an annotation experiment on French corpus data, this procedure allows us to highlight semantic differences and similarities between affixes by investigating the number and frequency of their semantic functions, as well as the relation between affix polyfunctionality and lexical ambiguity.

Keywords: derivation, affix polyfunctionality, lexical ambiguity, semantic annotation, nominalization

1. Introduction

Derived words (e.g. *arrival*, *impossible*, *exemplify*) constitute a large part of our mental lexicon. Their morphosemantic properties have attracted a growing attention in the last decades, with the development of studies investigating the relationship between form and meaning in derivation (Zwanenburg, 2000; Lieber, 2004; Bauer et al., 2015; Schulte, 2015; Lieber, 2019, a.o.). It has been observed that word-formation processes are often polyfunctional, i.e. each of them may serve a variety of semantic functions by producing derivatives with different types of meaning (Moortgat and van der Hulst, 1981; Lehrer, 2003; Plag et al., 2018; Prćić, 2019, a.o.). For example, the suffix *-er* in English can be used to derive nouns that denote agents (*writer*), experiencers (*hearer*), stimuli (*pleaser*), instruments (*amplifier*), patients (*scratcher*), locations (*smoker*), measures (*fiver*), and inhabitants (*New Yorker*) (Lieber, 2016). In addition, affix polyfunctionality can sometimes lead to the formation of ambiguous words, as in the case of nouns suffixed with *-er* that are ambiguous between an agent and an instrument reading, such as *player* in (1) and (2).

(1) One of the players is arguing with the referee. [AGENT]

(2) The player is damaged and needs to be repaired. [INSTRUMENT]

Previous works have focused on the identification of semantic functions of suffixes, without taking into account their realisation frequency among derived lemmas and tokens. Similarly, as far as lexical ambiguity is concerned, the focus has been put on the number of senses words have, rather than on the frequency of these senses.

In this study, we investigate the polyfunctionality of derivational processes, taking into account not only the number of functions they present, but also the distribution of these functions among tokens, as well as the ambiguity of the words they form. To do so, we annotate 4,500 corpus occurrences of 90 deverbal nouns ending with 6 different suffixes in French. Each occurrence is assigned two labels to account for the meaning of the noun: an ontological type corresponding to the description of the referent, and a relational type corresponding to the semantic relationship with the morphological base. While this annotation scheme allows us to investigate meaning regularities among words and suffixes, the corpus annotation brings three levels of observation for both affix polyfunctionality and derivative ambiguity: (i) the number of meanings observed; (ii) their realisation frequency; (iii) their distribution among items. The reliability of the method is evaluated by considering agreement scores between annotators.

The issue of the disambiguation of derived nouns and the modelling of their semantics is relevant in various areas of computational linguistics and natural language processing. Even though deverbal nouns constitute difficult cases for automatic word sense disambiguation, their processing is necessary for the identification of non-verbal events (Kolya et al., 2013; Zavarella and Tanev, 2013). The modelling of the semantics of derivational processes may also help in copying with the issue of data sparsity. Being able to model derivational semantics can allow to automatically infer the semantics of derived nouns not attested in corpora, for which representations in lexical resources or from word embeddings are not available.

In what follows, after a brief summary of related works (section 2), we introduce the annotation scheme used in the study (section 3), together with a description of the annotated sample, an evaluation of the reliability of the annotation, and a discussion of cases of inter-annotator disagreement (section 4). In section 5, we present some observations about the polyfunctionality of French suffixes and the ambiguity of deverbal nouns based on the sample we annotated.

2. Related work

Theoretical works on the semantics of derived nouns have frequently aimed at an exhaustive listing of their different possible meanings. Some studies made use of the analysis of corpus data, disambiguating specific instances of derived nouns. However, the annotation of senses of derived nouns in context has proved to be a difficult task even for human annotators. One of the main issue of disagreement is the annotation of ambiguous and semantically complex nouns (see Section 3), which are particularly frequent among deverbal nominalizations.

Martínez Alonso et al. (2013) conducted an annotation task on nouns presenting regular polysemy (not restricted to derived nouns) in three different languages. They found that the agreement score varied across the different polysemous types. While only one obtained a reliable value ($\alpha > 0.6$), i.e. the Animal-Meat type, other polysemous types had low scores of agreement, showing that not all cases of ambiguity can be equally identified.

Valdivia et al. (2013), in an annotation task on a sample of 323 Russian deverbal nouns extracted from the Russian National Corpus (RNC), obtained an average agreement of 0.296 (Fleiss' kappa). Four labels were assigned: 'event', 'state', 'result', and 'underspecified'.

Peris et al. (2010) report the annotation agreement obtained in a task where 5 non-expert annotators had to classify 300 Spanish deverbal nominalizations. Three categories were used: 'event', 'result', and 'underspecified'. After a training on one third of the sample, the annotators reached an agreement of 0.6 (Cohen's kappa).

Barque et al. (2020) annotated 5554 corpus tokens of French simple nouns using 23 WordNet Unique Beginners as semantic tags, reporting an agreement coefficient of 0.649 (Cohen's kappa). In their scheme, the annotation of complex types was allowed and proved to influence inter-annotator agreement. Indeed, considering partial agreement among complex types, the kappa score increases to 0.734.

Our annotation experiment inherits the difficulties of this kind of task, for which an agreement between 0.6-0.7 is already a good result.

3. Annotation scheme

In order to analyse French deverbal nouns in the context of real corpus sentences, we designed a scheme of semantic annotation that can provide reliable information about the semantics of these words. We used a classification of deverbal nouns that fundamentally distinguishes between ontological and relational types, and combines them into a unique class that is identified as their 'complete' semantic type.

The ontological type expresses the nature of the referent denoted by the noun and the category of entities that it represents linguistically. The relational type refers to the semantic relation between the derived noun and its morphological base. While many classifications of deverbal nouns proposed in the literature assimilate ontological and relational types in a single taxonomy, possibly creating conflicting identification issues, it appears that the two dimensions are not strictly interdependent. As can be seen in (3), the same ontological type (ARTEFACT) combines with different relational types, while in (4), the same relational type (RESULT) combines with different ontological types.

(3) a. bâtir 'build' → bâtiment 'building' [ARTEFACT-RESULT]
b. raser 'shave' → rasoir 'razor' [ARTEFACT-INSTRUMENT]
c. garer 'park' → garage 'garage' [ARTEFACT-LOCATION]

(4) a. bâtir 'build' → bâtiment 'building' [ARTEFACT-RESULT]
b. énerver 'irritate' → énervement 'irritation' [STATE-RESULT]
c. créer 'create' → créature 'creature' [ANIMATE-RESULT]

The ontological classification we used includes 14 simple types and 7 complex types, listed in Table 1. It is based on distributional tests taken from the literature on nominal semantics (Godard and Jayez, 1993; Flaux and Van de Velde, 2000; Huyghe, 2015, a.o.) and described in more detail in Salvadori et al. (2021). For example, a noun that can be used as the subject of the verb *avoir lieu* 'take place', such as *licenciement* 'dismissal' in (5), is classified as EVENT.

(5) Le licenciement de l'employé a eu lieu ce matin.
'The dismissal of the employee took place this morning'

Complex types (also known as *dot types*) characterise nouns that are semantically hybrid. They can refer simultaneously to different ontological aspects of entities and are contextually compatible with predicates that are distinctive of different ontological types (Copestake and Briscoe, 1995; Cruse, 1995; Pustejovsky, 1995; Kleiber, 1999; Asher, 2011; Dölling, 2020; Murphy, 2021). Such is the case of the noun *déclaration* 'statement' in (6), which denotes at the same time the act of making a statement and the content of this statement (i.e. an event and a cognitive object in our ontology, respectively).

As can be seen from the example, the co-existence of different facets of meaning is made explicit by the copredication: the eventive facet is selected by *effectuer*

Simple types	
ANIMATE	INSTITUTION
ARTEFACT	NATURAL
COGNITIVE	PHENOMENON
DISEASE	PROPERTY
DOMAIN	QUANTITY
EVENT	STATE
FINANCIAL	TIME
Complex types	
ARTEFACT*COGNITIVE	EVENT*NATURAL
ARTEFACT*INSTITUTION	EVENT*PHENOMENON
COGNITIVE*EVENT	EVENT*STATE
EVENT*FINANCIAL	

Table 1: Ontological types

'perform' and the cognitive facet by *selon lequel P* 'according to which P'.

(6) L'hôpital Legouest de Metz a effectué une déclaration selon laquelle il venait d'accueillir deux victimes blessées par balles. (web)
'The Legouest Hospital in Metz made a statement according to which they had just received two victims with gunshot wounds'

In order to account for collective nouns, i.e. nouns that have a plural reference when used in the singular (Flaux, 1999; Lammert, 2006; De Vries, 2019, a.o.), a COLLECTIVE label can be added to both simple and complex types. For instance, *assistance* 'audience' is assigned the label ANIMATE-COLLECTIVE, as it denotes a group of several people. The noun *déménageur* 'mover', by contrast, is annotated only as ANIMATE because it denotes a single animate entity.
Relational types are expressed by labels that correspond to semantic roles, considering that they are semantically equivalent to the roles that derived nouns fulfil with respect to base verb predicates. For example, the relational type of the noun *arrosoir* 'watering can' is INSTRUMENT because *arrosoir* denotes an entity that is used to perform the action denoted by the base verb *arroser* 'water'. We defined a set of 17 semantic roles adapted from VerbNet (Kipper-Schuler, 2005) and LIRICS (Petukhova and Bunt, 2008) (see Table 2 for the list). Since distributional tests cannot be used to differentiate semantic roles, we relied on explicit definitions to identify relational types, as described in Salvadori et al. (2021).
We supplemented the list of traditional semantic roles with a type called TRANSPOSITION for nouns whose role is actually that of transposing the verbal meaning into a noun. The noun *atterrissage* 'landing', for instance, can be considered a TRANSPOSITION, as it roughly denotes the same eventuality as its base verb *atterrir* 'land'. A FIGURATIVE label was also added in order to take into account metaphorical or metonymic meanings that are derived from a given role, but that are

AGENT	INSTRUMENT	RESULT
BENEFICIARY	LOCATION	SOURCE
CAUSE	MANNER	STIMULUS
DESTINATION	PATH	THEME
EXPERIENCER	PATIENT	TOPIC
EXTENT	PIVOT	

Table 2: Relational types

not semantically related to the base verb. It is attached directly to the role in question (e.g. *lacer* 'lace up' → $lacet_1$ 'shoelace' [INSTRUMENT] → $lacet_2$ 'zigzag' [INSTRUMENT-FIGURATIVE]).
It is important to note that, even if the labels used are the same as those of semantic roles, the annotation of relational types does not concern the semantic role of the derived noun in the sentence of occurrence. Relational types aim at capturing lexical semantic information that is not context-dependent. While a noun like *inspecteur* 'inspector' can be defined lexically as AGENT with respect to the base verb *inspecter* 'inspect', it can be assigned a variety of semantic roles that are not necessarily those of agent in discourse. For instance, *inspecteur* 'inspector' features as the agent in (7), but as the patient in (8) and as the beneficiary in (9). Whatever the semantic role is in context, the derivational relation with the base verb is stable and encoded as such by labels of relational types.

(7) L'inspecteur a interrogé les témoins.
'The inspector interviewed the witnesses'

(8) Le détenu a frappé l'inspecteur.
'The prisoner hit the inspector'

(9) Le commissaire a offert des fleurs à l'inspecteur.
'The superintendent offered flowers to the inspector'

It remains true that polysemous nouns can be lexically associated with different relational types, and therefore be assigned different relational types across sentences of occurrence.

4. Annotation experiment

In this study, we investigate the polyfunctionality of 6 French deverbal suffixes (*-oir*, *-ure*, *-is*, *-ment*, *-aire*, *-ade*) and the ambiguity of their derivatives. We analysed 15 nouns per suffix, based on the semantic annotation of 50 of their occurrences in the French web corpus FRCOW16A (Schäfer and Bildhauer, 2012; Schäfer, 2015). The nouns were randomly selected across different token frequency ranges, based on the frequency distribution of all the nouns derived with the 6 suffixes. We excluded lemmas with a frequency lower than 50, since we needed a sufficient amount of occurrences to investigate lexical ambiguity. Then, for each suffix, we selected 15 lemmas from three frequency ranges: 5

nouns with a token frequency up to the general median value (50-223), 5 nouns with a token frequency from the median value to the third quartile (224-3,799), and 5 nouns with a token frequency higher than the third quartile (3,800-3,966,941). For each lemma, we randomly selected 50 occurrences from the corpus and annotated the sense of the targeted derived noun in context for both ontological type and relational type. We did not consider tokens in which the meaning of the noun was not related to the meaning of the base verb, neither directly nor indirectly (i.e. by means of lexical figure). In total, our sample comprehends 4,500 tokens and 90 different lemmas.

In order to validate our annotation procedure and to assess the reliability of the annotation performed, two samples of the dataset were simultanously annotated by two authors of this paper and adjudicated with the help of the third author. Each sample contained 300 randomly selected tokens for a total of 18 lemmas. Annotators followed the guidelines previously defined to annotate the semantic types of the target words in the context of each sentence. The agreement among the two annotators was computed using Cohen's kappa coefficient[1].

In the first sample, the agreement for the relational type was already almost perfect (κ = 0.848), whereas it was only moderate for the ontological types (κ = 0.539). An analysis of cases of disagreement showed that the main difficulty encountered was the contextual analysis of nouns with complex types. The annotators partially disagreed on the annotation of 67 tokens involving a complex type, i.e. one annotator identified a complex type whereas the other identified a simple or another complex type partially overlapping the first one. For instance, the word *miaulement* ('meowing') in example (10) has been annotated by one annotator as PHENOMENON and by the other as the complex type EVENT*PHENOMENON, since it refers at the same time at something that can be heard and that takes place. In this case, we consider that the annotators only partially disagreed because at least the PHENOMENON facet was identified by both of them.

(10) Les petites chevêches d'Athéna font de jolis miaulements dans la journée mais c'est rare de les entendre.
'Athena's little owls make lovely meowing sounds during the day but it is rare to hear them'

When considering these cases of partial agreement as mere agreement, the kappa coefficient for ontological types increases from 0.539 to 0.786. More generally, it appears that many nouns with complex types are characterised by one dominant facet of meaning (e.g. COGNITIVE as opposed to ARTEFACT for the noun *argumentaire* 'argument document'). In the absence of a distinctive predicate specifically associated with a given facet of a complex type, the two annotators used different strategies, by considering the dominant meaning or the complex meaning as the default type.

We therefore refined the instructions for the contextual annotation of complex types. It was decided that complex types would be the default type when no clear contextual elements drive the interpretation in favour of a specific facet. In other words, in the presence of predicates that are underspecified with respect to facet selection, complex semantic types are annotated as such. This indication proved to be efficient since in the second sample, the agreement score for ontological types increased significantly (κ = 0.815). Indeed, the difference with the agreement score that also included partial agreement was almost null (κ = 0.877). The agreement score for relational types was assessed as substantial (κ = 0.717), albeit lower than that of the first annotation, which is probably due to intrinsic sample differences. After that, the rest of the sample was single-annotated by the three authors of the paper, but problematic cases were discussed in joint annotation sessions.

5. Annotation results

Twenty-three ontological types, 21 relational types, and 62 complete types are included in the final annotated sample. The distinction between ontological and relational categories proves to capture different aspects of the semantics of derived nouns. As can be seen in Fig. 1, the degree of polyfunctionality of the 6 suffixes investigated (i.e. the number of types realised) varies between ontological and relational types. A suffix like *-ment*, which realises a high number of ontological types, can present a low number of relational types. Conversely, a suffix like *-oir*, which realises a low number of ontological types, can present a high number of relational types. Considering the opposite behaviours of *-oir* and *-ment*, it seems that the former has a more cohesive referential meaning, whereas the latter has a more stable derivational relation with its base verbs. The number of complete types can leverage this difference, possibly showing a higher number of functions for suffixes with more ontological or more relational types. It can be noted that the relation between ontological and relational types is not uniform. In particular, there is no general inverse correlation between the number of ontological types and the number of relational types. This relation seems to be specific to each suffix.

The number of types realised per suffix can be regarded as a first measure of polyfunctionality: the higher the number of semantic functions, the more polyfunctional a suffix is. However, this measure does not provide a complete picture of the versatility of suffixes, because the realisation frequency of functions needs to be taken into account as well. It is theoretically possible that two suffixes, although they are associated with

[1]The computation was performed using the kappa2 function of the 'irr' package in R (Gamer et al., 2007; R Core Team, 2013).

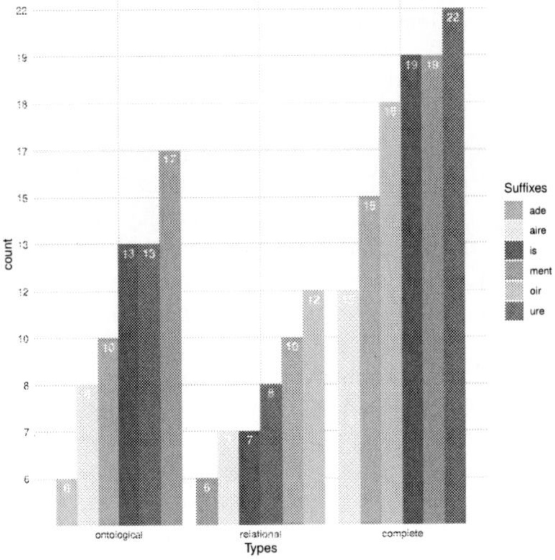

Figure 1: Number of function types realised by each suffix

a different number of semantic functions, can both have only one function that is represented in mostly all of the occurrences of the suffix. In addition to Fig. 1, Fig. 2 shows the proportion of ontological types realised among the corpus tokens of nouns ending with each suffix.[2] The plot illustrates what can be observed through token annotation.

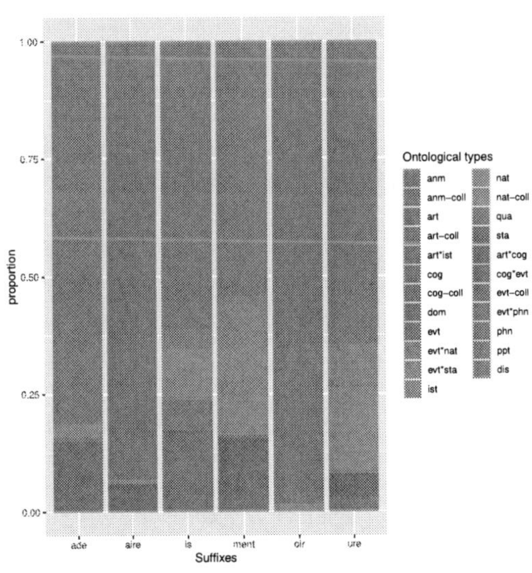

Figure 2: Token frequency of ontological types per suffix

[2]We do not include the plots for relational and complete types due to space limitation and to the large number of functions involved.

The suffix *-oir* realises the same ontological type (ARTEFACT) in most of the occurrences of its derivatives, with the other types covering less than 8% of its total occurrences. Similarly, *-aire* mainly realises animate nouns (e.g. *consignataire* 'consignee'), which constitutes 80% of its tokens. The suffix *-ade* also shows a clear preference for one given ontological type, but in a smaller proportion than *-oir* and *-aire*, with 64% of the occurrences of its derivatives referring to an event. For the last three suffixes, the distribution of ontological types is more diverse, with different types covering larger portions of occurrences. These observations about the distribution of functions go in the same direction as those about the number of ontological types attested: *-oir*, *-aire*, and *-ade* have a lower number of types and a less diverse distribution among tokens.

In a nutshell, the observations for suffix polyfunctionality based on our annotated sample of deverbal nouns relate to two different aspects: the number of types attested per suffix, and the number of tokens each type covers among the occurrences of each suffix. Borrowing terms from the ecological domain, we can think of these two observations as type abundance and relative abundance, i.e. richness and evenness of distribution of functions across suffix tokens, respectively. These properties are two sides of the same coin and should be considered together to fully assess affix polyfunctionality. A diversity index[3] such as the Hill-Simpson index (Hill, 1973; Jost, 2006; Roswell et al., 2021) can be used to consider these two properties together and determine which suffixes are more or less semantically diverse, and by how much. This diversity index not only takes into account the richness of the semantic functions of a suffix, but also the evenness of the token realisation of functions. More precisely, the Hill-Simpson index is equivalent to the inverse of the traditional Simpson index (Simpson, 1949) and is calculated from equation (1), where p_i corresponds to the number of tokens realizing a function i divided by the total number of tokens per suffix.

$$\frac{1}{\sum_{n=1}^{S}(p_i)^2} \qquad (1)$$

In Table 3, we report the Hill-Simpson values[4] for the 6 suffixes we investigated, computed for ontological types, relational types, and the combination of the two (i.e. complete types).

Considering only ontological types, the Hill-Simpson

[3]Diversity indexes are widely used in ecology to measure the diversity of species. A diversity index like Shannon's entropy has been used in computational linguistics to measure semantic content. See for example Santus et al. (2014) and Padó et al. (2015).

[4]Hill-Simpson indexes are computed using the MeanRarity package (Roswell and Dushoff, 2020) in R. We experimented also with Shannon's entropy and Hill-Shannon index and we found the same ranking of suffixes.

	Ontological	Relational	Complete
-ade	2.29	1.70	2.32
-aire	1.54	3.19	3.54
-is	5.85	2.25	7.08
-ment	4.16	1.80	4.21
-oir	1.16	3.90	3.96
-ure	5.37	2.71	6.64

Table 3: Hill-Simpson diversity index per suffix

index confirms what we already observed from previous analyses (Fig. 1 and Fig. 2): *-oir* and *-aire* have the lowest coefficients of diversity, due to their low number of ontological types and the low evenness of the distribution of their types among tokens. The suffix *-ade* has higher diversity than the previous two, but still lower diversity than *-ment*, *-is* and *-ure*. As for *-ment*, it presents the highest number of different ontological types, but the Hill-Simpson index only ranks it as the third most diverse suffix, given that the distribution of ontological types among its tokens is less even than those of *-is* and *-ure*.

We have discussed the results for ontological types as an illustration of our method, since it would have been more complex to examine a plot with the 60 complete types. However, we should consider complete types to fully represent the polyfunctionality of the suffixes. Looking at the Hill-Simpson index for complete types in Table 3, we can observe that *-ade* is the least diverse of the 6 suffixes. In 64% of the observed tokens, nouns ending in *-ade* refer to an event, whose relational type is always TRANSPOSITION. Despite the high number of complete types of the latter, *-aire* and *-oir* appear to be less diverse than *-is*, *-ment* and *-ure*, even if the difference with *-ment* is weaker. The most diverse suffix appears to be *-is*. Although *-ure* presents the highest number of complete types (fig. 1), it is distributed in less even ways among tokens, and finally evaluated as less diverse, than *-is*.

So far, we have focused on suffix semantics, investigating the semantic functions realised among corpus tokens of nouns ending with different suffixes. We have not considered yet the distribution of semantic functions among lemmas, nor the relationship between the ambiguity of derivatives and the polyfunctionality of suffixes. It can be asked how the different functions of suffixes are distributed among the nouns they derive, and whether more polyfunctional suffixes would derive more ambiguous words. Similarly to our observations for suffixes, we can infer from our annotated data different information for lemmas: the number of functions per lemma, the distribution (and degree of evenness) of these functions among tokens of lemmas, and a Hill-Simpson diversity measure combining these two for each lemma. We report these values averaged across lemmas for each suffix, in order to compare them with the values obtained above.

We first consider the number of semantic types realised by each lemma. In Table 4, we report the average number of different semantic types (considering as semantic types ontological, relational, and complete types) realised by the lemmas derived with each suffix, together with the standard deviation (SD) of these values. It appears that the suffix with the lowest number of complete functions (*-aire*) is also the suffix that produces the less ambiguous nouns (on average 1.53 complete type per lemma). However, this is the only suffix for which there is a direct correspondence between the two rankings. For the other suffixes, the degree of averaged lemma ambiguity is not parallel to the number of types. For example, *-ment* derives more ambiguous nouns than *-is* and *-ure*, although *-is* and *-ure* are associated with an identical and a higher number of complete types than *-ment*, respectively.

	Ontological		Relational		Complete	
	Avg	SD	Avg	SD	Avg	SD
-ade	2.07	1.28	1.80	1.01	2.27	1.49
-aire	1.53	1.19	1.20	0.41	1.53	1.19
-is	2.60	1.64	1.80	0.78	2.73	1.83
-ment	3.40	1.80	1.93	0.46	3.40	1.80
-oir	1.80	1.01	1.67	0.72	2.13	1.13
-ure	3.00	1.60	1.87	0.92	3.13	1.88

Table 4: Ambiguity of lemmas averaged per suffix

In addition to information about the ambiguity of nouns ending with the different suffixes, we should take into consideration the distribution of the different senses observed among these nouns. It can be argued that two words with two senses are not equally ambiguous if one of them realises only one sense among the majority of its tokens, whereas the other shows an even distribution of the two senses among its tokens. As before, we make use of the Hill-Simpson diversity index to consider together type frequency and token frequency of functions among derived words. More precisely, we computed for each lemma the Hill-Simpson diversity index, which tells us how ambiguous a lemma is and how evenly its senses are distributed among tokens. Then we averaged these values across the lemmas ending with each suffix. Results for ontological, relational and complete semantic types are reported in Table 5. We can observe that the ranking obtained is identical to that of the simple average ambiguity (column 6 in Tab. 4): higher ambiguity rates for lemmas per suffix correspond to higher diversity indexes.

We can conclude that the definition and the measurement of lexical ambiguity seem rather straightforward: the degree of ambiguity of derivatives remains the same if we consider the simple count of functions or if we combine it with the evenness of their distribution in the Hill-Simpson measure. The same is not true if we consider suffix polyfunctionality, for which we observed slightly different rankings for the different measures.

	Ontological		Relational		Complete	
	Avg	SD	Avg	SD	Avg	SD
-ade	1.48	0.88	1.31	0.57	1.50	0.91
-aire	1.27	0.61	1.17	0.36	1.27	0.61
-is	1.57	0.83	1.25	0.38	1.60	0.85
-ment	2.07	1.02	1.35	0.37	2.07	1.02
-oir	1.17	0.38	1.31	0.37	1.35	0.41
-ure	1.70	0.69	1.41	0.43	1.71	0.70

Table 5: Hill-Simpson diversity index for lemmas averaged per suffix

Therefore, it appears that suffix polyfunctionality and derivative ambiguity are not clearly correlated, since according to our analyses, each suffix presents its own characteristics for these two features.

6. Conclusion

In this paper, we have presented an annotation experiment on corpus data to investigate the semantics of nouns derived from verbs in French. We focused on 6 nominalizing suffixes, instantiated by 90 nouns and 4,500 corpus occurrences. The annotation represents word senses in a way that allows generalisations on meanings over suffixes and derivatives. It distinguishes semantically the ontological description of the referent and the relation between bases and derivatives. The results from our annotation experiment show that the relation between ontological and relational types is not uniform, but specific to each suffix.

The corpus annotation provides data for considering not only the number of semantic functions associated with suffixes, but also the distribution of these functions among tokens. We combined together these two levels of analysis and computed an index of diversity that can highlight various degrees of polyfunctionality and diversity across nominalizing suffixes. The ranking of suffixes obtained through this index is different from that obtained by simply counting the number of functions, confirming that it is important to take into account the realisation frequency of semantic types in the study of polyfunctionality. A similar evaluation can be conducted at the word level, assessing lexical ambiguity not just as the number of senses displayed, but also considering the evenness of their distribution among tokens.

The sample of nouns annotated in this study can be used as a gold standard for the evaluation of automatic word-sense disambiguation systems. Specifically, given the annotation at the token level, it can be used in the evaluation of contextualized embedding models (Peters et al., 2018; Devlin et al., 2018, a.o.), which seem promising in capturing word ambiguity. It can be hypothesised that (i) the similarity between pairs of token embeddings will be higher if the tokens share the same semantic functions, (ii) less polyfunctional suffixes will have a higher pairwise similarity among their tokens. These hypotheses will be the object of a further study.

7. Acknowledgements

This research was supported by the Swiss National Science Foundation under grant 10001F_188782 ('The semantics of deverbal nouns in French'). We thank the three anonymous reviewers for their helpful comments.

8. Bibliographical References

Asher, N. (2011). *Lexical meaning in context: A web of words*. Cambridge University Press, Cambridge.

Barque, L., Haas, P., Huyghe, R., Tribout, D., Candito, M., Crabbé, B., and Segonne, V. (2020). Frsemcor: Annotating a French corpus with supersenses. In *LREC-2020*.

Bauer, L., Körtvélyessy, L., and Štekauer, P. (2015). *Semantics of complex words*, volume 3. Springer.

Copestake, A. and Briscoe, T. (1995). Semi-productive polysemy and sense extension. *Journal of Semantics*, 12(1):15–67.

Cruse, D. A. (1995). Polysemy and related phenomena from a cognitive linguistic viewpoint. In P. St Dizier et al., editors, *Computational lexical semantics*, pages 33–49. Cambridge University Press.

De Vries, H. (2019). Collective nouns. *Oxford Handbook of Grammatical Number*.

Devlin, J., Chang, M.-W., Lee, K., and Toutanova, K. (2018). BERT: Pre-training of deep bidirectional transformers for language understanding. In *Proceedings of the 2019 Conference of the North American Chapter of the Association for Computational Linguistics: Human Language Technologies, Volume 1 (Long and Short Papers)*, pages 4171–4186, Minneapolis, Minnesota. Association for Computational Linguistics.

Dölling, J. (2020). Systematic polysemy. In Daniel Gutzmann, et al., editors, *The Wiley Blackwell companion to semantics*. John Wiley & Sons, Inc., Hoboken NJ.

Flaux, N. and Van de Velde, D. (2000). *Les noms en français : esquisse de classement*. Editions Ophrys.

Flaux, N. (1999). A propos des noms collectifs. *Revue de linguistique romane*, 63(251):471–502.

Gamer, M., Lemon, J., Fellows, I., and Gamer, M. M. (2007). The irr package.

Godard, D. and Jayez, J. (1993). Types nominaux et anaphores : le cas des objets et des événements. In Walter De Mulder, et al., editors, *Anaphores temporelles et (in-)coherence, Cahiers Chronos*, volume 1, pages 41–58. Rodopi.

Hill, M. O. (1973). Diversity and evenness: a unifying notation and its consequences. *Ecology*, 54(2):427–432.

Huyghe, R. (2015). Les typologies nominales: présentation. *Langue française*, (185):5–27.

Jost, L. (2006). Entropy and diversity. *Oikos*, 113(2):363–375.

Kipper-Schuler, K. (2005). *VerbNet: A broad-coverage, comprehensive verb lexicon*. Ph.D. thesis, University of Pennsylvania.

Kleiber, G. (1999). *Problèmes de sémantique: La polysémie en question(s)*. Presses Universitaires du Septentrion, Villeneuve d'Ascq.

Kolya, A. K., Kundu, A., Gupta, R., Ekbal, A., and Bandyopadhyay, S. (2013). Ju_cse: A crf based approach to annotation of temporal expression, event and temporal relations. In *Second Joint Conference on Lexical and Computational Semantics (* SEM), Volume 2: Proceedings of the Seventh International Workshop on Semantic Evaluation (SemEval 2013)*, pages 64–72.

Lammert, M. (2006). *Sémantique et cognition: les noms collectifs*. Ph.D. thesis, Strasbourg 2.

Lehrer, A. (2003). Polysemy in derivational affixes. In Brigitte Nerlich, et al., editors, *Polysemy: Flexible Patterns of Meaning in Mind and Language*, pages 217–232. De Gruyter Mouton.

Lieber, R. (2004). *Morphology and lexical semantics*, volume 104. Cambridge University Press.

Lieber, R. (2016). *English nouns: The ecology of nominalization*, volume 150. Cambridge University Press.

Lieber, R. (2019). 3. Semantics of derivational morphology. In Claudia Maienborn, et al., editors, *Semantics - Interfaces*, pages 75–102. De Gruyter Mouton.

Martínez Alonso, H., Sandford Pedersen, B., and Bel, N. (2013). Annotation of regular polysemy and underspecification. In *Proceedings of the 51st Annual Meeting of the Association for Computational Linguistics (Volume 2: Short Papers)*, pages 725–730, Sofia, Bulgaria, August. Association for Computational Linguistics.

Moortgat, M. and van der Hulst, H. (1981). Geïnterpreteerde morfologie. In Rob Knopper, editor, *Woordstructuur*, pages 17–53. Foris.

Murphy, E. (2021). *Linguistic representation and processing of copredication*. Ph.D. thesis, University College London.

Padó, S., Palmer, A., Kisselew, M., and Šnajder, J. (2015). Measuring semantic content to assess asymmetry in derivation. In *Proceedings of the Workshop on Advances in Distributional Semantics, London, UK*, volume 14. Citeseer.

Peris, A., Taulé, M., and Rodríguez Hontoria, H. (2010). Semantic annotation of deverbal nominalizations in the Spanish corpus ancora. In *Proceedings of the ninth International workshop on treebanks and linguistic theories: December 3-4, 2010, University of Tartu, Estonia*, pages 187–198. North European Association for Language Technology.

Peters, M. E., Neumann, M., Iyyer, M., Gardner, M., Clark, C., Lee, K., and Zettlemoyer, L. (2018). Deep contextualized word representations.

Petukhova, V. and Bunt, H. (2008). LIRICS semantic role annotation: Design and evaluation of a set of data categories. In Nicoletta Calzolari, et al., editors, *Proceedings of the Sixth International Conference on Language Resources and Evaluation (LREC'08)*, pages 39–45, Marrakech, Morocco. European Language Resources Association (ELRA).

Plag, I., Andreou, M., and Kawaletz, L. (2018). A frame-semantic approach to polysemy in affixation. *The lexeme in descriptive and theoretical morphology*, 4:467.

Prćić, T. (2019). Exploring the properties of English lexical affixes by exploiting the resources of English general-purpose dictionaries. *Lexikos*, 29:151–179.

Pustejovsky, J. (1995). *The generative lexicon*. MIT Press, Cambridge, MA.

R Core Team, (2013). *R: A Language and Environment for Statistical Computing*. R Foundation for Statistical Computing, Vienna, Austria.

Roswell, M. and Dushoff, J., (2020). *MeanRarity: Hill diversity estimation and visualisation*.

Roswell, M., Dushoff, J., and Winfree, R. (2021). A conceptual guide to measuring species diversity. *Oikos*, 130(3):321–338, March.

Salvadori, J., Barque, L., Pauline, H., Huyghe, R., Lombard, A., Monney, M., Schwab, S., Tribout, D., Varvara, R., and Wauquier, M., (2021). *The semantics of deverbal nouns in French: Annotation guide*. University of Fribourg, Switzerland.

Santus, E., Lenci, A., Lu, Q., and Im Walde, S. S. (2014). Chasing hypernyms in vector spaces with entropy. In *Proceedings of the 14th Conference of the European Chapter of the Association for Computational Linguistics, volume 2: Short Papers*, pages 38–42.

Schäfer, R. (2015). Processing and querying large web corpora with the COW14 architecture. In *Proceedings of Challenges in the Management of Large Corpora 3 (CMLC-3)*, Mannheim. IDS.

Schulte, M. (2015). *The semantics of derivational morphology: A synchronic and diachronic investigation of the suffixes* -age *and* -ery *in English*. Narr, Tübingen.

Schäfer, R. and Bildhauer, F. (2012). Building large corpora from the Web using a new efficient tool chain. In Nicoletta Calzolari, et al., editors, *Proceedings of the Eight International Conference on Language Resources and Evaluation (LREC'12)*, pages 486–493. European Language Resources Association.

Simpson, E. H. (1949). Measurement of diversity. *Nature*, 163(4148):688–688.

Valdivia, G. d., de Valdivia, G., Castellví, J., and Taulé, M. (2013). Morphological and lexical aspect in Russian deverbal nominalizations. In Irina Kor Chahine, editor, *Current studies in Slavic linguistics*, pages 267–280.

Zavarella, V. and Tanev, H. (2013). Fss-timex for tempeval-3: Extracting temporal information from text. In *Second Joint Conference on Lexical and Computational Semantics (* SEM), Volume 2: Proceedings of the Seventh International Workshop on Semantic Evaluation (SemEval 2013)*, pages 58–63.

Zwanenburg, W. (2000). Correspondence between formal and semantic relations. In Geert E. Booij, et al., editors, *Morphologie/Morphology: Ein internationales Handbuch zur Flexion und Wortbildung/An international handbook on inflection and word-formation*, pages 840–850. Walter De Gruyter.

Proceedings of ISA-18 Workshop at LREC2022, pages 142–149
Marseille, 20 June 2022

Annotating Propositional Attitude Verbs and their Arguments

Marta Ricchiardi, Elisabetta Jezek
University of Pavia
Corso Strada Nuova, 65, 27100 Pavia (PV)
marta.ricchiardi01@universitadipavia.it, jezek@unipv.it

Abstract

This paper describes the results of an empirical study on attitude verbs and propositional attitude reports in Italian. Within the framework of a project aiming at acquiring argument structures for Italian verbs from corpora, we carried out a systematic annotation that aims at individuating which verbs are actually attitude verbs in Italian. The result is a list of 179 argument structures based on corpus-derived pattern of use for 126 verbs that behave as attitude verbs. The distribution of these verbs in the corpus suggests that not only the canonical *that*-clauses, i.e. subordinates introduced by the complementizer *che*, but also direct speech, infinitives introduced by the complementizer *di*, and some nominals are good candidates to express propositional contents in propositional attitude reports. The annotation also enlightens some issues between semantics and ontology, concerning the relation between events and propositions.

Keywords: propositional attitude verbs, events, semantic types

1. Introduction

The object of this paper are propositional attitude reports, and precisely attitude verbs and propositional contents. Propositional attitude reports can be defined as sentences concerning cognitive relations people bear to propositions (see Nelson (2022) for an overview), such as:

(1) a. Jean believes what you said.
b. Jill hopes to be invited to the party.
c. Jack knows you are lying.

By attitude verbs, we mean the verbs that express that relation. By propositional content (or simply proposition) we indicate the propositional argument of an attitude verb. Syntactically, they are typically expressed by a clause. Semantically, they depend on verbs expressing a relation between humans and propositions: a propositional content is prototypically a human's mental representation, claim, assumption, question (Asher, 1987).

Traditionally, attitude verbs are identified in light of their behaviour concerning two puzzles (Pearson, 2015). The first is known as "Frege's puzzle", and concerns substitution failures with co-referring terms. For example, in sentences in the example (2):

(2) a. John believes that Joe Biden is eating a sandwich.
b. John believes that the President of the US is eating a sandwich.

it is clear that, even if the expressions Joe Biden and the President of the US refer to -at least at the moment we are writing - the same entity in the real world, (2-a) does not necessarily imply (2-b) - since John might not know that Joe Biden is actually the president of US. This is not true when the proposition is an independent clause, e. g. for verbs like *see* - 'John saw Joe Biden' logically implies 'John saw the president of US'.

The second puzzle concerns the possibility to establish the truth value of a sentence with empty predicates, as in (3):

(3) a. A unicorn is in the garden.
b. Sally believes a unicorn is in the garden.

Indeed, *unicorn* is an empty predicate, which makes it puzzling to determine the truth values of (3-a). However, the non-existence of unicorns in the real world does not affect the truth value of (3-b), which can be true or false depending on the mental representations of Sally – not on whether unicorns do or do not exist in the real world.

Even though these puzzles cannot be considered as acceptability tests (at least in linguistic terms), observing the behaviour of verbs in these contexts has been useful to identify attitude verbs.

Thus, we used these puzzles to verify whether some verbs were actually attitude verb or not applying them as tests, in the format:

- TEST 1: "John **verb** that Joe Biden is eating a sandwich" entails "John *verb* that the president of US is eating a sandwich"? If yes, *verb* is an attitude verb.
- TEST 2: The truth value of "Sally **verb** that **NP** is in the garden" changes whether **NP** refers to an entity that does not exist in the real world? If not, **verb** is an attitude verb.

Coherent systems of classification of attitude verbs have been proposed based on their syntactic and semantic behaviour. Pearson (2015) considers as prototypical the classes of *think*-like, *say*-like and *want*-like verbs. White et al. (2018) provide a reliable overview of the literature, summing it up in a classification based on the intersection of binary semantic features - namely: representational, preferential, factive, assertive, communicative, perception. We return on these features while discussing our data in section 4.

However, we believe that establishing which verbs are in fact attitude verbs is to some extent a language-specific issue, and thus it can be addressed in an empirical fashion. This is where our contribution to the debate is framed.

In this work, we approached the issue of propositional attitude reports in the context of an annotation task of typed predicate-argument structures of Italian verbs. The point where the issue arose was how to semantically annotate the propositional arguments of attitude verbs avoiding syntactic labels. We integrated our system of semantic types with a new label, [Proposition][1]. Then, since argument structures are acquired for more than 1100 Italian verbs, our purpose was to systematically annotate attitude verbs. The result of this process is a list of 179 argument structures based on corpus-derived patterns of use of 126 attitude verbs for Italian.

Based on our dataset of verbs and patterns of use involving propositions, it is possible to make some generalizations on the syntax and the semantics of propositional attitude verbs. In this paper, we overview the main syntactic configurations we found in the dataset, discussing why we consider them all as different syntactic realizations of the same semantic type for the argument – i. e. [Proposition]. The analysis of the lexical items that populate the arguments and the regularities in the alternation between different semantic types found in our patterns also provides supportive results towards the existence of the complex type (or dot type in Pustejovsky (1998)) Event • Proposition.

The paper is structured as follows. In section 2 we describe the methodology and the framework of the annotation process. Results and discussion of the annotation are provided in sections 3 and 4 respectively. In section 4.1 we discuss the classes of verbs we found; we discuss syntax issues in section 4.2 and semantics and ontology issues in sections 4.2 and 4.3 respectively. In section 5 we provide some concluding observations.

2. Annotation Framework

2.1. T-PAS

The annotation work is framed within the T-PAS project[2] (Ježek et al., 2014), a resource for Italian that provides argument structures annotated with the semantic type of the argument (Typed-Predicate Argument Structures). Argument structures appear as corpus derived patterns[3], and they are obtained through a procedure called Corpus Pattern Analysis (Hanks, 2004) based on co-occurrence statistics of syntactic slots in corpus instances[4].
The target corpus is a reduced version of ItWac (Baroni and Kilgarriff, 2006). An example of two patterns for the verb *guidare* ('to drive') is provided in Figure 1, in which the patterns, the sense descriptions, and some sentences that instantiate each pattern are reported[5].

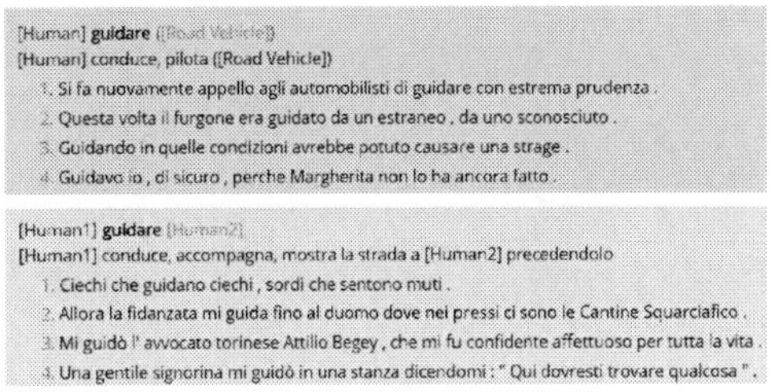

Figure 1: Two patterns of the verb *guidare* ('to drive' in the first pattern, 'to guide' in the second), provided with sense description and corpus instances.

Patterns are intended to be sense-stable objects, i. e. sentences where all the words are disambiguated. Since they are acquired from a random sample of 250 instances for each verb, they should provide a reliable overview of all the attested meanings of the constructions of each verb.

Syntax is also encoded in the system, although it is not visible in figure 1. Syntactic slots are subject, object, prepositional complement and clausal complement, and each argument occupies one syntactic slot (e. g. in the first pattern in figure 1, [Human] is in the subject slot, [Road Vehicle] is in the object slot).

2.2. System of Semantic Types

The annotation of the semantic types is performed manually: the annotator chooses which semantic type better generalizes over the set of lexical items that populates each argument slot. Semantic types are thus corpus-driven categories. They are organized in a hierarchy based on IS-A ("is a kind of") relations - e.g. [Human] is a kind of [Animate]; [Animate] is a kind of [Physical Entity], etc. An extract of the system is reported in Figure 2.

2.3. The [Proposition] type

The issue of propositional attitude reports arises from the labelling of the arguments expressing propositional contents in sentences such as (1-a), (1-b) and (1-c), or, to give a real corpus example in Italian:

(4) 'Pensavamo veramente che si avvicinasse un disastro.'[6]

[1] We use square bracket notation for semantic types.

[2] https://tpas.sketchengine.eu/.

[3] Henceforth we are referring to these argument structures as patterns of use, or simply patterns.

[4] For an explanation of how the pattern extraction and the semantic annotation is done, see (Ježek et al., 2014)

[5] We use round brackets to signal optional arguments.

[6] We use quotes to signal real corpus examples.

- Anything
  - Entity
    - Physical Entity
      - Inanimate
        - Artifact
        - Stuff
        - Light Source [Location, Inanimate]
      - Animate
        - Human
        - Human Group
        - Animal
        - Animal Group
      - Body
      - Part of Body
      - Plant
      - Location
    - Abstract Entity
      - Institution [Abstract Entity, Human Group]
      - Information Source
        - Document [Artifact, Information Source]
      - ......
  - Eventuality
    - Event
    - State
  - Property
    - Colour
    - Role
    - Weight
    - ......

Figure 2: Top-level of the Semantic Type System with a selection of leaf types.

Eng: 'We truly thought that a disaster was approaching.'

In T-PAS, each argument should be labelled with the correct semantic type from the system. Here the issue is to find the correct type for the propositional argument 'che si avvicinasse un disastro' (Eng: 'that a disaster was approaching').

First annotators (Ježek et al., 2014) alternatively used different strategies. One strategy way was to avoid the problem by applying labels whose definition was assigned on a syntactic basis. A type [Clause] was created and used for sentences introduced by complementizers. So, examples as (4) would have been generalized by patterns like:

(5) [Human] pensare che [Clause]
Eng: [Human] think that [Clause]

Similarly, [Quote] was used to label direct speech introduced by colons, as in:

(6) [Human] rispondere: [Quote]
Eng: [Human] answer: [Quote]

This was also the solution followed in the PDEV (Hanks, 2013) open-access dictionary. However, we preferred keeping the type system as a semantics-based categorization, and thus avoid any syntax-based definition for types.

Another strategy was to use the label [Event][7] or [Eventuality][8] - eventualities in Bach (1986) sense, i. e. including both states and events. Since every clause has a temporal structure, this choice could be considered as correct - as long as encoding information about the temporal structure is the essential property of eventualities.

However, considering the semantics of sentences like (4), the object of the act of thinking is not properly the eventuality, but rather what we defined thus far as propositional content. For this reason, we decided to use the semantic type [Proposition] that we defined as "a propositional content that is the object of an attitude verb, i.e. the content of a belief, a wish, a mental representation, a saying, etc."

Given that the system of semantic types should describe the relations between types, the position of the type in the system says something about the type itself. The [Proposition] type is positioned under the [Abstract Entity] > [Concept] branch.

One might be surprised that the position of the type under the [Concept] branch do not represent the relation between [Eventuality] and [Proposition]. Of course, propositions are expressed by clauses, and clauses, since they are tense phrases, involve temporal information, and thus they express eventualities. The point is that [Proposition] should be considered as a class of a higher order logic with respect to [Event] or [Eventuality]. However, so far only IS-A relations are represented in the system, thus the relation between [Eventuality] and [Proposition] is not traced yet in the system. However, the issue is worth to be discussed: we return to the relation between [Eventuality] and [Proposition]s in section 4.3.

3. Annotation results

We provide the complete list of annotations[9], i.e. of all the verbs that we consider as attitude verbs in Italian based on their patterns of use in corpus. As referenced in 1, the label [Proposition] was assigned to 178 patterns of use for 126 verbs. In Table 1 we provide a small excerpt.

One thing should be clarified concerning syntactic and semantic alternation. Patterns are induced on a semantic basis, i. e. they each capture a different sense of the verb. Syntactic alternations are signalled with the pipe, e. g. for the pattern of *giurare*, 'swear': '[Human] giurare che | di [Proposition] | : [Proposition]' means that the [Proposition] can be introduced by the complementizer *di*, *che* or through direct speech, indicated by the double colon. Semantic alternation is also signalled by the pipe, and it is used when more than one semantic type generalize over the lexical items that populate the argument slots of corpus instances. For example, in '[Human] | [Institution] ritenere che | di [Proposition]', the arguments in subject position are nouns denoting [Human]s or [Institution]s -and not, for example, other [Animate]s that are not [Human]s.

[7]Definition: "An [Eventuality] that involves movement, change, or development, unlike a [State]. An [Event] can either be a volitional [Activity] or a non-volitional [Process]"

[8]Definition: "It can either be an [Event] involving movement, change or development or a fixed [State]"

[9]available at `https://github.com/Rapazebu/Attitude-verbs-in-Italian`.

Verb		Pattern
annunciare	'announce'	[Human] annunciare [Event] | che | di [Proposition]
apprendere	'learn	[Human] apprendere [Information] | che [Proposition]
comprendere	'understand'	[Human] comprendere [Abstract Entity] | che [Proposition]
concludere	'infer'	[Human] concludere che [Proposition]
credere	'believe'	[Human] credere (che | di [Proposition])
dire	'say'	[Human] | [Institution] dire che | di [Proposition]
dimostrare	'prove'	[Human] dimostrare che [Proposition]
domandare	'ask'	[Human] domandarsi chi | come | cosa | perchè | se [Proposition] | : [Proposition]
giurare	'swear'	[Human] giurare che | di [Proposition] | : [Proposition]
immaginare	'imagine'	[Human] immaginare che [Proposition]
imparare	'learn'	[Human] imparare come | a [Activity] | che [Proposition]
pensare	'think'	[Human] pensare che | di [Proposition]
raccontare	'tell'	[Human1] raccontare [Concept] | [Event] | che | di [Proposition] (a [Human2])
ricordare	'remember'	[Human] ricordarsi che | di [Proposition] | di [Anything]
ritenere	'believe'	[Human] | [Institution] ritenere che | di [Proposition]
sapere	'know'	[Human] sapere [Information] | come | quale | cosa [Proposition]
sentire	'feel'	[Human] sentire che [Proposition]
spiegare	'explain'	[Human1] spiegare : [Proposition] (a [Human2])
...	...	...

Table 1: An excerpt of the annotation results, consisting of verbs and respective corpus-derived argument structures (patterns).

4. Discussion

In this section, we overview the classes of attitude verbs (4.1), together with the syntactic configurations (4.2) we found in our data, and some issues between semantics and ontology (4.3).

4.1. Classes of Attitude Verbs

We found many cases of what we called prototypical attitude verbs, i.e. verbs whose meaning is similar to those in the literature for English. However, we also found less prototypical cases, whose inclusion ought to be discussed here. In the discussion that follow, we refer to the classes used in White et al. (2018).

- Communication verbs like *dire*, 'to say'; *affermare*, ' to state', *ricordare*, 'to remind', *raccontare*, 'to tell', *spiegare*, 'to explain' are very common in the dataset. We considered as communication verbs also verbs like *rispondere*, 'to answer', *gridare*, 'to shout', *scrivere*, 'to write', i. e. verbs that introduce a proposition of the type "statement" just like 'say', but some additional information is also encoded in their meaning : 'to say as an answer', 'to say out loud', 'to say in writing'.

- Representional verbs like *pensare*, 'to think', *credere*, 'to believe', *sapere*, 'to know' are also very common.

- Similar to the prototypically representational verbs are also *verificare*, 'to verify'; *dimostrare*, 'to demonstrate', *concludere*, 'to infer', which refer to mental activities like reasoning and verifying truth conditions. Indeed, they roughly mean, respectively, 'to verify whether the propositional content is true'; to prove that [Proposition] is true' and 'to infer [Proposition] as the conclusion from some premises'.

- A (small) class of verbs that might be considered as communication and representational is that of the predicates of learning and teaching, which express a sort of transfer of some mental content from a person to another: *insegnare*, 'to teach'; *imparare*, 'to learn'; *apprendere*, 'to learn'. One should notice that patterns annotated with [Proposition] express epistemic knowledge, or knowledge-that, but not knowledge-how (Ichikawa and Steup, 2018). Consider as an example the verb *insegnare* that has patterns in which it is used for epistemic knowledge, as in example (7):

(7) [Event] insegnare che [Proposition] (a [Human2])
'Le varie esperienze insegnano, però, che è bene affrontare alcuni aspetti essenziali.'
Eng: 'However, various experiences teach us that is better to address some important issues.'

but also patterns that express knowledge-how, as example (8). We claim that this latter meaning does not involve attitude verbs, and thus we annotate the patterns with knowledge-how meaning with [Event] as object, as in:

(8) [Human1] insegna a [Activity][10] (a [Human2])
'Pomi mi ha insegnato a partire mettendo in leggero movimento la moto.'
'Pomi taught me to start the motorbike by slightly moving it.'

- Verbs of perception do not fall under the traditional definition of attitude verbs (Frege, 1892), (Moltmann, 2013), even though starting from Barwise and Perry (1981) some of them - such as *see* - are included (see also White et al. (2018)). It is plausible to assume that, in order to express an attitude towards a [Proposition], the [Human] should be an agent, while humans involved in argument structures of perception verbs are instead experiencers. We found some perception verbs that actually seem to behave like attitude verbs, especially in some patterns: *sentire*, 'feel (that)' and also 'hear (that)', '*notare*', 'to notice'. However, in our view, these cases are instead some particular kinds of representational and communication verbs, since the meanings of the patterns are, respectively: 'to know by feeling (that)', 'being told by someone (that)', 'to get aware (that)'.

4.2. Syntactic configurations

Attitude verbs and propositions are semantics labels. However, as with any linguistic issue that is analysed in terms of argument structure, it is hard to detach syntax from semantics. Here we explore to what extent this is possible. In the following sections, we illustrate all the syntactic configurations we found in the dataset. We claim that these cases are different syntactic realizations of the same semantic type for the argument, which represents the propositional content as the object of an attitude verb.

For sake of clarity, in the examples we provide the patterns complete with alternations, keeping in bold only the argument that are actually realized in the sentence of the example.

4.2.1. Complementizer *CHE* + finite

The most prototypical and well-known case, for explicit, finite-tense subordinate clauses whose subject can be different from the superordinates:

(9) **[Human] pensare che** | di **[Proposition]**
'Pensavamo veramente che si avvicinasse un disastro.'
Eng: 'We truly thought that a disaster was approaching.'

[10]Note that [Activity] is a subtype of Event.

4.2.2. Complementizer *DI* + non-finite

For implicit, non-finite tense subordinate clauses whose subject should be the same of the superordinate's.

(10) **[Human] pensare** che | **di [Proposition]**
'Saro' poco brillante , ma penso di essere pienamente nella media.'
Eng: 'I'm probably not very smart, but I think that I'm [lit. 'to be'] perfectly on average'

4.2.3. Embedded questions with *COME, DOVE, QUANDO, QUANTO, SE, CHI, COSA*, etc.

Like the complementizer *che*, many words behave as complementizers that introduce the so-called embedded questions, that are finite-tense subordinate clauses[11].

(11) **[Human1] domandare (a [Human2]) chi** | **come** | cosa | perché | se | di **[Proposition]** | : [Proposition]
'La gente lo assale domandandogli come ha fatto a entrare.'
Eng: 'People assault him asking how could he come in.'
'E se mi domando chi è lei , le risposte sono davvero deludenti'.
Eng: 'And if I ask myself who is she, answers are disappointing, really'.

We are not claiming, of course, that the meaning of these words is identical to that of the complementizer *che*: they all convey some additional information, such as place (*dove*, 'where'), time (*quando*, 'when'), person (*chi*, 'who'), reason (*perchè*, 'why'); some are semantically compatible with some types of attitude verbs and not with others (e. g. 'chiedi se vengono stasera', 'ask if they are going to come tonight', and '*ordina se vengono stasera"[12], '*order if they come tonight'), et cetera. However, these differences do not concern the attitude of a [Human] towards a [Proposition], and thus we consider them the same in their ability to introduce propositional contents.

4.2.4. Direct Speech

As it is well known, many attitude verbs, and especially communication verbs, also allow direct speech:

(12) **[Human] domandarsi** chi|come | cosa| perchè| se [Proposition]| **: [Proposition]**
'Piero si domanda : ho fatto la scelta giusta?'
Eng: 'Piero asks himself: did I make the right choice?'

[11]We are aware of the large literature distinguishing *that*-complements from embedded questions. We considered both structures as propositional complements if they satisfy the definition of proposition we are following in this paper

[12]Asterisk * is used here also to indicate semantic unacceptability.

4.2.5. Deverbal nouns

Propositions have been explored mainly when they are expressed by clauses, as in the examples we proposed thus far. However, some nouns express the propositional content that is the object of an attitude verb, as in the examples (13-a) and (13-b) from Pustejovsky (2005) and (14) from our data:

(13) a. John's belief is obviously false.
b. I doubt John's promise of marriage.

(14) **[Human1] suggerisce [Proposition]**[13] |: [Proposition] **(a Human2)**
'Non dobbiamo suggerirgli le risposte.'
Eng: 'We shouldn't suggest to him the answers.'

We will further discuss these cases in 4.3.1 in light of their semantic properties. By now, one should limit oneself to notice how also nouns can express propositional contents.

To conclude this section, in Table 2 we provide a summary of the syntactic configurations we found, provided with the number of patterns that show that configuration. Note that each pattern can have (and usually does have) more than one configuration, due to alternation.

Syntactic Configuration	n°	%
CHE + finite	134	76%
DI + non finite	122	69%
COME + finite	19	10%
QUANTO + finite	2	1%
SE + finite	10	%
CHI + finite	2	1%
COSA + finite	8	4%
PERCHE' + finite	4	2%
Direct speech	38	21%
Deverbal nouns	25	14%

Table 2: Syntactic configurations of [Proposition]s in argument position. Note that many patterns have alternations, thus they licence more than one configuration (e. g. many patterns allow both the *che* and the *di* construction)

4.3. Ontological issues: Events and Propositions

Once we move from syntax to semantics, some issues between semantics and ontology also arise. What are the relations between the semantic type [Proposition] and other semantic types – especially [Eventuality] and its subtypes?

[13]Here expressed by a noun.

4.3.1. The dot type Event • Proposition

The study of propositions expressed by nouns (see 4.2.5) enlightened the existence of complex types, or dot-types (Pustejovsky, 1998) whose facets are an [Eventuality] (or a subtype of) and a [Proposition]. Pustejovsky (2005) overviews these cases as an Act • Proposition dot type (also studied in Asher and Lascarides (2001)), as in:

(15) a. I heard John's quick promise (**[Event]**) from yesterday.
b. John's promise (**[Proposition]**) took months to realize.

and as a State • Proposition dot type (also discussed in Asher (1993)), as in:

(16) a. Nothing can shake John's belief (**[State]**).
b. John's belief (**[Proposition]**) is obviously false.

We found several cases of this type, i. e. several lexical items that, based on the pattern, may be [Eventualit]ies or [Proposition]s. Some examples of these items are *richiesta*, 'request'; *domanda*, 'question', *risposta*, 'answer', *affermazione*, 'statement', etc. They are, in fact, names of speech acts -intended as in the traditional sense (Searle, 1969), i. e. activities which are performed through words and have an illocutionary force; but they are also the propositional content of the speech act. Since speech acts do take place in time, [Speech Act], defined in this way, is a subtype of [Event] in T-PAS. Examples (17-a) and (17-b) are cases in which the word *affermazione* 'claim' is used as a [Proposition] or as a [Speech Act] respectively.

(17) a. **[Human]** | [Institution] **smentisce [Proposition]**
'Ma il sindaco ha smentito le affermazioni contenute nel documento.'
Eng: 'But the major has denied the claims contained in the document.'
b. **[Human] interrompe [Speech Act]**
A interrompere le affermazioni del segretario del Partito è proprio il Prefetto.
Eng: 'the one that interrupts the claims of the secretary of the Party is the Prefect himself.'

However, one should note that not only words referring to speech acts in the traditional sense can instantiate different facets of the [Event] • [Proposition] dot type, but also any word that refers to an object of an attitude verb: *pensiero*, 'thought', *frase*, 'sentence', *discorso*, 'speech' et cetera, e. g.:

(18) a. 'Ma il sindaco ha contestato il discorso (**[Proposition]**) del Prefetto'.
Eng: 'But the major has denied the Pre-

fect's speech'

b. 'A interrompere il discorso (**[Event]**) del sindaco è proprio il prefetto'.
Eng: 'The one that interrupts the major's speech is the Prefect himself'.

4.3.2. The alternation [Eventuality] | [Proposition]

As one could notice from the patterns of table 1, type alternations are present in the great majority of our patterns. Alternations are also insightful to analyse more complex semantic issues. In this matter, an interesting and very frequent alternation is that between nominal [Eventuality] -or its subtypes- and clausal [Proposition], as in:

(19) [Human1] | [Institution] annunciare [Event] | che | di [Proposition] (a [Human2])

Note that this issue is different from the issue discussed in 4.3.1 concerning the dot-type [Event] • [Proposition]; facets of dot types are activated by different selecting verbs, as in examples (17-a)-(17-b); while here we are discussing alternations with the same verb.

The fact that not all the verbs license all the three syntactic realizations (nominal proposition, verbal proposition, nominal event) is also puzzling:

(20) Annunciare l'arrivo del treno/che il treno è in arrivo/di stare arrivando/una notizia
Eng: 'to announce the arrival of the train'/'that the train arrived'/'to be arriving'/'a piece of news'

(21) Sapere che il treno è in arrivo/di arrivare/*le affermazioni di Marco/* l'arrivo del treno
Eng: 'knowing that the train is arriving'/'to be arriving'/'Marco's claims'/'to arrive'

The phenomenon is not easy to classify. We did not find enough evidence to consider this alternation as a coercion - assuming that the [Event] becomes a [Proposition] when coerced by the attitude verb's semantics - or as a very abstract kind of metonymy - in which the [Event] would be used instead of [Proposition] that expresses the [Event] itself. We then simply signal these cases as alternations, leaving them available for further investigation.

5. Conclusions

Annotating propositional arguments in a way that is coherent with the semantic annotation of any other verbal argument is not a trivial issue. That is the purpose of our work, framed in the context of the T-PAS annotation project. Through a procedure of automatic induction of argument structures (or patterns of use) from corpora, manually annotated with the semantic type of the arguments, we obtained 179 patterns for 126 verbs in which the [Proposition] type appears. Since T-PAS covers argument structures for about 1100 verbs in Italian, the results of our annotation should provide a reliable overview of what verbs are actually attitude verbs in Italian.

Generalizing on corpus data, we outline the main syntactic configurations of propositional arguments. The distribution of propositional arguments also enlightens ontological issues concerning the relation between events and propositions, and specifically the dot type [Event] • [Proposition]. Further study may refine this analysis.

6. Bibliographical References

Asher, N. and Lascarides, A. (2001). Indirect speech acts. *Synthese*, 128(1):183–228.

Asher, N. (1987). A typology for attitude verbs and their anaphoric properties. *Linguistics and Philosophy*, pages 125–197.

Asher, N. (1993). A theory of discourse structure for an analysis of abstract entity anaphora. In *Reference to Abstract Objects in Discourse*, pages 256–311. Springer.

Bach, E. (1986). The algebra of events. *Linguistics and philosophy*, pages 5–16.

Baroni, M. and Kilgarriff, A. (2006). Large linguistically-processed web corpora for multiple languages. In *EACL'06: Proceedings of the Eleventh Conference of the European Chapter of the Association for Computational Linguistics: Posters & Demonstrations; 2006 Apr 5-6; Trento, Italy. Stroudsburg (PA): Association for Computational Linguistics; 2006. p. 87-90*. ACL (Association for Computational Linguistics).

Barwise, J. and Perry, J. (1981). Situations and attitudes. *The Journal of Philosophy*, 78(11):668–691.

Frege, G. (1892). Über sinn und bedeutung. *Zeitschrift für Philosophie und philosophische Kritik*, 100:25–50.

Hanks, P. (2004). Corpus pattern analysis. In *Euralex Proceedings*, volume 1, pages 87–98. Université de Bretagne-Sud Lorient.

Hanks, P. (2013). *Lexical analysis: Norms and exploitations*. Mit Press.

Ichikawa, J. J. and Steup, M. (2018). The analysis of knowledge. In Edward N. Zalta, editor, *The Stanford Encyclopedia of Philosophy*. Summer 2018 edition edition.

Moltmann, F. (2013). *Abstract objects and the semantics of natural language*. Oxford University Press.

Nelson, M. (2022). Propositional attitude reports. In Edward N. Zalta, editor, *The Stanford Encyclopedia of Philosophy*. Metaphysics Research Lab, Stanford University, Spring 2022 edition.

Pearson, H. (2015). Attitude verbs. *Companion to Semantics. Wiley*.

Pustejovsky, J. (1998). *The Generative Lexicon*. MIT press.

Pustejovsky, J. (2005). A survey of dot objects. *Author's weblog*.

Searle, J. R. (1969). *Speech acts: An Essay in the Philosophy of Language*, volume 626. Cambridge University Press.

White, A. S., Hacquard, V., and Lidz, J. (2018). Semantic information and the syntax of propositional attitude verbs. *Cognitive science*, 42(2):416–456.

7. Language Resource References

Ježek, E., Magnini, B., Feltracco, A., Bianchini, A., and Popescu, O. (2014). T-pas; a resource of typed predicate argument structures for linguistic analysis and semantic processing. In *Proceedings of the Ninth International Conference on Language Resources and Evaluation (LREC'14)*, pages 890–895.

Author Index

Association for Computational Linguistics
209 N. Eighth Street
Stroudsburg, Pennsylvania 18360

ISBN 978-1-7138-6123-2

CURRAN ASSOCIATES INC.
proceedings.com